This is the first book to survey the performing practices in English choral music in the fifteenth, sixteenth and seventeenth centuries, including the period of the English Reformation. The essays, all written by specialists in the field, consider in depth such areas as the growth and development of the 'church' choir, related issues of vocal tessitura, performing pitch, the systems of pronunciation appropriate for Latin- and English-texted music, and the day-to-day training of choristers. There is also an investigation of the local circumstances under which many of the important manuscripts of the period were compiled, which reveals an unsuspectedly close interrelationship between domestic music and music for the Church. In addition, a study of surviving sources reveals that they give little more than a general guide as to their composers' and copyists' intentions.

English choral practice, 1400–1650

CAMBRIDGE STUDIES IN PERFORMANCE PRACTICE

This series provides a forum through which the most important current research may reach a wide range of musicologists, performers, teachers, and all those who have come to regard questions of performance practice as fundamental to their understanding of music. Each volume will contain contributory essays on various aspects of a particular theme in performance history.

Published titles

Perspectives on Mozart Performance
ed. R. Larry Todd and Peter Williams

Plainsong in the Age of Polyphony
ed. Thomas Forrest Kelly

Performing Beethoven
ed. Robin Stowell

Musical Performance during the Weimar Republic
ed. Bryan Gilliam

CAMBRIDGE STUDIES IN PERFORMANCE PRACTICE

ENGLISH CHORAL PRACTICE

1400–1650

Edited by
John Morehen

CAMBRIDGE
UNIVERSITY PRESS

Published by the Press Syndicate of the University of Cambridge
The Pitt Building, Trumpington Street, Cambridge CB2 IRP
40 West 20th Street, New York, NY 10011–4211, USA
10 Stamford Road, Oakleigh, Melbourne 3166, Australia

First published 1995

Printed in Great Britain at the University Press, Cambridge

A catalogue record for this book is available from the British Library

Library of Congress cataloguing in publication data

English choral practice 1400–1650 / edited by John Morehen.
  p. cm. – (Cambridge Studies in Performance Practice; 5)
Includes bibliographical references and indexes.
ISBN 0 521 44143 9 (hardback)
1. Choral music – England.   2. Performance practice (Music) – England.   3. Choirs (Music)
– England.   4. Church music – England.   5. Sacred vocal music – England – History and
criticism.   6. Latin language – Church Latin – Pronunciation.   7. English language –
Pronunciation.
1. Morehen, John.   II. Series.
ML3031.E54 1995
782.5'0942 – dc20   95–1966 CIP MN

ISBN 0 521 44143 9 hardback

CONTENTS

PLATES

GENERAL PREFACE

No doubt the claim, heard frequently today, that 'authentic performance' is a chimera, and that even the idea of an 'authentic edition' cannot be sustained for (most) music before the last century or two, is itself the consequence of too sanguine an expectation raised by performers and scholars alike in the recent past. Both have been understandably concerned to establish that a certain composer 'intended so-and-so' or had 'such-and-such conditions of performance in mind' or 'meant it to sound in this way or that'. Scholars are inclined to rule on problems ('research confirms the following …'), performers to make the music a living experience ('artistry or musicianship suggests the following …'). Both are there in order to answer certain questions and establish an authority for what they do; both demonstrate and persuade by the rhetoric of their utterance, whether well-documented research on the one hand or convincing artistic performance on the other; and the academic/commercial success of both depends on the effectiveness of that rhetoric. Some musicians even set out to convey authority in both scholarship and performance, recognizing that music is conceptual *and* perceptual and thus not gainfully divisible into separate, competitive disciplines. In general, if not always, the scholar appears to aim at the firm, affirmative statement, often seeing questions as something to be answered confidently rather than searchingly redefined or refined. In general, with some exceptions, performers have to aim at the confident statement, for their very livelihood hangs on an unhesitating decisiveness in front of audience or microphone. In the process, both sometimes have the effect, perhaps even the intention, of killing the dialectic – of thwarting the progress that comes with further questions and a constant 'yes, but' response to what is seen, in the light of changing definitions, as 'scholarly evidence' or 'convincing performance'.

In the belief that the immense activity in prose and sound over the last few decades is now being accompanied by an increasing awareness of the issues arising – a greater knowledge at last enabling the question to be more closely defined – the Cambridge Studies in Performance Practice will attempt to make regular contributions to this area of study, on the basis of several assumptions. Firstly, at its best, Performance Practice is so difficult a branch of study as to be an almost impossibly elusive ideal. It cannot be merely a practical way of 'combining performance and scholarship', for these two are fundamentally different activities, each able to inform the other only up to a certain point. Secondly, if Performance Practice has moved beyond the questions (now seen to be very dated) that exercised performance groups of the 1950s and 60s, it can widen itself to include any or all music written before the last few years. In this respect, such studies are a musician's equivalent to the cry of literary studies, 'Only contextualize!', and this can serve as a useful starting-point for the historically minded performer or the practically minded scholar. (The Derridaesque paradox that there is no context may have already affected some literary studies, but context is still clearly crucial across the broader field of music, the original Comparative Literature.) Cambridge Studies in Performance Practice will devote volumes to any period in which useful questions can be asked, ranging from at least Gregorian chant to at least Stravinsky.

Thirdly, Performance Practice is not merely about performing, neither 'this is how music was played' nor 'this is how you should play it in a concert or recording today'. (These two statements are as often as not irreconcilable.) In studying all that we can about the practical realization of a piece of music we are studying not so much how it was played but how it was heard, both literally and on a deeper level. How it was conceived by the composer and how it was perceived by the period's listener are endless questions deserving constant study, for they bring one into intimate contact with the historical art of music as nothing else can. It is the *music* we fail to understand, not its performance as such, if we do not explore these endless questions. As we know, every basic musical element has had to be found, plucked out of thin air – the notes, their tuning, compass, volume, timbre, pace, timing, tone, combining – and they have constantly changed. In attempting to grasp or describe these elements as they belong to a certain piece of music, it could become clear that any modern re-realization in (public) performance is a quite separate issue. Nevertheless, it is an issue of importance to the wider musical community, as can be seen from the popular success of performers and publications (records, journals, books) concerned with 'authenticity'. In recognizing this practical importance, Cambridge Studies in Performance Practice will frequently call upon authoritative performers to join scholars in the common cause, each offering insights to the process of learning to ask and explore the right questions.

PETER WILLIAMS

PREFACE

The death of Peter le Huray in Cambridge on 7 October 1992, only months after embarking on what had promised to be an exceptionally productive and fulfilling early retirement, was lamented particularly by thousands of Cambridge music graduates who had experienced at first hand his tutelage and counsel in a distinguished college and university career that spanned a period of some 40 years. The obituaries published in the national press at that time were unanimous in emphasizing Peter le Huray's unshakable commitment to his role as teacher, a commitment that does not always accompany distinguished scholarship.

It was characteristic of Peter le Huray's indefatigable dedication to intellectual enquiry that in the year following his retirement he organized an extended series of seminars at Cambridge devoted to performance practice in English choral music of the late fourteenth to the mid-seventeenth centuries. It was envisaged that the substance of the seminars would later be published in monograph form. In inviting a broad spectrum of scholars to contribute to those seminars, he drew on the expertise both of his Cambridge colleagues and those working elsewhere. Some contributors – such as Roger Bowers and Alison Wray – elected to develop areas in which they had already forged a formidable reputation, while others – such as Roger Bray, John Milsom and the present writer – availed themselves of the opportunity to use the seminars as a sounding-board for exploring new areas of interest.

Although the work of several of the original contributors is included in the present volume, some of those who participated in the Cambridge seminars felt that their sessions were unsuited to print or that their ideas were insufficiently developed for publication. Furthermore, Peter le Huray's own seminar was preserved only in note form, and, consequently, it was not possible to include it here. To compensate for the resulting shortfall, additional authors, including some of Peter's friends and former pupils, were invited to contribute essays in accordance with the broad thrust of the original seminars. This has enabled the editor to include contributions reflecting the researches of Jane Flynn on the education of English choristers in the sixteenth century (an area which was the subject of one of Peter's earliest published articles)[1] and to include David Mateer's

---

1 'The teaching of music in 16th-century England', *Music in Education* 30 (1966), pp. 75–7.

work on text underlay in English music, a domain which, unlike that of underlay in continental music, has traditionally been dismissed as being bedevilled by scribal idiosyncrasy and casualness. The shortfall has also enabled David Wulstan further to develop various aspects of the interrelationships between Byrd, Tallis and Ferrabosco which he first explored in abbreviated form in *Byrd Studies*.[2]

By design, none of the authors represented here has seen the work of the other contributors in advance of publication, since it was felt that unfettered exploration of controversial issues might otherwise be inhibited. Peter le Huray would undoubtedly have relished the robust debate that is represented, for instance, in the diametrically opposed views of Roger Bowers and David Wulstan on performing pitch in sixteenth-century choral music.

This volume is offered in respect, admiration and affection to the memory of a fine scholar, an inspiring teacher, and a most loyal friend.

JOHN MOREHEN
Nottingham 1994

2   Alan Brown and Richard Turbet (eds.), *Byrd Studies* (Cambridge 1992).

ABBREVIATIONS

The following abbreviations are used:

A	*Altus*, Alto	M	*Medius*, Mean
B	*Bassus*, Bass	*Mx*	*maxima*
B	*brevis*, breve	S	Soprano
C	*Contratenor*, Countertenor	S	*semibrevis*, semibreve
CF	*cantus firmus*	T	*Tenor*, Tenor
L	*longa*, long	Tr	Treble

COLLECTED EDITIONS, ANTHOLOGIES, ETC.

AECM	*Anthology of English Church Music*, comp. David Wulstan (London 1971)
BE	*The Byrd Edition*
CMM	*Corpus Mensurabilis Musicae*
EECM	*Early English Church Music*
EMS	*The English Madrigal School*
MB	*Musica Britannica*
TCM	*Tudor Church Music*
TECM	*The Treasury of English Church Music*, 2, ed. Peter le Huray (London 1965)

In the index, individual pieces within the above editions are designated as follows: *EECM* 3/10 indicates 'Piece no. 10 in volume 3 of *Early English Church Music*', and similarly with other series.

Clefs are shown by the use of subscript numbers; e.g. C_4 = C clef on the fourth line from the bottom. Voice designations use superscript numbers, e.g. T^2 = second tenor.

Pitch references are shown in the following example:

TO CHORUS FROM QUARTET: THE PERFORMING RESOURCE FOR ENGLISH CHURCH POLYPHONY, c. 1390–1559

ROGER BOWERS

In respect of the choral music of the church services in England, the fifteenth century witnessed a revolution in performance practice which established fundamental premises that have endured to the present day. At a point around 1390, the opening of the period under review here, choral execution in the music of the Church was a feature of the performance only of plainsong. The rendering of polyphonic music was the province exclusively of small ensembles of soloists, all adult males. By the end of the fifteenth century polyphony for performance by chorus, composed to a standard texture of five voices but not uncommonly for more, had emerged as one of the principal splendours of church practice in England, and involved the voices of the boys of liturgical choirs as well as those of the men. During the course of the century choirs originally constituted primarily to sing just the plainsong liturgy were perforce so re-modelled as to ensure supply of the resources, in terms both of personnel and of training, appropriate for the new musical medium. Correspondingly, founding authorities drawing up the constitutions of choirs newly established ensured that such provision was among their first priorities. Overall, the joint achievement of founders, chapters, composers and singers during this century was to develop and establish perhaps the most enduring of all vehicles for the performance of art music, namely the four-timbre chorus of treble, alto, tenor and bass voices – a concept over which the experience of 500 years and more has not been able to cast any substantive improvement.

(1) THE PERFORMANCE OF CHURCH POLYPHONY, c. 1390 – c. 1455

(a) The constituent voices: ranges and differentials

Problematic though it is, the attempt will be made here to establish defensible observations about such matters as size of ensemble, vocal timbre and sounding pitch, as each was practised at the commencement of this period, from the examination of contemporary evidence alone. It might be tempting to shrink at the prospect and fall back instead on the easier expedient of working backwards through time to the fifteenth century from more recent and more securely researched periods. Experience shows, however, that such procedures are fraught with hazards and pitfalls which, as hypothesis is piled on hypothesis, all too readily magnify exponentially through misconception to misunderstanding and finally to wholesale misrepresentation. The contemporary sources do, fortunately, yield materials susceptible of analysis which can provide reasonably soundly based conclusions, and it is this procedure which will be followed here.

Much information relating to the manner in which church polyphony was performed is encapsulated within the musical notes themselves. Analysis of such ingredients as the overall compass between the highest and lowest written notes and the differentials of pitch between the constituent voices discloses the existence of a number of pervasively consistent features that have much to reveal concerning the nature of the performing resource by which the composers expected their music to be sung and to which they tailored its composition in consequence.[1] It is the alignment of these internal musical consistencies with characteristics which archival sources reveal to be manifested by the performing ensembles themselves that permits conclusions to be drawn concerning the manner in which voices were used for the realization of the polyphonic music composed at this period.

These consistencies reveal that for the performance of polyphonic music the ensembles of (normally) four soloists maintained at each of the several institutions concerned consisted of personnel whose vocal constitution as a team was standardized according to a pattern that was as conventional and as fixed as that of the modern string quartet. In such a conclusion there is nothing fundamentally implausible. Throughout most of the fourteenth century polyphonic music was cultivated by groups of largely self-motivated enthusiasts, all of whom were members of the choirs of a relatively small number of cathedral and other major churches and private chapels that at no time exceeded some 35 to 40. Prior to about the 1380s the number of individuals in the whole of the kingdom who, at any one time, were able to understand the notation of polyphonic music, to write it and perform from it, may well have never exceeded a couple of hundred. These individuals created a lively culture that produced a good deal of music, and the considerable number of concordances among the surviving manuscripts indicates that compositions travelled quite freely around that relatively small number of groups of enthusiast-executants. In the straitness of such circumstances there was nothing to engender degrees of casual latitude or heedless experimentation in composing or performing manner. Rather, the performing groups, wherever they

---

[1] It may be observed here that although the church organ existed throughout this period, there is no shred of evidence to suggest that it was ever played simultaneously and as an accompaniment to the singing voices during the performance of polyphony, nor that it was ever used to give the pitch for the performance of any piece of polyphony.

were, had everything to gain from cultivating and maintaining a commonality of approach to composition and performance that established a common bond and means of expression. It may readily be appreciated that it is entirely consistent with the prevailing circumstances and constraints to suggest that wherever it was cultivated, polyphonic music was perforce performed in very much a single manner, by groups of executants all constituted in accordance with a single conventional and standard pattern – a pattern that had evolved in the light of experience and had been found to be logistically and aesthetically satisfactory.

If a representative selection of the surviving music of the period c. 1380–1450 be taken as a starting point, it will be seen that the great majority of pieces for church performance was composed for three voices, and most of the remainder for four. A certain number are in two parts only; almost all of these are not liturgical pieces but vernacular carols. There are eight examples of five-part writing, and no piece is written in more than five parts. In terms of overall compass this body of music, amounting to some 344 movements, exhibits a number of very conspicuous elements of consistency. Roughly equal numbers of pieces employ compasses of, respectively, thirteen, fourteen and fifteen notes, and between them these account for over 89 per cent of the total (see Table 1:1 below). A bare handful operate within a compass smaller than thirteen notes. Twenty-one pieces extend to sixteen notes and just two to seventeen; no piece uses a compass exceeding seventeen notes. It seems safe to conclude, therefore, that the performing medium available within choirs of all types to render polyphony at this period was best able to execute music composed within a compass of between one octave and a sixth and two octaves. Very few pieces exceed that upper limit (and then virtually never by more than one note), and two octaves may be taken as the normal upper working limit of overall compass.

Within these thirteen to fifteen notes the constituent voices were arranged not at random but according to a small number of particular predispositions. These were ubiquitous, and had first become established during the period c. 1330 – c. 1370.[2] Prior to c. 1390 all the commonest forms of composition had been written in score format and had adopted a 'terraced' design of vocal scoring based on the stratification of three unequal voices: high, middle and low. The very few exceptions employed two equal upper voices above a single lower voice. The contemporary motet repertory, copied in *cantus collateralis* format, included pieces in four as well as three parts, and in the case of the former the extra participant was always a second upper voice. Analysis of a substantial portion (111 pieces) of the surviving repertory of the period c. 1320 – c. 1390 has

---

2   For a full discussion see Roger Bowers, 'The performing ensemble for English church polyphony, c. 1320–1390', in Stanley Boorman (ed.), *Studies in the Performance of Late Mediaeval Music* (Cambridge 1983), pp. 161–92. The present chapter bridges the chronological gap between this article and my 'The vocal scoring, choral balance and performing pitch of Latin church polyphony in England, c. 1500–58', *Journal of the Royal Musical Association* 112 (1987), pp. 38–76. It supersedes my preliminary study, 'The performing pitch of English 15th-century church polyphony', *Early Music* 8 (1980), pp. 21–8. A few brief passages from these articles have been incorporated here.

Table 1:1: Overall compasses in music composed between c. 1370 and c. 1450

Compositions per vocal texture (VOICES)				Date of composition of contents: approximate span	Manuscript / Edition	Total number of compositions	Number of compositions observing each overall compass (NOTES)								
2	3	4	5				10 or fewer	11	12	13	14	15	16	17	18 or more
-	10	5	-	1370–1405	GB-Lbl Add. 40011B [a]	15	-	-	-	3	4	6	2	-	-
10	3	-	-	1400–20	GB-Ctc O.3.58 [b]	13	-	1	2	6	3	1	-	-	-
-	83	21	8	1380–1420	GB-Lbl Add. 57950 (first layer) [c]	112	-	2	10	40	34	18	7	1	-
-	29	-	-	1410–25	GB-Lbl Add. 57950 (additions) [c]	29	-	-	-	14	10	5	-	-	-
-	24	2	-	1400–45	Lionel Power: Complete 'Motets' [d]	26	-	-	2	6	8	8	1	1	-
-	56	6	-	1415–55	John Dunstable: Complete Works [e]	62	-	-	-	4	21	28	8	1	-
15	18	-	-	1420–35	GB-Lbl Egerton 3307 (carols) [b]	33	-	1	1	11	10	9	1	-	-
4	11	3	-	1420–35	GB-Lbl Egerton 3307 (liturgical) [f]	18	-	-	1	2	3	10	2	-	-
18	13	-	-	1420–35	GB-Ob Selden B.26 (carols) [b]	31	1	0	3	13	9	5	-	-	-
1	14	1	-	1420–35	GB-Ob Selden B.26 (liturgical) [f]	16	-	-	1	3	9	3	-	-	-
-	2	2	-	1440–55	GB-Ob Add. c.87	4	-	-	-	-	3	0	1	-	-
48	263	40	8		Sub-totals	359	1	4	20	102	114	93	22	3	-
-	12	3	-		SUBTRACT DUPLICATED ITEMS	15	-	-	2	1	6	4	1	1	-
48	251	37	8	1370–1455	TOTALS	344	1	4	18	101	108	89	21	2	-

disclosed that the working compasses of the individual voices commonly extended to, and only rarely exceeded, an interval of a tenth; and throughout this repertory the differentials between high, middle and low voices were not random, but constant. This analysis, that is, yields the noteworthy result that all composers ventured upon their work in the prospect of performance by ensembles of voices which all observed a uniform structure. If a clefless staff of seven lines be used to designate the two-octave overall working compass of these ensembles, and the first leger line above the staff to express the extension to a sixteenth occasionally employed, then the relative deployment of the voices in terms of pitch (and, by implication, of timbre) may be displayed as in Figure 1:1 below. All the four-part music in this repertory was performable by the complete ensemble, and the three-part music by singers representing voices 2a, 3^1 and 4 or (less commonly) 2a, 2b and 4. Figure 1:1 thus displays the prevailing vocal differentials being observed in the performing groups at the opening of the present period, c. 1390.[3]

voice: 2a   2b 3^1 4

Figure 1:1: Ranges and differentials of voices engaged in church polyphony, c. 1320 – c. 1390

At the very end of the fourteenth century, and evidently under the influence of the newly intensified contact with the music (and overall culture) of northern France that took place during the 1390s, this all-pervasive standard deployment of voices for polyphonic performance underwent a significant change. Of this the result was a revised pattern of vocal scoring which eventually entirely superseded its predecessor and predominated until c. 1450–60. Following the model set by the continental secular chanson, composers of church polyphony in England now adopted for the scoring of their three-part music a pattern involving a single high voice pitched above two lower and equal voices. The latter two employed the same range and commonly the same clef. Within the contrapuntal web they fulfilled

Notes to Table 1:1

a   Edward Kershaw (ed.), *The Fountains Fragments* (Newton Abbot 1989).
b   John Stevens (ed.), 'Medieval Carols', *Musica Britannica* 4 (London 1952; 2/1958).
c   Andrew Hughes and Margaret Bent (eds.), 'The Old Hall Manuscript', 3 vols., *Corpus Mensurabilis Musicae* 46 (Rome 1969).
d   Charles Hamm (ed.), 'Leonel Power: Complete Works', 2 vols., *Corpus Mensurabilis Musicae* 50 (Rome 1969–i.p.).
e   Manfred F. Bukofzer (ed.), 'John Dunstable: Complete Works', *Musica Britannica* 8 (London 1953; 2/1970, revised by Margaret Bent, Ian Bent and Brian Trowell; no. 73 excluded here for later consideration (pp. 27, 29).
f   Andrew Hughes (ed.), 'Fifteenth-century Liturgical Music', *Early English Church Music* 8 (London 1967); Gwynn S. McPeek (ed.), *The British Museum Manuscript Egerton 3307* (London 1963).

3   The number appended to each of the several voices is a point of reference intended to assist the identification of each through the successive Figures illustrating the text.

the function of *contratenor* and *tenor*, and commonly they were actually so labelled by the scribes of the manuscript sources. This internal modification to vocal scoring was accomplished without alteration of the prevailing upper working limit of overall compass, which remained at two octaves.

A source such as the 'Old Hall' manuscript,[4] compiled probably between 1418 and 1422 but containing pieces composed from c. 1375 onwards, includes music from both sides of this chronological divide. Of the 141 pieces sufficiently complete for this kind of analysis[5] 76 exhibit the long-established format of presentation in score while 65 observe the *cantus collateralis* layout employed both for the pieces in the style and scoring of the chanson and for those in motet and isorhythmic forms. Those in score format may be considered first. Of these, 63 are found in the original (c. 1418–21) and thirteen in the additional (c. 1421–2) layers; all are in three parts.[6] The very great majority observe the historic vocal scoring long established for such pieces. In 54 of the first-layer items and eight of the second-layer pieces the disposition of voices observes the standard terraced layout of voices 2a, 3^1 and 4 of Figure 1:1 above.[7] Just two pieces, copied consecutively (104, 105), observe the alternative vocal disposition of 2a, 2b and 4. In all cases, very few individual voices exceed a compass of a ninth.

All the remaining dozen pieces in score layout show how the traditions even of composition in this long-established format were modified at the turn and in the early years of the fifteenth century under the influence of the vocal scoring of the continental chanson, for all deploy the novel compositional layout of a single high voice pitched above two lower voices of equal range. Just seven out of the 63 first-layer pieces display this disposition, and all are among the most recent compositions and by named composers; two are by Cooke (7, 52), three by Chirbury (61, 102, 132) and one each by Roy Henry (94) and John Excetre (121). Five of the thirteen second-layer pieces in score also exhibit this scoring; they are by Sturgeon (9, 114), Damett (13, 54) and Burell (65). It is not uncommon for the ranges of individual voices in this repertory to extend to an interval of a tenth, one step wider than the upper limit encountered in the older-style pieces presented in score.

Among the 37 three-part pieces laid out in parts (*cantus collateralis*) 22 are found in the original layer and fifteen among the later additions. Nine are based on tenors disposed in isorhythmic layout; the remainder are in chanson style,

---

4   *GB-Lbl* Add. 57950. See fn. c to Table 1:1.

5   The items excluded are 69, 70, 91, 124, 143 and 144, of which all but the first belong in the original layer. For the completion of no. 147 see Margaret Bent, 'The progeny of Old Hall: more leaves from a royal English choirbook', in Luther Dittmer (ed.), *Gordon Athol Anderson: In Memoriam, Musicological Studies and Documents* 39 (Henryville 1984), pp. 11–18.

6   In the cases of both 4 and 139 the original core of the work will be included with consideration of the score repertory *a*3.

7   In 60, voice II's three excursions to a^1 extend one step above its limit, as does also voice II's single excursion to a^1 in 106 and voice I's single excursion to c^2 in 131. The single instance of pitch A in voice III of 136 produces a chord of 15-8-1 and appears certain to be an error; the true overall compass of this piece appears to be not A-c^2 but c-c^2.

founded on the duet established between *superius* and *tenor*. Among these 37 pieces a few traces of archaic fourteenth-century practice may still be found; they occur in three items in the original layer. A setting of the Credo (80) by Excetre observes most of the conventions of chanson style and layout in parts, but employs an old-fashioned terraced scoring adhering to the pattern 2a, 3[1] and 4 of Figure 1:1 above, slightly expanded to accommodate the wider individual ranges of (reading downwards) eleven, eleven and ten notes. Two isorhythmic pieces (19, 88) employ two equal high voices over a tenor, in the scoring 2a, 2b and 4 commonly encountered among fourteenth-century motets.[8] The remaining 34 pieces, whether in isorhythmic or chanson style, all exhibit a uniform scoring identifiable as that derived from the contemporary chanson, in which a single high voice is pitched a fifth above two lower, equal voices. The latter two are in *contratenor–tenor* relationship and almost invariably are actually identified as such by designations entered by the scribe on the manuscript. Individual voices, in all parts, commonly extend in range to a tenth and not infrequently to an eleventh.

The four-voice pieces, of which there are nineteen in the original layer and one among the subsequent additions, exhibit with only two exceptions the standard extension of this uniform scoring. In this the extra voice is a second *superius*, employing without exception the same range and tessitura as the first *superius*. Of the two non-conforming items, one is a piece exhibiting canonic structure (123), while the other is Dunstable's motet *Veni sancte spiritus / Veni creator spiritus*; both will be discussed later.[9]

Within its extensive repertory, therefore, the Old Hall manuscript incorporates the last of the traditions of scoring inherited from fourteenth-century music and inaugurates the adoption of the chanson-style scoring taken from continental example after c. 1390. All of the three- and four-part pieces which exhibit the older scoring could be performed by an ensemble of four voices stratified as in Figure 1:1 above. All of the three- and four-part music exhibiting the new scoring could be performed by an ensemble of voices slightly differently constituted, as delineated in Figure 1:2 below. The effective removal of the erstwhile middle voice will be seen to have allowed each of the two remaining vocal timbres to expand to respective ranges of an eleventh; that indeed is the extreme of range that can be accommodated on the five-line staff without

part-name: *contratenor*   *tenor*
voice: 2a   2b   3   4

Figure 1:2: Ranges and differentials of voices engaged in church polyphony, c. 1390 – c. 1455

8   Bowers, 'Performing ensemble', pp. 169–70.
9   See fn. 12 and p. 9 below.

recourse to leger lines. The need for an extra step permitting the realization of overall compasses of a sixteenth still remains, though it is required only for five of the four-voice pieces.[10]

As far as England is concerned, composition in five parts is unique to the Old Hall manuscript.[11] In four instances (the paired items 21 and 77, 36 and 82) a four-voice piece employing standard scoring exhibits a concluding section *a5*, in which the extra voice is created by the division of the topmost voice into two real parts of equal range. The remainder (27, 35, 71, 75) all accomplish composition *a5* through the device of canon at the unison, and in respect of their vocal scoring the results are uniform with those of the first four pieces. All eight engage a scoring realizable by the forces displayed as in Figure 1:3 below.[12] No new vocal timbre was involved; the five parts engage merely an expanded number of voices that answer to the parameters of relative pitch already established.

part-name: *contratenor*   *tenor*
voice: 2a   2a[1]   2b   3   4

Figure 1:3: Ranges and differentials of voices for five-part compositions in the 'Old Hall' manuscript

The conclusions derived from this study of the Old Hall manuscript are fully corroborated by the analysis of sources contemporary with it. Moreover, the practices of vocal scoring exhibited by the later music may be seen to become thoroughly consolidated and absorbed into the compositions of the generation following. Only a summary of this analysis can be given here. Of not every single piece does examination of the vocal scoring produce a result which fits perfectly into the fundamental matrix shown in Figure 1:2 above. Nevertheless, exceptions are strikingly few and, when they occur, almost invariably of negligible significance. Indeed, perhaps the most remarkable feature of this research has been the way in which countless pages of tables, charts, diagrams and figures concerning the analysis of many hundreds of pieces of music reveal and resolve into consistencies so all-pervasive that the data to be derived from them can be distilled into just a few simple sentences.

The fifteen complete pieces to be found in *GB-Lbl* Add. 40011B[13] (of which six concord with items in the Old Hall manuscript) exhibit the elements of this transitional period at an early stage. Nine are written out in score. Of these, all but one observe the terraced scoring and standard differentials of the fourteenth-

---

10   These are 28, 78, 118, 146, 147.
11   For present purposes the canonic piece 28 has been considered as a four-part composition.
12   The canonic piece 123, when realized as a canon 3-in-1 over a tenor, requires voices 2a-2a[1]-2b-4 of Figure 1:3.
13   For the compilation of this manuscript a date of 1407 has been suggested; see Roger Bowers, 'Fixed points in the chronology of English fourteenth-century polyphony', *Music and Letters* 71 (1990), pp. 317–20.

century repertory and display no part-names; the exception (7) observes chanson-style scoring. Among the remaining six pieces, whether for three voices or four, the *contratenor* and *tenor* parts are explicitly identified and marked as such on the manuscript, and only one makes any departure from the standard chanson-style scoring depicted in Figure 1:2 above. This is a canonic setting of the Gloria (3); its three written voices observe standard chanson scoring, but a fourth voice derived in canon from the tenor adds, in effect, a third low voice.

Examination both of the collection of works published as the complete 'motets' of Lionel Power and of the collected works of John Dunstable shows that the vocal scoring established by the later generation of Old Hall composers, as shown in Figure 1:2 above, became the standard for the composers at work in the period immediately following. The editor of the Marian antiphons of Lionel Power arranged them in perceived chronological order. The first five (which include three pieces from the Old Hall manuscript) exhibit the long-established style of terraced scoring. The remaining 21 are all composed to the standard disposition of *superius*, *contratenor* and *tenor* of either three voices or four (the two items *a*4 – nos. 7 and 12 – having double *superius*) as displayed in Figure 1:2 above. Strikingly few liberties are taken with this structure, and all are very slight.

Of the 63 complete pieces of sacred music published in the complete works of John Dunstable, one piece must await discussion as an early representative of the next generation of patterns of vocal scoring.[14] Of the remaining 62 all but one observe the standard scoring of *superius*, *contratenor* and *tenor* as displayed in Figure 1:2 above; the five four-part pieces (11, 12, 28–30) exhibit that scoring with double *superius*. Six of these items (3, 4, 16, 19, 29, 35) employ an overall compass of sixteen notes and extend to the extra step shown in Figure 1:2 above. As in the case of the music of Lionel Power the departures are strikingly few and of small significance. The single significant exception is the four-voice isorhythmic motet *Veni sancte spiritus* (32). In this the second texted voice (voice II) occupies a pitch-range markedly lower than that of the topmost voice.[15] It is not therefore a conventional second *superius*, and it observes a role different from that predicated by the pattern depicted in Figure 1:2 above; rather, it exhibits a range almost overlapping that of voice III.

There is no point in extending equally detailed investigation to the contents of the remaining principal manuscripts of this period. With only one exception the sixteen liturgical items in *GB-Ob* Selden B.26 observe the standard disposition of scoring. In *Nesciens mater* (13) the three voices consist of a *tenor* pitched a fifth below two equal high voices, creating a scoring realizable by voices 2a, 2b and 4 of Figure 1:2 above. It is clear that in *Sancta Maria virgo* (3) the sections engaging all three participating voices were composed for the standard disposition of *superius*, *contratenor* and *tenor*, while the intervening duos are (despite the

---

14 See below, pp. 27, 29.
15 This is also a feature of two out of the other three four-part isorhythmic motets (29, 30), though not to the point of negating adherence to the predominant pattern of vocal scoring.

manuscript layout) for a gymel of voices of *superius* pitch.[16] Among the eighteen liturgical pieces with which *GB-Lbl* Egerton 3307 begins, all but the first (which observes *cantus collateralis* layout, chanson scoring, and manuscript identification of the *contratenor* and *tenor*) are written out in the score format to which their musical style is well suited. Four pieces are in two parts only (*superius* and *tenor*). Among the rest the narrow ranges of the constituent voices often prevent the scoring from falling unequivocally into either classification, but if the pitch proximity of the two lower voices be taken as a yardstick, then eight (19, 23–25, 27, 29, 30, 35) employ terraced scoring and five chanson scoring (21, 22, 26, 32, 38). The carol repertories of these two manuscripts contain music which was not for liturgical use, but was executed by singers the same as those by whom the liturgical items were performed. The carols exhibit no conspicuous departures from the principles already enunciated.

This analysis of the music written between c. 1390 and c. 1455 points to a clear conclusion. Composers undertook their work in the expectation that their music would be performed by groups of singers who, no matter to which church or chapel they belonged, exhibited a single, recognized and conventional pattern of membership. Each group of singers was comprised of representatives of four standard participating parts (five in the exceptional case of the chapel for which the Old Hall manuscript was compiled). These consisted of two higher voices and two lower voices, each pair being comprised of voices of the same pitch and character. The two pairs occupied, respectively, the upper and lower elevenths of an overall sounding compass of two octaves, their ranges being separated by an interval of a fifth (Figure 1:2 above). In terms of the contrapuntal construction of the music the parts sung by the two lower voices were the *contratenor* and *tenor*, and commonly were specifically identified as such.

(b) Vocal timbre and sounding pitch

All that has been established so far is the number of parts included within a standard ensemble and the pitch of each relative to the others. Their timbre and actual sounding pitch remain unidentified by the above analysis. However, the uncompromising degree of uniformity exhibited by the vocal scoring of some hundreds of pieces of music certainly indicates that a single performing manner was adopted by the several ensemble groups, and this degree of uniformity necessarily predicates a roughly uniform level of sounding pitch and manner of vocal scoring. It is not inappropriate, therefore, to attempt to identify those points within the spectrum of pitch ostensibly available to the ensembles of performers at which that uniform level might actually have lain.

Clefs were, of course, identified and employed in the notation of this music, but these can give no assistance in determining the actual sounding pitch

---

16 The duos are for two voices pitched $g-c^2$; in the full sections a single voice of this pitch operates above a *contratenor* ($e-f^1$) and a *tenor* ($c-c^1$).

envisaged by the composer. No device to convey actual sounding pitch had yet evolved within musical notation, for the simple reason that groups of performers constituted according to a single pervasive pattern of vocal membership needed none. Rather, the manner in which the clef was deployed at this period shows that it was used with no more than the conventional meaning which it had always possessed in the context of the notation of plainsong within which it had evolved. It conveyed no indication of sounding pitch, but merely indicated the location of the diatonic semitones. Felicitous location of the semitones in such a way as to minimize the use of leger lines commonly resulted, in polyphonic music, in the engagement of a wide variety of configurations of clefs. Within the volume of the collected 'motets' published under the name of Lionel Power, for instance, the interval between the highest note occurring, written as f^2, and the lowest, F, is three octaves – that is, 22 notes.[17] Yet, as has been seen, no individual piece uses so wide an overall compass. One reaches seventeen notes and one sixteen, but none of the remaining 24 exceeds fifteen notes in compass. Comparable observations apply throughout this repertory. So if there really were voices which could sing up to f^2 and others able to sing down to F, it is strange indeed that they were *never* used simultaneously in the same piece. Rather, it is evidence that indications of sounding pitch ostensibly yielded by the original clefs are in fact wholly illusory, and arise only from assumptions and expectations concerning the nature and function of the clefs that are anachronistic. The composer's choice of clef configuration for any one piece discloses much concerning the nature of the composing process, but nothing about sounding pitch. To resolve this question, evidence of another sort must be used, namely archival evidence relating to the performing ensembles themselves.

The performance of the composed polyphony of this period was undertaken by the musically most literate members of the choirs of the major churches and of certain royal, aristocratic and episcopal household chapels. A survey of the institutions in England likely by c. 1450 to have maintained a musical culture which included the performance of written polyphony extends to some 65 establishments – a number that had grown considerably from the 35 to 40 of c. 1390. These included the nine secular cathedrals,[18] perhaps some thirty collegiate churches (including a few of the greater hospital establishments recently re-founded),[19] and some dozen to fifteen household chapels of the king (the Chapel Royal) and of the greater aristocracy, the richer bishops, and one or two lesser aristocrats and gentlemen of especial piety. These choirs included both men and boys; with them should be included some dozen or so ensembles which

17 Hamm, 'Leonel Power: Collected Works', I, nos. 6, and 4 and 26 respectively.
18 London (St Paul's), Salisbury, Chichester, Exeter, Wells, Lichfield, York, Lincoln and Hereford.
19 Including Arundel, Beverley, Cambridge (King's College), Crediton, Eton, Fotheringhay, Glasney, Hastings, Higham Ferrers, Leicester (St Mary Newarke), London (St Anthony), London (St Katherine), London (St Martin le Grand), Maidstone, Manchester, Ottery St Mary, Oxford (All Souls), Oxford (New College), Ripon, Southwell, Stoke by Clare, Tattershall, Wallingford, Warwick, Westbury-on-Trym, Westminster (St Stephen), Winchester (St Elizabeth), Winchester (St Mary), Winchester (St Cross) and Windsor.

consisted of men's voices only, including certain monastery Lady Chapel choirs of the oldest foundation,[20] a very few collegiate churches,[21] and a handful of ensembles of enthusiasts among the greater establishments of monks and regular canons.[22] Overall, the membership of these choirs in terms of numbers was very diverse. They ranged from 50 to 60 singers in the case of the largest cathedral choirs (Salisbury, Lincoln) down to around a dozen; indeed, the ensembles associated with monasteries (adult Lady Chapel choirs, and groups of enthusiasts among the monks) might number only three or four. There is no reason to suspect that any simple parish church yet maintained a professional choir, nor that the score or so of monastery Lady Chapel choirs consisting only of boys' voices under a professional Instructor yet performed any composed polyphony.

In determining the nature of the performing groups for polyphony, it is possible to exclude certain departments of the choirs from consideration from the outset. The monastic establishments excepted, these choirs included boys' voices as well as men's, but it is clear that at this period the voices of the boys were not used in the performance of written polyphony. The functions and duties then expected of the Instructor of the Choristers were thoroughly unexalted, and relegated him to possession of no great esteem or significance within any choral organization. By the statutes of New College, Oxford (1400), for instance, provision was made for the maintenance of sixteen choristers, but the actual arrangements for their teaching appeared of too little significance to merit any mention whatever, even in this most intricate, extended and ostensibly comprehensive document.[23] Even half a century later the statutes of King's College, Cambridge (1453), included only three very slight references to the choristers' Instructor, each purely incidental to other matters.[24] The demands of the liturgy required that the boys of any choir be taught their parts in its ceremony and plainsong, plus reading, writing and a command of Latin sufficient to enable them to recite the lessons of matins deputed to them.[25] In the most enterprising choirs provision was made at least from the early fifteenth century onwards to ensure that the boys were taught the skills of 'descant' – that is, the improvisation at sight of a line of melody above a given plainsong.[26] Nevertheless,

---

20 Including Worcester Cathedral Priory, Bristol Abbey and Westminster Abbey.

21 Including Hemingbrough, London (Guildhall Chapel) and Mettingham.

22 Including Westminster (St Peter), Canterbury (Christ Church), Winchester (St Swithun) and Durham.

23 Her Majesty's Commissioners, *Statutes of the Colleges of Oxford*, 3 vols. (Oxford and London 1853), I, pt. 5.

24 J. Heywood and T. Wright, *The Ancient Laws of the Fifteenth Century for King's College, Cambridge, and the Public School of Eton College* (London 1850), pp. 69, 108, 121.

25 See e.g. Statutes 15 and 16 of St George's Chapel, Windsor (1352): Windsor, Dean and Chapter, MS iv.B.1, f. 77^v; also statutes 4, 37: *ibid.*, ff. 75^v, 79^v.

26 For instance, the statutes of the collegiate church of Stoke by Clare (c. 1415–22) required that the boys be taught 'in lectura, cantu plano et discantu': London, Public Record Office (henceforth PRO) E315/3/50, f. 11^v. Lionel Power (d. 1445) served as Instructor of the Choristers of the chapel of the household of Thomas, Duke of Clarence and later as Master of the Lady Chapel choir of boys' voices at Christ Church, Canterbury; his 'Tretis upon the Gamme' is a manual of descant, written for one who would 'enforme a childe in his counterpoynt': Sanford B. Meech, 'Three musical treatises in English from a fifteenth-century manuscript', *Speculum* 10 (1935), p. 242.

although the English term 'pricksong' and some Latin equivalents were already
in use to denote written polyphony, no surviving set of statutes or act of chapter
prior to c. 1460 requires that this be among the skills taught to choristers.[27] It
is clear that it is possible to discard from consideration any proposition that the
voices of boys participated at all in performances of the polyphony of the period
c. 1390 – c. 1450.

The performing ensemble for church polyphony of this period therefore
consisted only of adult male voices. Modern taste and tradition divides the
naturally occurring timbres of these voices into three basic types: bass, tenor and
alto. It would not, of course, be safe to assume that early fifteenth-century throats
produced, or that early fifteenth-century ears perceived, the several vocal timbres
in precisely the same way as do their modern counterparts. Nevertheless, the
consistent layering and the standardized spacing of the voices used in this
repertory certainly suggest that a stratification of vocal timbres into self-contained,
discrete categories was perceived, and, moreover, exploited in the process of
composition. To avoid the possible anachronism of misnomer, reference will be
made to these timbres of voice, for the time being, by reference to the names
of the parts severally sung by each: *superius* (I and II), *contratenor* and *tenor*. Between
them, the three timbres of modern adult male voices can comfortably sustain
an overall working range of some nineteen notes, $F–c^2$ in terms of modern pitch
(a^1 = 440). The fifteen- or sixteen-note range of early fifteenth-century polyphony
did not, therefore, utilize the whole range realizable by adult male voices.
Consequently, the primary objective here is to identify that part of the spectrum
of nineteen notes or so ostensibly available which actually was *not* used in early
fifteenth-century performance.

This question cannot be resolved with complete conclusivity, but a number
of inferential lines of argument do all point to a single conclusion. First, it is
clear that something akin to the modern alto voice was well known in the
Middle Ages. Most references to its existence in England occur as prohibitions
forbidding members of certain of the more austere religious orders from using
it in their services. These references therefore rather pre-date the early fifteenth
century, but a continuum from these thirteenth-century instances can be established.[28] Since the alto voice seems unlikely to have had anything to contribute
to the performance of plainsong, it seems reasonable to propose that when used
at all it was in the performance of polyphony.

Secondly, it must be recalled that the choirs of which the singers of polyphony
were members were constituted principally and essentially to execute not
polyphony at all, but the plainsong liturgy. Since most plainsong melodies do

---

27 The contract of appointment of John Stele as Master of the Lady Chapel choir at Durham Cathedral Priory
     dated December 1430 required that he teach organ-playing and also 'Pryktenote Faburden deschaunte et
     counter', but his pupils were to include monks of the priory as well as the eight boys of the Lady Chapel
     choir: Durham, Archives of the Dean and Chapter, Priory Register III, f. 137ᵛ.
28 Bowers, 'Performing ensemble', pp. 179–81; Bowers, 'Performing pitch of English 15th-century church
     polyphony', p. 22 and fn. 8, with subsequent correspondence, *Early Music* 9 (1981), pp. 71–5.

not exceed a total overall compass of a ninth, one conspicuous characteristic of all such choirs was the absence of any call upon the singers as a body to be able to realize a range of pitch very much broader than that. Further, in the case of that large proportion of the plainsong repertory that was deputed by the consuetudinaries to performance by *omnes*, the men had to sing at a pitch that could comfortably be duplicated an octave higher by the voices of the boys. These considerations lead to the important conclusion that whatever the lowest pitches required for the performance of plainsong may have been, they would not have required voices able to descend any lower than about *c*. Genuine bass voices there may well have been among the membership of the choirs, but no call was made on their ability to sing in the lower part of their register.[29] Indeed, church authorities seem not to have approved of chanting at low pitch, and actually discouraged it if there was a danger of its becoming customary.[30] It has already been noted above that the bodies of singers to whom was committed the performance of polyphony can be shown to have eschewed recourse to a portion of the range of pitch ostensibly available to them. It seems fair to propose that the sector of range which they were discarding for polyphony was the same as that which they conventionally abjured in the performance of their prevailing repertory of plainsong chant.

All the available evidence, therefore, points to three conclusions that are evidently congruent. Within the ensembles by whom polyphonic music was performed, (a) the voices of boys were not engaged; (b) the lower reaches of the adult register, those below about *c*, were not engaged; (c) two basic timbres of voice were available, namely something akin to the modern alto voice, and a tenor or tenor/baritone not descending any lower than whatever pitch was necessary for plainsong. Given that the standard working overall compass of composed polyphony was two octaves, it does in fact become possible now to nominate a two-octave range which appears to meet all the criteria here established. If the highest working note of the alto be taken as c^2 (in modern terms), then the two vocal timbres represented in Figure 1:2 resolve into an alto singing at around $g–c^2$ (occasionally reaching d^2) and a lowish tenor singing at around $c–f^1$. This resolution is depicted in Figure 1:4 below, and appears notably felicitous. It does not employ boys' voices and it does not employ bass voices; it predicates the use of the two types of vocal timbre which, however slenderly, the evidence does suggest were available. It may be added here that there is nothing in these propositions that is at all novel or contentious. Writing nearly 40 years ago, Frank Harrison observed that 'it is clear that the range of polyphony

---

29 Doubtless, voices did exist which could descend lower than *c*, but in order to bring them into use in their lower register the liturgy had to express a specific stipulation to that effect – for instance, for the words of Christ in the recitations of the Passion story during Holy Week, which were expressly allocated to a low (*bassa*) voice.

30 For instance, in 1394 the cathedral chapter of Salisbury reprimanded both the vicars choral as a body for the low pitch of the singing (*precipue in depressione cantus*), and the succentor in particular for neglecting his duty to correct them: Salisbury, Archives of the Dean and Chapter, Reg. Dunham, f. 130[r].

until the second half of the fifteenth century corresponded to that of the tenor and countertenor [i.e. alto] of today'.[31] Harrison's intuition, born of long study of the music, and the present independent review of the full range of the evidence, such as it is, converge exactly upon the same conclusion.

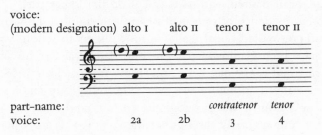

Figure 1:4: Timbres and ranges of voices engaged in church polyphony, c. 1390 – c. 1455

This is not, of course, to claim that every performance on every occasion emerged at this level of pitch. In the absence of any concept of fixed pitch in association with performance by unaccompanied voices, pitch would doubtless have varied somewhat from place to place, and from occasion to occasion. In the case of pieces engaging a compass of less than the full two octaves there was evidently some degree of leeway within that constraint. However, recognition of the fixed pattern of vocal scoring evident throughout the repertory does allow the concept of a range of performing pitch subject to boundaries represented by the two-octave compass $c–c^2$ to emerge with some clarity.

(c) Ensemble: solo quartet and proto-chorus

It transpires, therefore, that the ensembles singing the church polyphony of this period needed to be able to perform in up to four parts, in voices that may be thought of as akin to two alto and two tenor. Something can be said of the actual size of the ensemble. There is widespread agreement that the church polyphony of the fourteenth century and earlier was the preserve of ensembles of solo voices singing one to a part.[32] Some corroboration for this proposition is provided by the terms of the foundation charter of a small chantry college at Epworth in the Isle of Axholme, Lincolnshire, dated 1351. The college was to be staffed by a warden, two priests and four adult clerks, and the founders required of the latter that they be able to perform polyphony. For this purpose the warden was required to ensure that out of these four 'let one know adequately how to sing the tenor, and another the middle part, and the other two the third part'.[33] It will be seen

31   Frank Ll. Harrison, *Music in Medieval Britain* (London 1958; 2/1963), p. 311.
32   Manfred F. Bukofzer, 'The beginnings of choral polyphony', in *Studies in Medieval and Renaissance Music* (New York 1950), pp. 176–89.
33   'unus tenorem et alius medium et ceteri duo cantum tertium sciant canere competenter': Lincolnshire Archives Office, Cathedral Archives, MS Dij 51/3(4). 'Cantus tertius', 'trebyll' and the like were terms which at this

that the terms of this directive match perfectly the vocal scoring of the polyphony of its period, requiring two upper voices, one middle voice and one lower (cf. Figure 1:1 above). This configuration allowed performance one to a part of four-voice music. However, it also allowed three-part music to be sung either one to a part likewise, or, if desired, with two voices on the upper part.

There is other evidence of fourteenth-century origin to show that within the larger choirs there existed select teams of four singers to whom was committed the performance of polyphony.[34] At Lincoln Cathedral, for instance, the Lady Mass was performed every day with polyphony from at least 1368 onwards and probably from some time before that date. The sub-group among the 40 or so vicars choral by whom it was sung numbered four, and references to them and to their work occur regularly throughout the c. 1390 – c. 1455 period.[35]

In the recently founded choirs of the early fifteenth century it was from the newly introduced category of the professional lay clerks, rather than from the vicars or chaplains in priest's orders, that the performance of polyphony was expected,[36] and the number of clerks appointed for inclusion in these choirs shows a remarkable degree of consistency. There were to be four at Manchester (1421), Higham Ferrers (1422), Eton (1440, until c. 1445), Sherburn Hospital (1434) and Westbury-on-Trym (re-foundation 1439), while at Hemingbrough (1426), Warwick (St Mary, re-foundation 1439), Tattershall (1439, until c. 1460), Cambridge (King's College, c. 1445), Winchester (St Cross, re-foundation 1445) and London (St Katherine, re-foundation c. 1445) there were to be six.[37] At Eton College the ten chapel clerks for whom provision was made after c. 1445 included four specialist singers of polyphony and six ancillary staff, and a differential probably of the same nature obtained at Fotheringhay College (founded 1415) between the four clerks-gentleman (*clerici generosi*) and the four clerks-yeoman (*clerici valecti*).[38] Meanwhile, older-established colleges endowed with fewer than four clerkships now increased their membership to this number. For instance, a fourth clerkship (to be master of the choristers) had been added at New College, Oxford, by 1460, and at Leicester (St Mary) by c. 1450.[39] The pervasive efficacy of a group of four specialist singing-men for the performance

period had no association with the boy's voice. They designated merely the voice required to sing the topmost part in 'three-fold' (that is, three-part) polyphony, which at this period was an adult voice. See also p. 17 and fn. 43 below.

34   Bowers, 'Performing ensemble', pp. 175–8.

35   For further discussion of this evidence see Bowers, 'Performing ensemble', pp. 176–7, and for its institutional context see Roger Bowers, 'Music and worship to 1640', in D. Owen (ed.), *A History of Lincoln Minster* (Cambridge 1994), pp. 47–57.

36   For the genesis of the category and profession of lay clerk see Roger Bowers, 'Choral institutions within the English church: their constitution and development, 1340–1500' (Diss., U. of East Anglia 1975), pp. 4040–50, 5057–66, 5072–81.

37   For sources, see *ibid.*, pp. 4011, 4019–20, 5005–13.

38   *Ibid.*, pp. 4043–4, 5057–61.

39   A. H. M. Jones, 'Oxford: New College', in H. E. Salter and M. D. Lobel (eds.), *Victoria County History of Oxfordshire*, 17 vols. (London 1954), III, p. 157; A. H. Thompson, 'Visitations in the diocese of Lincoln, 1517–31', 3 vols., *Lincoln Record Society* 37 (1947), III, p. 240.

of polyphony is indicated most clearly by the provision made at Eton College. This foundation was most richly endowed; King Henry VI, its creator, was especially noted for his piety, and his college, for which he planned a chapel of cathedral dimensions, lacked for nothing wherewith to reflect a suitably edifying image of its founder's devotion as an exemplary son of the Church. Yet as late as 1453, when the statutes were finalized and promulgated,[40] a solo ensemble of four specialist singers was still all that was considered necessary to perform composed polyphonic music even at this most favoured of establishments.

Yet there is also evidence that certain choirs of especial prominence were already experimenting with the use of a small chorus for the performance of polyphony. It appears that Westminster Abbey may have been the first monastery to give effect to the novel type of Lady Chapel choir that consisted just of boys' voices under a single adult master; this was inaugurated, probably with four boys, in 1384. To this group at Easter 1393 was added a team of three further men, and at Michaelmas 1397, while the boys remained at four, the men were abruptly increased in number up to seven. This impressive enterprise lasted only two years, to Michaelmas 1399;[41] fortunately, during the summer of 1399 there was compiled a list of this team of seven men that identifies each by both name and a vocal designation,[42] and it is clear that all included among their abilities the competence to sing polyphonic music. The master, the composer John Tyes, was listed as *organista*, a term meaning 'singer of polyphonic music' generally. The vocal designation of one, William Causton, was not given, but he received exactly the same remuneration as John Byfield, designated 'Tenor'. All the remaining four, John Barker, John Grede, Peter Pleford and John Browing, were designated 'treble'.[43] In performing four-part music of this period, therefore – a time of overlap when both terraced and chanson scoring were current – there was scope for the master to deploy two voices on each upper part, while sharing the remaining two parts between the three other singers. In three-part music the availability of four men to sing the upper line gave scope for a genuinely choral sound to be developed.

The Westminster Abbey experiment was short-lived but not likely to have been unique at this time. Indeed, it appears to bespeak the intense interest in the abbey taken at the time by the king, Richard II,[44] and it is even possible

40 For the date of the Eton College statutes see Bowers, 'Choral institutions', pp. A026–A030.
41 Further, within a year or two more (by 1401) the practice of using boys' voices had lapsed altogether, leaving an ensemble just of men's voices – probably three from 1399 until c. 1416–19, and certainly the standard four thereafter until 1480. The history of the Lady Chapel choir from 1384 until 1399 can be pieced together from the following obedientiary accounts: Westminster Abbey muniments, 18627, 18732, 18878–81, 18999, 19004, 19371–87, 19651–7, 19871–9, 23187, 23188–97, 23340, 23346–7, 24540, 50733.
42 *Ibid.*, Book 1 (Liber Niger), f. 86ᵛ.
43 For the term 'treble', see above, fn. 33. Barker and Pleford were certainly adults; by chance it is known that each had completed his days as a singing-boy some twenty-odd years before, for both had been choristers of the household chapel of Thomas Arundel, Bishop of Ely, during 1381–4: Cambridge University Library, MSS EDR D(5)2, m.3ᵈ, D(5)6, m.2ᵈ; PRO E101/400/28(2), m.2ᵈ.
44 It may be noted that the abrupt disbandment of the expanded choir at Michaelmas 1399 coincided with the deposition of the king.

that this enterprise reflected contemporary practice in his own Chapel Royal. Overall it appears to represent an emerging appetite for tonal grandeur well realizable by the contrast of the traditional sound of the solo ensemble against the more opulent sound of a small chorus. Evidence corroborative of such a departure at this time is supplied by the Old Hall manuscript of c. 1418–22. Among its 147 surviving compositions ten display a conspicuous feature: composed principally either in three or in four/five parts, each incorporates passages which are distinguished by being written for only two voices, and for which the verbal texts were written in red ink (a feature occurring nowhere else in the manuscript other than at these points). It is a feature associated with large conception in composition. Of the ten pieces concerned, six are Gloria–Credo pairs, and two are a Sanctus–Agnus pair;[45] the remainder are a Gloria and Credo (20, 80), both by John Excetre but not forming a pair. It has been suggested that the use of red text indicates that the passages for reduced voices were to be performed by a solo duet while the surrounding passages for the full three, four or five voices were executed by a small chorus, and this seems to be a very plausible proposition.[46] Certainly the physical size of the manuscript is consistent with this proposal; each page measures 41.6 × 27.6 cm and the music would appear to be written with sufficient clarity for up to six or eight singers to be able to place it on a lectern and gather round to perform it as a group. There is every likelihood that its original users were indeed able to supply such forces. A case has been presented for considering that the manuscript was originally compiled in c. 1418–21 for use by the chapel of the household of Thomas, Duke of Clarence, eldest of the three younger brothers of Henry v. The management of this very large chapel placed a high priority on the supply of specialist musical expertise; its personnel consisted of a dean, eight chaplains, no fewer than sixteen lay clerks and four choristers.[47] That so large a body of lay clerks should be able to furnish up to eight singers of polyphony seems a very reasonable proposition.

Moreover, the Old Hall manuscript is not alone in this respect, but stands as merely the first in a considerable line of sources which appear to display a continuum of tradition for the use of red ink for the inscription of the texts of passages of music composed for a reduced number of parts. These include *GB-Cul* Pembroke College 314, of c. 1440,[48] some very small fragments of a slightly

45 21 and 77 (Power), 36 and 82 (Cooke), 39 and 93 (Damett); 116 and 140 (Power): see Andrew Hughes, 'Mass-pairs in the Old Hall and other English manuscripts', *Revue Belge de Musicologie* 19 (1965), pp. 15–23.

46 The occasional division of individual parts into two notes at cadences supports this conclusion. Further, see Andrew Hughes, 'Mensural polyphony for choir in 15th-century England', *Journal of the American Musicological Society* 19 (1966), pp. 363–9. The views expressed by Hughes in respect of music composed prior to c. 1450 in 'The choir in fifteenth-century English music: non-mensural polyphony', in G. Reese and R. J. Snow (eds.), *Musicological Studies in Honor of Dragan Plamenac* (Pittsburgh 1967), pp. 127–45, are much less convincing.

47 Westminster Abbey muniments 12163, f. 16ᵛ; Roger Bowers, 'Some observations upon the life and career of Lionel Power', *Proceedings of the Royal Musical Association* 102 (1975/6), pp. 104–10.

48 Entry by Roger Bowers, in Iain Fenlon (ed.), *Cambridge Music Manuscripts, 900–1700* (Cambridge 1982), pp. 103–6.

earlier date from Christ Church, Canterbury,[49] one of the two items added in c. 1455 to *Lbl* Egerton 3307,[50] and a fragmentary leaf from a setting of *Magnificat* of c. 1500, also from Christ Church, Canterbury.[51] This tradition culminated in the Eton Choirbook of c. 1502–5,[52] and in the context of music of the early sixteenth century there is independent evidence indicating the use of solo voices for the 'counterverses' – that is, the passages which in the musical sources were written for reduced voices and utilized red text.[53]

Meanwhile, in the principal manuscripts preserving the early carol repertory up to c. 1450 an explicit verbal instruction for the distinction of two-part from three-part sections of the same work by means of choral performance is found. The word *chorus* (or *cho:*) is inscribed adjacent to the three-part burden of one carol in *Lbl* Egerton 3307, of several in *Ob* Selden B.26, and at three out of four possible locations in a further source now very fragmentary.[54] There appears to be an implication that while a small chorus sang the burden, the two-part verses were performed by solo singers; such a procedure matches exactly the inference drawn above from the use of red text in Old Hall and other manuscripts. These vernacular carols were not sung in church in the course of the liturgy, but this manner of performance appears to have been transferred intact from the chancel to the fireside of the vicars' choral hall or of the residentiary's mansion, the likely locale for the singing of these evidently professional church compositions. Neither *Ob* Selden B.26 nor *Lbl* Egerton 3307 is physically large, but at 25.6 × 18 cm and 29.8 × 21.5 cm respectively it is readily possible to visualize up to six performers singing from either of them at once. Indeed, by the period c. 1430–50 the practice of contrasting three-part music with intervening passages in two parts was very frequently observed in the composition of music of many kinds, especially that written for the Mass and for the votive antiphon. In the churches and chapels of greatest distinction the contrast may well have been emphasized by allocation respectively to a minimal chorus and to solo ensemble.

It seems safe to conclude that in respect of the period c. 1390 – c. 1455 a solo ensemble of four voices was considered to be the fundamental and irreducible

---

49 Canterbury, Cathedral Library and Archives, Add. MS 128/66.

50 For *Cantemus Domino, socie / Gaudent in celis* see below, pp. 26–7, 29.

51 Canterbury, Cathedral Library and Archives, Add. MS 128/7 (photocopy of original source, now stolen); Nicholas Sandon, 'Fragments of medieval polyphony at Canterbury Cathedral', *Musica Disciplina* 30 (1976), pp. 48, 51–3.

52 Frank Harrison (ed.), 'The Eton Choirbook', 3 vols., *Musica Britannica* 10–12 (London 1956–61; 2/1967–73), I, p. xxii.

53 John Pratt (ed.), *The Acts and Monuments of John Foxe*, 8 vols. (London; 4/1887), v, p. 46: a roughly contemporary description of a performance in c. 1540 of a votive antiphon *Lauda vivi alpha et O* (the only surviving setting of this text is that by Fayrfax) in which two soloists sang the counterverse 'O redemptrix et salvatrix'.

54 Stevens (ed.), 'Medieval Carols', nos. 17, 18, 20, 27, 29, 30, 36, 51; also nos. 77–9, 91, 118 from the rather later 'Ritson' manuscript (*GB-Lbl* Add. 5665). Enigmatic markings appearing at the appropriate points within the music of several other carols in *Lbl* Egerton 3307 may also signify sections for chorus: Bukofzer, *Studies in Medieval and Renaissance Music*, p. 154; David Fallows, 'Oxford, Bodleian Library, MS Bodley 88*', in Roger Bowers and Andrew Wathey (comps.), 'New sources of English fifteenth- and sixteenth-century polyphony', *Early Music History* 4 (1984), pp. 321, 328.

medium for any major church to provide for the performance of polyphonic music. Indeed, that such a level of provision was considered to be perfectly self-sufficient is indicated by its maintenance even at an institution so prominent and copiously endowed as Eton College. Meanwhile, certain of the very grandest institutions – those equipped with substantial numbers of singing clerks – were already adding to this traditional mode of performance the innovation of contrasting (in a manner rather akin to the *concerto grosso* principle) the sound of a small chorus for full writing against solo ensembles for writing in a reduced number of parts. On the smallest scale, it was also within the capacity of the churches staffed by a team of singing clerks numbering six, relatively common among new foundations and re-foundations from c. 1420 onwards, to observe this distinction during performances of three-part pieces which included 'counterverses' for solo duet. Probably the objective was the securing of a certain opulence of sound to match the general magnificence of the manner in which – as good sons of the Church, and as proprietors of their several household chapels and founders and/or patrons of the permanent colleges – the great lords of the time ordered the observance of religious devotions in their name. It was a departure offering great scope for further development.

(2) THE PERFORMANCE REVOLUTION, C. 1450 – C. 1500

(a) The development of polyphonic repertory for full chorus

During the second half of the fifteenth century English composers of church polyphony began to break through and discard certain constraints of vocal scoring and overall compass within which their predecessors had been content to work for well over a hundred years. Crucial to the effectuation of this development was the progressive simplification at this time of the notation of polyphonic composition. The marginalization of major prolation, and the increasing resort to smaller, duple note-values in *tempus perfectum* and *imperfectum*, resulted in the emergence of a notation sufficiently straightforward to be teachable both to boys and to that generality of singing-men who thitherto had never contemplated performing any music more demanding than plainsong and improvised descant. The result was the creation between c. 1450 and c. 1480 of music for performance in true choral polyphony, executed by substantial numbers of singers, including the boys, singing several to a part.

The body of music contained in the Eton Choirbook shows the manner in which, by some time well before 1500, the former standard texture of three

Notes to Table 1:2

a   Margaret and Ian Bent, 'Dufay, Dunstable, Plummer – a new source', *Journal of the American Musicological Society* 22 (1969), pp. 394–9.
b   Stevens (ed.), 'Medieval Carols'.
c   Sydney R. Charles (ed.), 'The Music of the Pepys MS 1236', *Corpus Mensurabilis Musicae* 40 (Rome 1967).
d   See fn. 52 above.

Table 1:2: Overall compasses in music composed between c. 1450 and c. 1500

Compositions per vocal texture — VOICES					Date of composition of contents: approximate span	Manuscript / Edition	Total number of compositions	Number of compositions observing each overall compass — NOTES														
2	3	4	5	6 or more				10 or fewer	11	12	13	14	15	16	17	18	19	20	21	22	23	24 or more
-	2	-	-	-	1450–65	GB-Ob Lincoln College (e) lat. 124	2	-	-	-	-	-	1	-	-	-	1	-	-	-	-	-
-	1	2	1	-	1460–75	GB-Lbl Add. 54324/KRO MS PRC 50/5 [a]	4	-	-	-	-	2	-	-	-	1	-	-	1	-	-	-
-	47	2	-	-	1450–75	GB-Lbl Add. 5665 (first layer) [b]	49	-	-	3	6	7	19	7	7	-	-	-	-	-	-	-
33	67	6	-	-	1445–75	GB-Cmc Pepys 1236 [c]	106	13	10	1	16	15	18	22	8	1	1	-	1	-	-	-
6	20	-	2	-	1475–1500	GB-Lbl Add. 5665 (liturgical pieces in second layer)	28	1	2	2	3	2	4	3	6	1	2	-	1	-	1	-
-	-	22	52	18	1470–1505	The Eton Choirbook [d]	92	-	-	-	-	12	6	-	1	2	2	1	17	40	11	-
39	137	32	55	18	1450–1505	TOTALS	281	14	12	6	25	38	48	32	22	5	6	1	20	40	12	-

voices had been superseded by one of five voices, and in which the practical
constraint of overall compass of two octaves had been replaced by one of three
octaves and a second. At a total of 23 notes, this represented just about the
extreme working limit of compass of which men's and boys' voices together are
capable. The former parameters of texture and scoring were not discarded, but
now were largely eclipsed by the new and grander manner of composition. Of
the 92 pieces in the Eton Choirbook for which data can be established, just
eighteen observed the old constraint of fourteen, fifteen or sixteen notes of
overall compass. No fewer than 68 employed the newly expanded compass of
21, 22 or 23 notes; just six engaged the space in between, of between seventeen
and twenty notes (see Table 1:2). Meanwhile, out of the whole corpus of 92
pieces listed in the contemporary index, none was in three parts and 22 in four.
The bulk, 52, was in the new standard texture of five parts; thirteen were for
six voices, three for seven, one for eight and one for nine.

The expansion of the overall vocal compass by an octave and a second and
the addition of two new voices to the vocal texture were, of course, closely
related. The identity of the two new voices can best be detected by comparing
the music of the Eton Choirbook, composed between c. 1470 and c. 1505, with
the music of Dunstable and certain of his contemporaries, composed between
c. 1415 and c. 1455. Examination of the contents of the edition of the complete
works of John Dunstable (including a number of *opera dubia* probably composed
by others)[55] shows that of the 63 sacred works sufficiently complete for analysis,
56 are for three voices. In these the two lowest parts (whether the piece is in
chanson or isorhythmic style) are virtually invariably in *tenor–contratenor* relationship;[56] almost without exception these two parts are in the same clef, and even
when they are not (six instances only, as recorded in the edition), the compass
of one of the parts is such that it could have been written in the same clef as
the other without recourse to leger lines.[57] With very few exceptions (eight
instances) the clef of the *superius* of these 56 compositions is located a fifth
higher than that of the other two parts – and when not, could have been so
written without involving the use of leger lines.[58] Further, as a consequence of
the increasing propensity of composers to engage the whole potential range of
an eleventh realizable by each voice on its five-line staff, there had crystallized
by now from the formerly inchoate manifestations of configurations of clefs

55 See fn. e to Table 1:1 above (pp. 4–5).
56 Only no. 37 appears to display the old-fashioned terraced scoring.
57 I.e. nos. 9 (*tenor* in C_4 instead of C_5), 17 (*tenor* in C_3 not C_4), 19 (*contratenor* in C_4 not C_3), 27 (*tenor* in C_5
not F_4) and 62 (*contratenor* in C_4 not C_3). Indeed, only no. 37 seems to defy adjustment in this way. It is
possible that many of these adjustments were in fact made in the manuscripts without the fact being recorded
in the Critical Commentary of the edition. Certainly, most of the 'adjustments' suggested here are by no
means arbitrary but are actually commendable, since each would cause the music to lie within the staff more
conveniently than does the inaugurating clef recorded in the edition.
58 I.e. nos. 6, and 20 with 22: C_2 for C_1; no. 13: *tenor* and *contratenor* in C_4 not C_5. Only 19, 35, 60 and 62
cannot conveniently be adjusted in this way, and then not because of any significant departure from standard
scoring but merely because the *superius* of each engages the occasional upper note of the sixteen-note compass.

three more or less fixed lattices. Naturally these reflected the conventional differentials between the voices that were applied by all composers. In standard three-part music the upper voice was pitched a fifth above the *contratenor* and *tenor*, and in consequence the emerging lattices of clefs were crystallizing as C_1-C_3-C_3, C_2-C_4-C_4 and C_3-C_5-C_5. Indeed, of the 56 three-voice pieces under discussion here, no fewer than 51 either actually employ a clef configuration of C_1-C_3-C_3 (eighteen instances), C_2-C_4-C_4 (twenty instances) or C_3-C_5-C_5 (six instances), or engage vocal ranges which would allow them to be written in such clefs without the use of leger lines (seven instances).[59]

As has been observed above, all this music had been composed for performance by adult voices of something akin to alto and tenor timbre. Of the 51 pieces concerned, almost half (25) are found to be laid out (actually or potentially) in the clef configuration C_2-C_4-C_4. All of these use either all or part of the written compass c–c^2 (23 instances) or the compass B–b^1 (two instances). Of the remainder, seven employ the configuration C_3-C_5-C_5 and nineteen C_1-C_3-C_3; these use ranges that correspond to such configurations, respectively A–a^1 for the first and d–d^2, e–e^2 or f–f^2 for the second. Experience suggests that the music in the collected edition of Dunstable is typical for its period in its putting the configuration C_2-C_4-C_4 to commonest use. By sheer chance it is the configuration associated with the compass c–c^2. It does, therefore, happen – utterly and entirely fortuitously – to place the music very close to sounding pitch, for adult alto and tenor voices, judged by modern pitch standards.[60]

Alignment of these findings against those to be drawn from the Eton Choirbook demonstrates the precise nature of the achievement accomplished by composers and choirs between c. 1455 and c. 1500. Out of its original contents 54 pieces survive in a state sufficiently complete for analysis of this kind to be made. Of these, 31 are in the standard five parts, and of these 29 exhibit the newly broadened compasses of 21, 22 and 23 notes.[61] In all but five of these 29 the three middle parts have a very familiar look. The third and fourth voices are in identical clefs and have identical or virtually identical compasses; they are in fact in *contratenor–tenor* relationship, and in the manuscript are indeed commonly labelled *contratenor* and *tenor* respectively.[62] With only three

59 C_1-C_3-C_3: 17; C_2-C_4-C_4: 6, 9, 13, 20, 22; C_3-C_5-C_5: 27. Out of 56 pieces, only 19, 35, 37, 60 and 62 cannot be accommodated completely within this exposition, and then by only the smallest margin.
60 In *Lbl* Add. 5665, f. 84^v, there occurs one three-part piece, compass d–a^1, written in the C_2-C_4-C_4 configuration, which is actually marked *pro hominibus* – Thomas Packe's Mass *Gaudete in Domino*.
61 Nos. 21 and 35 are in five parts, for men's voices only.
62 Of the five exceptions one is no. 10, one of the earliest pieces in the manuscript. Here it is the fourth and fifth parts which are in *contratenor–tenor* relationship (see Harrison, *Music in Medieval Britain*, p. 308, and below, p. 30). In 33 there is no *contratenor*, since the five parts are scored for two trebles, alto, tenor and bass. The three genuine exceptions are 13, 23 and 24. In these the *tenor* is in a clef lower than the *contratenor* and is definitely pitched a tone or even a minor third beneath it. In 12 and 47 the *tenor* and *contratenor* could both have been written in the same clef (C_3 in 12, C_4 in 47) without the use of leger lines. In 3 the actual *tenor* and *contratenor* are labelled *medius* and *tenor* in the Eton manuscript, but are labelled correctly in a manuscript concordance, *GB-Oas* 18: Harrison, 'The Eton Choirbook', I, p. 142.

further exceptions the part above them, now labelled *medius*, is pitched a fifth higher;[63] between the lowest note of the *contratenor* and *tenor* and the highest note o f the *medius* the range is exactly and invariably two octaves. Out of the 29 applicable pieces, therefore, no fewer than 21 agree in having their middle voices lying in the same ranges, called by the same part-names and covering exactly the same compass of two octaves as the three-part music of the previous generation. The clef configurations agree as well. Of these 21 pieces, the clefs of the three middle parts are all either C_2-C_4-C_4 (15 instances) or C_1-C_3-C_3 (six instances).[64]

The exact nature of the innovations introduced by the composers active between c. 1450 and 1500 now stands clear. They inherited the standard compass, texture and chanson-style vocal layout of the music of Dunstable's generation, and retained it unchanged as the core round which they developed their own style of scoring. Above the core they added one new line, commonly designated *triplex* in the manuscript sources, lying above the *medius*; below the core they added a further new line, commonly designated *bassus*, lying below the *contratenor* and *tenor*. It was by these devices that they accomplished the increase of vocal texture to five parts and of the overall compass to three octaves and a second. The means by which this expansion was accomplished is indicated graphically in Figures 1:5a and 1:5b.

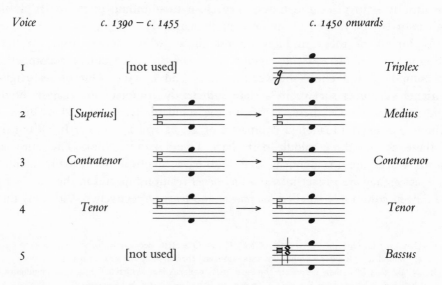

Voice	c. 1390 – c. 1455	c. 1450 onwards	
I	[not used]		Triplex
2	[Superius]		Medius
3	Contratenor		Contratenor
4	Tenor		Tenor
5	[not used]		Bassus

Figure 1:5a: The addition, c. 1450 – c. 1465, of two outer voices to historic three-part texture of composed polyphony

63 The exceptions are nos. 28, 29, 46; in these the *medius* contains isolated low notes and lies in a clef only a third above *contratenor* and *tenor*. In 17, 34 and 47 the clef of the *medius* would have been more felicitously located a fifth above that of the *contratenor* and *tenor*, on C_2 rather than C_3.

64 C_2-C_4-C_4: nos. 11, 14, 16, 17, 18, 19, 22, 25, 26, 30, 31, 32, 34, 44, 47. C_1-C_3-C_3: 12, 20, 27, 43, 45, 52.

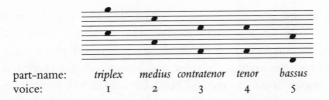

part-name:	*triplex*	*medius*	*contratenor*	*tenor*	*bassus*
voice:	1	2	3	4	5

Figure 1:5b: Ranges and differentials of voices engaged in church polyphony, c. 1455 onwards

It remains only to ascertain the exact nature of the two voices newly developed. As has been seen, when a three-voice piece exhibits an overall compass of two octaves written as $c-c^2$, then, by pure chance, its written pitch converts in transcription (in modern clefs) into just about its sounding pitch also, falling felicitously to voices of alto and tenor range. There seems to be no reason to imagine that the intended performing pitch of music in this vocal configuration altered at all when the two new outer voices were added to it; that is, any five-voice composition of which the three middle parts exhibit the clef-configuration C_2-C_4-C_4 will stand on paper at just about its correct sounding pitch also. The new top line in such compositions was invariably pitched a fifth above the *medius*, stood in the G_2 clef and occupied a range of up to eleven notes written as d^1-g^2; the new bottom line was invariably pitched a fifth below *contratenor* and *tenor*, stood in the F_4 clef and occupied a range of up to eleven notes written as $F-b$. At these sounding pitches the *triplex* is an eminently singable treble line for boys; the *bassus* is a perfectly viable part for the man's bass voice. The five-part vocal scoring fundamental to composition in the Eton Choirbook style, therefore, was conceived for performance by ensembles consisting of treble, alto, tenor, tenor and bass voices, within an overall compass sounding (in modern terms) at, or very close to, F to g^2.[65] The differentials and pitch of these voices are shown in Figure 1:6.

voice: (modern designation)	treble	alto	tenor I	tenor II	bass

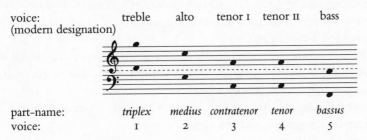

part-name:	*triplex*	*medius*	*contratenor*	*tenor*	*bassus*
voice:	1	2	3	4	5

Figure 1:6: Timbres and ranges of voices engaged in church polyphony, c. 1455 onwards

It may be noted that in music of the Eton Choirbook period the function of the clef continued to be the conveyance not of sounding pitch, but of just

---

65 Various permutations of these constituent voices could be applied as necessary for the performance of pieces in fewer than, or more than, the standard five parts.

the location of the diatonic semitones. The standard pattern of vocal scoring indicated in Figure 1:6 was applicable no matter which configuration of clefs was displayed by any given piece. Pitch was conveyed not by the clef but by the extremities of the staff; its highest and lowest pitches conveyed the singer's highest and lowest usual notes, and the clef (expanded, where necessary, by a staff-signature) merely purveyed the pattern of tones and semitones between them. Depending upon its 'tonality' (in the loosest sense of that word), therefore, the clef configuration of any given piece of standard five-part composition might be G_1-C_1-C_3-C_3-C_5, G_2-C_2-C_4-C_4-F_4 or C_1-C_3-C_5-C_5-F_5. Irrespective of the identity of its clef configuration, however, the singers embarked upon the performance of each given piece in their standard ensemble and at their standard pitch, and the resulting performances exhibited uniformity in these respects.

(b) The chronology of the performance revolution, c. 1450 – c. 1475

The Eton Choirbook discloses the new approach to compass and scoring as a completed process, and it yet remains to establish as precisely as possible the chronology of the transformation. Analysis of the contents of the small number of manuscripts surviving from the interim period c. 1455–1500 (see Table 1:2 above) helps to reveal the stages by which the revolution was accomplished.

The earliest instance yet traced of the use of composition in five parts in association with the newly broadened overall compass occurs in a manuscript compiled in the 1470s. This, *GB-Lbl* Add. 54324, contains an anonymous setting, now incomplete, of the Marian antiphon *Gaude flore virginali*. Of its five voices the two lowest are marked *Tenor* and *Bassus*, and the third and fourth voices stand in *contratenor–tenor* relationship. Its overall compass is 21 notes, written as F–e^2, and enough of the composition remains to show that in respect of ranges and differentials its five voices already agree perfectly with the lattice of voices that is characteristic of Eton Choirbook composition and is displayed in Figures 1:5b and 1:6 above.[66] The Eton Choirbook manner of vocal scoring, that is, had already emerged by c. 1475.

Prior to this point, it appears that of the two new voices the boy's voice was the earlier to be exploited in polyphonic composition. There occur at the end of *Lbl* Egerton 3307 two pieces added to the manuscript in c. 1455, of which one, in two sections, is a four-voice motet *Cantemus Domino, socie / Gaudent in celis*. Its overall compass extends to eighteen notes (written c–f^2). The two lowest voices are marked *Contratenor* (c–f^1) and *Tenor* (c–c^1) and above them lies a part a fifth higher (a–b^1); their clefs are C_2-C_4-C_4 and the voices engage an overall compass of fourteen notes. Above them lies the topmost voice, with clef G_2 and range d^1–f^2; this voice divides into a solo gymel (with verbal text in red ink) for the two-part passages introductory to each section. Since the lowest three

---

66 Margaret and Ian Bent, 'Dufay, Dunstable, Plummer', pp. 394–7, 399–403, 415–24.

voices clearly represent the historic core ensemble of *superius, contratenor* and *tenor* sung by an alto and two tenors, the upper voice seems certain to have been conceived for performance by boys. Indeed, the literary source of the text *Cantemus Domino, socie* presents it as having been sung, in the course of a celestial vision vouchsafed to St Dunstan, by a pair of female *precantatrices* to a chorus of virgins.[67] It is easy to appreciate, therefore, the reasons why it seemed appropriate to the composer that when setting this motet he should experiment with the engagement of the high voices of boys to sing the upper text.

Roughly contemporary with this piece is a four-part setting of *Descendi in ortum meum* attributed to Dunstable, of which two voices survive in the manuscript fragment of c. 1475 that contains the anonymous setting of *Gaude flore virginali* (*a5*) already discussed.[68] The disposition of its four voices likewise incorporates a single high voice pitched a fifth above three voices that correspond to the historic core; indeed, it matches exactly that of *Cantemus Domino, socie*, and it seems certain that its top voice also was conceived for performance by boys. If the attribution to Dunstable is correct, and there appears to be no good reason to doubt it, then in circles which may well be expected to have been at the forefront of enterprise and experiment, the very beginnings of the use of the boy's voice in composed polyphony were already in evidence by the early 1450s.

The first use of the bass voice, though not apparently contemporary with that of the treble, occurred very little later. A number of examples are to be found in *GB-Cmc* Pepys 1236 (see Table 1:2 above), a manuscript compiled over a number of years beginning in 1465 and stretching well towards 1480.[69] Much of the scoring manifested in the contents of this manuscript is as would be expected, departures from the prevailing matrix of scoring being few and of slight significance. In respect of compositions observing the traditional compasses of sixteen notes or fewer, those for three voices observe either chanson scoring or, especially for the simpler and slighter items in predominantly note-against-note counterpoint, the older style of terraced scoring. The two-part and four-part pieces engaging compasses of sixteen notes or fewer are likewise fully reconcilable with the established conventions of contemporary scoring.

However, of evident interest in the present context are the eleven pieces which enjoy an overall compass of seventeen notes or more, and thus share in the enlarged concepts of vocal usage emerging in the 1460s and 1470s.[70] Three

---

67 Bowers, 'Performing ensemble', pp. 191–2.
68 The remaining two voices survive elsewhere, in a fragment of a manuscript of c. 1500: Bent, 'Dufay, Dunstable, Plummer', pp. 394–9; Bukofzer (ed.), 'John Dunstable: Complete Works', no. 73.
69 This manuscript is unusual in bearing all the signs of being not a compilation of pieces for performance but a private individual's repository of items that interested him. Many of its items are very slight and brief and yield barely enough material to sustain analysis of pitch differentials and manner of scoring. Its contents vary widely in character and, particularly, in competence and quality of composition. A number of pieces bear the stamp of a non-professional ineptitude; when these display eccentricities of scoring, range and compass these infelicities may well be the consequence not of artistic imagination based on calculations of genuine practicality, but simply of maladroit composition.
70 The seventeen-note compass of no. 72 will be disregarded here as probably illusory, since its two discrete

of the items which use a seventeen-note compass (22, 51, 116) can be disregarded in the present context, since they appear to incorporate no novelties of vocal scoring. Rather, they merely show composers pushing to its limits the long-established chanson scoring for alto and two tenors, extending – for just one or two brief moments – the standard sounding compass of $c-c^2$ by up to a tone at both extremes. The remaining eight items, however, do appear to include genuine innovations of scoring, including instances of the adoption of the bass voice in certain pieces, of the boy's voice in others, and in one case, of both.

The piece engaging an overall compass of nineteen notes, John Tuder's three-voice *Gloria laus et honor* (101), consistently displays three voices of clearly terraced scoring. Its clef configuration is C_2-C_4-F_4, and the pattern of differentials and ranges matches exactly that of voices 2, 4 and 5 of Figure 1:6 above. Consequently there can be little doubt that this is an early piece for the ensemble of alto, tenor and bass. The very brief setting of *Alleluia V̇ Per te Dei genitrix* (40) displays the same characteristics, and does so within a compass of only seventeen notes.[71] Several other of the remaining compositions which use the seventeen-note compass likewise display a true manifestation of terraced scoring,[72] and probably should similarly be interpreted as items for alto, tenor and bass. These are nos. 20, 46, 94 and 108. They use an overall compass of seventeen or eighteen notes and their clef configuration is C_1-C_3-C_4. This represents a variant of the long-established C_1-C_3-C_3 matrix, in which the clef of the lowest part has been adjusted by the composer to C_4 in order to accommodate the extension of compass consequent upon the use of the bass voice.[73]

These earliest appearances of the bass voice appear to indicate that it originated as a substitute for the erstwhile *contratenor*, being deployed in three-part music in a pattern of terraced scoring newly revived for the purpose. Not until c. 1470 does it occur in surviving four-part writing. The music of the 'Saxilby Fragment' of about this date employs an overall compass of eighteen notes. The upper three voices, which use the clef configuration C_1-C_3-C_3 and cover a compass of two octaves (written $f-f^2$), clearly represent the historic core ensemble of parts for alto and two tenors. The fourth part, pitched a fourth below this matrix (written $c-e^1$), appears certain to have been conceived for performance

---

stanzas (one a3, the other a4) appear not to come from the same composition. Individually they exhibit normal compasses of fifteen and sixteen notes respectively.

71 Immediately comparable to these pieces is a three-part setting of *Kyrie eleison* preserved imperfectly in a fragment of a manuscript which looks as if it was written not much later than c. 1465: *GB-Ob* Lincoln College (e) Lat. 124, f. 222[v]. The total compass of this piece is nineteen notes; its clef configuration is C_1-C_3-F_4, and the lowest voice is actually marked *Bassus*.

72 That is, the distance between the highest note of the middle voice and the lowest note of the lowest voice is too great (twelve notes or more) to enable them to be comprehended as performable by voices of the same timbre, or to have been composed as *contratenor* and *tenor*. Many examples in this manuscript show that for simple and unambitious homespun composition, as opposed to the sophisticated work of the professionals, terraced scoring in the fourteenth-century manner had never been abandoned.

73 This conclusion applies equally to no. 20, even though it appears to be a factitious composition – intended to serve as a Jesus antiphon – concocted from two or three pre-existing pieces.

by the bass voice.[74] Indeed, the differentials and range of these four voices correspond neatly with voices 2, 3, 4 and 5 of Figure 1:6 above.

The Pepys manuscript is a further source of items engaging the boy's voice in composed polyphony. The anonymous four-voice setting of *Salve festa dies ... astra tenet* (no. 17) occupies an overall compass of seventeen notes. The three lowest voices (clefs C₂-C₄-C₅ [for C₄]) display a compass of fourteen notes (written *c–b¹*); the two bottom voices engage the same lowest note and almost identical range (*c–f¹* and *c–d¹*), and together these three voices clearly represent the historic core of a *superius* with *contratenor* and *tenor*. Superimposed upon this matrix is a topmost voice pitched a fifth above (*d¹–e²*). The three lower parts are evidently written for the established ensemble of an alto and two tenors; the topmost voice, consequently, appears certain to have been conceived for performance by a boy's treble. Indeed, the differentials and ranges of the four voices of this piece make a virtually perfect match with those of Dunstable's *Descendi in ortum meum* and the motet *Cantemus Domino, socie / Gaudent in celis* discussed previously, as is shown in Figure 1:7 below. Moreover, in the case of all three compositions their four voices establish a neat correspondence with voices 1, 2, 3 and 4 of Figure 1:6 above, offering strong corroboration for the vocal scoring which has been suggested.

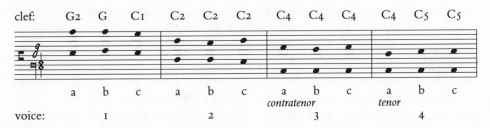

(a) *Cantemus Domino, socie / Gaudent in celis* (Egerton 3307, ed. McPeek, no. 51);
(b) John Dunstable, *Descendi in ortum meum* (*Complete Works*, no. 73);
(c) *Salve festa dies ... astra tenet* (*Pepys 1236*, ed. Charles, no. 17).

Figure 1:7: Vocal ranges and differentials in three early compositions incorporating the boy's voice

The anonymous setting for four voices of *Salve festa dies ... qua caro Messie* (no. 65) occupies an overall compass of 21 notes. This is only one step less than three octaves, and the piece must have been conceived for realization by an ensemble incorporating both low men's voices and the boy's treble. The three lower parts exhibit the standard chanson scoring, ranging through an overall compass of sixteen notes written *c–d²* (expanded to seventeen by a single rogue *e²* in the upper voice of these three) and deploying the clef configuration

74 Margaret Bent and Roger Bowers, 'The Saxilby fragment', *Early Music History* 1 (1981), pp. 1–28; Reinhard Strohm, *The Rise of European Music, 1380-1500* (Cambridge 1993), pp. 356, 388.

C_1-C_4-C_4. Pitched high above this foundation is the topmost voice, written a^1–bb^2 and laid out in the G_1 clef. The very wide differential left between this and the highest of the three foundation voices indicates that this composer understood the incorporation of the top voice effectively to push lower the sounding pitch of the supporting voices. The interpretation most plausible for this scoring, and most consistent with the findings already made, is that the voices envisaged were the standard treble, standard alto and a pair of baritones, sounding respectively at about f^1–g^2, g–c^2 and A–c^1.

The experimental nature of this scoring is made plainer by its similarity to that of a unique item in the Eton Choirbook, stylistically identifiable as one of its earliest pieces.[75] This is a five-part setting of *Salve regina* by William Horwood.[76] In this the overall compass is likewise 21 notes, and likewise the pair of equal voices is the two lowest (a feature found in no other Eton Choirbook piece in five or more parts). In clefs and ranges the top, second and two lowest parts of this *Salve regina* make a virtually perfect match with the four voices of *Salve festa dies … qua caro Messie*. Evidently such an approach to scoring was experimental; its involvement of two equal voices at the bottom of the range was found to be unsatisfactory, and perseverance was not made with it.

It would appear, therefore, that the first experiments with the use of the boy's treble voice in composed polyphony were under way by the early 1450s, and that this was accomplished through the superimposition of the treble voice upon the core of alto and two tenors already long established, so creating music in four parts. Roughly contemporaneously, and entirely independently, the first experiments were being made with the incorporation of the bass voice; this was introduced through a strategy wholly different, since it was engaged primarily in three-part music through the substitution of a *contratenor bassus* for the erstwhile plain *contratenor*. By the 1470s, and probably to add a foundation tone with which to balance the new treble voice, composers were beginning to experiment with the addition of the bass voice underneath the ensemble of treble, alto and two tenors already devised. The result was evidently found to be satisfactory – and thus was created the five-part scoring for treble, alto, two tenors and bass that is fundamental to the style of composition of pieces represented by the Eton Choirbook.

Fortunately much corroboration for the interpretations of vocal scoring offered above is supplied by archival evidence arising from the institutions by which the performers of this music were employed. The principal innovation for which accommodation had to be made was the novel involvement of the chorister boys in the singing of composed polyphony. Any institution wishing to keep abreast of this development now had to address two particular necessities – to ensure firstly that it engaged an Instructor qualified to teach the boys, and

75 Harrison, *Music in Medieval Britain*, p. 308.
76 Harrison, 'The Eton Choirbook', I, no. 10. On this occasion the scribe's identification of the four lowest voices as *Medius, Contratenor, Tenor* and *Bassus* clearly failed to match the reality of the compositional layout.

secondly that it maintained them in numbers sufficient to allow a musically satisfactory balance to be established within the choir.

The post of Instructor of the Choristers had ceased to be one that could satisfactorily be executed merely by one of the existing vicars or clerks.[77] It was from the beginning of the 1460s that the major churches began to recruit as Instructor musicians specializing in this newly professional employment, engaged under specific contracts to teach the boys in the skills of performing their part in polyphonic music. Among the first were the cathedrals of Lincoln, where the composer William Horwood was appointed in 1461, and Salisbury, where John Cacherew was engaged in the same year and was succeeded by John Kegwyn in 1463. The corresponding step was taken at Wells in 1479 (Richard Hygons), at St George's Chapel, Windsor, in the same year (Walter Lambe), and in 1484 at Worcester Cathedral Priory (John Hampton).[78]

Simultaneously there is evidence of a widespread effort to increase the number of choristers at institutions originally staffed with only modest numbers. At York Minster seven boys were increased to twelve in 1472, at St George's Chapel, Windsor, six to thirteen between 1477 and 1482, and at St Paul's Cathedral, London, eight to ten by the early sixteenth century. The boys of the Lady Chapel choir of the cathedral priory of Winchester were doubled in numbers from four to eight in 1482 and increased to ten by 1511. Boys were added to the choral staffs of monastery Lady Chapel choirs and collegiate churches originally equipped with none: at Worcester Cathedral Priory, for instance, in 1478, at Bristol Abbey in c. 1490, at Mettingham College by c. 1500, at Rushworth by 1501, and at Pleshey at much the same period.[79]

It is certainly hard to avoid the conclusion that the motive informing this widespread strategy was the creation and moulding of a corps of singing-boys sufficiently numerous to cope with the novel requirement that they be able to sustain the top line in five-part polyphony and establish a suitable balance with the lower voices. Indeed, the use of spare income at Tattershall College to increase the numbers of lay clerks and of choristers from the six of each established by the founder in c. 1444 to ten of each by the end of the century seems to bespeak comprehensively the adjustments necessary to adapt a choir from the solo-orientated polyphony of the first half of the century to the chorus-orientated polyphony of the second.[80]

77 Cf. above, pp. 12–13.
78 For these and numerous other examples see Bowers, 'Music and worship to 1640', pp. 38–9; Bowers, 'Choral institutions', pp. 6052–4, 6066–74.
79 For these and several further examples see: *ibid.*, pp. 6035–55, 6060–2; Harrison, *Music in Medieval Britain*, pp. 11–12; Roger Bowers, 'The musicians of the Lady Chapel of Winchester Cathedral priory', *Journal of Ecclesiastical History* 45 (1994), pp. 224–8.
80 Bowers, 'Choral institutions', pp. 5007–8.

(3) THE CONSOLIDATION OF CHORAL PRACTICE, C. 1500–1559

(a) The proliferation of choral endeavour

Fully established in mainstream circles by the beginning of the 1480s, the fundamental characteristics of compass, scoring and texture manifested by the Eton Choirbook repertory became ubiquitous and remained standard for the composition of Latin church music until its second and final extinction in 1559. In writing for full choir composers worked consistently within an overall compass of 21, 22 or 23 notes and employed four timbres of voice (treble, alto, tenor and bass) of which one (tenor) was conventionally doubled to create the standard five-part texture (see Figure 1:6). In terms of modern pitch this sounded at, or close to, the 23 notes F–g^2. Composition in fewer than five parts was accommodated by selection from the standard five. Composition in more than five parts was most commonly accomplished simply by the doubling of one or more of the established vocal timbres. Alternatively (or in addition) composers might use a baritone voice pitched between bass and tenor, sounding at A–d^1. This was already being used in certain Eton Choirbook compositions for men's voices, and in writing in six or more parts for full choir.[81] Presumably any reasonably competent choir included basses who could also manage these baritone parts.

The forces available to sing this music were, by the second quarter of the sixteenth century, extraordinarily diverse. The capacity to make an offering of polyphonic music during the course of divine worship became a coveted objective at churches far beyond those great institutions which thitherto had been its sole preserve. It was from c. 1470 or so that there began the explosive expansion in the cultivation of church music in England which took its numbers of professional practitioners from no more than a few hundreds in around that year to several thousands by the time that all was overtaken by the Reformation of the 1540s and 1550s. In particular, from the last quarter of the fifteenth century onwards the fraternities and gilds of devout laity, founded within the richer parish churches of cities and market towns throughout the land, began to organize the recruitment of professional choirs of men and boys by whose music their offering of worship could be enlarged and enhanced. In addition, many monastery Lady Chapel choirs thitherto consisting only of boys' voices began to be converted into full choirs using the broken voices either of professional singing-men or of the abler religious.[82] By the early 1540s – the apogee of their cultivation, since the establishment of sixteen New Foundation choirs in 1538–40 more than offset the loss of monastery choirs during the dissolutions of 1535–40 – there may have been some 200 professional liturgical choirs in England. These doubtless covered a broad spectrum of competence from the very finest to the fairly

81 Harrison, 'The Eton Choirbook': respectively nos. 6, 7, 35; 4, 9, 15, 51.
82 See, for instance, Bowers, 'The musicians of the Lady Chapel of Winchester Cathedral priory', pp. 223–31, and numerous other instances quoted in Bowers, 'Choral institutions', pp. 6055–9.

threadbare, but all were professionally engaged in a vocation which by then was probably employing a perceptible proportion of all educated males in the country over the age of eight.

Where the strength of forces permitted, the performance of this music had by c. 1520 become truly choral.[83] Prior to around the last years of the fifteenth century no evidence has yet been found to suggest that among the adult members of the choir any other than the professional singers – the lay clerks of the second form – were expected to be able to perform the polyphonic repertory. It is evident, however, that in the most prominent choirs efforts were being made from about the 1490s onwards to ensure that the priests of these choirs – whether vicars choral or chaplains – were equally able to contribute to the performance of polyphony. Such a step was rendered possible, of course, by the existence from about the 1470s onwards of increasing cohorts of former singing-boys who had learnt to read from polyphonic notation during their careers as choristers. As early as 1483 the residentiaries of Lincoln Cathedral were admitting to only a provisional place as a vicar choral any man who was not yet able to sing polyphony, allowing him a period of six months or a year to become perfect 'in Playnsong, Pryksong, discant et Faburdon'. In 1503 the chapter of the collegiate church of Ripon ordered that thenceforth no one should be admitted as a priest-vicar unless he knew how to sing both plainsong and polyphonic music, while in 1507 at York Minster the vicars themselves set up an incentive through their decree that thenceforth no vicar should draw benefit from certain of the endowments of the vicars' college unless he were able to sing *perfecte* both pricksong and faburden.[84]

It is unlikely that these three churches were unique in this respect. In chantry colleges, in which the chaplains of the choir served also as the managing fellows of the college, prime responsibility for singing polyphony probably continued perforce to lie with the clerks alone, since the principal criterion for the appointment of at least many of the chaplains had to be their possession of managerial and administrative abilities. In respect of all other choirs, however, it is probably safe to conclude that by the 1520s at the latest it was normal for the polyphonic chorus to consist not only of the clerks and boys but also of a high proportion of the priests of the choir as well. It may not always have been easy to fill vacancies among the latter with men who both were ordained and possessed the skills of singing polyphony. Nevertheless, the effort was certainly made, and it was not until the onset of the Protestant values of the Edwardian Reformation after 1547 that the difficulty of finding priests who were also skilled

---

83 The evidence perhaps most evocative of the transition from solo-orientated to chorus-orientated composition and performance is the manner in which, over the period from c. 1420 to c. 1525, the individual pages of choirbooks steadily increased in size to accommodate the steadily increasing numbers of performers.

84 Lincoln, Dean and Chapter Archives, MS A.2.37, ff. 15ᵛ, 63bᵛ; J. T. Fowler (ed.), 'Memorials of Ripon', 4 vols., *Surtees Society*, 74, 78, 81, 115 (1882-1908), IV, p. 275; York Minster, Archives of the Vicars Choral, MS VC 1/1, p. 12. For the teaching of plainsong, pricksong, descant and faburden to choristers in the sixteenth century see Chapter 8 (ed.).

singers of polyphony was quoted as an excuse for the reduction of the numbers of priests in certain of the major choirs.[85]

Estimation of the proportion of the skilled singers in any choir who actually participated on each occasion in the performance of polyphony remains problematic, however. The attendance of singers at the daily Lady Mass and the evening votive antiphon was commonly laid down in each particular case by act of chapter or by statute or ordinance; commonly an attendance of less than the full choir was specified. At High Mass on Sundays and festivals a substantial proportion of the choir was engaged about the ceremony of the service and was thus unavailable for much of its duration to participate in the singing. Indeed, in 1515 the abbot of Ramsey Abbey (Co. Huntingdon) claimed that he needed the attendance of at least fourteen of his monks at High Mass to ensure that there was always the minimum number of two sufficiently unoccupied elsewhere to be able to sing the choral chants from the choirstalls[86] – and the ceremonial of Mass as celebrated at the great secular churches was no less elaborate than that of the Benedictine Mass. At the observance of the Office it was common practice for one side of the choir, week and week about, to undertake the recitation of the monotoned parts of the services (especially the lessons), while the other side alone took responsibility for supplying singers of the solo passages in the more elaborate (i.e. responsorial) chants. It is at least likely that this practice was commonly extended also to the performance of the polyphony of the Office, which thus was sung by just one side of the choir from the partbooks that for this period do indeed survive universally in single, not double, sets. All these considerations suggest that on a high proportion of occasions the singing of polyphony was undertaken by substantially less than the full choral force; the principles and aesthetic underlying the composition and performance of polyphony were always essentially those of chamber music.

(b) Local diversities in the patterns of vocal scoring and dispositions of voices

By the early sixteenth century choirs of many different kinds and constitutions were undertaking to tackle the performance of polyphony composed in the standard five parts (TrATTB), and some degree of variety in the practical disposition of the vocal forces available becomes evident. The determining factor was the relative numbers of boys and men. In most choirs the men outnumbered the boys by a substantial degree, and such relative abundance made it readily possible to allocate four out of the five parts to men, and the top part to the boys, while maintaining a satisfactory balance. At Chichester Cathedral, for instance, the choral strength from 1526 onwards consisted of twenty men and eight boys. Four of the men

85 Walter Howard Frere and William McClure Kennedy, 'Visitation articles and injunctions of the period of the Reformation', 3 vols., *Alcuin Club* 14–16 (1910), II, pp. 161–2, 316.
86 Lincoln Archives Office, Diocesan Archives, MS vj/6, f. 22ᵛ.

were the lay clerks of the foundation of Bishop Robert Sherburn that was inaugurated in that year, and the qualifications required of the members of this group were specified with care. It was to consist of

four lay clerks having mutually blending voices and learned in music, of whom one at least is always [to be possessed] of a natural and audible bass voice; while let the voices of the other three be sweet and melodious, so that by the joint application of their voices they may naturally and freely encompass fifteen or sixteen notes.[87]

The four voices were thus to consist of one bass, and three others which between them could cover a compass of fifteen or sixteen notes. This evidently relates to the two-octave compass covered by the next three parts reading upwards, namely the *tenor*, *contratenor* and *medius* sung by, respectively, two tenors and an adult alto, leaving the top part alone to be sung by the boys.[88]

This disposition of one boy's voice and four men's was probably the standard for five-part polyphony written for TrATTB, but it was not the only disposition possible and in the case of certain early sixteenth-century choirs it was not in fact the most suitable. These latter were choirs in which either the absolute number of men was only small, or the normal proportion of boys to men was reversed, the boys so far outnumbering the men that the division of the latter into four real parts could result only in their being overwhelmed by a superfluity of trebles. In these choirs only the three lowest voices were allocated to the men. Both of the upper two parts were allotted to the boys; the boys' choir, that is, consisted of two divisions, and the parts in five-part polyphony generally designated as *triplex* and *medius* were sung by, respectively, ordinary trebles and boy (rather than adult) altos. These were known respectively as 'trebles' and 'meanes'.

This strategy was applied in the tiny choir of the Lady Chapel of the priory of Llanthony Secunda (located in the suburbs of Gloucester). Here, where the lower voices were sung probably one to a part by the Instructor and a couple of religious, the boys' department in 1533 consisted explicitly of 'foure childerne well and suffycyently enstructed that is to say too meanys and too trebles'.[89] There is evidence to suggest that the same division was maintained in the choirs of Magdalen College and New College, Oxford. In each of these the boys numbered sixteen and the singing-men probably between only five and ten. The division of the boys into trebles and altos would be an obvious strategy to establish an acceptable balance.[90]

Best documented of the choirs in this class is that of the household of Henry Percy (1478–1527), 5th Earl of Northumberland.[91] Probably Percy set up his

---

87 Oxford, New College, archive 9432, ff. 21ᵛ-22ʳ (translated).
88 Bowers, 'Vocal scoring', pp. 49–52.
89 PRO, E315/93, f. 231ᵛ.
90 Bowers, 'Vocal scoring', pp. 65–6.
91 The history and constitution of this chapel is considered in Bowers, 'Vocal scoring', pp. 57–64, 68–76. For a recent study of Percy see Mervyn James, 'A Tudor magnate and the Tudor state: Henry, fifth Earl of Northumberland', in *Society, Politics and Culture* (Cambridge 1986), pp. 48–90.

chapel soon after attaining his majority in 1499, and the administrative archives of his household contain numerous accounts of the vocal constitution of the chapel personnel as it stood between c. 1505 and c. 1522.[92] The lifetime of this earl represented rather a trough in the fortunes of the Percy family, and compared with those of some of his aristocratic colleagues his chapel was only quite meanly staffed. It was managed by a dean, and its sacerdotal staff was completed by a sub-dean and two other priests; none of these was specifically accounted as competent to perform polyphony, and in this respect the chapel may be accounted rather old-fashioned. The boys numbered five in c. 1505 and six thereafter. In c. 1518 they were specifically recorded as divided into three 'first trebles' and three 'second trebles' and in c. 1505 into two 'trebles' and three 'meanes'; apparently both terminologies refer to a division into trebles and altos.

This division was rendered necessary by the relatively small number of the singing-men. Their total number varied between eight and thirteen, but not all of these sang polyphony. In the English vernacular in which the lists were compiled, the singing-men were divided into 'countertenors', 'tenors' and 'basses'. In the context of the administrative documentation which is the sole source of this information, this terminology identified departments of the adult choir for executive (recruiting and remuneration) purposes, and evidently it did not identify separate timbres of voice. At the time at which these lists were being compiled, c. 1505 − c. 1522, the music in the standard five-part repertory was being scored for TrATTB voices, and once the two top parts had been allocated to the boys, the broken voices were required to provide not three but only two timbres of voice, the tenor being doubled. Indeed, it must be recalled that the contemporary *contratenor* and *tenor* parts were, and always had been, sung by voices of the same pitch and timbre; consequently it would be perverse to imagine that *at this period* their vernacular equivalents, 'countertenor' and 'tenor', could possibly refer to voices of different and contrasting timbre. Rather, the two vernacular terms evidently refer to voices of much the same timbre, the distinction between them being made for administrative purposes and arising from their doing different work.

In certain contemporary continental usages the term *tenor* or *tenorista* referred to a singing-man whose expertise extended only to the singing of plainsong,[93] and in respect of the Earl of Northumberland's chapel there is evidence to suggest that in like fashion the clerks designated as 'tenors' were not engaged in the singing of polyphony.[94] Meanwhile the chapel lists show that those listed

92 The principal source is the 'Northumberland Household Book': Alnwick Castle, Estates Office, MS 98A.
93 See e.g. Craig Wright, *Music and Ceremony at Notre Dame de Paris, 500–1500* (Cambridge 1989), pp. 322–4. Writing of Notre Dame during the period between the mid-fifteenth and the mid-sixteenth centuries, Wright explains that the term *tenorista* 'did not denote a vocal part or range, but rather a function: a tenor was one who assured a slow, steady, forceful rendering of the plainsong'. In 1544 these singers were described as 'tenoristae tenentes planum cantum et psalmodiam'.
94 For instance, the only one of three lists of weekly duties that is not compromised by evident errors conspicuously omits the 'tenors' from those expected to be able to play the organ, and the presence of two 'tenors' on the lists of 1511 may well explain the simultaneous existence of two singing-men who were engaged on rates of pay significantly lower than those awarded to their colleagues; see Bowers, 'Vocal scoring', pp. 58–62, 73–5. In the early sixteenth century, 'tenor' would have been a natural term to choose in order to identify and designate an exclusively plainsong entity existing with an essentially polyphonic context.

as 'countertenors' were more numerous than any other voice, consistently possessing sufficient strength of numbers to perform two parts. The manifest conclusions to be drawn are: (1) that those singing-men of the Northumberland household chapel who were designated as 'tenors' sang only plainsong and not polyphony, and (2) that those designated 'countertenor' sang the *contratenor* part in polyphony and also its twin, the *tenor* part, and were for this reason maintained at twice the number of any other division of the choir.

It is worth pursuing the details of the constitution of the Northumberland household chapel choir to this point, since these lists provide a clear, and unique, insight into the distribution of voices and concepts of vocal balance within an early Tudor choir. For polyphonic performance this choir was only ever of very modest dimensions, extending to five or six boys and six to eight men; by timbre the voices were allocated as in Table 1:3 below. The voices emerge as evenly distributed through all the parts, and essentially such a conclusion is remarkably unsurprising. Nevertheless, the small number of trebles serves as a salutary reminder of the extent to which in the English early sixteenth-century 'soundscape' the treble part constituted no pre-eminent melody requiring a large number of executants for its performance, but was merely a constituent line of the polyphony, a thin thread of high sound superimposed from c. 1450–1455 onwards upon a pre-existing and already dense texture of adult voices.

Table 1:3: Disposition of voices for performance of five-part polyphony in the household chapel choir of Henry, Earl of Northumberland, c. 1505 – c. 1522

	Boys		Men			Other staff		
Part:	*Triplex*	*Medius*	*Contratenor*	*Tenor*	*Bassus*			
Voice:	Treble	Meane /	Counter-	Counter-	Bass	Tenors	Chaplains	Dean
Date		2nd treble	tenor I	tenor II				
c. 1505	2	3	2	2	2	2	3	I
c. 1509	3ᵃ	3	2	2	2ᶜ	2	3	I
1511	3ᵃ	3	3	3	2	2	3	I
1516	3ᵃ	3	3	3	2	2	3	I
c. 1518	3	3	2	2	3	4	3	I
c. 1520	[3]ᵇ	[3]	3	3	2	5	3	I
c. 1522	[3]ᵇ	[3]	3	3	4	3	4	I
Modern Designation:	Treble	Boy alto	Tenor I	Tenor II	Bass			

a   Total boys given as six; division into 3 + 3 by inference from list of c. 1518
b   No information. Total boys given as six on list of c. 1520; division by inference, as above
c   Instructor of Choristers, and Epistoler: voices unspecified but apparently both basses

In choirs such as that of the Earl of Northumberland the division of the boys' voices into trebles and altos was evidently a permanent feature of its constitution. Very many other choirs of prominence and distinction may well have likewise applied such a two-way division of the voices of the boys, though in their cases only under particular, though daily, circumstances.

In many collegiate churches founded since c. 1400 the statutes provided that daily Lady Mass be observed with the attendance just of the boys and their Instructor. Originally intended to furnish a plainsong performance by boys' voices, the subsequent extension of competence in polyphony to the choristers eventually gave rise to a special body of Lady Mass music, specifically designed for the voices just of the boys and their Master. Most evidently characteristic of this repertory is the weekly cycle of three-part *alternatim* Lady Masses by Nicholas Ludford (c. 1490–1557), dating from the 1520s. Each mass in this cycle exhibits an overall compass of eighteen or nineteen notes, and terraced scoring for three separate timbres of voice. The clef configuration G_2-C_2-C_4 occurs in all seven masses, and clearly it forms the basic configuration for the set.[95] These voices seem certain to represent the standard voices 1, 2 and 4 of Figure 1:6 above. Ludford's choir at St Stephen's, Westminster, consisted of seven boys and eighteen men (thirteen priest-vicars, four lay clerks and himself as Instructor of the Choristers).[96] Such proportions indicate that when the choir sang as a body the boys undertook only the treble line; the men would take the remaining four out of the standard five parts, adult altos taking the 'meane' part. Lady Mass, meanwhile, would appear to have been sung not by the whole choir but by the Instructor and boys. The nineteen-note compass of each Lady Mass would be realized through performance of the lowest part (sounding $c-f^1$) by the Instructor while the remaining upper parts were sung by the boys, now divided into trebles (d^1-g^2) and altos ($g-c^2$).

There were a few further liturgical occasions to which application of this principle was particularly felicitous. Throughout the surviving sixteenth-century repertory polyphonic settings of the appropriate sections of the responsories *Audivi vocem Ṽ Media nocte* and *Hodie nobis celorum rex Ṽ Gloria in excelsis* were composed consistently in restricted compasses of fourteen to sixteen notes. These in fact were the two most splendid of the set pieces deputed by the liturgy to performance specifically by the boys of the choir.[97] Each of these settings is in four parts, and most engage two pairs of equal voices, one high and one low, spaced about a fourth or a fifth apart. In these cases performance by boys' voices appears certain to have been envisaged, divided into two trebles and two altos.[98]

---

95 Four masses are scored in this configuration throughout. In the Tuesday and Wednesday masses it occurs for the alleluia and sequence, while the remaining movements stand in the configurations C_2-C_4-C_5 and G_1-C_1-C_3 respectively. In the Saturday mass the sequence is located in C_2-C_4-C_5. In performance, of course, the respective movements of these three masses emerge not at different pitches, but at the same pitch with different locations for the diatonic semitones.

96 Bowers, 'Vocal scoring', pp. 54–5, fn. 38.

97 Harrison, *Music in Medieval Britain*, p. 107.

The likelihood overall, therefore, is that from the early sixteenth century onwards the boys' voices of the choirs of all the greater churches were trained to render both treble and alto parts, and that the ability to do so was ubiquitous. It was part of the standard vocal disposition for those occasions – especially, but not exclusively, the daily Lady Mass – on which the boys sang alone and without the adult altos who were present only when the full choir assembled.

The executants of the 'meane' part, therefore, were – in any given choir – just as commonly boys as men, and the 'meane' voice was as much that of a boy alto as of an adult. It is this circumstance that explains the way in which, after the Reformation, the term 'meane' rather than the term 'treble' became that by which the single standard boy's voice was known. Many instances from the Eton Choirbook onwards demonstrate the conventional manner in which part-names were allocated to the several voices in a polyphonic composition by working – as was natural – from the tenor outwards. In the early years of the Reformation period most composition of church music was in only four parts, the duplication of the tenor having been abandoned. Named from the tenor outwards that part (now for adult altos) immediately above the tenor was called the 'countertenor' and the part next above that the 'meane'. This was the topmost part, composed for performance by boys – a part to which the name 'meane' was easily attached, since singing the *medius*/'meane' had long been part of the work to which boys' voices could be directed.[99] The term 'treble' was perforce discarded in respect of church music, and so was available for resuscitation early in the seventeenth century as a name for the very high boy's voice which briefly became fashionable then.

(c) The bifurcation of the tenor voice, c. 1520–1559

The premises fundamental to the scoring of Latin choral music of the whole period c. 1470–1559, as discussed so far, were enriched from about the 1520s onwards by the adoption of an optional refinement which was beginning by

---

98 See May Hofman and John Morehen (comps.), 'Latin Music in British Sources, c. 1485 – c. 1610', *Early English Church Music*, Supplementary Vol. 2 (1987): Cowper, Sheppard, Tallis, Taverner; see also David S. Josephson, *John Taverner* (Ann Arbor 1979), pp. 158–60. Christopher Tye's setting of another liturgical setpiece for boys, the Palm Sunday processional hymn *Gloria laus et honor*, is composed in the clefs G_2-G_2-C_2-C_4; here the scoring appears to be for three-part boys (two trebles, one alto) and a tenor sung, on the analogy of Ludford's Lady Masses, by their Instructor.

99 The use of boy altos to contribute to the performance of the second line in polyphony may not have disappeared everywhere with equal rapidity at the Reformation. In 1580 John Farrant 'the elder' was engaged at Salisbury Cathedral as Instructor of the Choristers, his obligation being to 'furnishe the quier of the said Cath[edral] churche with eight choristers havinge good and commendable voyces for trebles and meanes' (Salisbury, Cathedral Archives, indenture without reference). The revival of this practice at Salisbury is readily explained, and its rationale is the same as that which had applied prior to the Reformation. By this period the adult department of the choir at Salisbury was staffed with only seven vicars choral (Stanford Lehmberg, *The Reformation of Cathedrals* (Princeton 1988), p. 183), and evidently the contemporary criteria for choral balance required that some contribution to the lower voices be made by one or two of the boys, singing alto.

the later 1530s to achieve a perceptible significance. This was the application of the tenor voice in two slightly different manifestations. One was a conventional tenor operating within a very slightly contracted range of a tenth, sounding around $c-e^1$; the other was a full-range tenor operating within a range expanded by one step beyond its previous upper limit and so sounding within the twelfth $c-g^1$.

The first stage in this incipient bifurcation of the manner of scoring for the tenor voice may be exemplified by comparison of two votive antiphons by Robert Fayrfax (c. 1460–1521). The traditional equality of the *contratenor* and *tenor* parts, both sung by tenor voices, is manifest in his early *Salve regina*, a composition from the end of the fifteenth century preserved in the Eton Choirbook.[100] Of its five parts, the *contratenor* and *tenor* show virtually identical ranges (respectively $c-f^1$ – once g^1 – and $c-f^1$) and stand in the same clef (C_4). Their respective tessituras are likewise identical. Calculation reveals that the mean pitch of the *contratenor* lies 8.46 semitones above c and that of the *tenor* 8.19 semitones; the difference between them extends to barely a quarter of a semitone. However, in the much later *Maria plena virtute* a perceptible divergence has become apparent.[101] Its *contratenor* part persistently explores the higher sector of the tenor vocal range, yielding a mean pitch 11.05 semitones above c; meanwhile the *tenor* part engages principally its lower reaches, yielding a mean pitch 6.93 semitones above c. The gap is substantial, representing a divergence exceeding the major third g to b. Indeed, a full analysis of the five-part works by Fayrfax which survive complete (eleven items) discloses that while the first tenor (singing the *contratenor* part) continued to sing in its conventional range ($c-f^1$, sometimes $d-f^1$), the second tenor voice (singing the *tenor* part) might not be asked to extend to the upper semitone (five items) or even minor third (five items) of its erstwhile range at all. Nevertheless the impact and consequences of this development up to this point (c. 1520) should not be overemphasized. Most commonly both parts were still written in the same clef, and even in a piece such as *Maria plena virtute* the two parts remained, in terms of overall range, almost identical (*contratenor*: $d-f^1$, *tenor*: $c-e^1$). Both, that is, were still clearly written for performance by the same basic timbre of voice.

Certain of the composers of the next generation chose to expand upon this departure, presenting it in a guise yet further developed. The five-part and – *mutatis mutandis* – also the four- and six-part music of John Taverner, written between c. 1520 and 1545 and together comprising much the greater part of his surviving output,[102] provides an illuminating body of material. Of his 31 surviving liturgical works for four or more voices, five survive in a state too

---

100 Harrison, 'The Eton Choirbook', I, no. 6.
101 Edwin B. Warren (ed.), 'Robert Fayrfax: Collected Works', 3 vols., *Corpus Mensurabilis Musicae* 17 (Rome 1959–66), II, p. 59.
102 Hugh Benham (ed.), 'John Taverner: Complete Works', 5 vols., *Early English Church Music*, 20, 25, 30, 35–36 (London 1978–90).

incomplete to sustain the present analysis. Of the 26 remaining, five engage an overall compass of fifteen or sixteen notes, and for immediate purposes are not particularly illuminating.[103] Two use a compass of nineteen notes, one being *a*4 and one *a*5. Both are for the lower voices, and the choirs which used the manuscripts in which each survives certainly engaged a boy's alto voice for the highest part.[104] Of the nineteen pieces remaining, one (*a*5) uses a compass of 21 notes, twelve extend to 22 notes (two *a*4, nine *a*5, one *a*6) and six to 23 notes (two *a*4, one *a*5, three *a*6).[105] These nineteen show that Taverner's scoring for the fundamental five-part choir consistently observed the standard relative disposition of the five basic voices (as in Figure 1:6), except insofar as the vocal timbre represented by the third and fourth voices now displays a certain perceptible degree of instability and divergence.

Taverner's treble, alto and bass voices adhere to conventional ranges and differentials,[106] and in each of the four instances of four-part writing these are supplemented by an equally conventional tenor. Among the fifteen items *a*5 and *a*6 which engage a compass of 21, 22 or 23 notes, the scoring of six observes the conventions of the later Fayrfax era. In these, the first tenor voice observes both the standard range of an eleventh (sounding pitch $c-f^1$) and the standard differential from the other voices, while the second tenor engages a range extending up from c by either a seventh (two instances, both *cantus firmus*), a ninth (one instance) or tenth (two instances).

It is in the remaining nine pieces that the instability mentioned above may be detected, and it seems most likely to be best resolved and interpreted as an incipient bifurcation of the tenor timbre into two no longer quite equal voices. The major point of novelty is exhibited by the first tenor. Effectively increasing its range to a twelfth by virtue of extending one step higher than formerly, this

---

103 This category extends to six when the arrangement *a*4 of *Dum transisset sabbatum* (1) is included. Taking liturgical considerations into account, the intended scorings appear to be as follows. Two trebles and two boy altos: *Hodie nobis* ℣ *Gloria in excelsis* (realized a major second above edited pitch); *Audivi* ℣ *Media nocte*. Two full-range tenors, tenor and bass: 'Playnsong' Mass, *Magnificat a4*, *Dum transisset a4*. Three full-range tenors, tenor and bass: *Te Deum a5*.

104 The four-voice *In pace* is inscribed 'for iij men and a childe' in each partbook of the 'Gyffard' set (*GB-Lbl* Add. 17802–5); the five-voice 'Meane mass' is inscribed in *GB-Cp* 487 'for iiij men and a childe'. These performance directions are unique. The universal absence of such inscriptions elsewhere indicates that under normal circumstances the scoring of any piece was self-evident. The inference to be drawn here is that normally in the choirs for whose use these manuscripts were prepared an alto part would be sung by a man or men; only by explicitly directing that the part be sung by a boy would the scoring particularly desired in these cases be accomplished.

105 Of the eleven pieces which use full compasses of 21–23 notes and are scored for the standard five-part choir, the *tenor* is lost from four: these are the Mass *Mater Christi*, the Mass 'Small devotion', the *Magnificat a5*, and *Christe Iesu pastor bone*. Of the treble of the *Magnificat a6* only two sections survive; these appear sufficient to supply the identity of the treble's highest pitch, g^2. The remainder of the four six-part works are complete. Of the nine pieces *a*4, all but three are small-scale and relatively brief.

106 To this, only one significant exception appears. In the Mass *Gloria tibi trinitas* the exigencies of scoring the *cantus firmus* in the *medius* part appear to have constrained the composer into extending its compass regularly by a factor of one note above its predicated range. If this interpretation is correct, the composer appears to have had only boys' voices in mind for its performance.

manifestation of the tenor voice was beginning to show a concentration upon its upper reaches (occasionally eschewing use of its lowest tone or even minor third altogether) and was consistently entered into the *contratenor* partbooks. Meanwhile, the second manifestation is identifiable as the voice of more limited compass; it used only the lower tenth of its erstwhile range, and was consistently entered into the *tenor* partbooks.[107] Nevertheless, the two voices yet remained within the same established range for the tenor voice and, in view of the small degree of differentiation yet apparent between them, were essentially of still the same timbre. The first may now be designated 'full-range tenor' to distinguish it from the tenor of somewhat restricted compass.[108] The vocal ranges available to Taverner during his last twenty years or so, and to his contemporaries and successors as composers of Latin church music, are tabulated, with the differentials between them, in Figure 1:8.

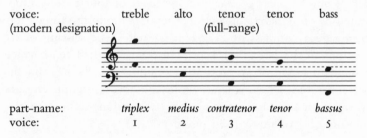

voice: (modern designation)	treble	alto	tenor (full-range)	tenor	bass
part-name:	*triplex*	*medius*	*contratenor*	*tenor*	*bassus*
voice:	1	2	3	4	5

Figure 1:8: Ranges and differentials of voices engaged in church polyphony, c. 1520–1549, 1553–9

The surviving six-part music of the Chapel Royal composer John Sheppard (c. 1512–1559), much of which appears to date from the reign of Mary I (1553–8), shows the persistence of this pattern of vocal scoring right up to the end of Latin liturgical composition in England. However, it has to be recalled that the overall pattern of clefs and ranges of voice engaged in Sheppard's music are not those of conventional choirs of the Marian period. Rather, they witness the forces available in the contemporary Chapel Royal. This was uniquely the largest, finest, and last, of the pre-Reformation choirs in England, and following the depredations of the Edwardian Reformation no other choir in the land could match the potential for richness of scoring offered by its staff of 32 gentlemen and twelve boys. Such opulence allowed Sheppard to score regularly in six-part combinations that included five adult voices, usually extending to alto, two full-range tenors, tenor and bass. His patterns of vocal scoring, therefore, were

107 Of the four pieces in six parts, the *Magnificat a6* and the Mass *Gloria tibi trinitas* both add a baritone voice (clef C5, range *A–d¹*) to the standard five-part ensemble; the Mass *Corona spinea* adds a second bass part (clef F4, range *G–b*), and the Mass *O Michael* adds a second full-range tenor (clef C4, range *c–f¹*).

108 Although in many instances the restriction of range arose from the identity of the tenor as a monorhythmic *cantus firmus* from plainsong, the limit of range still applied even in compositions in which this was a fully polyphonic part.

exceptional, and do not constitute a standard against which the usages of other composers (especially his successors, composing to the vernacular texts of the Protestant Church) can be compared – except, of course, for those of his Chapel Royal colleagues. This six-part writing was created by adding to the five voices of which the standard scoring was constituted either a baritone voice sounding *A–d* or, much the more commonly, an extra full-range tenor sounding *c–g¹*. In those instances in which the latter voice made little use of its lowest one or two notes, it might be found convenient to locate its clef one line of the staff 'higher' than formerly. Commonly therefore, though far from universally, it was located in the C_3 clef rather than C_4, and under these circumstances could thus be designated a 'high-range' tenor. The voice-ranges and clef configuration common in the six-part (and, *mutatis mutandis*, the seven- and eight-part) writing of John Sheppard are indicated in Figure 1:9.

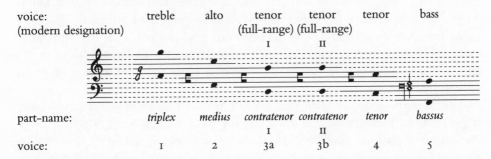

Figure 1:9: Timbres and ranges of voices, Chapel Royal composition *a*6, 1553–1559 (John Sheppard)

Probably during the 1530s or 1540s this bifurcation of the erstwhile pair of equal tenor parts became sufficiently wide to gain some genuine significance for vocal scoring. It was this divergence in the nature of the tenor voice, abetted by the habit of entering the full-range/high-range tenor part into the *contratenor* partbooks, that led, in post-Reformation composition for vernacular texts, to the compression of the differential between the alto and tenor voices from a fifth to a third, and helped to cause the term *contratenor*/countertenor eventually to become attached to the adult male alto voice.[109]

(d) The 'high pitch' theory

It may have been noticed that the interpretation of vocal scoring and performing pitch offered here is not compatible with another that has been expressed elsewhere (in relation just to the music of the Eton Choirbook period onwards) and has been given extensive exposure through adoption in performance over the last

---

109 These developments will be considered in Roger Bowers, 'The vocal scoring of English church polyphony: "choir pitch" and the origins of "organ pitch", c. 1547–70' (forthcoming).

twenty years or so. This alternative theory may be called the 'high pitch' theory, since the vocal scoring and consequent sounding pitch that result from its application produce performances for music of the period c. 1470–1559 startlingly higher in pitch than those advanced here.[110]

According to this theory, the clef had already by the third quarter of the fifteenth century taken on its modern role of conveying to the singers the precise performing pitch intended by the composer for each piece. This, however, was communicated not directly but through a phenomenally complex 'clef code', acknowledged even by its propounder to be 'labyrinthine, cumbersome and often contradictory', and for the evolution of which no coherent rationale has ever been produced.[111] This 'code' is conceived as having conveyed to the performers specific degrees of transposition applicable to the written music in front of them. For music of the Eton Choirbook and onwards to 1559 these transpositions respond to an alleged need for scoring for five (not four) distinct vocal timbres. Three are held to have been exclusively adult voices: a bass, sounding $Ab–db^i$, a tenor sounding $eb–gb^i$ and a 'countertenor (or alto)' sounding $eb–bb^i$. The upper two timbres are produced exclusively by boys' voices: a mean, sounding $bb–eb^2$, and a treble sounding at the extraordinarily high pitch of $eb^i–bb^2$ or even, exceptionally, c^3.

This hypothesis differs from that offered here in four principal respects. First, it purports to perceive in the music of the period c. 1465–1559 five entirely distinct vocal timbres rather than the four reported above. Secondly, it interprets the voice second from the top of the matrix as exclusively a boy's voice, leaving no scope for the alternatives of performance by either adults or boys as suggested here. Thirdly, it interprets the composer's choice of clef configuration as communicating not simply the location of the diatonic semitones, but – by a complex sequence of processes of transposition – actual sounding pitch. Fourthly, and most strikingly, it recognizes the evident concept of standardized differentials between the voices, but in terms of sounding pitch locates the matrix of timbres a whole minor third higher than the optimum indicated here.

It will already be evident that such conclusions do not fit with the continuum of vocal scoring from c. 1320 onwards that has been indicated above. Indeed, the 'high pitch' theory has been formulated without regard to the practices of scoring from which the five-part writing of the Eton Choirbook style evolved. Yet it seems impossible to deny the validity of Figure 1:5a above, showing how five-part scoring was developed during the third quarter of the fifteenth century from the erstwhile three-part scoring through the addition of one new voice above and one below. The 'high pitch' theory locates the sounding pitch of the two octaves covered by the three middle voices of five-part scoring as $eb–eb^2$. Were this so, then it would have to be accepted that this was also the sounding pitch of the music of the period of Lionel Power and John Dunstable, being

110 David Wulstan, *Tudor Music* (London 1985), pp. 192–249.
111 *Ibid.*, p. 212. In fact, this 'clef code' appears to be entirely imaginary.

produced by an ensemble consisting of a lowish boy's voice $bb-eb^2$ with two adult voices whose pitch, at $eb-ab^1$, would seem to identify them as particularly high tenors. Yet not only is this conclusion negated by the indications that prior to c. 1450 or so the boy's voice was not used in polyphonic music; it also seems unacceptable on simple empirical grounds. It appears impossible to conceive a scenario compatible with the known evidence that could result in the evolution of so peculiar a scoring and so strained a pitch for performance of the three-part music of the first half of the fifteenth century, and its antecedents.

Such ruminations merely emphasize the fact that the primary and principal consideration invalidating the 'high pitch' theory is the realization that there has been produced not a single shred of genuinely contemporary evidence to support it. It has been generated from the imposition upon the musical and other evidence available from the period c. 1465–1559 of material arising exclusively from a substantially later age, namely the early seventeenth century. As has often been pointed out, certain commentators of the 1620s and 1630s described a five-part disposition of voices, used within contemporary church music for a minority of compositions, which employed a compass of 23 notes, sounded at or close to the overall compass of $Ab-bb^2$ and engaged five distinct timbres of voices. These were distinguished especially by the very highest, a boy's high treble sounding at around eb^1-bb^2 or even c^3. The statements of these commentators certainly constitute good evidence for interpreting the scoring of relevant music of the early seventeenth century.[112] However, it is manifestly unsafe to apply this evidence indiscriminately to the interpretation of the scoring of music from a period some 100 to 150 years earlier. No corroborative evidence from the intervening period is available to establish a continuum of practice as a bridge over which the transfer of evidence can take place. Moreover, the intervening period, far from exhibiting the prevailing stability of the years c. 1465 – c. 1535, witnessed an era of unprecedented turbulence in all aspects of church affairs. Given what is now known of the history of liturgical choirs during the years of the English Reformation, say c. 1530 – c. 1585, it is clear that there is no ingredient within performance practice for church music for which a continuum can be safely assumed in the absence of firm evidence in its favour.[113] And for the existence of the 'high treble' voice prior to 1600 there is not a shred of evidence of any kind.

It has been pointed out that the words used to describe the five timbres of voice available in the early seventeenth century (c. 1620–1630) – bass, tenor, countertenor, mean and treble – coincide exactly with the words chosen to identify the departments of the choir of the Percy household chapel in the early

---

112 Peter le Huray, *Music and the Reformation in England, 1549–1660* (London 1967; Cambridge 2/1978), pp. 121–3.
113 Much evidence remains unpublished; however, see Lehmberg, *The Reformation of Cathedrals, passim* but especially pp. 182–225; Ian Payne, *The Provision and Practice of Sacred Music at Cambridge Colleges and Selected Cathedrals, c.1547–1646* (New York and London 1993), pp. 10–58; and, more generally, Eamon Duffy, *The Stripping of the Altars* (Yale 1992), pp. 377–593.

sixteenth century (c. 1505–1522).[114] So they do. However, a coincidence of two lists of words separated in origin by no fewer than 120 very turbulent and eventful years must be interpreted with care, and detailed examination shows that the ostensible parallel and similarity is false; the comparison is simply not of like with like. The lists furnished by the early seventeenth-century commentators are indeed of *timbres of voice* for the singing of polyphony; but the lists to be extracted from the Earl of Northumberland's volume of household regulations are of *departments of the choir*, identified not for musical but for administrative reasons (primarily, for recruitment). The two are not the same. As has been shown above, and as close examination of the music will verify, the music of the period to which the Percy chapel lists relate displays not five but four timbres of voice; those listed as 'tenors' belonged to a department of the choir which was not involved in the singing of polyphony. No true analogy between early seventeenth-century and early sixteenth-century scoring can be drawn on the basis of these lists, therefore; and without that analogy the whole foundation of the 'high pitch' theory for early Tudor polyphony evaporates.

Indeed, application of this analogy produces at least one result of such implausibility that it defies credibility. The analogy can be sustained only if the music of the period c. 1505–1522 can be shown to have engaged the five separate timbres of voice mentioned in the sources of the 1620s and 1630s. This can be accomplished only if in the standard five-part scoring of the early sixteenth century the third and fourth voices, consistently marked with the contrapuntal identifications *contratenor* and *tenor*, were sung by voices of different timbre – the first by a 'countertenor' voice of alto character, the second by a tenor voice.[115] Yet for all this period (i.e. up to c. 1522) these two voices were composed in the same clef and engaged the same range, and there can be no doubt that they were performed by two representatives of one and the same vocal timbre. The 'high pitch' theory is constrained to posit for the performance of these two parts an 'alto or countertenor' voice for the third and a 'tenor' voice for the fourth which represent two different timbres but whose bottom pitches are wholly identical and whose overall ranges are almost so.[116] So infelicitous a result does appear to invalidate wholly the theory which produced it. The perception within the scoring of five-part music of the period c. 1500–1520 of five distinct vocal timbres emerges as patently misconceived, and the analogy with early seventeenth-century scoring thus vanishes. The 'high treble' voice may therefore be recognized as a phenomenon exclusively of early seventeenth-century composition; to interpret the vocal scoring of music of any earlier period to accommodate and engage it clearly represents a serious misunderstanding.

Only one further shred of evidence has ever been produced to locate usage

---

114 Wulstan, *Tudor Music*, pp. 233–7.
115 *Ibid.*, pp. 242–5.
116 See especially *ibid.*, Example 117, p. 212; the voices labelled 'alto' and 'tenor' are accorded the same lowest pitch, *eb*.

of the 'high treble' voice within composition of the late fifteenth and sixteenth centuries. There have survived skeleton scores for organ of three or four settings of anthems and Services by composers known to have been active in the early Elizabethan period, particularly Sheppard and Tallis, which are described in the manuscript which is their sole source as 'for trebles'. This source, however, is once again not of sixteenth- but of seventeenth-century origin. The music survives uniquely in *GB-Ob* Tenbury 791, an organ-book compiled (possibly for use by John Tomkins) during the 1630s – which is indeed the major source of music 'for trebles'.[117] All that the evidence available indicates, therefore, is that these early Elizabethan settings were revived during the 1630s and performed at a pitch requiring use of the then fashionable 'high treble' voice. It gives no grounds for imagining that at the time of their composition 60–70 years earlier their composers envisaged performance at such a pitch and with such forces. Again, this is evidence of the performance practice of the 1630s, not of the 1550s.

In performance the application of the 'high pitch' theory has proved unfortunate. The sonority of music conceived as consisting of a dense texture of four adult voices and an ordinary boy's treble is substantially misrepresented when executed by a scoring that is top-heavy, dominated by high voices and performed around a minor third above the level of pitch envisaged by the composer. Moreover, the foundation and heart of the original five-part scoring lies in the twinning of two tenor voices singing in the naturally stronger parts of their register. The integrity and character of this scoring is seriously compromised when these two tenor parts are raised in pitch by a minor third and allocated instead to two alto voices, who have to sing predominantly in the weaker sections of their register. By this process the whole intended core of the choral sound is enfeebled, leaving in the middle of the texture insufficient tone to hold together the two outer ends of the tonal spectrum.

It seems clear that the revolution in performance forces for polyphony which took place in the second half of the fifteenth century was not compounded and exaggerated by any radical revision in the prevailing aesthetic of character of sound inherited from the past. The key to the sonority of early Tudor polyphony needs to be recognized as not a shallow brilliance but a searching richness of sound, such as had characterized its antecedents in an unbroken tradition since the Middle Ages.

(The author records with pleasure his thanks to the relevant authorities for their permission to consult and reproduce material from the archival sources quoted in the footnotes, and to the British Academy, whose generous award of a Research Readership provided the opportunity for this chapter to be prepared for publication.)

117 It may be added that the considerable lapse of time between the composition of these pieces and their inscription into this much later source may render the attributions somewhat doubtful. The remaining composers of 'high treble' parts were all active in the early seventeenth century.

2

EDITING AND PERFORMING
MUSICA SPECULATIVA

ROGER BRAY

Nearly 70 years ago H. B. Collins, editing the anonymous early Tudor Mass *O quam suavis*,[1] and decoding the manuscript's obscure instructions explaining how the notes of the *tenor* were to be arrived at, became the first editor to face the problem of editing *musica speculativa*, a term which I define and discuss elsewhere,[2] but which for present purposes we may briefly describe as music which is conceived and presented in an esoteric format for academic presentation (skill in *musica speculativa* and *musica practica* being required by Cambridge of candidates for their music degrees in the early years of the sixteenth century, indicating that *musica speculativa* involved something beyond simple compositional skill, *musica practica*). Collins naturally and rightly concluded that the notes of the *tenor* of this mass were not performable in their manuscript layout, since they were presented to suit an esoteric purpose, arranged either with fictional lengths or in the wrong order, and they needed arrangement and realization to form part of an edition that would make sense to modern readers and performers. However, the mass would have been just as unperformable to musicians of the time, and even though no contemporary arrangement survives there can be no doubt that a sixteenth-century performance edition, at least of the *tenor*, would have been essential.[3]

At least in the surviving version of this mass it is obvious that the *tenor* is in an esoteric format because of the evidently strange notation and the canons telling how it is to be realized, and until recently it was thought that this was the only mass of the period conceived in this way, and it was looked upon as a unique oddity: 'there is nothing to equal its degree of artifice among the surviving English choral music of the period'.[4] However, I suggest[5] that the work

1 *Plainsong and Mediaeval Music Society* (London 1927). The source is *GB-Cul* Nn.6.46.
2 Roger Bray, 'Music and the quadrivium in early Tudor England', *Music and Letters* 76 (1995), pp. 1–18.
3 It would have been even more essential for the accompanying antiphon *Ave regina celorum*.
4 Frank Ll. Harrison, *Music in Medieval Britain* (London 1958), p. 268.
5 Bray, 'Music and the quadrivium'. I suggest also that the name of John Lloyd be reunited with this mass as the solution to the cryptic ascription. If it is the work of Lloyd, we have Sir John Hawkins's statement that he was a Cambridge graduate (*A General History of the Science and Practice of Music*, 5 vols. (London 1776), II, p. 522), together with the ascription to a puzzle canon in *GB-Lbl* Add. 31922, f. 27ʳ: 'Flude in armonia graduat'.

is not a unique oddity in its esotericism and that there are several other English masses which are equally academic and learned. The academic provenance of *O quam suavis* is shown by its complex layout and its presentation with its accompanying antiphon, thus fulfilling the stipulation most commonly found at Oxford and Cambridge after, respectively, 1507 and 1515; its uniqueness lies in the fact that it survives only in its cryptic format, whereas the others survive only in their performance arrangement. We are therefore introduced to the figure of the sixteenth-century editor, whose task was to make performable an obscurely notated original illustrating *musica speculativa*, and we have to ask ourselves what the remit of the twentieth-century editor is to be in relation to such works, and how far we should go in trying to establish what form a lost prototype of a surviving arrangement might take.

Nowadays the editor is used to preparing two kinds of edition: the scholarly edition and the performance edition, which can sometimes be combined though they can on occasion sit uncomfortably on top of each other. Most of the editorial interventions necessary for performance editions are uncontroversial these days as long as it is clear what has been added or changed, with prefatory staves indicating original note-values and pitch, and a system of showing accidentals that makes clear what the editor has done. The establishment of the notes themselves of the original version should be an easy task compared with the intricacies of *musica ficta*, transposition, vocal scoring and underlay.

But what is the original version: the esoteric version, illustrating *musica speculativa*, or the performance version, illustrating *musica practica*? Which should the editor attempt to re-create? Elsewhere[6] I explain that Fayrfax's Mass *O quam glorifica* survives only in a contemporary arrangement for performance. It is an academic Exercise, for his Oxford doctorate in 1511, and, as such, it would have been presented to the Oxford masters in a format as esoteric as the surviving version of the Mass *O quam suavis* and quite as incomprehensible to performers. In its surviving version Fayrfax's mass is complicated enough, but it is possible to see beyond the arrangement and deduce something of an even more complex original. The complexity hinges on the mensuration, and it is the practical difficulty of performing some of the music in its original mensuration that has necessitated the preparation of a contemporary performance version.

Briefly, the work has been arranged so that three of the voices appear to be in O and the remaining two voices in C throughout. The double mensuration of this sixteenth-century edition is a neat and simple conceit and creates no serious performance problems in itself, because the imperfect *semibrevis* (worth two *minimae*) is common to both signatures and even the *breves* coincide every two or three bars; indeed the adoption of imperfect *semibreves* is specifically

---

6   See my edition of Fayrfax's masses *O bone Iesu* and *O quam glorifica* for *EECM* (forthcoming), and my 'Music and the quadrivium'. There is a modern edition by Edwin B. Warren, 'Robert Fayrfax: Collected Works', 3 vols., *Corpus Mensurabilis Musicae* 17 (Rome 1959), I, p. 64, but this is not recommended.

designed to solve, not create, problems.[7] Yet the mass is unusual within the Tudor mass repertory in having no change of mensuration in the course of each movement; most Tudor festal masses start each movement in ○ and change to ₵,[8] usually at 'Qui tollis peccata mundi' in the Gloria, 'Et incarnatus est' in the Credo, 'Benedictus' in the Sanctus, and either the second or third 'Agnus Dei' in the Agnus, and many revert to ○ for a final section. Analysis of the structure of the mass, of the note-values of the *tenor* part and of the curious layout of rests shows that *O quam glorifica* was originally conceived in ⊙ for the first section of each movement and ○ for the second. For most of the mass this in itself is not a particular problem for performers; although ⊙ is rarely found by 1500 it is not much more difficult than ₵, which is commonly found. The problem lies in the passages during which Fayrfax writes in 3:2 proportion within ⊙. This is most easily understood in modern-day values, in which the triplet figuration within groups of three basic quavers can be readily seen (Ex. 2:1).

Example 2:1

There are four such passages in the mass, one each in the Credo and Sanctus, and two in the Agnus, which would surely have proved unperformable in ⊙, because the dotted-crotchet pulse is almost impossible to maintain while it is still present, and even this pulse disappears in passages such as 'Pleni sunt celi' in the Sanctus and the second 'Agnus Dei' passage of the Agnus, where all the voices eventually move to the triplets, making retention of the original beat even more difficult because no voice has it. Although this is technically 3:2 proportion (three triplet quavers for every two basic quavers), it is actually 27:18 because it is two complete bars in 9/8 before the pattern repeats, which in turn means that the barline of alternate bars becomes lost for the voice(s) in triplets.

This sixteenth-century edition tells us something of the speed of the music, for there would have been no practical problem if the choir were reckoning its beat as the *minima* (quaver), so the effort expended in re-arranging the music indicates that the beat or pulse is the *semibrevis*, not *minima* (dotted-crotchet, not quaver), which gives us some indication of the lilt, and probably therefore the approximate speed, of the music (viz. three, not nine, in a bar, in modern parlance).

7   In the following discussion original note-values are given their Latin name, in italics, to distinguish English semibreves from Latin *semibreves*. In the original notation a quaver is a *minima*, a dotted crotchet a dotted *semibrevis*, and a dotted minim a dotted *brevis*, though it is the unusual use of chains of (original) dotted *semibreves* and dotted *breves* in ₵, instead of undotted *semibreves* and *breves* in a perfect signature such as ⊙, that provides an indication that something strange has happened to the note-values and the mensuration.
8   By the late 1520s this had become ⊘ and ₵.

More important, proof is provided of the relationship of one mensuration to another; since ○ is used for three voices, and C for two, throughout all movements in the surviving edition, with no mensural change, it follows that the *minima* (quaver) is constant throughout, and therefore even when the original mensuration is restored to ⊙ for the first section of each movement and ○ for the second the *minima* is still constant, a relationship which in turn should be applied to all masses which change between ○ and C for all of their movements.

The chosen method of arrangement takes into account the fact that singers can perform triplets only against groups of two, and therefore the basic pulse must be arranged so as to provide groups of two against which they sing their triplets. The price paid for the performability is worth noting, however: the whole of the first section of each movement has had to lose its 9/8 rhythm and pulse. To present-day performers, who rely on a time-signature and barlines to tell us of the pulse of a work, this is a serious handicap, and it is doubtful that we would be able to sing music in ○ or C as if it were in ⊙. To sixteenth-century musicians it seems that this was not such a problem, probably because they did not, of course, have barlines, and were able to take each note and group of notes as an entity to which its own rhythm was applied. This is particularly noticeable in the work of Fayrfax, where the music seems to us to float in a timeless way because the changes of the *cantus-firmus* note and the chord frequently do not occur on strong beats.

Example 2:2: Fayrfax, Mass *O quam glorifica* (opening of Credo in 9/8)

The prevailing 9/8 mensuration of the first half of each movement, including a passage using the triplet proportion, may be seen in Example 2:2, from the beginning of the Credo. This may be compared with the same passage as it appears in the surviving sources, with (at this point) one voice in 3/4 and one in 2/4 (Ex. 2:3).

Example 2:3: Fayrfax, Mass *O quam glorifica* (opening of Credo in 3/4 and 2/4)

The triplet passage in 9/8 (Ex. 2:2) is unperformable, while the layout in 3/4 and 2/4 (Ex. 2:3), though certainly performable, loses the 9/8 rhythmic lilt. An incidental illustration of the unconvincing nature of the contemporary arrangement lies in the fact that in this opening duet, the first few bars of which are common to all four movements, the music of the lower of the two voices alternates between voice III (in O or 3/4, Gloria, Sanctus) and voice IV (in C or 2/4, Credo, Agnus); the reason for the same music's alternating between O and C lies, of course, in the fact that originally it was in neither.

Some of the passages when presented in O/C, do not even have a whole number of *semibreves*, still less *breves* (respectively crotchets and bars in transcription).

Example 2:4 shows the lead into the first full passage of the Sanctus; the barring (i.e. the implication of O and C) has been faithfully followed from the beginning of the passage, and it may be seen that we have three orphan quavers

Example 2:4: Fayrfax, Mass *O quam glorifica* (Sanctus in 3/4 and 2/4)

(original *minimae*) necessitating a bar of 3/8. The careful structure of the early Tudor mass demands that each passage has a whole number of *breves*, and in many masses a whole number of *longae* and even (for whole sections) larges or *maximae* is produced. So these fractions and odd bits of bars (*breves*) cannot represent Fayrfax's original conception.

Example 2:5: Fayrfax, Mass *O quam glorifica* (Sanctus in 9/8)

Example 2:5 shows this passage in 9/8, also counting the bars faithfully from the beginning of the movement, and here we do find a whole number of bars and no need for any irregularity.[9]

9 Harrison, *Music in Medieval Britain*, pp. 263–4, barred one extract in 3/4 without noticing that it looked more like 6/8, while in another extract he briefly used 9/8 without comment. There are several passages in which the total number of *minimae* is divisible only by nine, so 6/8 will not do, and 9/8 it must be.

The fact that the only surviving version is a contemporary performance edition poses a series of problems for the editor. A scholarly edition should restore the music to the mensuration of Fayrfax's original conception, which means that for this mass the editor must therefore aim at an 'authentic' version not of the surviving sources but of a prototype original. But even the restoration of the 9/8 mensuration of this prototype original is unsatisfactory because a presentation version for the Oxford masters (similar to that of *O quam suavis*) would almost certainly have been arranged to look very learned and would have had notation of several colours for the notes of the *cantus firmus*,[10] which at that stage would have been presented in very long notes and not yet divided into shorter note-values to fit the syllables of the text. So there are three potential original versions: the presentation version, with highly formalized notation using several colours; Fayrfax's assumed working version using ⊙ but not the different colours; and the surviving sixteenth-century performance edition. None of these is entirely satisfactory. A version similar to *O quam suavis* in coloured notation with complex canonic instructions can be ruled out because we have no means of inventing the canons, though the inscriptions in *O quam suavis* and the puzzle canons of *Lbl* Add. 31922 provide an indication of the sort of riddles at which we would aim. A representation of the original notation in ⊙ cannot be faithfully achieved in modern scored format for two main reasons: the original perfect *semibreves* had to appear in the contemporary arrangement as *dotted semibreves* because the music was arranged into imperfect *prolatio* (O or C), but the dots would be unnecessary in ⊙ and yet would have to be shown for modern readers; and, more generally, the layout of the notes of the *tenor* in the arrangement was disposed to fit the syllables of the text, but the prototype *tenor* was evidently conceived in note-values some of which are very long indeed (up to 72 *minimae*), which could have been notated in *longae* and *maximae* (and even *duplex maximae*). If we decline to admit these features we are already imposing editorial decisions and re-notation and interpreting the text, aspects of editorial policy which appear to be at odds with the developing fashion to apply 'original' note-values.

On the other hand, a performance edition could follow the surviving contemporary performance edition, but in this case it loses all suggestion of 9/8, or ⊙ rhythm. The seminars arranged by Peter le Huray in Cambridge in 1990/91 provided the opportunity to try out with his choir some editorial principles and practical strategies for this mass, and it was found that, in order to maintain 9/8 for as long as possible and yet permit performance of the passages in triplets, the music still needs to be arranged, but arranged in a manner different from that of the early sixteenth century, so that modern notational devices and performing techniques, such as barlines and our modern ability to change mensuration readily, may be recruited to achieve the required effect. The solution

10 As described by John Tucke in his lecture notebook, *GB-Lbl* Add. 10336. See Ronald Woodley, *John Tucke: a Case Study in Early Tudor Music Theory* (Cambridge 1993). I am very grateful to the author for allowing me to see his manuscript before publication.

is therefore to edit in 9/8 as much as possible of the music in ⊙, but, when the triplet passages are looming, to go first into 6/8 (which is not difficult to do from 9/8) and thence to 3/4 (which is not difficult to do from 6/8), the quaver remaining constant at all times (Ex. 2:6).

Example 2:6: Fayrfax, Mass *O quam glorifica* (opening of Credo in modern performance version)

This, then, is what is necessary for a modern performance edition which captures as much as possible of the perfect (9/8) mensuration of the original while allowing a modern choir to deal with the passages in triplets.

The fifteenth-century choir was capable of passages in quite complex cross-rhythms achieved by cross-mensuration, including those achieved in some of the more complicated works of the 'Old Hall' manuscript (*GB-Lbl* Add. 57950), such as the anonymous Credo[11] which uses three colours in its notation, but it appears that the sixteenth-century choir was less capable of cross-mensuration or complex proportions than its fifteenth-century counterpart, perhaps because it was larger. The fact that the whole of *O quam glorifica* has had to be re-arranged to be performable illustrates both the rarity of complex cross-mensurations by this time and the lengths to which somebody was prepared to go to get the mass performed.

[11] No. 75, ff. 62^v–63.

This leads us inexorably to ask who our sixteenth-century editor was. Elsewhere[12] I cite the case of Dr Newton, an ill-fated composer whose work we do not know today because, according to Whythorne,[13] he appears to have been unable or unwilling to get his music performed (and it was therefore never copied out). This might seem to suggest that it was the composer's task to prepare the performance edition as well as the esoteric original, but, although all surviving sources of *O quam glorifica* are fairly well agreed on most aspects of its re-notation, they disagree in three important respects: the method of showing rests covering lengthy periods of silence, of breaking up the very long notes of the *tenor*, and of showing some of the passages in triplets. Thus, for example, in the passage 'in nomine' in the Sanctus, the silent Mean voice (II) has twelve *longa* rests in the 'Lambeth Choirbook' (*GB-Llp* 1) and eighteen *longa* rests in the 'Caius Choirbook' (*GB-Cgc* 667) for its 216 *minimae* of silence; either is potentially correct, depending how much the *longa* is worth (respectively eighteen or twelve *minimae*), though the simultaneous presence of two kinds of *longa* is yet more evidence of the inconsistency of the arrangement. One of the most significant examples proving re-notation occurs at the end of the opening passage of the mass, where the alto voice (III) actually has a *semibrevis* and *minima* rest completing a perfection in ⊙ (even though ostensibly it is in ○) before embarking on the remainder of the rests.

The different manner of breaking up the *tenor* is seen at the word 'de' in the phrase 'de celis' in the Credo, where there are two notes each to the total value of eighteen *minimae*; both are shown in Caius as dotted *brevis* followed by dotted *longa*, but in Lambeth the first is shown as *longa* + *semibrevis* + *longa* (*LSL*), and the second as *maxima* + *semibrevis* (*MxS*); eighteen *minimae* in each case certainly, but sufficiently different to deny a common ancestry, one version with its dotted *brevis* and dotted *longa* reflecting the ⊙ original, the other with its undotted notes reflecting a more thorough-going transformation into C. It is important to note that at this point there is no change of syllable necessitating the breaking-up of the original eighteen-*minima* note in the first place; that is to say, the tinkering which has led to these revealing differences need never have happened if the mensuration had not needed re-arrangement.

The work survives also in the Peterhouse 'Henrician' partbooks (*GB-Cp* 471–4).[14] The loss of the *tenor* book from this set is unfortunate because it is particularly in the *tenor*, as we have seen, that evidence of a difference between the Lambeth and Caius versions is to be found, and it is all the more unfortunate because there is evidence that the Peterhouse version was indeed different from the Lambeth and the Caius versions. In the triplet passage in voice III on the word 'Dei' in the second 'Agnus Dei' the Peterhouse version uses four separate proportional signs: for the first nine triplet *minimae* it has .96., for the next six

---

12 Bray, 'Music and the quadrivium', pp. 9–11.
13 See James M. Osborn (ed.), *The Autobiography of Thomas Whythorne* (London 1961), p. 300.
14 *Olim* 40, 41, 31 and 32. See Nick Sandon, 'The Henrician Partbooks at Peterhouse Cambridge', *Proceedings of the Royal Musical Association* 103 (1976/7), pp. 106–40.

it has $\mathbb{C}$, for the next eighteen it has $\bigcirc$ 6.4., and for the last 93 it has $\odot$ 3.2. This suggests that the Peterhouse books of 1539/41 were indeed based (as has been suggested by Sandon) on a reputable but older version, perhaps a Magdalen exemplar, part of the collection assembled there between 1518 and 1524,[15] which presented the mass in a transitional stage halfway between the lost prototype of 1511 and the surviving Lambeth or Caius arrangements of the 1520s, which in turn suggests that the ability to cope with these complex passages decreased during the first 20 or 30 years of the century.

These details are significant enough to indicate three slightly different ancestors. It is unlikely that all three versions are by Fayrfax and therefore one must doubt that any are by him (for if a version was available carrying the authority of the composer it would surely have been the only acceptable exemplar). Indeed, an examination of errors and inconsistencies in other masses suggests that the sixteenth-century editions were made by scribes, not composers, for it is impossible to believe that some of the mistakes or variants in the surviving versions can have been made by a composer to his own work.

Fayrfax's *Albanus* is a case in point. Indeed, if it were not for the fact that we are told that *O quam glorifica* was his doctoral Exercise, we would suspect *Albanus* of having served in this capacity, for it even has its associated antiphon (*O Maria Deo grata*), satisfying a requirement commonly specified at Oxford from 1507. More important, not only could its *cantus-firmus* layout have been presented in esoteric fictional notation, but there is actually one passage in which it is still presented thus. In the antiphon there is even a remnant of the canonic instruction which ensured correct interpretation of this conceit and, moreover, this instruction appears in the Peterhouse version, providing again (as in *O quam glorifica*) direct evidence of a transitional phase in the work's notational history. In both mass and antiphon Fayrfax uses a type of isorhythm for the presentation of the nine-note *cantus firmus* in prime, retrograde, inverted and retrograde-inverted forms, a conceit susceptible of esoteric presentation. Each form of statement is usually presented in the same rhythm, though in various different mensurations. So, for example, the inverted form is presented in the values *BBBSSBBBB* under four different mensural signatures, yielding the rhythms shown in Example 2:7 in modern values as they appear in the mass and the antiphon *O Maria Deo grata* (and it is important to note that the antiphon is particularly closely integrated with the mass in ways other than this).

Three of these statements are themselves repeated three times at different pitches, so an esoteric layout of this passage could have presented the *cantus firmus* in its prime form with a clef or canon indicating that inversion was necessary, a mensural sign indicating the conversion of note-values and a canon indicating that there was to be a repetition on different degrees of the scale.[16]

15 Harrison, *Music in Medieval Britain*, p. 431, and Sandon, 'The Henrician Partbooks', p. 117.
16 As is achieved in the textless work by Lloyd in *Lbl* Add. 31922, f. 27ʳ, where a three-note rising *cantus firmus* is designated as a three-note falling *cantus firmus* to be repeated a tone lower by means of a canon.

Example 2:7: Fayrfax, *Mass Albanus* (isorhythmic layout of inverted form of *cantus firmus*)

In the final passage of the antiphon and of the Agnus of the mass the *cantus firmus* is presented in equal *semibreves* moving through all the voices before finally settling in the *tenor*. The notation of the Lambeth, Caius and 'Forrest-Heyther' (*GB-Ob* Arch. f. e. 19–24)[17] versions of the mass, and of the Peterhouse version of the antiphon, presents the nine notes of the *cantus firmus* in a smaller note size using ligatures, making it look like plainsong; it may be that the esoteric version of this passage survives because there were no syllables to be fitted to it. Not only are these ligatured notes the wrong length (all notes should be *semibreves*) but also the rhythm presented at this point in the Agnus by Lambeth and Caius is *BLLBBBLLL*, the rhythm actually found in an earlier statement of the prime form (at 'Cum sancto spiritu' in the Gloria), while Forrest-Heyther gives this rhythm for some of the statements in the *tenor*, and very nearly so for the statements in other voices. The Peterhouse version of the mass yet again represents a different ancestry, for the note-values are correct *semibreves* and there is no hint of esoteric notation. However, in the final passage of the antiphon *O Maria Deo grata*, where the *cantus firmus* is treated in very similar fashion (in equal *semibreves* moving through the voices before settling into the *tenor*), Peterhouse not only gives fictitious values that look like plainsong, but in one voice feels the need to explain what the real values should be; in voice II the copyist has added the note 'ij menoms', all that remains of the original canon

17 *Olim* Mus. Sch. e. 376–81.

telling how these *longae* and *breves* were to be read as equal *semibreves* and indicating that the correct value is indeed two *minimae* (= one *semibrevis*) instead of the *longae and breves* actually presented in the archaic-looking ligatures.

The final passage of the mass (see Ex. 2:8) reveals itself as one to which contemporary editing has been applied also by the fact that the arrangement of this passage has led to different layouts of the nine-*semibrevis* periods of rest as they occur in various voices (*LLS, SLL, SBLB*, etc.): incidentally each nine-note statement follows immediately upon the heels of the preceding statement and the crotchet (original *semibrevis*) rest between the second and third, which has crept into the modern edition, is incorrect.[18]

Example 2:8: Fayrfax, Mass *Albanus* (beginning of final section of Agnus)

18 Warren (ed.), 'Robert Fayrfax: Collected Works', I, p. 62.

Once one sees how this passage was originally notated and measured, it becomes an easy matter to restore the original mensuration, which is O not C, with perfect *modus*, giving 9/4 or groups of three bars of 3/4. The final passage of the antiphon *O Maria Deo grata* is very similar musically, and has been similarly arranged from 9/4 into 2/4.

In *O quam glorifica* we could see why the music had been edited into a different mensuration. In *Albanus* the reason is by no means so clear, but it may indicate performers' unease in perfect mensuration, as in *O quam glorifica*. Whatever the reason, it is certainly the editor's duty to uncover passages like these, whether for scholarly purposes as a matter of correctness or for performance purposes in order to achieve the correct accentuation and flow of the music.

Despite its esoteric layout of the *cantus firmus*, *Albanus* cannot be an academic Exercise because Fayrfax only ever had to write one (*O quam glorifica* for Oxford in 1511), having been exempted by Cambridge from any formal requirement for both his Mus. B. and Mus. D., and anyway there is no record of what the requirement was when he took these degrees (1501–2).[19] If *Albanus* is non-academic and yet written in the esoteric tradition,[20] we should look at other masses not submitted for music degrees, to see if nevertheless they show esoteric approaches. In so doing we know, from the two Fayrfax examples, that a likely indication of a lost, complex, original is the presence of confused notation, especially of the *tenor*, and clusters of mistakes or variant readings.

Three such masses have already been identified: Ashwell's *Iesu Christe* and *Ave Maria*, and Taverner's *Corona spinea*.[21] John Bergsagel has pointed to notational features of Ashwell's Mass *Iesu Christe* that present 'an interpretation provided by the Forrest-Heyther scribe for the benefit of singers no longer able to cope with an older tradition',[22] and Benham has shown that in Taverner's Mass *Corona spinea* 'we have a kind of sixteenth-century performing edition'.[23] Both these comments refer to the layout of the *cantus firmus*, but Woodley[24] has noted a non-*cantus-firmus* passage in the Credo of Ashwell's *Ave Maria* where the 'clumsy ... notation' is betrayed by 'gross use of the *punctus additionis*, strange mensuration signs, a figured proportion 8:3, and a written instruction backing this up which is itself garbled ("dupla superpartiens" instead of "dupla superbipartiens tertias")', and a passage in the third 'Agnus Dei' of the same mass where

---

19 Bray, 'Music and the quadrivium', p. 7.

20 The structure of *O quam glorifica* is discussed at some length in my edition for *Early English Church Music* (forthcoming) and in Bray, 'Music and the quadrivium', pp. 15–18. In *Albanus*, once the re-mensuration of the final passages of the Agnus has been applied, and only then, it transpires that Fayrfax has contrived the structure outlined in the Appendix (see pp. 66–7 below). See also fn. 26 below.

21 Modern editions, respectively, in: John D. Bergsagel (ed.), 'Early Tudor Masses: ii', *Early English Church Music* 16 (London 1976), p. 1, and *idem*, 'Early Tudor Masses: i', *Early English Church Music* 1 (London 1963), p. 61; Hugh Benham (ed.), 'John Taverner: i, Six-part Masses', *Early English Church Music* 20 (London 1978), p. 75.

22 Bergsagel (ed.), 'Early Tudor Masses: ii', p. 206.

23 Benham (ed.), 'John Taverner: Masses: i', p. xvi.

24 Woodley, *John Tucke*, p. 112.

the 'clumsiness' of the notation is shown by 'three of the four verbal proportional indications being incorrect'.[25]

Since all three of these masses are in the Forrest-Heyther partbooks (as is *Albanus*) we must look more closely at this collection to see if any further masses show evidence of having been arranged for performance. Sure enough, a cluster of variant readings reveals yet another edited mass, none other than Taverner's *Gloria tibi trinitas*, in which it is likely that the final passage of every movement has been put into a different mensuration; certainly, the end of the Credo, the Sanctus and the Agnus appear in other sources which are demonstrably[26] better than Forrest-Heyther.

The complete mass survives in Forrest-Heyther and also in the Baldwin partbooks of the 1580s and 1590s (*GB-Och* 979–83, lacking the *tenor* book).[27] Two extracts, scored and barred, also survive in another Baldwin manuscript, his 'Commonplace Book' (*GB-Lbl* R.M.24.d.2).[28] The last passage of the Agnus is the most straightforward to deal with first, for the superior version of the Baldwin partbooks has quite rightly been preferred by Benham, the modern editor, even though the source itself is at least 50 years later than Forrest-Heyther; the Forrest-Heyther version is inconsistent and confused, and one perfect *semibrevis* too long, i.e. 55 perfect *semibreves*, a length which does not yield a whole number of *breves* in any mensuration. The Baldwin version has 54 *semibreves*, which on analytical as well as musical grounds is demonstrably correct. At the end of the other two movements mentioned above, the Credo (see Ex. 2:9) and the

Example 2:9: Taverner, Mass *Gloria tibi trinitas* (end of Credo)

25 *Ibid.*, p. 117.
26 Demonstrably, that is, in analytical terms. See fn. 31 and the Appendix below.
27 See Roger Bray, 'The part-books Oxford, Christ Church, MSS 979–983: an index and commentary', *Musica Disciplina* 25 (1971), pp. 179–97. Modern edition in Benham (ed.), 'John Taverner: 1, Six-part Masses', p. 1.
28 See Roger Bray, 'British Library, MS Royal 24.d.2 (John Baldwin's Commonplace Book): an index and commentary', *[Royal Musical Association] Research Chronicle* 12 (1974), pp. 137–51.

'Benedictus' from the Sanctus, it is the other Baldwin source, his Commonplace Book, that gives the correct version. In the Credo this version is slightly shorter (66 *semibreves*) than the version presented in Forrest-Heyther and Christ Church (which both have 68) and, most significantly, it is scored and barred in ⏀ (modern 3/4) rather than the ₵ (2/4) of the other versions.[29]

Example 2:10: Taverner, Mass *Gloria tibi trinitas* (final passage of Benedictus)

29 Admittedly, in his Commonplace Book Baldwin sometimes bars in ⏀ music which one would expect to be in ₵, and indeed he gives ₵ as his mensuration sign, but the significant feature is the actual barring.

Baldwin uses Φ again for his Commonplace Book extract from the end of the Benedictus, and on this occasion his version is exactly the same as the other versions, except, of course, for the effect of its being in Φ rather than ₵, making the 54 *semibreves* into eighteen *breves* in Φ rather than 27 *breves* in ₵.

In Example 2:10 the dotted point of imitation in bars 1–2 in the two *contratenor* parts is now consistent within a 3/4 bar, and the four-note rising point of imitation in bars 4–5 (*contratenor*), 5–6 (*tenor*) and 6–7 (*bassus*) is also consistent within the bar, while the slightly altered version of this imitative point a third lower behaves similarly in the highest voice (bars 8–9) and finally in the *bassus* at the cadence.

So one or other of the Baldwin sources presents a different, and better, version of the end of three of the movements, and in two cases a reversion to Φ is indicated. Many composers, certainly including Taverner, revert to Φ for the final passage of various movements of their masses, and indeed we have just seen Fayrfax doing so covertly at the end of the Agnus of *Albanus*. Finally, the end of the movement of *Gloria tibi trinitas* for which the Forrest-Heyther partbooks and the Baldwin partbooks are agreed, and Baldwin's Commonplace Book does not provide a concordance, provides the passage that on musical grounds alone presents the clearest case for re-mensuration into Φ (Ex. 2:11).

Example 2:11: Taverner, Mass *Gloria tibi trinitas* (final passage of Gloria)

If we re-bar the last passage of the Gloria into 3/4 we find that the rising scalic point of imitation now appears consistently within our bar. Incidentally, we also have our attention drawn to the difference between the treble and the altos at the top of this rising scale; clearly the work represents an interesting stage in the upward extension of both voices (to G or not to G),[30] unless, of course, the difference reflects yet more sixteenth-century editorial intervention. If three movements are to be re-barred into perfect *breves*, we should re-examine the end of the Agnus, which we have already agreed is 54 *semibreves*, and I believe it should be in perfect *breves* like the other movements, except that, since the *semibrevis* is itself perfect, this means 9/8 or ☉ (Ex. 2:12).[31]

Example 2:12: Taverner, Mass *Gloria tibi trinitas* (final passage of Agnus)

I have discussed Baldwin's activities as copyist elsewhere;[32] here it is sufficient to note that he obviously had access in the 1580s to three different versions of

---

30 After transposition, to B♭ or not to B♭.

31 In *Gloria tibi trinitas*, once the re-mensuration of the final passages has been applied, and only then, we may see that Taverner has contrived the structure outlined in the Appendix (see p. 70 below). See also fn. 26 above.

32 See fn. 27 above, and also Roger Bray, 'John Baldwin', *Music and Letters* 56 (1975), pp. 55–60, and *idem*, 'Sixteenth-century *musica ficta*: the importance of the scribe', *Journal of the Plainsong and Mediaeval Music Society* 1 (1978), pp. 57–80.

Gloria tibi trinitas (for his partbook version does not tally with his Commonplace Book version, and neither tallies with Forrest-Heyther which he also possessed at this time). Indeed, the final passages of the Credo and Agnus are the only two passages of this mass included in his Commonplace Book, and it seems that he copied them there because he found a different version and wished to record its different mensuration and length, despite the fact that he owned the Forrest-Heyther books and had already made one complete copy in his partbooks. The most important feature here is that, on all three occasions when there is a Baldwin reading of some kind, the correct reading is found in Baldwin and the incorrect reading in Forrest-Heyther, a source generally reckoned to be very closely associated with Taverner himself, with *Gloria tibi trinitas* given pride of place as the first work in the manuscript and copied (it is assumed) to accompany his taking up his post at Cardinal College, Oxford.[33] Having failed to find an official Fayrfax version of *O quam glorifica*, we have failed to find an official Taverner version of *Gloria tibi trinitas*. Furthermore, we have shown that the earliest surviving source is not necessarily the most trustworthy. Peterhouse transmits an apparently earlier version of one of the proportional passages of *O quam glorifica* and one of the fictionally notated passages of *Albanus* than do the earlier Lambeth and Caius sources; likewise, Baldwin's two sources present versions superior to that of Forrest-Heyther, even though they are 50 years later. Since no fewer than seven masses (*O quam suavis, O quam glorifica, Albanus, Iesu Christe, Ave Maria, Corona spinea* and *Gloria tibi trinitas*) have been shown to present some sort of problem with the music text, the task of editing this complex music requires constant vigilance, especially if singers are to be able to perform it.

33 John D. Bergsagel, 'The date and provenance of the Forrest-Heyther collection of Tudor masses', *Music and Letters* 44 (1963), pp. 240–8.

APPENDIX

The structure of Fayrfax's Mass *Albanus* and Taverner's Mass *Gloria tibi trinitas.*

Fayrfax: Mass *Albanus* and antiphon *O Maria Deo grata*

Table 2:1: Fayrfax, Mass *Albanus*

sig.	text	voices	S	B	*cantus firmus* form	rhythm	no.
	Gloria						
⊕	Et in terra	1,2,3	81	27			
	Gratias agimus	Full/*CF*	54	18	P	A	1
	Domine Fili unigenite	3,4,5	45	15			
	Domine Deus	Full/*CF*	45	15	R	D	1
¢	Qui tollis ... miserere	2,3,4	56	28			
	Qui tollis ... suscipe	1,3,5	90	45			
	Qui sedes	Full/*CF*	66	33	P+R	A+D	1+1
	Quoniam	1,2,3	20	10			
	Tu solus	3,4,5	24	12			
	tu solus	1,2,3	32	16			
	Iesu	Full	8	4			
	Christe	1,2,3	16	8			
⊕	Cum sancto	Full/*CF*	45	15	P	B	1
	Credo						
⊕	Patrem omnipotentem	1,2,3	72	24			
	Et in unum Dominum	3,4,5	63	21	I	E	3
	Et ex Patre	Full/*CF*	144	48			
¢	Et incarnatus	1,4,5	84	42			
	Crucifixus	3,4,5	96	48			
	Et resurrexit	2,3,4	114	57			
	Et iterum	Full/*CF*	66	33	RI	G	3
⊕	Et exspecto	Full/*CF*	72	24	I	F	1
	Sanctus						
⊕	Sanctus	1,2,3	63	21			
	Sanctus, Sanctus	3,4,5	45	15			
	Dominus Deus	Full/*CF*	54	18	P	A	3
	Pleni sunt caeli	2,3,4	81	27			
	gloria tua	3,4,5	60	20			
	Osanna	Full/*CF*	45	15	R	D	3
¢	Benedictus	1,4,5	60	30			
	qui venit	2,3,4	50	25			
	in nomine	3,4,5	88	44			
	Osanna	Full/*CF*	66	33	RI	G	3

Table 2:1: *(cont.)*

sig.	text	voices	S	B	cantus firmus form	rhythm	no.
	Agnus						
Φ	Agnus Dei 1	1,2,3	54	18			
	qui tollis	3,4,5	66	22			
	miserere nobis	Full/*CF*	45	15	R	D	3
[¢]	Agnus Dei 2	2,3,4	50	25			
	qui tollis	1,2,3	74	37			
	miserere nobis	Full/*CF*	36	18	RI	G	3
¢	Agnus Dei 3	1,4,5	86	43			
	qui tollis	Full/*CF*	48	24	I	E	3
[Φ]	dona nobis	Full/*CF*	45	15	P	C	5
	pacem	Full/*CF*	45	15	P	C	5

Table 2:2: Fayrfax, Mass *Albanus*, movement structure (breves)

Gloria

Full/*CF*		18	15		/			33						15
Reduced/non-*CF*	27		15		/	28	45		10	12	16	4	8	/	
Total	27	18	15	15	/	28	45	33	10	12	16	4	8	/	15

Credo

Full/*CF*			48	/				33	/	24
Reduced/non-*CF*	24	21		/	42	48	57		/	
Total	24	21	48	/	42	48	57	33	/	24

Sanctus

Full/*CF*			18			15	/				33
Reduced/non-*CF*	21	15		27	20		/	30	25	44	
Total	21	15	18	27	20	15	/	30	25	44	33

Agnus

Full/*CF*			15	/			18		24	/	15	15
Reduced/non-*CF*	18	22		/	25	37		43		/		
Total	18	22	15	/	25	37	18	43	24	/	15	15

Table 2:3: Fayrfax, Mass *Albanus*, overall structure

	Gloria	Credo	Sanctus	Agnus	Total
Total	246	297	248	232	1023
Full/*CF*	81	105	66	87	339
Reduced/non-*CF*	165	192	182	145	684
Section 1	75	93	116	55	339
Section 2	156	180	132	147	615
Section 3	15	24	–	30	69

Table 2:4: Fayrfax, O *Maria Deo grata*

sig.	text	voices	S	B	cantus firmus form	cantus firmus rhythm	cantus firmus no.
Φ	O Maria		24	8			
	Deo grata		84	28			
	Christo		30	10			
	isto mundo		30	10			
	Te Maria		30	10			
	ubi sanctam		48	16			
	O Maria mater bona	Full/*CF*	171	57	RI+I	G+F	3+3
¢	O Maria mater Dei		156	78			
	O Maria spes		184	92			
	O Maria pro me	Full/*CF*	156	78	R+P	D+B	3+3
Φ	O Sancta Maria	Full/*CF*	99	33	P	C	11

Table 2:5: Fayrfax, Mass *Albanus*, and antiphon O *Maria Deo grata*, overall structure (breves)

	Gloria	Credo	Sanctus	Agnus	Antiphon	Total
Total	246	297	248	232	420	1443
Full/*CF*	81	105	66	87	168	507
Reduced/non-*CF*	165	192	182	145	252	936
Section 1	75	93	116	55	139	478
Section 2	156	180	132	147	248	863
Section 3	15	24	–	30	33	102

Notes:

(a) Tables 2:1 and 2:4 give, in the right-hand columns, details of the layout of the *cantus firmus*, as described above. Thus, for example, the form of the *cantus firmus* already discussed appears here as **R** (= Retrograde), **D** (rhythm **D** in my analysis), and then the number of times it is repeated (e.g. three times in the Agnus, as shown in Example 2:7). In the 'form' column, **P**, **I** and **RI** stand respectively for Prime, Inversion and Retrograde Inversion, while the 'rhythm' column shows that a particular form usually receives its peculiar rhythm.

(b) Table 2:2 shows the structure of each movement of the mass, arranged so that the carefully judged Boethian proportions may be seen clearly.[34] These work in various different ways:

---

34 For an introduction to Boethian proportions and the Platonic/Pythagorean theory, see Brian Trowell, 'Proportion in the music of Dunstable', *Proceedings of the Royal Musical Association* 105 (1978/9), pp. 100–41; Margaret V. Sandresky, 'The continuing concept of the Platonic/Pythagorean system...', *Music Theory Spectrum*

(i)   within a single category, e.g. Full/*CF*; for example, in the Gloria the first two such passages (18 + 15 = 33) balance the third passage in this category (33), while the second passage alone (15) balances the last (15);

(ii)   within a single combination of passages of music; for example, in the Gloria the first *finalis* occurs at the end of the first Full/*CF* passage and thus completes a combination of passages for reduced and full choir of 45 breves (= 27 + 18), which is as 3:2 to the next such combination of passages (15 + 15 = 30);

(iii)   across sectional divisions of a movement; for example, in the Credo the first five passages (24, 21, 48, 42, 48) alternate between lengths based on 21 and 24; furthermore, in this movement the opening 45 (= 24 + 21) is as 1:2 to the two combined passages of 90 in section 2 (respectively 42 + 48 and 57 + 33), leaving the intervening 48 as 2:1 to the final 24;

(iv)   across movements; for example, the only lengths used for *cantus-firmus* passages in the mass are 15, 18, 24 (and its multiple, 48) and 33; in this case the consistency is found even between works, for the *cantus-firmus* passages of *O Maria Deo grata* maintain not only the same method of rhythmic application to particular forms of the *cantus firmus* but also the lengths of **R** and **P** respectively (36 being in the scheme based on 24 and 42 being 18 + 24);

(v)   individually or in combination with neighbours as symbolic or cabbalistic numbers, the most common of which in Tudor music is 33 representing Christ, 33 being the age at which Christ was thought to have been crucified; the 33 in the Gloria may be an example, its use here (at 'Qui sedes') providing a symbolic reminder of the aftermath of the Crucifixion.

(c)   Table 2:3 gives the total lengths for the various categories; for example, the length of all the Full/*CF* passages in the Gloria (18 + 15 + 33 + 15 = 81) is listed in the total Full/*CF* figures. The extent of Fayrfax's erudition may be seen from the precise balance between Full/*CF* music and section 1 music for the whole mass (339 breves). A moment's thought should be sufficient to show that this is no mean feat (see also note (d) below).

(d)   Tables 2:4 and 2:5 repeat the process for the antiphon *O Maria Deo grata*. Although the work survives in incomplete form it is nevertheless possible to tell where the *cantus firmus* may be fitted, from which it is apparent that Fayrfax uses the same rhythms for each form of the *cantus firmus* as those in the mass. The extent of Fayrfax's even greater erudition may be seen from Table 2:5, where the total length of Gloria + Agnus (246 + 232 = 478) precisely balances the total length of all section 1 music (478), and therefore Credo + Sanctus + Antiphon balances section 2 + section 3 music (965). It is difficult to see how a mathematical formula could be designed both to achieve this and the relationships mentioned in paragraph (c) above, and also, moreover, to maintain the internal careful proportions. This is further evidence of the close relationship between the antiphon and the mass.

---

1 (1979), pp. 107–20, and Marcus van Crevel's lengthy Introduction to his edition of Obrecht's Mass *Maria Zart* in Jacob Obrecht, *Opera Omnia: Missae* 7 (Amsterdam 1964), pp. i–clxiv. The simplest such proportions are those found in the simplest musical intervals, 2:1, 3:2, 5:4, 9:8, etc.

(e) The division between passages occurs at the point just before they reach their *finalis* (or, where voices arrive at different times, just before the first voice to arrive does so); the *finalis* is therefore excluded whether the music continues to another passage or comes to a final cadence with *fermata*.[35]

(f) Original note-values are used. In this respect the present approach differs from that of earlier writers. Harrison[36] counted breves in O but longs in C, and Benham[37] followed Harrison. Warren[38] counted twice those bars where one passage ended and another began. Messenger[39] was not concerned to count, though his analysis of the formal and choral layout is interesting. The logic of the approaches of Harrison, Benham or Warren is not apparent. One possible explanation for their view, that O and Φ mean different things, is not relevant by 1500 in England; the inconsistency of the use of the stroke may be seen in the Gloria of *Albanus*, the three sections of which originally used O–C–O, where both the Caius and Lambeth Choirbooks present voice II (but only voice II) in Φ–C–O (which also means that this voice has Φ against the other voices' O) as an intermediate stage in the process which led to this mass appearing in Forrest-Heyther and Peterhouse in Φ–₵–Φ.

(g) This approach to structure, or something like it (sometimes even more erudite than this), is found (or occasionally only aimed at) in all but two Tudor festal masses that are in an analysable state.

35 See also Bray, 'Music and the quadrivium', which provides similar details for Fayrfax's Mass *O quam glorifica*. See also my edition of Fayrfax's masses *O bone Iesu* and *O quam glorifica* for *Early English Church Music* (forthcoming).
36 Harrison, *Music in Medieval Britain*, p. 314.
37 Hugh Benham, 'The formal design and construction of Taverner's works', *Musica Disciplina* 26 (1972), pp. 189–200, at p. 194.
38 Edwin B. Warren, *The Life and Works of Robert Fayrfax*, Musicological Studies and Documents 22 (Rome 1969), p. 81.
39 Thomas Messenger, 'Texture and form in the masses of Fayrfax', *Journal of the American Musicological Society* 24 (1971), pp. 282–6.

Taverner: Mass *Gloria tibi trinitas*

Table 2:6: Taverner, Mass *Gloria tibi trinitas*

sig.	text	voices	CF stmnt	S	B	No. CF notes
	Gloria					
Φ	Et in terra	F	CF1	42	14	12
	Laudamus te	3,5,6		54	18	
	Gratias agimus	F	CF1	96	32	27
	Domine Fili unigenite	1,4,6		78	26	
	Domine Deus	F	CF1	54	18	15
¢	Qui tollis ... miserere	2,4,6	CF2	76	38	22
	Qui tollis ... suscipe	1,3,5		84	42	
	Qui sedes	F	CF2	64	32	32
	Quoniam tu solus	1,4		28	14	
	Tu solus Dominus	3,5,6		16	8	
	tu solus altissimus	1,2,4		20	10	
[Φ]	Cum sancto	F	CF3	60	20	54
	Credo					
Φ	Patrem omnipotentem	F	CF1	36	12	12
	visibilium	3,4,5		24	8	
	Et in unum Dominum	1,6		60	20	
	Et ex Patre	F	CF1	120	40	42
¢	Et incarnatus	2,3,4,5	CF2	84	42	22
	Crucifixus	1,1,6		84	42	
	Et resurrexit	F	CF2	108	54	32
[Φ]	Et exspecto	F	CF3	66	22	54
	Sanctus					
Φ	Sanctus	F	CF1	30	10	12
	Sanctus, Sanctus	2,5		30	10	
	Dominus Deus	F	CF1	78	26	27
	Pleni sunt caeli	2,3,4		60	20	
	gloria tua	1,5,6		54	18	
	Osanna	F	CF2	48	16	15
¢	Benedictus	4,5,6		48	24	
	in nomine	1,2,3,6	CF2	112	56	54
[Φ]	Osanna	F	CF3	54	18	54
	Agnus					
Φ	Agnus Dei 1	F	CF1	36	12	12
	qui tollis	2,3,4,5,6	CF1	24	8	18
	miserere nobis	F	CF1	72	24	24
¢	Agnus Dei 2	4,5,6		80	40	
	miserere nobis	2,4,5,6		88	44	
	Agnus Dei 3	1,3		86	43	
[⊙]	dona nobis pacem	F	CF2	54	18	54

Table 2:7: Taverner, Mass *Gloria tibi trinitas*, movement structure (breves)

Gloria

CF	14		32		18	/	38		32				/	20
Non-CF		18		26		/		42		14	8	10	/	
Full	14		32		18	/			32				/	20
Reduced		18		26		/	38	42		14	8	10	/	
Total	14	18	32	26	18	/	38	42	32	14	8	10	/	20

Credo

CF	12			40	/	42		54	/	22
Non-CF		8	20		/		42		/	
Full	12			40	/			54	/	22
Reduced		8	20		/	42	42		/	
Total	12	8	20	40	/	42	42	54	/	22

Sanctus

CF	10		26			16	/		56	/	18
Non-CF		10		20	18		/	24		/	
Full	10		26			16	/			/	18
Reduced		10		20	18		/	24	56	/	
Total	10	10	26	20	18	16	/	24	56	/	18

Agnus

CF	12	8	24	/				/	18
Non-CF				/	40	44	43	/	
Full	12		24	/				/	18
Reduced		8		/	40	44	43	/	
Total	12	8	24	/	40	44	43	/	18

Table 2:8: Taverner, Mass *Gloria tibi trinitas*, overall structure (breves)

	Gloria	Credo	Sanctus	Agnus	Total
Total length	272	240	198	189	899
CF	154	170	126	62	512
Non-CF	118	70	72	127	387
Full	116	128	70	54	368
Reduced	156	112	128	135	531
Section 1	108	80	100	44	332
Section 2	144	138	80	127	489
Section 3	20	22	18	18	78

Notes:

(h) (See the notes to the Tables for Fayrfax's Mass *Albanus* for general points.)

(i) Table 2:6 gives details of the layout of the *cantus firmus*; in the column headed 'CF stmnt' the number of statements in each movement is described, and in the column 'No. of CF notes' the disposition of the statement is indicated. The CF consists of 54 notes and is sometimes stated complete, so, for example, in the Gloria there are three statements, the first two of which are divided and the third of which is complete and unbroken, and in the first statement (CF1) it is broken into three segments, of 12, 27 and 15 notes.

(j) Table 2:7 analyses more categories than Table 2:2 did for *Albanus*, because Taverner sometimes gives the *cantus firmus* to reduced-choir passages. The same careful proportions apply, however (see note (b) above), and the intricacy of Taverner's design may be judged by the reader; in the Gloria, for example, the first two passages (14 + 18 = 32) are balanced by the next (32) and by the passage at the end of section 2 (32, followed by 14 + 8 + 10 = 32), while, on a much larger scale, in the Sanctus the whole of section 2 (24 + 56 = 80) balances the latter part of section 1 (26 + 20 + 18 + 16 = 80) and both are as 4:1 to the opening of the movement (10 + 10 = 20).

(k) Table 2:8 reflects the greater number of categories analysed in Table 2:7. Taverner's erudition may be seen from the fact that Gloria + Credo (272 + 240 = 512) balances all the music for *cantus firmus* (512).

3

THE SOUND OF LATIN IN ENGLAND BEFORE AND AFTER THE REFORMATION

ALISON WRAY

For many centuries Latin was the *lingua franca* of religion and scholarship in Europe, promoting the speedy dissemination of knowledge amongst those with the suitable education and background. As the language of worship in the Catholic Church, it inevitably also predominated in musical settings of scriptural and devotional texts for liturgical purposes, a fact which should not deceive us into the assumption that it enjoyed uniformity in its spoken and sung form. Erasmus, whose keen observations are one of our most useful sources of information about the pronunciation of Latin in Europe in the first half of the sixteenth century, noticed, for example, that:

Italians [outside Florence] make virtually no distinction between *homine* 'a man' and *omine* 'a portent'. We in Holland make the distinction too obvious. Each of us is wrong, but each of us laughs at the other.[1]

Thus, in order to establish the pronunciation of Latin texts for any period from the breakup of the Roman Empire to the twentieth century, the traditions of each country or region need to be considered separately, because the local linguistic environment is known to have had a major influence upon the way the words on the page were realized, so that Latin sounded different – often considerably so – in different countries.

We refer to these versions of Latin as *vernacular Latins* because the difference between them resided in the superimposition on to Latin of the sound-spelling rules of the local languages. The effect of this could be striking. Erasmus recounts how a Frenchman, making, in Latin, a speech of welcome to Emperor Maximilian I, was thought to be speaking French, 'he spoke it with such a French accent'. Amongst the speakers to make a formal reply to his words were a Dane and a Zeelander, whose Latin was pronounced so much like their respective native languages that 'you would have sworn that neither was speaking Latin'.[2]

---

1 Erasmus, 'De Recta Latini Graecique Sermonis Pronuntiatione Dialogus' (1528), in J. K. Sowards (ed.), *Collected Works of Erasmus* (Toronto 1985), XXVI, pp. 347–625 (transl. M. Pope), p. 442.
2 Erasmus, 'De Recta Latini Graecique', pp. 472–3.

In England, the vernacular pronunciation was used[3] until relatively recently, when it was replaced by the two pronunciations most familiar to us today. The classical pronunciation, which students of Latin now use, was adopted early in the twentieth century,[4] with reaction against it still strong in the late 1930s in the public schools.[5] Although it was also briefly adopted in the ecclesiastical context in a few places in the first quarter of the twentieth century[6] it was never a serious contender for use outside of the study of the Classics.

The other of our two 'standard' pronunciations of Latin in late twentieth-century Britain is the so-called italianate Latin, used in choral music. This first gained ground on the vernacular version in the mid-nineteenth century via the Oxford Movement, but was slow to spread, as might be expected of an innovation seriously threatening a cultural institution. Brittain suggests that amongst Britain's Roman Catholics italianate pronunciation may have taken over in services by the turn of the century,[7] but Copeman associates the beginnings of pronunciation reform with pressure from Pope Pius x in 1903.[8] Either way, the Anglican choral tradition did not see fit to align itself with such changes for at least another quarter century. This is nicely illustrated by Brittain himself, originally in 1934:

The Italian pronunciation does not appear to have made much headway in Anglican Cathedrals or college chapels up to the present.[9]

This contrasts starkly with the position 60 years on, where the only pronunciation of Latin conceivable in a church context is the italianate,[10] and where, as regards sacred music in a secular context, the only threat to italianate Latin comes from the adoption of 'authentic' pronunciations by the more specialist ensembles. However, despite the fact that most other countries have also embraced the classical and italianate versions, so that international differences have diminished, vernacular phonologies continue to leave enough of an imprint to make it possible to guess a user's native language or variety.[11]

---

3   'The grammar-school [vernacular] pronunciation of the early nineteenth century was the lineal descendant of the grammar-school pronunciation of the fourteenth century' (Henry Bradley, 'On the English pronunciation of Latin' (Introduction to Sargeaunt, S. P. E. Tracts, 4) in *Collected Papers of Henry Bradley* (Oxford 1928), p. 159).

4   G. C. Moore Smith, 'The English language and the 'Restored' pronunciation of Latin', in N. Børgholm, Aage Brusendorff and C. A. Bodelsen (eds.), *A Grammatical Miscellany Offered to Otto Jespersen on his 70th Birthday* (Copenhagen and London 1930), p. 167.

5   W. Sidney Allen (ed.), *Vox Latina: The Pronunciation of Classical Latin* (Cambridge 1965; 2/1978), P. 106.

6   See F. Brittain, 'Latin in church', *Alcuin Club Tracts*, 28 (Cambridge 1934; London 2/1955), pp. 74 ff.

7   Brittain, 'Latin in church', pp. 71–2.

8   Harold Copeman, *Singing in Latin* (Oxford 1990), p. 12.

9   Brittain, 'Latin in church', p. 80.

10 Moreover, memories are short, it seems:
    Many persons who would never attend a Roman Catholic church listen to its services from their homes. As the Latin pronunciation which they hear is an Italian one, the popular belief that the Roman church never changes, and that it is the same everywhere, helps them to jump to the conclusion that the pronunciation which they hear has been used by the church at all times and in all places. (Brittain, 'Latin in church', p. 14).

11 Cf. Brittain, 'Latin in church', pp. 70–1.

For most people today, the traditional English pronunciation of Latin is quite unfamiliar, except in certain words which have appended themselves to the vocabulary of English itself:

We cannot say *genus* and *species*, *Julius Caesar*, *Venus* – in fact we can hardly speak a sentence – without using the English pronunciation of Latin.[12]

Lawyers are more conversant with this pronunciation than most, because legal jargon abounds in Latin phrases which continue to be pronounced in the traditional way. A similar conservation of the old pronunciation has occurred in the sciences. Although William Stearn recommends the adoption of the classical pronunciation for botanical names, he concedes that gardeners and botanists generally use the traditional English one.[13]

As the English vernacular pronunciation of Latin was still in use well into the twentieth century, it would not be unreasonable to assume that this marked the tail end of a continuous tradition of considerable standing. However, although it is consistently both attested in commentaries and demonstrated in rhyme schemes from at least around 1500 through to this century, two weighty events of the sixteenth century require us to question very carefully our assumptions about the sound of Latin in English specifically at the time of the Reformation. One was the demotion of Latin from its liturgical role; the other was the promotion, at around the same time, of classical pronunciation by some scholars. In what follows, the predominance of English vernacular Latin before and after this period will first be demonstrated and explained. We shall then return to these sixteenth-century events to focus on their likely effects on the pronunciation of Latin.

The earliest contrasts in spoken Latin in different linguistic communities were linked to the very development of the Romance languages from varieties of Latin[14] that originated in different parts and periods of the late Roman Empire. The Germanic and Celtic communities inherited their Latin as a trapping of later Christian conversion, in forms heavily influenced by the native languages of the missionaries. All of these already differing Latins continued to evolve individually through the interaction of, on the one hand, natural sound mutations concomitant with diachronic phonological change in the host vernacular and, on the other, sporadic doctoring as and when some external tradition became, albeit temporarily, preferred. Thus we find that variation in Latin pronunciation occurred in response to both linguistic and politico-cultural pressures, and that there was no single 'correct' version.

---

12 Moore Smith, 'The English language and the 'Restored' pronunciation of Latin', p. 171.

13 William T. Stearn, *Botanical Latin* (Newton Abbot 1966; 2/1973), p. 54. Stearn provides a table comparing the two pronunciations, and although it lacks the *phonological* detail that we require to effect reconstructions – that is, it tells us *what* to say but not *when* to say it – it is a very useful checklist for the state of English vernacular Latin in modern times, something which has direct relevance to our study of its pronunciation in the past.

14 For discussions of the intricacies of this process see Roger Wright, *Latin and the Romance Languages in the Early Middle Ages* (London and New York 1991).

To suggest, then, as Erasmus did, that vernacular-based pronunciations were the product of ignorance, is to miss the point. They were 'no invention of English [*or other*] wrongheadedness, but the product of the unconscious historical evolution of centuries'.[15] All the same, it is less wide of the mark to consider the survival of the vernacular pronunciations, especially through certain key periods of cultural change, to be the product of obstinacy, or, at least, of a strong sense of national cultural identity.

The first English vernacular pronunciation of Latin was most likely established within a generation or two of the adoption of Roman Christianity (to the exclusion of the older Celtic tradition) at the Conference of Whitby in AD 663. Users probably remained essentially faithful to that phonology until the Norman conquest, after which Latin was taught through the medium of French, using a French-based vernacular phonology.[16]

English re-appeared as the medium of Latin instruction in the mid-fourteenth century,[17] by which time French was no longer the native language of the nobility and was, as Chaucer observed, increasingly as likely to be modelled on 'the scole of Stratford-atte-Bowe' as the 'Frenssh of Parys'.[18]

Ever since the Norman Conquest, English had been spelt according to the conventions of French, such that, for example, [u] was spelt 'ou' and 'c' was used to represent both [k] and [s], 'g' both [g] and [dʒ], with the pronunciation indicated by the following vowel. Once French was ousted and it became customary to learn to read English before anything else, a subtle change to the reader's perception of Latin was able to occur. Whereas before, Latin *venite* had [i:] in its middle syllable because French read 'i' in this position as [i:], now it had this sound because English did. For as long as French and English shared a common sound-symbol correspondence, this shift would have had no outward effect on Latin. However, when the pronunciation of English began to change, as it did in a process known as 'the Great Vowel Shift' (see Chapter 4 below), it was not only for English that long i came to be associated with the diphthong [əi] but also for Latin. The changes in all the long vowels that came about during the Great Vowel Shift, and which finally left us with the phonetic values we associate with the *names* of the vowels today, thus changed [i:] to [əi] and later [ai] not only in English 'side' but also in Latin 'Maria': [mari:ə] → [marəiə] → [məraiə]; [a:] became [ɛ:], [e:] and finally [ei] not only in English 'made' but also in Latin 'Ave': [a:ve:] → [ə:vi:] → [e:vi:] → [eivi:].

The English-based phonology for Latin, as all of Europe's vernacular-based systems, was easily sustained because, by definition, it featured the inventory of familiar vernacular sounds and mirrored in its own sounds the changing sounds

15 Moore Smith, 'The English language and the 'Restored' pronunciation of Latin', p. 171.
16 Bradley, 'On the English pronunciation of Latin', p. 158.
17 Allen, *Vox Latina*, p. 102.
18 Chronologies of linguistic usage are set out by John Nist, *A Structural History of English* (New York 1966), pp. 141–2, and Joseph M. Williams, *Origins of the English Language: A Social and Linguistic History* (New York 1975), pp. 71 ff.

of the host language. The national traditions were viewed as a part of a country's heritage; not to speak Latin like an Englishman if you were English, or like a Frenchman if you were French, was tantamount to conceding points to the other side.[19]

In fact, this jingoistic attitude can make it difficult to establish just how much genuine breakdown of communication could occur. For while Erasmus, always eager to promote his belief in reform, makes much in his anecdote of genuine misunderstanding, others seem to have coped perfectly well. Englishman John Chapman walked from Calais to Rheims in 1579 communicating entirely by means of Latin,[20] and in 1608 Thomas Coryate traversed Europe in the same way.[21] Indeed, Samuel Johnson (1779) thought the problems were minimal:

> He who travels, if he speaks Latin, may soon learn the sounds which every nation gives to it, that he need make no provision before his journey; and if strangers visit us, it is their business to practise such conformity to our modes as they expect from us in their own countries.[22]

Yet the very fact that a traveller was inevitably confronted with these variations in Latin means that at any point a local pronunciation of Latin, within, say, a monastery, school or church, could be displaced by some other, brought back by a travelling clergyman or musician or introduced by a foreign visitor. But whether such changes lasted long is questionable. Such a person would have been an expert in a favoured foreign pronunciation only for as long as they were alive to remember and impart it. After that, the vernacular version, the default, is likely to have soon returned, particularly in such periods as the mid- to late fourteenth century, when the monasteries, at least, recruited 'large numbers of uneducated men whose wives had died of the plague'.[23]

That English vernacular Latin continued to be the norm until the late nineteenth century is witnessed by Latin–English (macaronic) rhymes, such as *jure ecclesiae* – *if it please ye* and *ad infinitem* – *still to bite 'em*, both from Swift.[24] R. L. Pearsall, in his early nineteenth-century translation of the carol *In Dulci Jubilo*, rhymed *O Jesu parvule* with *My heart is sore for thee*. The latter now reads *I yearn for thee alway*,[25] presumably as a match for the italianate Latin pronunciation.

---

19   The jingoism was not restricted to the treatment of Latin, either:

> According to Burney a like principle was followed by Burke when he read French poetry aloud. He read it as though it were English. Thus on his lips the French word <u>comment</u> was pronounced as the English word <u>comment</u>. (John Sargeaunt, *On the Pronunciation of English Words Derived from Latin*, S. P. E. Tracts, 4, 1920, p. 9.)

   Presumably he is referring to the novelist Fanny Burney (1752–1840) and the politician Edmund Burke (1729–97).

20   Charles Nicholl, *The Reckoning: The Murder of Christopher Marlowe* (London 1992), p. 123.

21   Stearn, *Botanical Latin*, p. 53.

22   Samuel Johnson (ed. George Birkbeck Hill), 'Life of Milton', *Lives of the English Poets* (Oxford 1905), p. 133.

23   Williams, *Origins of the English Language*, p. 69.

24   Moore Smith, 'The English language and the 'Restored' pronunciation of Latin', p. 173.

25   Reginald Jacques and David Willcocks, *Carols for Choirs*, 1 (London and New York 1961), p. 42.

Returning now to sixteenth- and seventeenth-century England, we shall first examine the general status of Latin in the secular and church context, and how this was altered by the Reformation. Knowledge of Latin was a benchmark which represented an enormous divide within the English population. Latin had always been a marker of education and aspiration, and was, by the sixteenth century, part of the staple educational diet of the grammar-school boy:[26]

By 1600 there were about 360 grammar schools in the kingdom or one for every 12,000 people, a much better ratio than in Victorian England. ... Furthermore, Latin – not English – was supposed to be the language used in schools, even if this ideal was not always adhered to, and exposure to a good deal of colloquial, spoken Latin, both in class and out, would have reinforced the grammatical drills. This intensive study of Latin, carried on for long hours each day, with few holidays, meant that an Elizabethan child who had spent a few years at grammar school was saturated in the language.[27]

And whilst Ben Jonson claimed that Shakespeare knew only 'small Latin and less Greek', the standards of the day seem to have been very high:

a boy educated at an Elizabethan grammar school would be more thoroughly trained in classical rhetoric and Roman (if not Greek) literature than most present-day holders of a university degree in classics.[28]

Although sermons had been given in English since the ninth century,[29] both the Bible and the liturgy had remained in Latin. For the grammar-school educated this was no problem, but to those in a congregation who had not had the benefit of any tuition in Latin the words of the liturgy, however often they might be explained, did not have the immediate impact that English words could have.

The Protestant movement in Europe, with its emphasis on personal salvation and plain, comprehensible teaching, must, however, have had an impact on both the educated and the uneducated, given that when in 1540 an English translation of the Bible was issued to every parish church, it was in response to considerable demand, met up until then by unofficial, 'heretical' translations.[30]

As the Reformation gained pace, the problem of securing general access to the message carried in the scriptures and liturgy was tackled further, on two major fronts. In one, English continued to gain ground on Latin in tandem with

---

26 Thomas Whitfield Baldwin, *William Shakespeare's Small Latine and Lesse Greeke* (Urbana Ill. 1944).

27 J. W. Binns, *Intellectual Culture in Elizabethan and Jacobean England: The Latin Writings of the Age* (Leeds 1990), pp. 4 and 292.

28 'General introduction' in Stanley Wells and Gary Taylor, *The Complete Oxford Shakespeare* (Oxford 1987), p. x.

29 Brittain, 'Latin in church', p. 16. The tradition was not unbroken, though, as the following extracts from Williams's chronologies indicate (initial numbers signify century and decade, hence 12.5 = 1140-9):

   12.8 ... a poem complains that although 500 years ago Bede taught and preached in English, it is now no longer done.

   12.9 About this time, Abbot Samson, a famous churchman, encourages his monks to preach in French rather than in Latin and better yet in English, as he is able to do.

   13.4 Robert Grosseteste, Bishop of Lincoln, encourages preaching in English and does so himself (Williams, *Origins of the English Language*, pp. 78-9).

30 Owen Chadwick, *The Reformation* (Harmondsworth 1964; 3/1972), p. 116.

wider changes. Whilst the introduction of the English Bible occurred only one year after the Act of Six Articles had fiercely defended central Catholic doctrines such as transubstantiation and celibacy for priests, by 1549, two years after Edward VI's accession, when anti-Catholic doctrine was permitted both in the pulpit and in print and the clergy were permitted to marry, the Gospel and Epistle readings could be in English,[31] and, through the first Act of Uniformity, English became the official language of the liturgy, using translations by Cranmer collectively known as the *Book of Common Prayer*.

The other attack was on the use in church music of intricate, particularly melismatic, musical settings, which were considered to distort the text.[32] Erasmus had remarked on the problem as early as 1519 when he said:

Modern church music is so constructed that the congregation cannot hear one distinct word. The choristers themselves do not understand what they are singing. ... Words nowadays mean nothing.[33]

The response to this is illustrated by Archbishop Holgate's injunction in 1552 to the Dean and Chapter of York Minster:

we will and command that there be none other note sung or used ... saving square note plain, so that every syllable may be plainly and distinctly pronounced, and without any reports or repeating which may induce any obscureness to the hearers.[34]

In the context of these musical reforms and also various changes to the format of worship, such that the overall number of Masses was reduced and there was an increased emphasis on sermons and Bible readings,[35] it is reasonable to conclude that the English Church's main objection to Latin was that it was a language that was incomprehensible to most of the participants in the worship, rather than that, for example, it represented a tempting target for a well-aimed blow at the very essence of Catholic tradition.

Once simplicity and comprehensibility were a high priority,[36] then the composition of Latin settings had little point, except amongst the recalcitrant Catholic community.[37] Indeed, the use of Latin texts for English sacred music *since the*

---

31 *Ibid.*, pp. 115 ff.
32 Peter le Huray, *Music and the Reformation in England, 1549–1660* (London 1967; Cambridge 2/1978), pp. 8 ff.
33 Erasmus 1519, Commentary on *I Corinthians XIV* 19. See J. A. Froude, *Life and Letters of Erasmus* (London 1895), p. 130.
34 *Statutes etc. of the Cathedral Church at York* (Leeds; 2/1900), Article 13, p. 74.
35 Le Huray, *Music and the Reformation in England*, pp. 8 ff.
36 Not everyone easily conceded to this, however. Bishop John Hooper, in December 1549, writing of the clergy's reluctance to accept the first Act of Uniformity, observed that the replacement of the word 'Mass' with 'Communion' was being accompanied by little genuine change:
    They still retain their vestments and the candles before the altars;... and that popery may not be lost, the mass priests, although they are compelled to discontinue the use of the Latin language, yet most carefully observe the same tone and manner of chanting to which they were heretofore accustomed in the papacy (Letter 36 in H. Robinson (ed.), *Original Letters Relative to the English Reformation*, Parker Society (Cambridge 1847), I, p. 72.
37 Brittain, 'Latin in church', p. 63, considers that Latin, in continued use by Catholics in their secret worship, would have retained its English character; if their priests could consistently call their French seminary 'Doway'

Reformation is more than anything indicative of its successful demotion from any position of power as a tool of politico-religious statement.

Against this backdrop of moves to oust Latin from the Church, came the promotion of Erasmus's new pronunciation of Latin. In England Erasmus's ideas were championed by two Cambridge Regius professors, Thomas Smith and John Cheke, who, in the 1540s, introduced the classical pronunciation of Latin and Greek to the University.[38] The reaction from the establishment was unequivocal. Stephen Gardiner, Bishop of Winchester and Chancellor of Cambridge University, issued in 1542 a decree including the words

Let no one who recognises my authority dare to affix, to Greek or Latin letters, sounds which differ from the public usage of the present time.[39]

Severe penalties were threatened, including expulsion from the Senate and exclusion from degrees.[40]

There is good reason to believe that Smith and Cheke's efforts came to very little,[41] despite the fact that Dobson claims that the reformed pronunciation had

(Douai), then their sense of Englishness must have been intact. Brittain also speculates, however, that they might have retained a sixteenth-century pronunciation through to the nineteenth. This seems rather less plausible, precisely because of the phonological status of a vernacularized pronunciation, which relies upon a continuing direct relationship between the host language and Latin.

38 In the introduction to the National Federation of Music Societies, *Choral Latin: Some Notes for the Guidance of Choirs in the Pronunciation of Latin* (London 1960), it is the traditional English vernacular pronunciation which is, mistakenly, referred to as 'the Erasmian pronunciation'; the term seems to have been independently coined in the article to refer to the pronunciation which Erasmus criticized. However, Erasmus did this in the context of justifying his reformed pronunciation, which is therefore customarily the one referred to in this way.

39 Brittain, 'Latin in church', p. 47.

40 Allen, *Vox Latina*, p. 104.

41 The failure of the classical pronunciation to recover from the initial opposition may perhaps be attributed, at least in part, to the turbulent times and, in particular, to the need felt by most people in the public eye to keep their head down (and on) whilst monarchs and religious policies came and went; it was not a good time to be controversial. But it is unlikely that the attempt at pronunciation reform coincided with the Reformation by design rather than chance.

First, if the classical pronunciation had been part of the English Reformation package, aimed at creating distance from Catholic practice, the simultaneous bid to abolish the use of Latin in church services would have rendered it rather pointless. Secondly, Cheke and Smith were not primarily concerned with church practices, but rather with the scholarly study of the Classics. Thirdly, Catholics do not appear to have associated the Reformation with *this* type of change to Latin pronunciation, though some apparently believed that it was responsible for successfully *introducing* the English vernacular pronunciation, to replace an older, traditional *italianate* one! This is what Brittain ('Latin in church', p. 44) is referring to when he writes of a Jesuit contemporary of his (presumably in the 1930s) who 'asserted that English scholars deliberately smashed the pre-Reformation pronunciation of Latin and replaced it by a new, insular, Protestant, and purely artificial one'.

As Brittain soon explains, such an account is fanciful and flies in the face of considerable evidence, not least the writings of Erasmus. And, as Copeman (*Singing in Latin*, p. 80, fn. 36) points out:

Gardiner's opposition to reformed Latin (italianate or Erasmian) confirms that the traditional English Latin pronunciation was not, as used to be asserted by Catholics, a Protestant invention. It cannot even be that, as John Sargeaunt[*] argued, the Reformation arrested 'the growing tendency to Italianisation of English Latin'.

[* This observation was in fact made by Bradley in his introduction to Sargeaunt's article.]

'clearly been accepted by the overwhelming majority of well-educated South-
erners'.[42] Dobson bases his assumption upon the pronunciation of words borrowed from Latin into English in the years following the promotion of the
reform. On the other hand he is forced to concede that usually two pronunciations co-existed, viz. a reformed and an 'unreformed' one, and that the one
which prevailed was, in many cases, the latter. Furthermore, he observes that
our view of the predominant pronunciation of such words at that time is very
much distorted by the fact that the orthoepists, upon whose reports we rely,
were prescriptive in favour of the more 'learned' reformed versions.[43]

Evidence *against* any wide-ranging or long-lasting adoption of the reformed
pronunciation can be found in an examination of the main teaching text of the
time, commonly referred to as *Lily's Grammar*. This was in fact a joint work by
Lily and Colet properly called *A Short Introduction of Grammar*. It remained the
standard textbook for Latin through many generations, and, although it was
available in its final form only in the 1540s, its precursors, constructed separately
by the two authors, began to appear as early as 1513.[44] Colet knew and indeed
had some influence upon Erasmus. As regards Lily, Colet employed him at his
school and dedicated one of his books to him. Erasmus and Lily shared an
interest in and commitment to 'correct' Latin, based upon the classical model,
but it is not clear to what extent Lily supported Erasmus's bids to reform
pronunciation to the classical standard; Colet, a traditionalist,[45] almost certainly
did not.

Of central importance here is that there is very little about pronunciation in
either *A Short Introduction* or the *Brevissima Institutio, seu Ratio Grammatices*, a
commentary on (and in) Latin which was normally bound with it, despite the
latter having a section dedicated to 'Orthœpia' (the art of correct pronunciation).
There are warnings about one or two consonants, such as over-zealous aspiration
on final 'd' and 't' and the difference between 'f' and 'v'. But as far as the vowels
are concerned there is only a plea against excessive 'ioticism' (probably a reaction
to the then current realization of long 'i' as [əi] in English (see Chapter 4), and
the observation that 'æ' and 'œ' are pronounced as 'e', their value in the English
vernacular Latin pronunciation. All of these notes on pronunciation are really
no more than half-hearted correctives – they state how various sounds are *not*
to be pronounced. What is striking is that we do not see any primary information
about how the Latin language was supposed to sound, as an integrated whole.

Lily's *Grammar* had been carefully compiled to impart the information that a

More than anything, then, the account provided by Brittain's Jesuit simply indicates how quickly a long
tradition can be totally forgotten once it has been replaced – in the 1930s it was still barely a couple of
generations since italianate Latin had been a novelty to English Catholics.

42 E. J. Dobson, *English Pronunciation, 1500–1700*, 2 vols. (Oxford 1968), II, §110 and §127. In line with Dobson's
own practice, subsequent references are to vol. I by page number and vol. II by section number.
43 Dobson, *English Pronunciation*, §110.
44 Copeman, *Singing in Latin*, pp. 60 ff.
45 Brittain, 'Latin in church', p. 46; Copeman, *Singing in Latin*, p. 80, fn. 36.

student required to learn good Latin. If part of the package had been the mastering of a pronunciation which was new and controversial, one which the young learner may not be able to hear in use, especially amongst the older generation or those who had not gone to the *right* schools, then surely there would have been substantial coverage of it in the book. There would have been instruction in reading the letters, such as we find in primers for foreign languages of the day, and perhaps even an essay on the merits of the new pronunciation over the traditional one. So how are we to explain the absence of this? Copeman suggests that

there was strong disagreement between traditionalists (including Colet) and reformers ... when Colet, Lily and Erasmus were drafting the original parts of the Grammar, and ... this had not been resolved by the 1540s when the Brevissima Institutio was first included.[46]

If this is so, then the writers' intentions could either have been that the new pronunciation be adopted, and the instructions just didn't get into the book, or that the traditional pronunciation continue unchallenged in the classroom. In the latter case, no pronunciation guidance would have been necessary, for not only every school master, but every learner, already knew, through their mastery of English phonology, the phonology of English vernacular Latin; and there is no sense in mending something that is not broken. Either way, the effect of there being no instructions was that there was no revolution.

On this basis, then, we can proceed on the assumption that the vernacular pronunciation of Latin was the major, if not the only one in use in England (outside of the circle of the most learned university classicists) in not only the period up to Erasmus's attempted reforms but also right through the sixteenth and seventeenth centuries and beyond. Our reconstruction of the sounds of Latin texts can therefore take as its starting point the sound system of the English of the time. The reconstruction of pronunciation for any language is not simply a matter of haphazardly inserting phonetic values. To get to the whole picture of an integrated system of sound relationships requires an understanding of the phonological principles which underlie it.[47]

In the case of English Latin, this means that we must find out how the phonological system and phonetic values of English were applied to Latin. In other words we must establish how a given sequence of letters constituting a Latin word would have been related to the spoken phonology of English. Any sequence never seen before, whether because it was Latin or simply a new English word, would necessarily be subject to such an analysis, in the same way as our present-day knowledge of the grapheme–phoneme correspondences of English enables us to agree on the pronunciation of modern acronyms such as NATO and CAMRA; in the former case the 'a' is 'long' because it is stressed at the

46 Copeman, *Singing in Latin*, pp. 63–4.
47 Cf. A. C. Gimson, *An Introduction to the Pronunciation of English* (London 1962; 4/1989), pp. 74–5.

end of the penultimate syllable, whilst in the latter, both 'a's are short, the first because it is stressed before two consonants, the first of which ends the first syllable[48] and the second because it is unstressed in final position, where it is reduced to [ə]. The same system of assigning length according to stress and position accounts for how the vowels change between related forms, as in *televise/ television*, *redeem/redemption* and *major/majority*.

In order to determine how a Latin word was pronounced on English phonological principles it is necessary, therefore, to have a clear grasp of the relationship which English itself maintains between spelling and pronunciation. Where English has a 'long vowel',[49] English vernacular Latin will also. The rules that apply today are on the whole the same as those of the sixteenth century:[50] it is the *phonetics*, not the phonology, that has undergone most change since then. Therefore, it is possible to build up the historical system from what we know of the modern one. Of particular help in doing this are Sargeaunt,[51] and Larsen and Walker.[52] Having established whether a particular vowel is long or short, it can be assigned a phonetic value appropriate to the date in question by using tables like those given in Chapter 4.

Two other considerations may be briefly mentioned here. One concerns whether spoken Latin differed in religious and secular contexts and the other, whether sung Latin differed from spoken. Regarding the first, Brittain suggests that there may have been a delay of up to 50 years in the adoption into liturgical Latin of new English sounds, presumably because of a general deference to conservatism.[53] In this case the phonetic values adopted should be those of an appropriately earlier date than might otherwise be selected. As regards the second consideration, it is well known that singing today draws on a different phonetic repertory from that of speech. However, discussion in Chapter 4 explores the likelihood that vocal production in church music before the eighteenth century did not involve much compromise to the spoken phonetic values.

---

48 For a clear account of English syllabification see Charles Kreidler, *The Pronunciation of English* (Oxford 1989), ch. 5.

49 The terms 'long' and 'short' are used to label pre-Vowel Shift pairs, which subsequently diverged phonetically (see Chapter 4). As a rule of thumb, the 'long' vowels are identical to the vowel names, such that their modern Southern British English values (some of which are phonetically diphthongal) are: A [ei] as in *cake*, E [i:] *keep*, I [ai] *kite*, O [ɛʊ] *cope*, U [ju] *cute*; the short vowels are those that correspond to the sound of the vowel in words like the following: a [a] as in *cap*, e [ɛ] *kept*, i [ɪ] *kit*, o [ʊ] *cot*, u [ʌ] *cut* and [ʊ] *put*. Besides 'long' and 'short' vowels, English also has 'diphthongs', some of which are, phonetically speaking, monophthongs (see Chapter 4, Table 4:3).

50 Major exceptions to this are the [ʌ]–[ʊ] contrast, which did not exist, and the various divisions of short 'a' which give us modern contrasts such as *hat/half/ancient/want/all*, etc. (see Chapter 4, Table 4:2).

51 Sargeaunt, *On the Pronunciation of English Words Derived from Latin*.

52 Thorleif Larsen and Francis C. Walker, *Pronunciation: A Practical Guide to American Standards* (Oxford 1930). That Larsen and Walker work to 'American Standards' is of no consequence, for, as already mentioned, it is in most cases only on the phonetic level that differences occur. In any case, they frequently note both the English and American pronunciations.

Another American to have produced pronunciation guidelines for (in this case) legal Latin is E. H. Jackson, *Latin for Lawyers* (London 1915; 2/1937).

53 Brittain, 'Latin in church', p. 25.

We can see the process of reconstruction in action in what follows, a study of the phrase 'Quia respexit humilitatem ancillæ suæ...' from the *Magnificat*.

QU was pronounced [kw] as today, being an Old English cluster whose spelling was changed from 'cw' to 'qu' by the Normans.[54]

I   before a vowel was long.[55] At some point long i changed from its Middle English value of [i:] to [əi]. Dobson's view is that this diphthongization began as early as 1400, despite some descriptions of [i:] as late as 1686.[56] If we accept Brittain's view about a delay in the phonetic progress of Latin relative to English, then it would be reasonable to use [i:] up to, say, 1490, but no later. Resistance to this phonetic change, presumably, accounts for the criticism of 'ioticism' criticized in the *Brevissima Institutio*.

A   in final position was unstressed, hence [ə].[57]

R   in this position was probably, as today, a post-alveolar fricative[58] or even a frictionless continuant, but certainly not a trill, though the acoustic benefits of the trill may have made it an attractive alternative in church music.

E   when unstressed and followed by two consonants other than stop + liquid, was short.[59] Short e was [ɛ], as today.[60]

S   as today.

P   as today.

E   stressed, before two consonants ('x' = [ks]) was short.[61] Short e was [ɛ].

X   was as today, viz. [ks].

I   unstressed in non-initial syllables was short.[62] Short i was [ɪ].

T   as today.

54 Barbara Strang, *A History of English* (London and New York 1970), p. 227. Moore Smith, 'The English language and the 'Restored' pronunciation of Latin', pp. 169–70, provides some evidence in support of [k]. However, Larsen and Walker and Sargeaunt favour [kw].

55 Larsen and Walker, *Pronunciation*, p. 139.

56 Dobson, *English Pronunciation*, § 137. See Roger Lass, 'How early does Modern English get modern?', *Diachronica* 6 (1989), pp. 75–110, for an alternative view of the timing of this and other vowel changes.

57 Larsen and Walker, *Pronunciation*, p. 137.

58 Dobson, *English Pronunciation*, § 370.

59 Larsen and Walker, *Pronunciation*, p. 138; Sargeaunt, *On the Pronunciation of English Words Derived from Latin*, p. 9.

60 However, the analogy of English *respect* which has a phonetically reduced (i.e. shortened and centralized) version of *long* e ([i:] → [ɪ]) supports the treatment of this 'e' as syllable-final. In this case, the phonetic realization would be [ɪ], being a reduced version of long 'e', which the Vowel Shift had modified to [i:] from its earlier value [e:]. Before that (say, up to about 1500 (Dobson, *English Pronunciation*, § 132)), it would presumably have been [e] if shortened at all. In practice, unstressed vowels are phonetically less distinct than stressed ones, so none of the possibilities [ɛ], [ɪ] and [e] would sound particularly odd.

61 Larsen and Walker, *Pronunciation*, p. 138; Sargeaunt, *On the Pronunciation of English Words Derived from Latin*, p. 9.

62 Larsen and Walker, *Pronunciation*, p. 138; Sargeaunt, *On the Pronunciation of English Words Derived from Latin*, p. 12.

H was pronounced in initial position in English Latin.[63]

U in non-final syllables followed by one consonant was long. Long U in this context
   refers not to Middle English [u:] (→ modern [au]) but Middle English [y:] and [iu]
   (→ modern [ju]),[64] which Dobson believes to have been pronounced [iu] 'from at
   the latest the beginning of the sixteenth century', though Sargeaunt thinks that the
   'parasitic y', i.e. the [j] component, 'is perhaps not of very long standing'.[65]

M as today.

I unstressed in non-initial syllables was short (see fn 62). Short i was [ɪ].

L as today.

I unstressed in non-initial syllables was short (see fn 62). Short i was [ɪ].

T as today.

A stressed in the penultimate syllable, before one consonant, was long.[66] According to
   Dobson[67] long a began as [a:] (not [ɑ:]) in Middle English and developed through
   [æ:], [ɛ:] and [e:] to modern [ei]. Dobson gives [æ:] as the pronunciation in careful
   speech until 1650 but gives [ɛ:] as the less careful form in the sixteenth century. The
   choice of one or the other therefore depends on one's opinion about how 'careful'
   Latin pronunciation was, as well as whether, as Brittain suggests, it lagged behind
   English.

T as today.

E in a final syllable ending in a consonant other than s was short.[68] Short e was [ɛ].

M as today.

A in a non-final syllable, followed by two consonants other than stop + liquid, was
   short.[69] Short a was pronounced [a] until at least 1600 in careful speech, with
   sixteenth-century vulgar [æ] gaining ground after that.[70]

N as today.

C before i was [s].[71]

---

63 Dobson, *English Pronunciation*, § 426, fn. 3. Discussing the pronunciation of 'h' in English, Dobson mentions
    words which have no initial /h/, e.g. *heir, honest, honour*, etc., because they were adopted from Latin via Old
    French which omitted it. He goes on to say that words like *harmony* and *habitation* have /h/ because they
    were re-adopted directly from the Latin which must, then, in its usual English pronunciation, have manifested
    the /h/, even in the cognates of established words of English that omitted it.

64 See Dobson, *English Pronunciation*, § 178–89, and M. K. Pope, *From Latin to Modern French* (Manchester 1934),
    § 1142.

65 Sargeaunt, *On the Pronunciation of English Words Derived from Latin*, p. 8.

66 Larsen and Walker, *Pronunciation*, p. 137.

67 Dobson, *English Pronunciation*, 98.

68 Larsen and Walker, *Pronunciation*, p. 138; Sargeaunt, *On the Pronunciation of English Words Derived from Latin*, p.
    10.

69 Larsen and Walker, *Pronunciation*, p. 138; Sargeaunt, *On the Pronunciation of English Words Derived from Latin*,
    p. 9.

70 Dobson, *English Pronunciation*, § 59, specifically p. 548.

I   in a non-final syllable, before a double consonant, was short.[72] Short i was [ɪ].

LL   as today.

Æ   was pronounced as e[73] and was, in syllable final position, long.[74] Long e changed from [e:] to [i:] by 1500.[75]

S   as today.

U   before another vowel was long.[76] Long u was [iu].

Æ   was [i:] by 1500 (see fnn. 73–5).

This extract, plus the text which immediately follows it in the *Magnificat*, thus turn out as follows for a date of around 1500:

Quia   respexit   humilitatem   ancillæ   suæ
[kwəiə   rɛspɛksɪt   hiumɪlɪtæːtɛm   ansɪliː   siuiː]

ecce   enim   ex   hoc   beatam   me   dicent   omnes   generationes
[ɛksiː   iːnɪm   ɛks   hɔk   biæːtam   miː   dəisɛnt   ɔmniːz   dʒeneræːsiɔːniːz]

Changing it for c. 1580 and c. 1620 gives the following differences:

humilitatem becomes [hiumɪlɪtɛ̱ːtəm] and then [hjumɪlɪtɛ̱ːtɛm]
hoc becomes [ho̱k] by 1620
beatam becomes [biɛ̱ːtam] and then [biɛ̱ːtam]
dicent becomes [da̱isɛnt] by 1620
omnes becomes [o̱mniːz] by 1620
generationes becomes [dʒenɛrɛːsio̱ːniːz] and then [dʒenɛrɛ̱ːsio̱ːniːz]

One test of such a prediction is to compare it with the pronunciation that can be reconstructed from contemporary accounts, even though the latter method is highly problematic because, as with descriptions of English, it is so difficult to judge the status of the remarks that are made and to fit together fragmentary details from different sources.[77] Here we shall use Copeman's version of the pronunciation of the *Magnificat* for c. 1450 onwards,[78] comparing it to the 1500 version above.

---

71 Larsen and Walker, *Pronunciation*, p. 140; Sargeaunt, *On the Pronunciation of English Words Derived from Latin*, p. 9.
72 Larsen and Walker, *Pronunciation*, p. 139; Sargeaunt, *On the Pronunciation of English Words Derived from Latin*, p. 9.
73 Larsen and Walker, *Pronunciation*, p. 140; Sargeaunt, *On the Pronunciation of English Words Derived from Latin*, p. 8.
74 Larsen and Walker, *Pronunciation*, p. 137; Sargeaunt, *On the Pronunciation of English Words Derived from Latin*, p. 10.
75 Dobson, *English Pronunciation*, § 132.
76 Larsen and Walker, *Pronunciation*, p. 139; Sargeaunt, *On the Pronunciation of English Words Derived from Latin*, p. 11.
77 Alison Wray, 'Authentic pronunciation for early music', in John Paynter, Tim Howell, Richard Orton and Peter Seymour, *Companion to Contemporary Musical Thought* (London and New York 1992), p. 1055.
78 Copeman, *Singing in Latin*, p. 295.

Copeman: . [kwəia respeksɪt hʏmɪlɪtæːtem ansɪli[79] sʏi]

Wray: [kwəiə respeksɪt hiumɪlɪtæːtem ansɪliː siui:]

Copeman: . [ɛkse enɪm ɛks hɔk biæːtam mi dəisent ɔmniz dʒeneræːsiɔniz]

Wray: [ɛksi iːnɪm ɛks hɔk biæːtam miː dəisent ɔmniːz dʒeneræːsiɔːniːz]

Copeman makes less use of the colon, which is the sign for length. It is hard to tell whether this is simply a difference in transcription style. If it is not, then provided it is only disagreements about phonetic length that are implied, these are inconsequential for sung texts, where the duration of the vowel is determined by the note-value.[80]

Apart from this, the only differences in this admittedly short passage are:

(1) the precise phonetic identity of unstressed, word-final short a. This discrepancy is no more major than that of whether the last sound in modern English *sofa* is [a] or [ə] – on this point it is reasonable to prefer Copeman's vowel for singing, as it is a more suitable sound for extended length and is brighter than [ə].

(2) [ʏ] (the sound of short ü in German) for [iu]. As noted above, the developments of Middle English [iu] and [yː] were closely associated and are discussed in some detail by Dobson, who is himself unable to be sure which was being described by contemporary commentators. [ʏ] is the slightly retracted short equivalent of [yː], paralleling the relationship of [ɪ] to [iː].

(3) Copeman has [eː] in *ecce* and *enim*, not [iː]. In his commentary[81] he identifies long e as a 'close vowel' and gives the phonetic value from the fifteenth century as [iː]. He attributes a 1580 attestation of [ɛː] to the influence of Erasmus's reformed pronunciation. Yet ultimately, he plumps for [eː] in singing,[82] seemingly to be on the basis of intuition rather than hard evidence. Whilst his preference for [eː] over [iː] is essentially a matter of opinion, his mixing of [eː] and [iː] for long e within the same text is less easy to understand.

The above exercise illustrates one method by which Latin pronunciation may be re-created for any date: the assignment of long and short values to vowels may be assumed to operate more or less consistently and the phonetic values by which they were realized at the specific time may simply be inserted into the static phonological framework. That such an approach relies on the principle of systematicity is both its strength and its weakness. It is a strength because the

---

79 In the hardback version Copeman gives [e] for [i] in the first occurrence (only) of 'ae'. This is a printing error and it is corrected in the paperback version.

80 However, Copeman states that he has 'included IPA marks of length only where it seemed helpful to indicate the right *quality* of vowel' (my emphasis) (p. 295), implying that a mark of length also gives information about the phonetic identity of a vowel; this is a practice normally reserved for phonemic transcriptions. Just what that difference in quality might be is not explicit. In my own version, length marks indicate that a vowel is phonologically and phonetically long; 'long vowels' which are curtailed because of their environment (e.g. [i] in [biæːtam]) have, as the transcription suggests, the phonetic identity of a long vowel, without the length.

81 *Singing in Latin*, p. 123.

82 *Ibid.*, p. 124.

underlying sound patterns of language are systematic. By exploiting the genuine link between Latin and a known system (English) we are more likely to establish plausible patterns than we are if we rely solely on the piecemeal descriptions in the contemporary literature.

The weakness of this approach, however, lies in the reliance on systematicity. Latin was, at the end of the day, a foreign language learnt by youths and adults. As such it may have been subject to various non-systematic features the like of which cannot be acquired by the young child but can be learned in class, or by imitation in later years. Ultimately, of course, we simply cannot know how Latin was pronounced at a particular time in the distant past. We can only experiment with different methods in the hope of achieving something that makes sense at as many levels as possible.

4

ENGLISH PRONUNCIATION,
c. 1500 – c. 1625

ALISON WRAY

The purpose of this chapter is to consider how the texts of church anthems and other English-texted music might have been pronounced in the sixteenth and seventeenth centuries. The practical process of reconstructing pronunciation for performance purposes, illustrated later for texts set c. 1505, c. 1580 and c. 1622, relies upon a range of assumptions, some more contentious than others. Formal study in the field of the history of the English language can inform us only so far, for reasons which will be outlined below.

Leaf through any anthology of Tudor anthems and one is left in no doubt that music in the late sixteenth and early seventeenth centuries was set to an English very little different from today's. Although spellings were rather erratic,[1] there is almost no difficulty in understanding the words or grammatical structures. Like Shakespeare's works, the texts of both sacred and secular music during the Elizabethan and Jacobean periods were in modern English, albeit a form technically known as *Early* Modern English. However, the similarity in appearance belies differences in pronunciation. A closer look will in fact uncover discrepancies, even to the untrained eye, though we are, as readers both of song-texts and of poetry in its own right, remarkably adept at overlooking and, indeed, misinterpreting the signs. We take for granted, for example, 'eye-rhyme',[2] placing into that category many pairings which were originally true rhymes. If we were

---

[1] Henry Bradley, 'Shakespeare's English', in *Shakespeare's England*, 2 vols. (Oxford 1917), II, ch. 30, pp. 546 ff.

[2] It is not at all easy to pinpoint the beginnings of eye-rhyme (see A. C. Gimson, *An Introduction to the Pronunciation of English* (London 1962; 4/1989), p. 79). C. L. Wrenn, *Word and Symbol – Studies in English Language* (London 1967), p. 146, places the origins of what he terms 'traditional spelling rhymes' as early as Marlowe and Spenser's rhymes of *love* and *grove*, which 'at no time could … have rhymed truly, since the one in Middle English would have had a tense and the other a slack ō'. In such a case, the alignment of the spelling, along with the confusion about what was 'proper' English pronunciation at the time, might have been enough to invite such artistic licence.

In general, however, eye-rhyme probably owes its existence to discrepancies in pronunciation; the writer and his contemporary reader might not have agreed about whether a rhyme was true or not. Later readers, being more distant to, and in general ignorant of, the sounds of the writer's language, would be obliged either to accuse him of poor workmanship or to attribute to him the deliberate intention of not rhyming words.

Dennis Freeborn, in *From Old English to Standard English* (Basingstoke 1992), p. 175, illustrates this effectively with examples of apparent eye-rhymes from the translation of Vergil's *Aeneid* by John Dryden (1631–1700). These include: *appear(s)* rhyming with *steer*, *bares* and *stares*, and *sea* rhyming with *display*, *obey* and *decree*. Some

more accustomed to expecting true rhymes in works of this period then we might more readily attribute the failure of rhyme to subsequent changes in the language rather than to any deliberate choice on the part of the poet.[3] Of course, words fail to rhyme today where they did before only if alterations in their pronunciation have taken them in different directions. Words which have shared a development will still rhyme today, though often with a different sound from that originally intended by the poet. Of equal importance when looking at texts of earlier centuries are words which are never rhymed. For example, words spelt with '-ee-' and '-ea-' such as *meet* and *seat* did not, in standard English,[4] converge in their pronunciation until after 1700.[5]

Our sources of information regarding the pronunciation of Early Modern English are manifold, for there was a considerable interest in the sounds of speech from the points of view of orthoepy (the 'art of correct pronunciation'), spelling reform and indeed phonetic study in its own right. The books and pamphlets written on these subjects between 1500 and 1700 have been carefully examined by Dobson, to whom much reference will be made in what follows. The question of how English should be pronounced and spelt was a contentious one for those with the leisure to consider it, for English had, since around 1400, been undergoing considerable changes to its vowel system in the course of the so-called 'Great Vowel Shift', whose main trends are summarized in Tables 4:1–4:4.

of Dryden's rhymes are only sustainable if one is prepared to admit of alternative pronunciations, e.g. *victory* rhyming with *sky*, *high* [ai] and *see* [i:], and one may legitimately ask whether the poet himself would have used both in normal conversation.

A poet today could rhyme *scone* with *stone* in one place and with *gone* somewhere else, yet his own conversational usage might consistently be one rather than the other. If as his *contemporaries* we cannot tell which of the available pronunciations the poet himself uses – nor yet whether he intends us (a) to sustain the rhyme at the cost of changing *scone* to fit it or (b) to treat one or other rhyme as false – what chance would any future student have of ascertaining his pronunciation? E. J. Dobson, *English Pronunciation, 1500-1700*, 2 vols. (Oxford 1957; 2/1968), § 109, illustrates that this argument applies even as early as Chaucer, whose rhymes of ME ę̄ and ME ẹ̄ he defends:

> It seems to me improbable that these are inexact rhymes, as is often assumed...; so cultivated a poet is not likely to have held on occasion that a rhyme between the markedly different sounds [ɛ:] and [e:], which were distinct elements in meaning ... was near enough. I would rather hold that these rhymes show Chaucer making occasional use of ME ẹ̄ variants in 'ME ę̄ words' – variants which had already begun to come into the language of London from that of Essex... .

With historical texts, the temptation is to find legitimate pronunciations of the day (even if some be a little antiquated) which permit a full-rhyme, but these may be somewhat contrived.

3 There were many ways of making words rhyme, such as using deliberately archaic pronunciations or regional ones. See Henry Cecil Wyld, *Studies in English Rhymes from Surrey to Pope* (London 1923; re-issued New York 1965) for a full descriptive account.

4 The term 'standard English' will be used to refer to the English which developed into modern Southern British English.

5 Dobson, *English Pronunciation*, § 107 (in line with Dobson's own practice, references are to vol. I by page number and vol. II by section number. References to vol. II, § 4, are, exceptionally, provided with a page reference too, as the section covers a number of pages). Dobson argues convincingly that this change, in which words normally spelt '-ea-' today and formerly pronounced [e:], converged in pronunciation with [i:], actually involved the adoption by standard English of a regional pronunciation, perhaps a northern one, but more likely an eastern (§ 108). This means that rhymes of '-ee-' and '-ea-' may have been possible much earlier for writers in the north and east of England.

However, there can be problems in relying too heavily upon the information given in the contemporary commentaries. One difficulty which is immediately obvious from even a cursory glance at Dobson's compilation is that the writers did not agree. Even taking account of differences in transcription practices, the age of the writers and their origins, there are disagreements at every turn. Some of these, incorporating internal inconsistencies, are simply inaccuracies of analysis or printing errors, but others clearly reflect genuine variation in the language itself.[6] An additional difficulty arises because our aim today is to establish what was actually being done whereas the writers of the day were mostly in disagreement with the current practice and mentioned it only disparagingly in passing, if at all, and often then with rather less accuracy than the conservative or even outdated form they were promoting. The sounds that were actually current in ordinary usage, including those of song- and anthem-texts, are likely to have been rather advanced in relation to what is found in the books of the time.[7] Thus, much as we may begin to work out the sounds of a text by using the orthoepical evidence from its date of composition, the text itself also informs us about the pronunciation, by containing rhyming and scansion patterns which would simply not have been possible a few years before or after.[8]

As the structure of Tables 4:1-4:4 suggests, a major clue to the pronunciation of a particular word is its spelling, though there are also numerous exceptions and false friends. Configurations of letters tend to reflect historical groupings, so that, for example, within the set of words mentioned earlier, which are now pronounced with the vowel sound [i:], those spelt with '-ee-' (*meet*, *street*) had a different development to those spelt with '-ea-' (*meat*, *seat*).[9] In the same way, words now spelt with the same configuration of letters but pronounced differently (*bead*, *bread*) originally belonged to one group.[10] The spelling system failed to change when the pronunciation did, because written English was just that little bit too institutionalized:

If the shift had happened a century or two earlier our spelling would probably have reflected it; but because it occurred only after some of our spelling conventions had at least begun to solidify, it left us with our very curious habit of using the same letters to indicate phonetically unrelated vowel sounds. Our ancestors simply continued to spell with the letters they were used to, even when they had greatly changed their habits of pronunciation. The shift does not explain all our odd spellings of vowel sounds, because other factors are involved in many words; but it does account for the greatest single peculiarity.[11]

6   Bradley, 'Shakespeare's English', pp. 540–1.
7   Spellings in the Paston family letters similarly support the likelihood of earlier change than is reported by the orthoepists; see, for example, R. E. Zachrisson (1913), *Pronunciation of English Vowels 1400-1700* (New York 1971), who considers the Great Vowel Shift to have been more or less complete by as early as 1500. It should be borne in mind, however, that the Pastons were of East Anglian origin and, as such, were speakers of the variety of English which appears to have led standard English into the Great Vowel Shift.
8   Though see Wrenn, *Word and Symbol*, pp. 144–6, for an examination of the dangers.
9   Cf. Gimson, *An Introduction*, p. 72.
10 See Barbara M. H. Strang, *A History of English* (London 1970), p. 114, for an explanation of the divergence.
11 L. M. Myers and Richard Hoffman, *The Roots of Modern English* (Boston Mass. 1966; 2/1979), p. 160.

The historical linguist can rejoice in the fact that, as English spelling did not keep up with the changes in pronunciation, it has preserved for us the general shape of its earlier sound system.

Yet to what extent is anything that we might establish about the pronunciation of the spoken word, relevant to singing? This is a tricky issue. Is there likely to have been any deliberate attempt to modify singing in relation to speech? Two questions lie behind this. Firstly, was sung English specifically antiquated, regional or classbound – that is, would beginner singers have to be taught a pronunciation they did not use in their normal speech? The evidence of the rhymes, mentioned above, tends to suggest that the compiler of a text, at least, paid little heed to the linguistically reactionary element. And as for the expunging of any regional or class accent, Potter doubts that this was necessary or expected.[12] He considers the neutralizing of such accents to be a later phenomenon, linked at least in part to changes in vocal production, which increasingly divorced the sung language from the phonetic possibilities of the spoken one.

The second issue which lies behind the question of modification in singing is that of how vocal production has changed since Tudor times. The outstanding singers of today base their vocal production upon the principles of *bel canto*, though the term is now used in a rather loose way and its precise meaning has almost certainly changed over the centuries. Manén both dates the true *bel-canto* technique back to that of Giulio Caccini (c. 1545–1618)[13] and defines it in quite specific terms, as the method of vocal production in which 'the larynx is activated from the trigeminal region of the face' which triggers a secondary but crucial laryngeal mechanism, the ventricle of Morgani.[14] The effect of this is to generally lower the vowel formants and to reduce the strength of the high overtones.[15] Caccini was directly involved in the late sixteenth-century development of virtuoso solo song, which, in contrast to consort music, required the voice to stand out clearly from the instrumental sound and to express a wide range of human emotions.[16] In Manén's opinion:

The ventricular mechanism is the particular instrument for which classical Italian music was composed and with which alone classical Italian music should be sung, just as a violin sonata must be played, and can be played adequately, only with a violin.[17]

Tudor church music was not of this type. Although the Italian style and sound would ultimately revolutionize the English scene, we can be fairly sure that *bel*

---

12 John Potter, 'Reconstructing lost voices', in Tess Knighton and David Fallows (eds.), *Companion to Medieval and Renaissance Music* (London 1992), pp. 311–16.

13 The term *bel canto* itself appears to be of nineteenth-century origin; see Lucie Manén, *The Teaching of the Classical Italian Song-Schools, its Decline and Restoration* (Oxford 1987), p. 3.

14 Manén, *The Teaching of the Classical Italian Song-Schools*, p. 13. Salaman, on the other hand, defines *bel canto* as 'a school of vocalising "at the larynx – the power station"'. See E. Salaman, *Unlocking your Voice* (London 1987).

15 Manén, *The Teaching of the Classical Italian Song-Schools*, p. 14.

16 *Ibid.*, p. 18.

17 *Ibid.*, p. 15.

canto did not arrive until well into the seventeenth century. The alternative to *bel canto*, the more 'natural' *voix ordinaire* in which the speaking voice is used for singing,[18] is more likely to have been the basis of the Tudor church sound. In Potter's opinion, this entailed 'a relatively high larynx position and a relatively forward jaw position'.[19] Hillier agrees that modern singing employs a production unlike that of speech, while sixteenth-century singing did not, and feels that the former suffers from a 'barrier of produced sound, a continual deposit of "expressive" sonority', such that 'the physical properties of the language do not seem to be felt, either physically or emotionally, by the singers, at least not as they are when the language is spoken'.[20]

the voices of earlier generations were probably lighter and more agile, smaller and less able to project but with a more speech-like clarity of vowels.[21]

Although Manén's contention is that only *bel canto* fully expresses the human emotions,[22] Hillier, Potter and Manén herself agree that vocal music is compromised by the employment of a production other than that which was intended by the composer.

It seems, then, as if the sung language of the period in question had the potential to resemble very closely the singer's own speech, in terms of both general sound production and linguistic variety. If this is so, then we can freely apply to vocal music the information that is available about the sounds of speech of the time. Beyond the question of production, we may speculate that in post-Reformation church music there was a certain preference for clear diction, seeing as the texts were in English and the music had been simplified precisely for the purpose of rendering the words comprehensible.[23]

Table 4:1: General progress of long stressed vowels of Middle English[a]

Modern spelling	Modern sound	Examples	Stage I (pre-1500 -1600)[b]	Stage II (post-1500 -1650)	Stage III (post-1600 -1700)
aCe	[ei]	made	[æ:]	[ɛ:]	[e:]
ee, ie	[i:]	green, field	[i:]	[i:]	[i:]
ea, ei, eCe	[i:]	meat, conceit, complete	[ɛ:]	[e:]	[e:]→[i:]
ea	[ei]	break	[ɛ:]	[e:]	[e:]
ea	[ɛ]	breath	[ɛ:]	[ɛ]	[ɛ]
i, y, iCe, ie	[ai]	child, eye, pie, tide	[əi][c]	[əi]	[ai]
oo, o, oCe	[u:]	goose, who, move	[u:]	[u:]	[u:]

18 *Ibid.*, p. 10.
19 Potter, 'Reconstructing lost voices', p. 313.
20 Paul Hillier, 'Framing the life of the words', in Knighton and Fallows (eds.), *Companion*, p. 308.
21 Potter, 'Reconstructing lost voices', p. 312.
22 In fact while Manén cites Caccini as the originator of *bel canto*, Potter cites him as clear proponent of the speech-based production.
23 See Chapter 3.

Table 4:1: *(cont.)*

Modern spelling	Modern sound	Examples	Stage I (pre-1500 -1600)[b]	Stage II (post-1500 -1650)	Stage III (post-1600 -1700)
oo	[ʊ]	look	[uː]	[uː]	[ʊ]
oo, o	[ʌ]	blood, mouth	[uː]	[uː]→[ʊ]	[ʌ]
oa, oCe, o, oe	[əu]	boat, so, hope, foe	[ɔː]	[oː]	[oː]
oCe	[ɒ]	gone	[ɔː]	[ɔ]	[ɒ]
oa	[ɔː]	broad	[ɔː]	[ɔ]	[ɒ]→[ɔː]
ou, ow	[au]	house, now	[əu]	[əu]	[au]

Key to Tables: **C** = single consonant **N** = nasal consonant **#** = word break

Phonetic symbols without modern equivalents in the Table:
[ɛː] current Southern British English pronunciation of *air* (not the diphthong [ɛə])
[eː] French 'é', German 'eh'
[əi] as *Percy* without the 'p' or the 'c'
[ɒː] longer version of [ɒ]

a   Tables 4:1–4:4 have been constructed from the information provided in a variety of commentaries, including Dobson, Charles Barber, *Early Modern English* (London 1976), and Wilhelm Viëtor, *A Shakespeare Reader* (London 1906). The examples are mostly Barber's and the format has been adapted from his to incorporate the modern spelling configurations. The phonetic values are drawn mostly from Dobson. The reader is invited to compare this information with the tables and/or descriptions of other researchers, such as Bradley, 'Shakespeare's English', pp. 539 ff.; A. A. Prins, *A Synopsis of the History of English Tonic Vowels* (Leiden 1966), pp. 21 ff.; John H. Fisher and Diane Bornstein, *In Formes of Speche is Chaunge: Readings in the History of the English Language* (Lanham Md. 1984), pp. 366–70; and Roger Lass, *The Shape of English – Structure and History* (London 1987), pp. 129 ff.
    The Tables have been simplified in the interests of clarity, and as such they represent a general pattern only. There are numerous exceptions not included here, not least involving words which gained a new spelling by false analogy with an unrelated group. A good example of this is *delight*, which gained its 'gh' by analogy with the spelling of *light*, even though, unlike the latter, it had never been pronounced with the sound [ç] (Gimson, *An Introduction*, pp. 78–9).
b   The dates given for these 'stages' should amply demonstrate the range of variation in the sound changes of this period. It is likely that at any one time at least two pronunciations of the same word could be heard. The reader should also avoid the assumption that all the sounds entered a new stage at the same time. The level of chaos in the language is clear from Dobson's descriptions and comparisons of the contemporary writings.
    The stages originate with Barber, *Early Modern English*, and are intended simply as a means of demonstrating the general patterns of change which ultimately emerged. At the time, such patterns would have been entirely obscured.
c   John Williams Clark, *Early English: A Study of Old and Middle English* (London 1957; 2/1967) suggests that the earliest stage of the diphthongization of ME ī must have been [əˈi], 'i.e., the original sound preceded by a faint and unstressed (and unconscious) schwa' (p. 57). Constance Davies, *English Pronunciation from the Fifteenth to the Eighteenth Century* (Westport Conn. 1970), p. 7, inserts a stage of [ei] before [əi]. The precise phonetic quality of the initial element has in fact been identified in various ways (see, for example, Robert P. Stockwell and Donka Minkova, 'The Early Modern English vowels, more o'Lass', *Diachronica* 7(2) (1990), p. 210, fn. 14, for some discussion of these).

Table 4:2: General progress of short vowels of Middle English

Modern spelling	Modern sound	Examples	Stage I (pre-1500 -1600)	Stage II (post-1500 -1650)	Stage III (post-1600 -1700)
a	[a]	hat, man	[a]	[æː]	[æː]
w(h)aC★, quaC★	[ɒ]	want, was, quarrel	[a]	[a]	[a]→[ɒ][a]
alC	[ɔː]	all, chalk	[au]	[ɒː]	[ɒː]→[ɔː]
alC	[ɑː]	calm, half	[au]	[ɑː]	[ɑː]
auN, awN	[ɔː]	haunt, lawn	[au]	[ɒː]	[ɒː]→[ɔː]
aN	[ei]	angel, fame	[au]	[au]→[ɛː]	[eː]
aN, auN	[ɑː]	aunt, dance	[au]	[ɒː]	[ɒː]→[ɔː]
afC, asC, ath	[ɑː]	ask, path, staff	[a]	[a]	[a]→[ɑː]
e	[ɛ]	set, bed	[ɛ]	[ɛ]	[ɛ]
i, y	[ɪ]	sit, symbol	[ɪ]	[ɪ]	[ɪ]
o	[ɒ]	dog, fox	[ɔ]	[ɔ]→[ɒ]	[ɒ]
u, o, ou	[ʌ]	cut, son, country	[ʊ]	[ʊ]	[ʌ]
u, o	[ʊ]	bull, wolf	[ʊ]	[ʊ]	[ʊ]
a, o, u (unstressed)	[ə]	about, obey, submit	[ə]	[ə]	[ə]
-ed (unstressed)	[ɪd][b]	haunted	[ɪd], [əd]	[ɪd],[əd]	[ɪd]
eC (unstressed)	[ɪ]	eleven, embark	[ɪ]	[ɪ]	[ɪ]

★ = not [k], [g], [ŋ].

a   In some varieties, [a] in this position was already [ɒ] much earlier (Barber, *Early Modern English*, p. 311).
Wrenn, *Word and Symbol*, p. 145, notes that Sir John Paston, writing in the late fifteenth century, was already
spelling words such as *wash* with 'o'.
b   i.e. only after /t/ and /d/; elsewhere 'ed' is realized as a consonant with no preceding vowel.

Table 4:3: General progress of diphthongs of Middle English

Modern spelling	Modern sound	Examples	Stage I (pre-1500 -1600)	Stage II (post-1500 -1650)	Stage III (post-1600 -1700)
ai, ay, ey	[ei]	nail, day, whey	[ɛi]	[ɛː]	[eː]
au, aw	[ɔː]	cause, law	[au]	[ɒ]	[ɒː]→[ɔː]
ew, eu, eau	[juː], [uː]	dew, neuter, beauty	[əu]	[iu]→[juː]	[iu]→[juː]
ew, ue, uCe, ui, ieu, iew	[juː], [uː]	new, blew lute, suit	[iu]	[iu]→[juː]	[iu]→[juː]
oi, oy	[ɔi]	noise, royal	[ɔi]	[ɔi]	[ɔi]
ou, ow	[əu]	soul, know	[ɔu]	[ɔː]	[oː]
ou	[ɔː]	bought	[ɔu]	[ɔː]	[oː]→[ɔː]
oi, oy	[ɔi]	boil, coin	[ui][a]	[ui]→[əi]	[ɑi]→[ɔi]

a   There was an alternative pronunciation with [ɔi] at all three stages.

Table 4:4: General progress of stressed vowels of Middle English followed by 'r'

Modern spelling	Modern sound	Examples	Stage I (pre-1500 -1600)	Stage II (post-1500 -1650)	Stage III (post-1600 -1700)
arC, ar#, erC, er#	[ɑ]	barn, clerk, sergeant	[ar]	[ar]	[ar]
w(h)arr, quarr	[ɒ]	warrant, quarrel	[ar]	[ar]	[ar]→[ɒr]
w(h)arC, quarC	[ɔ:]	warble, quart	[ar]	[ar]	[a:r]→[ɔ:r]
e(a)rC, er#	[ə:]	herb, earn	[ɛr]	[ər]	[ər]
irC, ir#	[ə:]	birth, stir	[ɪr]	[ər]	[ər]
orC, or#	[ɔ:]	corn, lord	[ɔr]	[ɔr]	[ɒr]→[ɒ:r]
urC, ur#	[ə:]	curse, burn	[ʊr]	[ʊr]	[ər]
are	[ɛ:], [ɛə]	hare	[æ:r]	[ɛ:r]	[ɛ:r]
eer, ier, ere	[iə]	peer, pierce, here	[i:r]	[i:ər]★	[i:ər]
ear, ere	[ɛ:], [ɛə]	bear, where	[ɛ:r]	[ɛ:r]	[ɛ:r]
ear	[iə]	beard, dear	[ɛ:r]→[i:r]	[i:ər]★	[i:ər]
ire, iar	[aiə]	fire, briar	[əir]	[əiər]	[aiər]
oor	[ɔ:], [ɔə], [uə]	door, poor	[u:r]	[ɔ:r], [u:r]	[ɔ:r], [u:r]
ore, oar	[ɔ:], [ɔə]	more, soar	[ɔ:r]	[ɔ:r]	[ɔ:r]
our, or, oar	[ɔ:]	pour, afford, hoard	[u:r]	[ɔ:r]	[ɔ:r]
ower, our	[auə]	flower, hour	[əur]	[əuər]★	[auər]
air	[ɛ:], [ɛə]	pair, stair	[ɛir]	[ɛ:r]	[ɛ:r]
ure	[juə]	pure	[iur]	[iur]→[ju:r]	[ju:r]

★ = Disyllabic, but rarely set as such in vocal music.

In what follows we shall consider the pronunciation(s) of English that may be legitimately associated with a selection of pieces of sacred music, examining for each what we can be sure of and where we must guess. Key points in the development of English pronunciation will be mentioned as they are relevant, but the more technical aspects of the discussion have been relegated to the footnotes, so that the outline of the methodology is not obscured by detail. A fuller picture of the development of the English language may be found in any of the standard texts.[24]

24 E.g. Strang, *A History of English*; Gimson; *An Introduction*; Albert C. Baugh and Thomas Cable, *A History of the English Language* (London 1951; Cambridge 4/1993); Charles Barber, *The English Language: A Historical Introduction* (Cambridge 1993); short, simplified accounts relating the pronunciation of Early Modern English to vocal music can be found in Alison Wray, 'Restored pronunciation', in Knighton and Fallows (eds.), *Companion*, pp. 292–9, and Alison Wray, 'Authentic pronunciation for early music', in John Paynter, Tim Howell, Richard Orton and Peter Seymour, *Companion to Contemporary Musical Thought* (London and New York 1992), pp. 1051–64.

Study number 1: *Ah my dear, ah my dear son* (anon.), from the 'Fayrfax' manuscript[25] (c. 1505)

BURDEN: Ah my dear, ah my dear son said Mary...
Kiss thy mother, Jesu, with a laughing cheer.

Verse 1: This enders <u>night</u> I saw a <u>sight</u> all in my <u>sleep</u>
Mary that <u>may</u>, she sang lul<u>lay</u>...and sore did <u>weep</u>
To keep she <u>sought</u> full fast a<u>bout</u> her son fro <u>cold</u>
Joseph said <u>wife</u>, my joy, my <u>life</u>, say what ye <u>would</u>.
Nothing, my <u>spouse</u>, is in this <u>house</u> unto my <u>pay</u>;
My son, a <u>king</u>, that made all <u>thing</u> lieth in <u>hay</u>.

Verse 2: My mother <u>dear</u>, amend your <u>cheer</u>, and now be <u>still</u>;
Thus for to <u>lie</u> it is sooth<u>ly</u> my father's <u>will</u>.
Deris<u>ion</u>, great passi<u>on</u>, infinite<u>ly</u>,
As it is <u>found</u>, many a <u>wound</u> suffer shall <u>I</u>
On Calva<u>ry</u> that is so <u>high</u> there shall I <u>be</u>,
Man to re<u>store</u> nailed full <u>sore</u> upon a <u>tree</u>.

This text has a tight rhyme pattern of AABCCB, DDEFFE, etc., and we must start from the assumption that there are no exceptions to the pattern and no half- or eye-rhymes.[26] We rely strongly on the evidence of rhymes to give us the key relationships from which we can work out the remaining words, so this example is valuable for its three rhymes to a line. Most of the rhymes still work today. The only ones that do not are: *sought/about*, *cold/would*, *lie/soothly*, *found/wound*, *infinitely/I* and *Calvary/high*. Of these, three involve the same phenomenon, viz. the rhyming of modern [ai] (*lie, I, high*) with the ending '-ly' or '-y'. Let us begin there.

In the Middle English period, at the tail end of which Chaucer was writing, words with modern [ai] were pronounced [iː], so that the word *line* would have sounded like modern *lean*. This group is normally referred to by its Middle English vowel: ME ī. Of the words in question here, the first person singular pronoun *I* is most reliably a member of the ME ī group, so we shall deal with

25 *GB-Lbl* Add. 5465; see John Stevens (ed.), 'Early Tudor Songs and Carols', *Musica Britannica* 36 (London 1975), no. 50, pp. 78–9. The history and the various contents of the Fayrfax manuscript must raise the question of whether the religious pieces were composed for use in church or were simply religious songs (see Stevens's discussion on p. xv). David Wulstan, *Tudor Music* (London 1985), p. 70, considers them to have been 'purely domestic devotional music'. The date of 1505 may be slightly late, as Fayrfax was made Doctor of Music in 1504 and this title is not mentioned in the manuscript (see Wulstan, *Tudor Music*, p. 69). A recording of this piece, using restored pronunciation, can be found on The Sixteen's *The Flower of All Virginity*, Collins Classics, COLL 1395-2.

26 John Stevens, 'Early Tudor Songs and Carols', p. xvii, encourages our confidence in the artistry of the text: [The Fayrfax Manuscript] has a strong claim on the attention of anyone who is interested in the musical setting of English words. The composers of the Fayrfax Manuscript effected a minor revolution; the results have come to seem so natural in subsequent centuries that their revolutionary character can easily be overlooked. The novelty was to attend to the words of the poems they chose in such a way as to see them, and set them, as physical sound-objects of an individual kind. So successful were the composers in this, and so conscientious the scribe, that the editor seldom has difficult decisions to make. The Fayrfax Manuscript is the earliest source in which one finds the careful and observant copying of English speech sounds.

this first. The progression of ME ī to its modern pronunciation began perhaps as early as 1400,[27] becoming [əi]; in careful Southern English speech it remained so until 1700.[28] Therefore, we may safely assume that in 1505 *I* was pronounced [əi]. As *I* rhymes with *infinitely* the '-y' ending must also be pronounced [əi]. Dobson[29] confirms that although the pronunciation [ɪ] from ME ī was also common, word-final -y and -ly, derived from Old English -īc, did indeed often follow the pattern of ME ī.[30] Moving to the words *soothly* and *Calvary* we find that the final '-y' in these too can be pronounced with either [ɪ] or [əi]. Therefore we must consider their rhyming partners. *Lie* was pronounced with [əi], but Dobson notes an alternative with [ɪ] which he views as 'a widespread tendency which affected pronunciation in the sixteenth and early seventeenth centuries'.[31] *Lie* and *soothly* could, therefore, have rhymed on either [ɪ] or [əi]. The fact that *lie* is a strong monosyllable falling on a stress beat suggests that the vowel is likely to be [əi]: [ɪ] was the *un*stressed ending and would not normally carry a rhyme with a stressed syllable. Our preference for the latter on the grounds of stress remains valid. *High* does not offer the option of [ɪ], so we must assume that it rhymed with *Calvary* on [əi], though the first description of *high* with this pronunciation is as late as 1566.[32]

To summarize the above discussion, despite alternatives which might be difficult to choose between in words in non-rhyming position, we have been able to establish with reasonable confidence that the words *lie, soothly, infinitely, I, high* and *Calvary* should all contain the vowel [əi]. The least convincing is *high* because it is not recorded by contemporary writers until the 1560s, but the phonetic argument presented by Dobson and the supporting rhyme evidence from such as Cornysh,[33] draw us inevitably to one of two conclusions: that the orthoepists were way behind the times, or that this text displays regional features that had not yet reached London.

Turning now to the other rhymes in the text, *sought* and *about* rely for their rhyme upon the early loss of [χ] for -gh. Dobson[34] believes that the consonant was shed in the English of eastern England, whilst the standard language retained

27 Dobson, *English Pronunciation*, § 137.
28 *Ibid.*
29 *Ibid.*, § 275.
30 Although never the carrier of primary stress, when -y carried secondary stress in polysyllabic words it was pronounced [əi]. Dobson observes:
    Tonkis (1612) lays it down as a general rule that final -y is pronounced 'anglice' (i.e. with the English 'long i', [əi]) not 'gallice' (i.e. with [i(:)]); his example is the last syllable of ability, which he contrasts with the i's of the second and third syllables (§ 275).
31 Dobson, *English Pronunciation*, § 40.
32 Dobson, § 140–3. Dobson argues here that to exist at all, *high* must have aligned itself with regular ME ī words in time for the shift from [iː] to [əi], i.e. by around 1400. The lateness of any recognition of this pronunciation by the contemporary commentators must, then, either mean that they were extremely conservative, or that *high* operating with ME ī was a non-standard variant for some major proportion of that intervening century and a half.
33 *Blow thy horne hunter* by William Cornysh (1468–1523) displays this rhyme, with *on hye* and *dye*.
34 Dobson, *English Pronunciation*, § 424.

it throughout the sixteenth century and adopted the non-standard form in the seventeenth; some evidence attests its survival as late as 1650. For a text of 1505 the rhyme is, then, according to Dobson, likely to be non-standard and, specifically, typical of the east of England. As for the vowel, it would have aligned with ME ū[35] and matched the vowel in *about*, also from ME ū. The phonetic identity of this was a diphthong which Dobson[36] defines as [ʌu] but which is also commonly described as [əu]. The only difficulty, then, in matching the words in rhyme is that the text is rather earlier than we would expect for the rhyme to work.

In modern English *cold* and *would* fail to rhyme on two counts – they have different vowels and the 'l' in *would* is silent. In Early Modern English, pronunciations of *would* (and also *should* and, by analogy, *could*) with and without the 'l' existed. Of the two with 'l', [wu:ld] was the more common, and also the ancestor of our modern [wʊd].[37] However, *cold* is not attested as [ku:ld] and is unlikely to have been pronounced so in any variety in which *cooled* was so pronounced. The other pronunciation of *would* with 'l' was [wʌuld][38] and amongst the various realizations of *cold*, [kʌuld] is listed.[39] Indeed one commentator, Price, listed *cold* and *could* as homophones with this vowel.[40] However, Price was writing in the 1660s, considerably later than our text, and it is hard to know how much support we may draw from him for a so much earlier occurrence.[41] The rhyming of *found* and *wound* presents no problem, as they had the same vowel, [ʌu], until the seventeenth century.[42] The other rhymes still work today, but in most cases use different sounds. What these are will become clear below. Only one, *dear–cheer*, requires mention because it might not have been expected quite so early (see Table 4:4). However, as already observed,[43] [i:] in words spelt '-ea-' had long existed in some pronunciations outside London and, as a comparison of Tables 4:2 and 4:4 indicates, 'ea' + 'r' led the way.[44]

35 *Ibid.*, § 170.
36 *Ibid.*, § 160.
37 *Ibid.*, § 4, p. 457.
38 *Ibid.*, § 4, p. 451.
39 *Ibid.*, § 169, fn. 4. Both would then be associated with the development of ME ou, according to which pattern *cold* has achieved its modern pronunciation. The stage of ME ou which Dobson describes as [ʌu] is also identified as [əu]; the difference is minimal, relating only to the amount of lip-rounding on the first element.
40 *Ibid.*, § 4, pp. 451 and 462.
41 In The Sixteen's recording of this piece (see fn. 25 above), I recommended [kɔld] and [wu:ld], thus forfeiting the rhyme. In retrospect, the rhyming pair would probably have been preferable, despite the reservations already expressed.
42 Dobson, *English Pronunciation*, § 162. The present pronunciation [wu:nd] comes from non-standard varieties where there was no diphthongization of ME ū when a /w/ preceded. This pronunciation was subsequently adopted in standard English. The past participle of the verb *wind*, which ought to have been subject to the same conditions, appears to have diphthongized by analogy with other past participles, such as *found* and *bound* (Dobson, §§ 162–3).
43 See fn. 5 above.
44 See also Dobson, *English Pronunciation*, § 126.

Reconstructing the pronunciation of the remainder of the words is more difficult because there are no rhymes to provide clues. Where there is more than one possibility to choose from, decisions can only be made from the point of view of consistency. Thus, a word with the same history as one which is rhymed, should normally be given the same treatment. If more than one text of the same period is being reconstructed, there is more information of this kind to draw on, though it cannot be guaranteed that two texts of the same age will reflect the same pronunciation. Clearly, expediency from the performance point of view will encourage the use of as little variation as possible, so absolute accuracy – if one can ever make a claim so bold – can sometimes be at odds with the practical demands of performance. Printed below is a possible pronunciation for c. 1505 of the complete text of *Ah my dear, ah my dear son*. Brief comments on the choice of sounds follow; as is customary, vowel classes are referred to by their Middle English (ME) value.

BURDEN: [ɑ: məɪ diːr sʊn sɛid mæːrɪ...
           kɪs ðəi mʊðər dʒeːziu wɪθ ə lauxɪŋg tʃiːr]

The first line is reconstructed according to the regular development of vowels from Middle to Modern English. The vowel in *dear* has been given as [iː] because this word occurs later on, rhyming with *cheer*. The final [r] in *dear*, which does not occur in modern RP,[45] would not have been rolled in speech[46] but rather would have sounded like a modern American final 'r' (a frictionless continuant/approximant). The adoption of a rolled 'r' for modern concert performance is, however, justifiable, as the unrolled one does not carry well in large halls; recordings, of course, can support the quieter sound. The second syllable of *Mary* is unstressed, hence [ɪ], in contrast to the rhyming words discussed before which had [əi]: in disyllabic words there was not normally secondary stress; the only exception might be where a strong rhyme was required, which is not the case here.

In line 2 *with* has a voiceless final consonant [θ]; some speakers even today use this, though the predominant pronunciation has the voiced equivalent [ð]. The reverse was true in Early Modern English, with [wɪθ] the strong, stressed and citation form.[47] In a sung context either [wɪθ] or [wɪð] might have occurred, depending in part upon the attention paid to diction. The other word of particular

---

45 Post-vocalic /r/ existed in standard (British) English until the eighteenth century and is one of the main reasons why Shakespeare's English is often said to have sounded rather American. Although we may say that it was then lost (cf. Gimson, *An Introduction*, p. 83, for example), it is more accurate to say that it became vowel-like, changing short preceding vowels into phonetically similar long ones (e.g. *cart*: /kart/ → /kɑːt/) or appearing as [ə] (*square*: /skwɛr/ → /skwɛə/, now increasingly commonly pronounced /skwɛː/). Dobson describes the considerable influence of [r] on surrounding sounds in some detail (*English Pronunciation*, §§ 198–218).

46 Except intervocalically (Dobson, *English Pronunciation*, § 370). But J. W. H. Atkins, 'The language from Chaucer to Shakespeare', in Sir A. W. Ward and A. R. Waller (eds.), *Cambridge History of English Literature*, 15 vols. (Cambridge 1909), III, ch. 20, p. 460, suggests that all 'r's were 'strongly trilled, for "fire" and "hire" appear in Shakespeare as disyllabic, "Henry's" and "angry" as trisyllabic'.

47 Dobson, *English Pronunciation*, § 4, p. 462.

interest is *laughing*. The '-gh' developed from [χ] to [f][48] in dialectal speech and was borrowed from there into standard English in the early seventeenth century.[49] The vowel is, at this stage, the regular development of ME au.[50] The final [g], which is absent today except in a few regional pronunciations, existed in standard English until the late sixteenth century.[51]

Verse 1:   [ðɪs ɛndərz nɪçt əi sau ə sɪçt aul ɪn məi sli:p
mæ:r'ɪ ðat mei ʃi: saŋg lʊlei and sɔ:r dɪd wi:p
tu ki:p ʃi səut fʊl fast əbəut hɛr sʊn frɔ kɔuld
dʒɔ:'zɛf sɛid wəif məi dʒɔi məi ləif sɛi hwat ji wɔuld
nʊ'θɪŋg məi spəus ɪz ɪn ðɪs həus ʊn'tu məi pɛi
məi sʊn ə kɪŋg ðat mæ:d aul θɪŋg ləi'ɛθ ɪn hɛi][52]

The word *enders*, which has not survived to modern times, meant 'recent'; thus the opening phrase translates as 'The other night'. The rhyme of *night* and *sight* involves not only the short vowel [ɪ] where today there is a long one, but also an extra consonant [ç], still represented in the modern spelling by 'gh'; in these words the development is from ME ĭç not the ME īç of *high*.[53] While *saw* is pronounced in accordance with the regular progression of ME au to modern [ɔ:], *all* belongs to the ME ă class which fragmented; some words in which [l] + consonant followed the vowel joined the ME au group, so that *all*, *false*, *chalk*, etc. have in modern Southern British English the same vowel as *saw*, *cause*, etc. (see Table 4:2). In line 2 all the words conform to the general patterns. The final [g] in *sang* is pronounced as it was in *laughing* (see above). In line 4 *what* is given an initial [hw],[54] as in a Scottish pronunciation; [w] replaced it in the eighteenth century.[55]

Verse 2:   [məi mʊðər di:r əmɛnd ju:r tʃi:r and nəʊ bi stɪl
ðʊs fɔr tu ləi ɪt ɪz su:θ'ləi məi faðərz wɪl

48 The change occurred where '-gh' was final or before final /t/. Thus *daughter* and *slaughter* were unaffected; they underwent different changes.
49 Dobson, *English Pronunciation*, § 371 and § 424. Of this Dobson says:
    In the sixteenth and early seventeenth centuries [χ] must be regarded as the normal pronunciation of good speech, but [f] was also used and from about 1625 onwards was normal in those words in which it is now accepted and occurred occasionally (probably chiefly as a vulgarism) in other cases. (§ 371)
50 The modern pronunciation of the vowel is due to the shortening of ME au to ă (= [a]) before word-final [f] and the subsequent lengthening of [a] to [ɑ:]. *Laughter*, in which the [f] is not final, must have changed by analogy with *laugh*; otherwise, like *daughter* and *slaughter*, it would have undergone neither the [χ] to [f] nor the ME au to ă changes (Dobson, *English Pronunciation*, § 28).
51 Dobson, *English Pronunciation*, § 399.
52 Stress on normally unstressed syllables is marked with ' immediately before the syllable.
53 By the end of the sixteenth century two pronunciations co-existed:
    Shakespeare has many rhymes like night and white, but during and after his lifetime there were many who continued to pronounce the gh like the German ch in licht, or with some fainter modification of this sound (Bradley, 'Shakespeare's English', p. 542).
    For a date of 1505 we may safely choose the older form, viz. [-ɪçt].
54 It is phonetically more accurate to write '[ʍ]', representing a voiceless [w], rather than '[hw]' which suggests two successive sounds, viz. a (voiceless) glottal fricative followed by a voiced labio-velar approximant. However, '[hw]' is more transparent and I have yet to find anyone pronouncing it as anything other than '[ʍ]'!
55 Dobson, *English Pronunciation*, § 414.

dirizi ˈɔn grɛːt pasi ˈɔn ɪnfəinəit ˈləi
az ɪt ɪz fəund ma ˈnɪ ə wəund sʊ ˈfər ʃaul əi
ɔn kalva ˈrəi ðat ɪz sɔ həi ðer ʃaul əi biː
man tu rɪstɔːr nei ˈlɛd fʊl sɔːr ʊpɔn ə triː]

A number of words in this verse have unexpected stress on the last syllable: *soothly, derision, passion, infinitely, many, suffer, Calvary, nailed* (the stress is marked in the transcription by a ˈ before the appropriate syllable). We can account for this in the polysyllabic words by recognizing that they carried a secondary stress on (in these cases) the final syllable. However, the disyllabic words cited here cannot be explained this way; neither do they belong to the (quite sizeable) set of words whose stress was different then to now. Rather, we must assume that the placing of the stress is simply awkward in relation to the rhythm of the scansion and deal with it exactly as we would a modern piece with the same problem.

The word *infinitely* raises another problem, namely whether the middle two syllables should have a long vowel [əi] or a short one [ɪ]. Dobson[56] demonstrates that the '-nite' part of the word was pronounced both ways. As to the first of the central syllables, 'fi-', the modern pronunciation of *finite* versus *infinite* sufficiently indicates that the vowel varies (indeed both do) according to its position in relation to the stress. Amongst many modern churchgoers there is a practice of pronouncing *infinite* as [ɪnfainait] (e.g. in Wesley's hymn *Ye Servants of God*[57]),[58] where, perhaps, the length of the notes countermands the sequence of short vowels. One might argue similarly here as well, hence the transcription given. However, [ɪnfəinɪtlɪ] is equally possible; from the point of view of the rhythm, [ɪnfɪnəitləi] seems less likely, for the primary stress appears to be on the second syllable, not the third, thus rendering the third syllable's vowel phonologically short.[59] The first vowel in *many* is another example from the fragmented ME ă class, raising under the influence of the following nasal consonant to join the ME ĕ class at [ɛ] (Table 4:2). However, this happened considerably later, so the pronunciation here is [a].

56 *Ibid.*, § 275.

57 *Hymns Ancient & Modern New Standard Edition* (London 1983), no. 149.

58 Cf. John Sargeaunt, *On the Pronunciation of English Words Derived from Latin*, S. P. E. Tracts, 4 (Oxford 1920), p. 13: '"infinit"* (I must be allowed to spell the word as it is pronounced except in corrupt quires)'. Philip Moore, Organist and Master of the Music at York Minster, prefers the Minster choir to sing the spoken pronunciation, but notes that the singers can find this strangely counter-intuitive and difficult. In addition to *infinite* he has encountered problems with *testimonies*, in which the third syllable is pronounced [əu] rather than [ə] (personal communication). As we are dealing here with 'reduced', and, crucially, unstressed, versions of various vowels (see Table 4:2), we should hardly be surprised that the full sound is restored when there is stress or length added by the music.

* This represents [ɪnfɪnɪt].

59 The process of assigning vowel length in syllables is briefly described in Chapter 3.

Study number 2: *Out of the Deep* (Psalm 130) Thomas Morley, c. 1580[60]

Verse: Out of the deep have I called to thee, O Lord:
            Lord, hear my voice.

Chorus: O let thine ears consider well:
            the voice of my complaint.

Verse: If thou, Lord, wilt be extreme to mark what is done amiss:
            O Lord, who may abide it?

Chorus: ...For there is mercy with thee:
            therefore shalt thou be feared.

Verse: I look for the Lord; my soul doth wait for him:
            in his word is my trust.

Chorus: My soul flyeth unto the Lord:
            before the morning watch, I say...

Verse: O Israel, trust in the Lord,
            for with the Lord there is mercy:
            and with him is plenteous redemption.

Chorus: And he shall redeem Israel: from all his sins. Amen.

As this text does not rhyme, we have none of the clues which the first study provided. Instead, we must simply launch in, working from a general knowledge of the sound of English at the end of the sixteenth century and aiming for consistency within the text. As this piece predates by only about a decade the earlier works of Shakespeare, there has been rather more attention paid to the pronunciation of this period than those that precede or follow it.

Verse: [əut ɔv ðə diːp hæv əi kauləd tu ði: oː lɔrd
            lɔrd hiːr məi vuis

Chorus: oː lɛt ðəin iːrz kɔnsɪdər wɛl ðə vuis ɔv məi kɔmplɛːnt

Verse: if ðəu lɔrd wɪlt bi ɛkstreːm tu mark hwat iz dʊn əmɪs
            oː lɔrd wuː mɛː əbəid ɪt

Chorus: ...fɔr ðɛr ɪz mɛrsi wɪθ ði: ðɛrfɔr ʃalt ðəu bi fiːrɛd]

A few points are of particular interest in the above. In the word *called*, ME ă before /l/ + consonant was pronounced [au]. According to Barber the next stage of the change, to [ɒː], did not occur until 1600.[61] Regarding *hear*, Barber gives this a disyllabic pronunciation, viz. [hiːər].[62] Morley, however, as most[63]

---

60 John Morehen (ed.), 'Thomas Morley: I, English Anthems; Liturgical Music', *Early English Church Music* 38 (London 1991), no. 3.

61 *Early Modern English*, p. 301. Of course, it means very little to give exact dates as sound changes did not take place overnight. Furthermore, we can once again ask the question, were the orthoepists not the last ones to know about (or acknowledge) sound changes? If so, many people, no doubt, said [kʊːld] in 1580. However, there is a clear disadvantage to an *ad hoc* speculative adoption of sounds in advance of the date given by the experts, namely that unless one adjusts *all* the sounds one cannot be sure of retaining a workable system.

62 *Ibid.*, p. 310.

63 The only exception to this that I have encountered is Wilbye.

composers of the time, sets this class of words as monosyllabic. For this reason I have transcribed it as [hi:r]; the movement of the articulators in changing from [i:] to [r] automatically creates a diphthong with [ə], so in fact nothing is lost except the syllable break. The word *voice* belongs to a small class from ME ui. In standard English this remained separate from the ME oi class (noise, boy, rejoice) until the eighteenth century. This might lead us to expect no rhymes between the two classes until then. However, in Byrd, we do find such rhymes. In *From virgin's womb this day did spring*, the text of which is by Francis Kindelmarsh (fl. 1570s), the refrain rhymes *voice* and *rejoice*. It is most likely that Byrd was rhyming the words on the ME oi sound [ɔi], which might appear to suggest that the classes coincided much earlier. However, Dobson[64] provides an alternative explanation, namely that *voice* could belong to both groups, manifesting a variation that dated from Anglo-Norman times.[65] In this text, as there is no rhyme, either pronunciation is possible; however, the ME ui version appears to have been more usual; Dobson offers a ratio of 5:1 in the orthoepical records. As Table 4:3 indicates, the ME ui route means that [vəis] is also a candidate realization of the word at this date.

In line 4, the word *extreme* is worthy of remark. According to Dobson[66] the second syllable of this Latin loan-word existed in two pronunciations, [ɪkstri:m] and [ɪkstre:m], the latter considered rather more learned. These two pronunciations co-existed until around 1700,[67] when words with [e:] from ME ę̄ altered to [i:] (e.g. *meat, complete*), merging the two forms at the modern value. Selecting [e:] or [i:] for the word in this text is therefore dependent upon one's opinion of singers' social attitudes and aspirations.[68] My choice of [i:] here reflects the fact that the adoption of [e:] would have been a deliberate and pretentious gesture. In the final line of the extract above, *mercy* is given the pronunciation [mɛrsi]. The lowering of unstressed ME ě under the influence of following /r/, giving [ər], was already attested in the mid-sixteenth century; in stressed position, however, it changed rather later. Indeed, more at question is whether *mercy* was pronounced [marsi].[69] The word *feared* has been given, exceptionally, an [ɛd]

64 Dobson, *English Pronunciation*, § 255.

65 One pronunciation of *voice*, then, developed as in Table 4:3: [vuis]→[vəis]→[vaɪs], by coinciding at [əi] with the ME ī group and collapsing with it. The other pronunciation collapsed in Anglo-Norman times with ME oi (Dobson, *English Pronunciation*, § 255), giving [vɔis] at a much earlier date, but this pronunciation was non-standard until it displaced the [ai] form in the eighteenth century (Barber, *Early Modern English*, p. 304). It is not so difficult to imagine how such variation can exist, even within the same variety, when one considers some of the differences that exist in standard Southern British English today, e.g. *scone* [skˑon]~[skəun]; *broom* [bru:m]~[brʊm]; *schedule* [skɛdjul]~[skɛdʒul]~[ʃɛdjul]~[ʃɛdʒul]; etc.

66 Dobson, *English Pronunciation*, § 110.

67 *Ibid.*, § 110.

68 It is, of course, far from settled that one should be reconstructing the practice of the singers rather than the intentions of the composer; see Alison Wray, 'Restored pronunciation', pp. 294–5.

69 Dobson, *English Pronunciation*, § 66, fn. 4. The pronunciation of stressed -er- as [ar], fast-spreading in the late sixteenth and early seventeenth centuries, seems to have been most in evidence in London though it may not have originated there; Edmund Coote (*English Schoole-Master*, 1596) called it the 'barbarous speech of your country people' (Dobson, *English Pronunciation*, § 66). This phenomenon was part of a general muddling

ending, simply because it falls on a final cadence. Elsewhere, [ə] is to be generally preferred, though modern performers may in any case be accustomed to modifying sustained [ə] into [ɛ] or [œ].

Verse: [əi luːk fɔr ðə lɔrd məi sɔːl duθ wɛːt fɔr hɪm
          ɪn hɪz wʊrd ɪz məi trʊst

Chorus: məi sɔːl flɛiθ ʊntu ðə lɔrd bɪfɔr ðə mɔrnɪŋg watʃ

Verse: ɔː ɪzraɛl trʊst ɪn ðə lɔrd fɔr wɪθ ðə lɔrd ðer ɪz mɛrsi
          ænd wɪθ hɪm ɪz plɛntius rɪdɛmsiɔn

Chorus: ænd hi ʃal rɪdiːm ɪzraɛl frɔm aul hɪz sɪnz ɛːmɛn]

In line 3 of this section *flyeth* is given as one syllable only because Morley sets it so. It is possible that the monosyllabic version was not [flɛiθ] but [flɛiz]. Late sixteenth-century writers regarded the third-person singular verb ending -s as poetic,[70] but it must have been increasingly common in ordinary speech. By 1643 Richard Hodges (*Special Help*) was remarking that 'whensoever *eth* cometh at the end of any word, wee may pronounce it sometimes as *s*, sometimes like *z*';[71] just as today we read and write '-gh' for [f] in *laugh* and 'ps-' for [s] in *psychology*, so the seventeenth-century reader/writer understood '-eth' to be the common spelling of [s] and [z] at the end of the third-person singular verb.[72] In line 3 *watch* provides yet another example from the now-fragmented ME ă class, but its development to [ʊ], which occurred after /w/ (including 'qu' = [kw]) except where a velar consonant followed,[73] did not take place until the seventeenth century in standard English,[74] so the vowel is still [a] at this date. *Redemption* (line 5) has [siɔn], not [ʃiɔn] or [ʃən]. In speech at this date [sjən] is likely to have been heard, that is, a single syllable but without the [ʃ], which developed naturally from the fast articulation of [s] + [j] in the mid-seventeenth century.[75] The disyllabic version with [i] for [j] and the unreduced vowel [ɔ] recognizes the practice in musical settings of giving separate notes to each component. Of the two modern pronunciations of *amen*, viz [ɑːmɛn] and [eimɛn], the latter represents ME ā, from which the late sixteenth-century pronunciation would have regularly developed.[76] Certainly, this is the one which appears in a 1685 phonetic transcription of the Lord's Prayer (Francis Lodwick, *An Essay Towards an Universal Alphabet*).[77]

---

of -ar- and -er- words, which left us with the pair *parson* and *person* and with -er- spellings of what are now -ar- pronunciations like *clerk* and *sergeant*.

70 Observe that [ɛθ] was not replaced by [ɛz] and [ɛs] but by [z] and [s] (Dobson, *English Pronunciation*, § 313).

71 Dobson, *English Pronunciation*, I, p. 168.

72 [s] appears after voiceless consonants and [z] after voiced consonants and vowels. However, sibilant consonants take [ɪz] (or [əz]) so that the vowel can separate them from the sibilant ending: e.g. *catches, judges, hisses, buzzes, pushes, vexes*, etc. Hodges proceeds to list the sounds that take this ending.

73 Hence *swan* but *swag* and *swank*, *quality* but *quack*, etc.

74 See fn. a to Table 4:2 (p. 96).

75 Dobson, *English Pronunciation*, § 388.

76 The pronunciation with [ɑː] is likely to have been a 'reform'.

77 See Dobson, *English Pronunciation*, I, p. 272.

Study number 3: *When David heard*, Tomkins, 1622[78]

> When David heard that Absalom was slain
> He went up to his chamber over the gate and wept;
> and thus he said, O my son Absalom, my son...
> Would God I had died for thee...

> [hwɛn deːvɪd hæːrd ðæt æbsælom waz sleːn
> hi wɛnt ʊp tu hɪz tʃeːmbər oːvər ðə geːt ænd wɛpt
> ænd ðʊs hi seːd oː mai sʊn æbsælom mai sʊn
> wuːld god ai hæd daid for ðiː]

There is much less to say about this text, not only because it is short but also because the language has almost reached its modern sound. The change of ME ī words from [əi] to the much more modern [ai] (*my*, *died*) and the parallel development of ME ū from [əu] to [au], of which there are no examples here (but *out* and *house* would be two), do a great deal to de-exoticize the sound.[79] Outstanding in relation to modern Southern British English are: [r] preceded by a vowel and followed by a consonant or word-end, which was still pronounced then but is silent now; [hw] for 'wh' (see Study number 1); monophthongs where there are now diphthongs, e.g. *David*, *slain*, *over*; [l] in *would*, which was already optional. Few points remain.

The word *heard* does not conform to normal patterns. Gil in 1619 gives the pronunciation provided above. It is discussed at some length by Dobson.[80] It is still too early for the vowel in *was*, subject to the same process as *watch* in Study number 2, to have changed. Although it occurred as early as the Middle English period in some varieties, for standard English the process was a slow one during the seventeenth century, with some speakers still using [a] as late as 1750.[81] Although *said* was already attested with the short vowel [ɛ], it was considered dialectal.[82]

In conclusion it may be observed that identifying the "correct" pronunciation for a given piece is not only impossible but also nonsensical. There simply was no single way of pronouncing English, but rather an enormous diversity of varieties, determined not only by social class and place of origin, but also age. Furthermore, this was as much the case in the higher as the lower echelons of society:

---

78 Although this analysis is based on the setting in Thomas Tomkins's *Songs of 3. 4. 5. and 6. Parts* (1622), the principles may be broadly applied to the settings by Weelkes (manuscript sources only) and Michael East (*The Fourth Set of Books*, 1618). The vocal scoring and nature of the sources leave no doubt that all the surviving settings of David's Lament were intended for domestic use. See Peter le Huray, 'The English anthem, 1580–1640', *Proceedings of the Royal Musical Association* 86 (1959/60), p. 9.

79 As mentioned earlier, Zachrisson (1913) considers these changes to have occurred over a century earlier.

80 *English Pronunciation*, § 65, and I, pp. 145–6.

81 Barber, *Early Modern English*, p. 311.

82 Dobson, *English Pronunciation*, § 26.

It is probably safe to assume that even in the inmost circle of the Court there were many whose speech was strongly marked by the dialectal peculiarities of the part of England from which they came, and that the pronunciation of the mercantile classes in London was much less of one type than it would have been found to be a century or two later.[83]

83   Bradley, 'Shakespeare's English', p. 541.

5

BYRD, TALLIS AND FERRABOSCO

DAVID WULSTAN

I remember many years ago reading an article in an American newsletter devoted to computer-aided textual criticism and analysis in the Greek and Latin classics. The details are vague now, but the author's main point sticks vividly in the mind: it was a somewhat plaintive question as to whether we, commanding sophisticated gadgetry, are any more appreciative of Vergil than those nineteenth-century amateurs who relied simply on a few pencilled marginal notes. Telephones do not breed good conversationalists, nor do word-processors engender stylists; but there is a happy belief that computers can somehow convert base instructions into conclusions of gold. The sentiments of that half-forgotten article are thus still germane fifteen or so years later, when understanding has by no means kept pace with verbiage.

There are exceptions, however: as John Morehen has shown[1] by asking the right questions problems of authenticity can be greatly illumined, even solved, by computer methods. Penelope Rapson demonstrated[2] that seemingly intractable problems of textual criticism and stemmatics can be side-stepped by algorithms. And in a previous article[3] I reported the late John Duffill's work on the question of pitch in Byrd's church music. There, unfortunately, his statistics could not be properly presented, and the article had to be truncated in several other ways, notably in regard to a discussion of aspects of Ferrabosco's influence on Byrd. These omissions are made good here, and Duffill's more recent statistics concerning the elder Ferrabosco have been included.[4] For the sake of intelligibility, some of the findings of the previous article are repeated here.

The enquiry began by discussing the common assumption that Byrd was Tallis's pupil; it concluded that certain technical features, notably the ranges and disposition of voices, differed markedly between the two composers. These were shown up by the computer analysis by John Duffill which also confirmed that, in common with the English language equivalent, the Latin church music of

1 John Morehen, 'Byrd's manuscript motets: a new perspective', in Alan Brown and Richard Turbet (eds.), *Byrd Studies* (Cambridge 1992), pp. 51–62.
2 Penelope Rapson, 'A technique for identifying textual errors and its application to the sources of music by Thomas Tallis' (Diss., U. of Oxford 1981).
3 David Wulstan, 'Birdus tantum natus decorare magistrum', in Brown and Turbet (eds.), *Byrd Studies*, pp. 63–82.
4 John Duffill died suddenly after preparing them for the press.

the time was meant to be sung at a consistent pitch, based on that of the organs of the time, and which was slightly below a minor third above present-day 'concert pitch' ($a^1 = 440$).

The assumption that the church music of Gibbons, Tomkins and their contemporaries was sung at a pitch higher than ours goes back to Ouseley. It was not until Peter le Huray published an edition of Weelkes's Fourth (Evening) Service ('for Trebles'),[5] however, that the implications of this pitch in regard to the high treble voice were generally realized. My own work of the same time pointed to the extensive use of the same voice-ranges and pitch standard in earlier English church music with Latin texts by Tallis, Sheppard, Taverner and others. The strange phenomenon is that these exegetical advances of le Huray, myself and many others, have lately met up with a renewed bout of fundamentalism, and not only in regard to pitch; there has been a recent regression to the long note-values ridiculed by Thurston Dart. So, too, the other Snark-like belief – that the written note of Byrd, despite the known vacillations of pitch standards between then and now, mysteriously corresponded with $a^1 = 440$ – has returned. And if its adherents should have a sudden access of understanding that this notion is indeed preposterous, it obligingly changes to that of the Boojum: despite the care with which sixteenth-century composers exploited the limits of specific vocal compasses, the insouciant singer may choose any pitch (though this always turns out to be Snark pitch). What is particularly odd is that authentic pitch (not to speak of temperament) is assiduously sought for Bach and Telemann, even for their instrumental music; and though no one would dream of singing Britten or Tippett at an eccentric pitch, Byrd and Tallis are treated more cavalierly, at least in their Latin compositions (and this is another oddity, for their English text pieces are usually transposed).

The computer statistics presented here show once more that the Latin-text music of Byrd and Tallis was sung according to the same pitch base as their English-text music; they also make clear that continental music, as represented by Ferrabosco, was no different. At the same time they also shed light on the important question of the formative influences upon Byrd's style, which will be the concern of the following pages.

Alfonso Ferrabosco the Elder, as Richard Charteris[6] has shown, was in England for three periods in the 1560s and 1570s. As will shortly be seen, one of his connections with Byrd was probably through Robert Parsons. The researches of Watkins Shaw[7] and others have revealed the dates when Byrd was at Lincoln and the Chapel Royal. If these and a few other meagre facts are put together, the chronology of what is known of his early life is as follows:

5   Stainer and Bell's *Church Services*, no. 327 (London 1962).
6   Richard Charteris, 'New information about the life of Alfonso Ferrabosco the Elder (1543–1588)', *[Royal Musical Association] Research Chronicle* 17 (1981), pp. 97–114.
7   Watkins Shaw, 'William Byrd of Lincoln', *Music and Letters* 48 (1967), pp. 52–9. John Harley has established, however, that Byrd was almost certainly born in London.

1542 (or 3)	Byrd born, probably in London
1553–8	Mary Tudor's reign; William possibly at Chapel Royal
1562–3 (?)	Ferrabosco in England
1563	Parsons sworn as Gentleman of the Chapel Royal (April) Byrd at Lincoln as Organist
1564–9	Ferrabosco's second visit
1570	(February) Byrd sworn as Gentleman of the Chapel Royal
1572	Death of Parsons
1571–7	Ferrabosco's final visit
1575	Tallis–Byrd *Cantiones ... sacrae* published
1585	Death of Tallis
1589	Byrd's *Cantiones Sacrae* I published
1591	Byrd's *Cantiones Sacrae* II published

The publications of 1589 and 1591, and even the first book of *Gradualia* (1605), contain what seem to be early works; to begin with, however, the following discussion will concentrate on the music which can be assigned with reasonable certainty to the period leading up to the 1575 *Cantiones ... sacrae*.

Byrd's earliest musical experience may well have been in London. According to Anthony à Wood he was 'bred up to musick under Thomas Tallis'; Kerman is surely correct in taking this phrase to mean that during Mary's reign of 1553–8, William may have been at the Chapel Royal under Tallis.[8] There is no direct evidence for William's tenth to fifteenth years being spent there as a chorister, but his apparent progress as a composer is most easily explicable in the light of this supposition.

The earliest English works circulating under his name include *Out of the deep* (his rival for the ascription is Gibbons, but no great credit attaches to the authorship of this indifferent anthem) and *Save me O God* (again, so poor as to be accepted into the canon with the utmost reluctance). Whatever the attributions of these English pieces, however, they presumably come from after the time of Mary. The question arises as to whether any of the Latin works date from her reign, that is, before Byrd was yet sixteen. As with the English pieces just mentioned, the problem is whether an untypical work is authentic and early, or is simply by another composer. There are several manifestly untypical works to which the name of Byrd is attached: the curious hymn-setting *Christe qui lux es et dies* (a5) is generally admitted to the canon, as *Christus resurgens* (which Peter le Huray described as 'a remarkably mature piece')[9] must be, since it was printed in *Gradualia* (I). Thomas Byrd has been suggested for *Similes illis fiant* (the middle section of the collegiate setting of the processional psalm *In exitu*

---

8   Joseph Kerman, *The Masses and Motets of William Byrd* (London 1981), p. 23.
9   Peter le Huray, 'Some thoughts about cantus firmus composition', in Brown and Turbet (eds.), *Byrd Studies*, p. 22.

Israel) and *Reges Tharsis*, though Kerman is inclined to regard both of these as tyro efforts by William; he rejects *Sacris solemniis*, however, and a few other items that need not detain us here.

John Morehen's stylistic analysis[10] has rejected the dull but worthy *Similes illis fiant*, so the ascription to 'Mr Bird' makes Thomas a reasonable choice since he was active at the Chapel Royal at the time, and was apparently of the right generation to collaborate with William Mundy and the presumably even more senior Sheppard in the setting of *In exitu Israel* found in the 'Gyffard' partbooks (*GB-Lbl* Add. 17802–5). As David Mateer shows,[11] the later layers of this source represent, at second hand, music by predominantly London-based composers mostly active in the early 1550s. Its repertory seems to reflect the struggle of Queen Mary's musicians, after the desert years of the Edwardine interregnum, to re-assemble or create a working corpus of music in the months leading up to that first Easter of her reign, and to train a choir to sing it. It must be emphasized that this remark applies to the contents, not to the source as we have it. Much of its music is for men's voices[12] and its four-part texture is but a shadow of the five- or six-part festal polyphony which would shortly rise again under the *aegis* of Tallis and Sheppard. So it is difficult to picture William as the 'Bird' of the Gyffard books; but it is easy to see him as the perpetrator of *Reges Tharsis*, as is confirmed by John Morehen's analysis.[13] Byrd's efforts may be somewhat uncouth, and the few resemblances with Sheppard's great setting serve only to make the comparison more unfortunate; but this display of youthful vigour may readily be interpreted as a first tilt in the lists. If this be so, then *Similes illis fiant* recedes into further unlikelihood: its canonic technique and a couple of high notes at the end are the only arguments for William, and everything else, especially the supposed recrudescence of *Reges Tharsis*, stands against these two works being by the same composer.

Nonetheless, *Reges Tharsis* displays features which are not consonant with a very early date. It is an example of the genre that Harrison dubbed 'paraliturgical', in that the repeats from 'Reges Arabum' and 'Domino' are precluded by the overlapping of the preceding points when the *cantus firmus* has these words. It also has the chant incipit written out in the alto part and repeats the words of the incipit at the opening of the polyphony. This last feature is not unique, but is found in Sheppard's *Verbum caro* and also in the anonymous setting of *Spiritus sanctus procedens* of the Gyffard books. These latter pieces, however, are liturgical responds, in common with Taverner's *Dum transisset sabbatum* (I), though this setting is found converted into a 'respond-motet' in the surviving sources of the five-part version. It seems unlikely that its scribes (Baldwin and Dow) were

10 Morehen, 'Byrd's manuscript motets', pp. 61–2.
11 David Mateer, 'The Gyffard Partbooks: composers, owners, date and provenance', *[Royal Musical Association] Research Chronicle*, 28 (1995). See also David Wulstan, *Tudor Music* (London 1985), p. 294.
12 By no means all, however: Kerman's assertion, *The Masses and Motets*, p. 24, is presumably a slip of the pen.
13 Morehen, 'Byrd's manuscript motets', pp. 61–2.

responsible for the bowdlerizing of *Dum transisset*, since they do not accord the same treatment to any other responds. Since it is not possible to restore Byrd's setting as a liturgical respond, its paraliturgical features cannot be ascribed to scribal meddling. Though the 'respond-motet' had gained ground as a para-liturgical genre during the Marian period, there is evidence that it was already in use, even as a devotional piece for domestic music-making, in Edwardian times.[14]

In *Christe qui lux* the young Byrd may again be seen as sizing himself up to his elders, this time Robert White. To go one better on the model setting (the first of a sequence of several by White), Byrd puts the *cantus firmus* first into the bass, then up a fifth in the tenor, then back at the octave of the original pitch in the middle part, and so on up to the top of the five-part texture. But instead of following White in setting the hymn in the traditionally *alternatim* fashion, Byrd treats the middle five verses polyphonically, framing them with a chanted first verse and *Gloria* (the latter is often omitted in modern editions, which not only does violence to the words, but also to the key balance) and ending with a polyphonic *Amen*. Though it is a bold experiment, it shows that the cadet has yet to win his colours. The difficult note-against-note harmonic style, well managed in the model, is awkward in Byrd's effort, whose part-writing is also angular and vocally ungracious.

Christe qui lux is paraliturgical in that it is not set *alternatim*; though this of itself does not rule for a late date, there is an additional feature which must be considered. The third verse of Byrd's setting has the chant in the tenor: its underlay does not correspond with any of the known (through-set) printed Sarum Hymnals that I have seen, from 1525 to 1555. In these, at the phrase 'nec caro illi consentiens' the hiatus of 'caro illi' has to be served by an additional note to 'con-', filling in the third between the two notes set to the adjacent syllables. Byrd, however, follows the outline of the unmodified chant, and squeezes '-senti-' into shorter note-values, almost as if the syllables 'ti-ens' were elided. This may mean that he followed the text of the Sarum Antiphoner which gives only the first verse (rather than following a through-set Hymnal), and forgot what he had sung at the Chapel Royal as a boy in Lent;[15] a less likely alternative is that Byrd's version comes from a continental source; if a corresponding continental source were to be identified, then the circumstances would certainly point to a post-Marian date. All of this points to *Christe qui lux* being Elizabethan. It is quite unlike *Sacris solemniis*, a dull hymn so traditional in form, technique and vocal scoring that, as Kerman suspects, it is probably not by Byrd.

The Lamentations may plausibly have been written under the tutorship of Tallis, whose influence is more notable here than in any other work. The low ranges are typical of the Lamentations of the Parsley–Tallis–Mundy tradition

14 See Owen Rees, 'The English background to Byrd's motets: textual and stylistic models for *Infelix ego*', in Brown and Turbet (eds.), *Byrd Studies*, pp. 24–50.

15 A lapse of memory of this kind is posited by Rees, *ibid.*, in connection with *Infelix ego*.

(but not of White); although the paraliturgical usage of the words does not of itself indicate a date after Mary's death, it is certainly suggestive of the Elizabethan period. Despite some shortcomings, the Lamentations are not as unremarkable as is often claimed: they are considerably less dull than the settings by Ferrabosco[16] or Parsley, and if they have not the sustained intensity of Tallis or White, there are many fine moments, not least at 'Jerusalem, convertere'.

Whether or not the Byrd of the Lamentations had now left the Chapel Royal, he seems to have studied Van Wilder's *Aspice Domine quia facta* at about this time, for Byrd's obviously early setting of the same text, printed in 1575, is clearly dependent upon Van Wilder.[17] And, in London, Byrd might have had something to do with Ferrabosco in 1562 or so, though both had left London in 1563. Meanwhile, it is more than likely that Tallis had taken Byrd under his wing in the years up to William's appointment to Lincoln. The three sections of *Tribue Domine*, printed in the 1575 collection, show marked English traits, and might reasonably be credited to Tallis's influence, but this work may date from after Byrd's Lincoln days; *Laudate pueri Dominum* and *Memento homo quod cinis est*, which both have continental characteristics, may also be of this later vintage, together perhaps with *Diliges Dominum*.

Laudate pueri, as has been known for some time, is an underlaid version of an earlier piece for viols;[18] and *Memento homo* also may originate in a viol fantasy. As Kerman has shown, *Memento* has close links with Tallis's *Salvator mundi* (1), but it is not impossible that this, too, was originally an instrumental piece. John Milsom[19] has demonstrated that *O sacrum convivium* and its English version *I call and cry* originated in this way, so it might be that *Salvator mundi* and perhaps *O salutaris hostia* are part and parcel of this fashion for 'dittying' instrumental pieces.[20] As to Byrd's *How long shall mine enemies*, it seems to be closely modelled on Tallis's *I call and cry*,[21] a dittying which could well have been Tallis's own, and may have preceded the Latin version.

It is notable that much of the early anthem repertory consisted of contra-factions: the miserable uncertainties of the Edwardine period, the sharp about-turn to Marian Catholicism and the subsequent lurch to Elizabethan Anglicanism had left their marks on the repertory. The anthems and Services of Tallis, Sheppard and Mundy are, on the whole, a pale reflection of their Latin works, and a substantial part of the early Elizabethan English repertory is as dull as ditchwater.[22]

16 The Ferrabosco settings, having the appearance of being liturgical, are unlikely to have influenced Byrd.
17 Kerman, *The Masses and Motets*, p. 102.
18 Oliver Neighbour, *The Consort and Keyboard Music of William Byrd* (London 1978), p. 62.
19 John Milsom, 'A Tallis fantasia', *The Musical Times* 126 (1985), pp. 658–62.
20 The term *contrafactum* does not properly apply to a piece with added words, but only to one with a *substitute* text.
21 Craig Monson, 'Authenticity and chronology in Byrd's church anthems', *Journal of the American Musicological Society* 35 (1982), pp. 280–305.
22 As is now known from the discovery of his will – see David Wulstan, 'New light on John Sheppard', *The Musical Times* 135 (1994), pp. 25–7 – Sheppard's English church music was composed in the Edwardian period. Although the style of his Second Service may have had congeners in the work of some composers in early Elizabethan times, it must now be ascribed itself to a pre-Marian date.

Small wonder, then, that the meagre, often shoddy, stock of the Elizabethan stall should have been filled out with some reach-me-downs which, despite inelegances of fit, were at least of good quality material.

By studying the Elizabethan English repertory, Byrd might have learnt this aspect of his trade at Lincoln; or he might have learnt to write for the English rites earlier, first hand, with Tallis in London. The view that Tallis used someone else's adaptation of *O sacrum convivium* as a last on which to show Byrd how to cobble together an English anthem is not only against common sense, but also against the facts as we now know them. Although the early, and dubious, anthems may date from pre-Lincoln days (but presumably before the more accomplished Lamentations), the more assured, though hardly mature, *How long shall mine enemies* may date from this time. Yet, in view of the number of Byrd's Latin works which circulated as contrafactions, it seems unlikely that he had composed much of his extant English church music before or during the Lincoln years. For Lincoln, Byrd may have composed the First Service, at least in an early version, and some Preces and psalms (e.g. *O clap your hands* and *When Israel came out of Egypt*). Meanwhile, however, there is no reason to doubt that Byrd continued to keep his hand in for more elaborate music, including the Latin polyphony for which there would have been little or no call at Lincoln. Furthermore, it is likely that Byrd's polyphonic style was crucially and lastingly influenced during his time at Lincoln.

The profound sea-change which Byrd's Latin style then underwent was due to the influence of Ferrabosco. Kerman[23] has identified several specific examples of this influence; little or none of it can be ascribed to direct contact in the 1562–3 period when Ferrabosco was in London, for Byrd was at Lincoln in 1563 or thereabouts. Parsons, however, was sworn as a Gentleman of the Chapel Royal in that year; he, also clearly influenced by Ferrabosco, may have had contact with the Italian during the period 1564–9 on his return to England. Kerman has plausibly suggested that the propinquity of his three Lincolnshire livings may have linked Parsons with Byrd and, in turn, with London and Ferrabosco. Byrd did obvious homage to Parsons in his *Libera me Domine de morte* of 1575, probably occasioned by Parsons's untimely death by drowning in the Trent at Newark. The latter's admiration for Ferrabosco can be gauged from his *Credo quod redemptor*, whose opening virtually paraphrases Ferrabosco's (compare Ex. 5:1(a) with Ex. 5:1(b)).[24]

In turn, as Kerman has shown, Byrd's *Emendemus in melius* is heavily indebted to Ferrabosco's *Qui fundasti* (the third section of his *Benedic anima mea … Domine deus meus*).[25] So, too, the Sapphic rhythms (reflecting the humanist interest in quantitative classical metre), black notation (*note nere*), and through-setting of

23 Kerman, *The Masses and Motets* and earlier writings.
24 In this and the following examples the transpositions discussed later in the article need to be applied.
25 The second section of this piece – *Extendens caelum* – probably provided the idea for the opening point of *Hodie beata virgo Maria* of the *Gradualia*.

Example 5:1(a): Parsons, *Credo quod redemptor* (opening), clefs C₁–C₂–C₃–C₄–C₄–F₄.

Siderum rector are clearly dependent upon *Ecce iam noctis*, as is *O lux beata trinitas*, which also leans upon Ferrabosco's *Aurora diem nuntiat*. The latter also provided ideas for *Ne irascaris Domine* (1589) and *Laudibus in sanctis* (1591). Finally, *Domine secundum actum meum* and *Domine secundum multitudinem* are both dependent on *Domine non secundum peccata nostra* in a curious way. The first of the Byrd pieces, printed in 1575, takes up the idea of using the second phrase of the point separately, but cribs only the first phrase from the model; on the other hand, the work printed in 1589 (though not necessarily composed later than 1575) takes the second Ferrabosco phrase as its point (see Ex. 5:2, pp. 118–19 below).

Ferrabosco's music circulated in English manuscripts of the period, though mostly later copies are now extant. Although Parsons is a likely intermediary by which Byrd may have seen some of this music, the *Peccantem me quotidie* settings by the two composers have little in common, nor do they resemble Ferrabosco's setting, with its paired and reverted opening point. Other continental music, however, had also been known in England for some time, such as that of Lassus, Clemens and others, and, of course, Van Wilder, who was a member of the Royal Household; this influence had already percolated, if sporadically, into the native music. Jeremy Noble[26] has convincingly argued that Tallis's *Suscipe quaeso* (printed in 1575) was heard in 1554–5 when the Spanish *capilla flamenca* (including Monte) sang at the Chapel Royal. The scoring, with two equal mean parts, is continental,

26 *Apud* Paul Doe, *Tallis* (London 1968; 2/1976), p. 40.

Example 5:1(b): Ferrabosco, *Credo quod redemptor* (opening), clefs C_1–C_3–C_3–C_4–C_4–F_4.

and it displays an up-to-date use of close-knit imitation which was both uncharacteristic of the older style insular music, and which took several more years to gain a proper foothold on English soil. The use of paraliturgical texts is another possible cross-channel influence evident in the Chapel Royal repertory.

Example 5:2(a): Ferrabosco, *Domine non secundum peccata nostra* (opening), clefs C_1–C_1–C_3–C_4–C_4–F_4.

Example 5:2(b): Byrd, *Domine secundum actum meum* (opening), clefs C_1–C_3–C_3–C_4–C_4–F_4.

It is unfortunate that the word 'motet' is often employed in connection with liturgical settings (e.g. those of Byrd's *Gradualia*), for this blanket usage of a continental term clouds the important issue of function.[27] Apart from the votive

27 See fn. 28.

Example 5:2(c): Byrd, *Domine secundum multitudinem* (opening), clefs G₂–C₂–C₃–C₃–C₄.

antiphon, most Henrician polyphony was liturgical, i.e. it was a set part of the Mass or Office whose appointed texts (and chants, as appropriate) were followed by the composers. Settings of Mass and *Magnificat*, hymn and respond, all conformed to this liturgical usage. The paraliturgical pieces were, much like the hymns and anthems of today, outside this regimen, and though they might often have apparently liturgical texts, they were not designed to have a properly liturgical function. Thus the form of Tallis's *In jejunio* or *O nata lux* (1575) rules out liturgical usage as a respond or hymn, as does Byrd's *Christe qui lux*. The Lamentations of White, Tallis, Mundy and Byrd (though not those of Parsley) also fall into this same category. These paraliturgical usages are typical of the Elizabethan period, but the extent to which they can be cited as examples of the influence of Lassus and other continental composers is problematic.[28]

28 See Rees, 'The English background to Byrd's motets', who also despite the title of his article, rightly inveighs against the indiscriminate use of the word 'motet'.

This being so, any supposed influence of Ferrabosco on Parsons and Byrd must therefore be traced to substantive, rather than to supposed, continental traits. One of the most important manifestations of this specific influence concerns the question of vocal scoring. As Examples 5:1 and 5:2 demonstrate, the vocal ranges of Parsons and Byrd are very like those of Ferrabosco. This is significant only when compared with the ranges of other Parsons works, or with those of Sheppard and Tallis. The alto range (up to a sounding c^2 or db^2) and the use of two tenor parts, are typical of Ferrabosco, and of Parsons and Byrd under his influence; these features are alien, however, to the general run of English music.

Most of Byrd's Latin music exists in 'partitive' sources with names such as *discantus*, *sextus*, etc. This nomenclature does not indicate what voices are involved (which might differ from piece to piece in the same partbook); although there may be a correspondence (e.g. the *bassus* book is generally for a bass voice) it does not necessarily follow, particularly in the case of *contratenor* or *tenor* books. The part-names are therefore of little value in regard to the vocal scoring. We do know, however, the names of English voices and their ranges from 'eponymous' sources, such as those containing much of Byrd's English church music. Here, the partbooks have names such as *medius cantoris*, *secundus contratenor decani*, which are specific and exclusive to the intended voice. The ranges found in these eponymous sources, linked with the known organ pitch of the period, can be traced back to earlier music,[29] and thus the vocal scoring for the Latin music can be established, provided that the functions of the original clefs are taken into account.

H. K. Andrews pointed out[30] that several works by Byrd existed in alternative sources which displayed differing pitches and clefs. The clef of the lowermost part is usually significant of itself, though the clef configuration may additionally involve the clef of the highest part. Of the *Cantiones* of 1575, several works exist also in *GB-Lbl* Add. 30810–5 (wordless) where the clefs and written pitches differ, as follows (the lowermost clef only is given here, F_4 and C_4 indicating conventional bass and tenor clefs respectively):

	1575	*Lbl Add. 30810–5*
Aspice Domine	F_4	C_4, flat in key-signature, up a fourth
Attollite portas	F_4	C_4, flat in key-signature, up a fourth
O lux beata trinitas	F_4	C_4, flat in key-signature, up a fourth
Memento homo	F_4	C_4, no flat in key-signature, up a fifth
		(see Appendix 1, however)

The manuscript versions confirm the formula given by Praetorius[31] that if the

---

29 Wulstan, *Tudor Music*, ch. 9.

30 H. K. Andrews, 'Transposition of Byrd's vocal polyphony', *Music and Letters* 43 (1962), pp. 25–37.

31 Michael Praetorius, *Syntagma Musicum*, 3 vols. (Wolfenbüttel 1614–19; facs. Kassell 1958), III, pp. 80–1; discussed by Arthur Mendel, 'Pitch in the 16th and early 17th centuries', *The Musical Quarterly* 34 (1948), pp. 39–40.

tenor clef is found in the lowest part (Praetorius also includes the C_3 and F_3 clefs as having the same effect), the score must be transposed down a fourth if there is a flat in the key-signature, or down a fifth if there is no flat. As to the F_3 clef, it is found in Byrd's *Emendemus* of 1575, in which there is a (two-) flat key-signature. Here, downward transposition of a fourth is again appropriate; the same is true of *Peccantem me quotidie* which has C_5 (= F_3) and a (two-) flat key-signature. Neither of these pieces, however, has a confirmatory manuscript source in conflicting pitch and clef. None the less, Ferrabosco's *Timor et tremor*, printed by Lindner in his *Sacrae cantiones* (1585), has an F_3 clef (flat signature). This work is found in several sources of English provenance, but 'Tregian's' manuscript (*US-NYp* Drexel 4302) has the piece in normal clefs (F_4 in the bass) written a fourth lower in relation to the printed pitch. It is worth mentioning Ferrabosco's *In monte Oliveti*, also printed by Lindner in 1585, which has an F_5 clef (used by Tallis in *In jejunio* of 1575); this piece, again found in several English manuscripts, is written a fourth higher in *Lbl* Add. 30810–5 in normal clefs (F_4 in the bass), thus confirming the *upward* transposing function of the somewhat unusual F_5 clef.

These, and many other sources, confirm that large transpositions had to be made, in conformity with what amounted to a clef code. The alternative conclusion, that wide-ranging music was sometimes sung at a distance of a fourth or fifth from the original pitch, is not plausible.

If Byrd's Latin corpus is to be transposed according to the clef convention and in conformity with the organ pitch of the time, two difficulties arise. The first concerns anomalies or complications in connection with the clef convention, which are comparatively few.[32] The second concerns his voices' ranges, which differ markedly between Byrd and Tallis, or even between Byrd's English and Latin church music. Could there be a lingering doubt that some of his Latin music was somehow pitched differently from his English-texted music and the music of Tallis and others?

In order to test this question as scientifically as possible, John Duffill analysed the voice-ranges of Byrd's English church music found in volume 2 of *Tudor Church Music*, and of the Tallis and Byrd *Cantiones* of 1575, printed in volumes 6 and 9 of the same series. In these editions, the music is printed at the original written pitch, and there is no indication of the clefs of the sources. Duffill did not know of the possible significance of the clefs, in any case, nor of the possibility of transposition, nor yet of my own or others' work on the subject. The request I therefore made was in the nature of a 'blind tasting', for in my asking as to whether the works in *TCM* 9 relate to the same, or different, pitch base(s) in respect of those in *TCM* 2, Duffill had no idea of what I should expect, nor indeed how to go about the task. This should be borne in mind in connection with the method he chose, as described in Appendix 3.

The works by Tallis and Byrd in the 1575 *Cantiones*, and the three masses

---

32 See Appendix 1, p. 126 below.

and other works by Byrd found in *TCM* 9, showed remarkable correlations between their probable pitch level and the clef configurations of the sources. The level was the same as that found in Byrd's English church music, which because of the associated organ parts can be established as being a minor third higher than modern pitch, and was the level eventually taken by Duffill as his computer bank base pitch.

The most remarkable consistency in the calculations was seen in connection with *O nata lux*, *In manus tuas*, *Dum transisset* and *Candidi facti sunt*, since (unknown to the computer) these works are all scored for upper voices quite unlike those displayed by Byrd's English church music. The 'mean' is the highest voice used by Byrd in his English church music, ascending to eb^2 (taking the minor-third pitch difference into account) or sometimes f^2; the four Tallis works mentioned, on the other hand, employ the 'treble' voice a fourth or fifth higher. The top bb^2s of *Candidi* or the rather high mean range of *In jejunio* caused no problems to the computer once it had developed a 'soprano' range combining mean and treble voices. The ranges i–v given in Example 5:3 are those employed by Tallis and others in earlier music involving the 'treble' voice;[33] those of ii–v correspond with those of Byrd's church music and earlier music without 'trebles'. The highest notes of the treble and mean ranges are particularly significant: the mean can be seen rising in compass (*In jejunio*) as the century progresses, but the treble, before dropping more or less entirely out of use (apart from a brief revival in the 1610s or so), tended to descend slightly from the bb^2 favoured by Sheppard

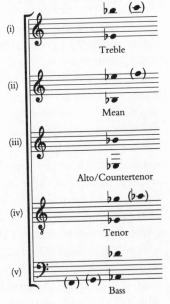

and the earlier Tallis (*Candidi*) to ab^2 (*O nata lux* and *Dum transisset*). The alto range is remarkably stable. This typical range, together with that of the tenor, often contrasts sharply with that employed by Byrd in his Latin music, as will shortly be seen.

Note that in the general run of English music the alto voice (iii) was frequently, whereas the tenor (iv) was infrequently, doubled. As has been seen, however, the doubling of the tenor (and indeed mean) voice was a particular characteristic of Byrd's style. And although the computer successfully negotiated the peculiarities of his voice-ranges,[34] it is significant that its difficulties were caused by marked differences between the ranges of works such as *Reges Tharsis*, which are in an obviously English style, and of works such as *Emendemus* which, in common with its Ferrabosco model *Qui fundasti*, has 'terraced' scoring rather than the characteristic doublings of the insular style.

Example 5:3

33 Wulstan, *Tudor Music*, ch. 9.
34 For a more detailed commentary see Wulstan, 'Birdus tantum'.

The peculiarities of Byrd's voice-ranges are often so unlike Tallis's, so like Ferrabosco's, that they must be accounted as an integral part of the influence of the Italian. That this correspondence of Ferrabosco's and Byrd's voice-ranges is pointed up by new computer statistics[35] gives additional credence to the references by Morley and East concerning the friendly rivalry between the two composers. Other important aspects of style should also be taken into account of course, but must be left severely alone for the present.[36]

Some account of the significance of these correspondence ranges in showing the evolution of Byrd's style in response to Ferrabosco's influence has been given elsewhere.[37] Two characteristics may be singled out, however. The first is Byrd's propensity for doubling the tenor part, which as has already been noted does not stem from Tallis and the English school, but it is typical of Ferrabosco. This doubling is found thrice in Byrd's *Cantiones* of 1589 (*Defecit in dolore, Aspice Domine de sede, Domine secundum multitudinem*) and five times in 1591 (*Fac cum servo tuo, Apparebit in finem, Domine non sum dignus, Domine salva nos* and *Haec dies*), and of course in the five-part mass printed in 1594–5. The second, and most telling trait of all, however, is the increase of terraced scoring: *Vide Domine, Vigilate, In resurrectione tua, Ne irascaris, Tribulationes civitatum* and *Laetentur caeli* (1589) and *Salve regina, Tribulatio proxima est, Haec dicit Dominus, Exsurge Domine, Miserere mei Deus, Afflicti pro peccatis* and *Cunctis diebus* (1591).

These latter pieces include several having a specifically 'recusant' message (e.g. *Vide Domine* and *Civitas sancti tui*, the second section of *Ne irascaris*) as pointed out by Kerman.[38] They also show an often pronounced influence of Ferrabosco, quite apart from matters of scoring. Byrd's more entrenched recusant position seems therefore to be associated with the time in which he became especially influenced by Ferrabosco, surely when he can be presumed to have met him in the period 1571–7. But Ferrabosco can hardly have been an evangelist in this regard, for as Charteris has shown,[39] he was himself in fear of the Roman Church. At best Ferrabosco was an intermediary, bringing over continental Catholicism through music of the counter-reformation, and which may have inspired Byrd to adopt a more assertively recusant stand; this seems to have happened well before the time Byrd moved to London in 1571 or so. The question is clouded by two curiosities, discussed in Appendix 2: the supposed correspondence with Monte, and the setting of *Ad Dominum cum tribularer*.

There is much in Byrd's music to suggest that he was susceptible to many different continental influences: the mark of Clemens, Lassus, Van Wilder[40] and

---

35 See Appendix 4, p. 134 below.
36 The question of underlay is mentioned briefly in Appendix 2, p. 127 below.
37 Wulstan, 'Birdus tantum'.
38 Kerman, *The Masses and Motets*.
39 Charteris, 'New information'.
40 Van Wilder's *Aspice Domine* influenced Byrd's setting of these words, and indeed *Civitas sancti tui*, as David Humphreys points out. See David Humphreys, 'Aspects of the Elizabethan and Jacobean polyphonic motet, with particular reference to the influence of Alfonso Ferrabosco the Elder on William Byrd' (Diss., U. of Cambridge 1976).

other foreign composers can be traced in particular works. Nonetheless, the pervasive influence of Ferrabosco is demonstrable not only in matters of vocal ranges and scoring, but in the melodic outlines displayed in a remarkable number of pieces, to be found everywhere in Byrd's printed collections. I confine myself to a couple of instances. Ferrabosco's *Surge propera*[41] opens with this compound point (the opening point is also taken up, modified, in the second section of the piece) (see Ex. 5:4).

Example 5:4: Ferrabosco, *Surge propera* (opening)

It can readily be seen that (a) corresponds with a host of Byrd's opening points, from *In resurrectione tua* (1589), *Circumspice* (manuscript sources only) to *Alleluia ... Vespere autem, Ave maris stella, Salve regina, Felix es* and *Felix namque* of the *Gradualia* (see Ex. 5:5).

Example 5:5(a): *In resurrectione tua*

Example 5:5(b): *Circumspice*

Example 5:5(c): *Alleluia ... vespere autem*

Example 5:5(d): *Ave maris stella*

41 See Richard Charteris (ed.), 'Alfonso Ferrabosco the Elder (1543–1588) Opera Omnia', *Corpus Mensurabilis Musicae* 96, 2 vols. (Stuttgart 1984), II, p. 89.

Example 5:5(e): *Salve regina*

Example 5:5(f): *Felix es*

Example 5:5(g): *Felix namque*

Note the similarity of the phrases to the word 'Felix'. In *Salve regina* (1591), *Salve sancta parens* and *Salve sola Dei genetrix* from the *Gradualia*, the word 'salve' seems to conjure up a motif similar to that of *Felix namque*. Many words – e.g. 'Domine' already instanced – seem to suggest a particular idea in Byrd's mind (illustrating his concept of the *aptissimi numeri* mentioned in the *Gradualia* preface), as for example the word 'senex' in the two *Gradualia* settings. In the same collection *Hodie beata virgo, Hodie Christus natus est* and *Hodie Simon Petrus* also use motifs seen in Example 5:5, though the *Hodie beata* point might instead be ascribed to Ferrabosco's influential *Qui fundasti*. Similar kinds of points are abundant in both Ferrabosco and Byrd. The use of these and other particular scalewise figures in central or concluding melismata are also a distinctive mark of Byrd's style which can be traced to Ferrabosco. Point (b) of Example 5:4 is familiar, too, as the opening of *Haec dies* (*Cantiones* of 1591) (see Ex. 5:6).

Example 5:6: Byrd, *Haec dies* (opening)

Similar (it would be a mistake to say 'derived') figures abound in Byrd's work.

Tallis and other English composers may have had a formative influence on Byrd's style, particularly in his earlier pieces; but much of what we tend to regard as typical Byrd, and especially his 'recusant' works, is pervaded by characteristics which can be traced to Ferrabosco. The 'English' scoring, as is shown by Duffill's computer statistics given in Appendix 3, has a great deal less correspondence with that of Byrd than Ferrabosco's use of the voices, analysed in Appendix 4. This is not to say that Byrd's was derivative, certainly not to the extent of being a pale imitation: far from it, for very little of the Italian composer's music has the grandeur and power of the Englishman's; but it can safely be said that Byrd would not sound like the Byrd we know had Ferrabosco not exerted a profound influence at a crucial stage in Byrd's development.

APPENDIX 1

A more meticulous analysis of the *Gradualia*, and indeed of Byrd's repertory as a whole, would doubtless reveal other facets of vocal scoring of interest; but this must be left for another occasion, and, indeed, for a different author. It is necessary to point out, however, that May Hofman pioneered the way by tabulating Byrd's voice-ranges for each of his works (in common with those of all English composers of Latin church music between 1485 and 1610).[42] As she showed in 1977, the transpositions demanded by the clef configurations result in remarkably few exceptions or anomalies. May Hofman discusses these at some length (particularly in her Appendix VII), where she makes clear that the three-part extracts from votive antiphons excerpted by Baldwin, Paston and others can be disregarded: in common with the arrangements for voice and lute of Fayrfax, masses and the like (including pieces of limited range extracted from the *Gradualia* in Paston sources), these *disjecta membra* for domestic music-making have nothing to do with the performance of their parent works by the original choral forces.

If these kinds of arrangements are discounted, the exceptions to the proper working of the clef convention are few. They are even fewer than May Hofman suggests, for she assumed that the C_4 clef in the bass implies only one transposition, whereas the evidence of the Byrd sources confirms the Praetorius formula, that when there is no flat in the signature C_4 implies the same transposition as F_3. Accordingly, many of the items in the Paston books which she regards as irregular are in conformity with normal transposition, for example the items from the 1575 *Cantiones*, mentioned on p. 120, found in *Lbl* Add. 30810–5. *Memento homo*, however, is peculiar in that in the latter source the top part is in a different pitch to that of the other manuscripts in the set: the lowermost parts are written a fifth lower from the printed pitch (correctly, in view of the C_4 clef in the bass, no flat) but the top part is only a fourth lower. This anomaly (a similar jumble may be seen in the Lamentations found in *GB-Ob* Tenbury 369–73) implies either a mistake (assuming an F_4 transposition) or that a different intermediary was used as exemplar for this particular part (again, an F_4 in the bass would be implied).

42 May Hofman, 'The survival of Latin sacred music by English composers, 1485–1610' (Diss., U. of Oxford 1973). It is singularly unfortunate that space considerations dictated the exclusion of these important data from her catalogue published in the *Early English Church Music* series.

The same partbooks contain three items from the 1591 *Cantiones*. Of these, *Domine non sum dignus* and *Domine salva nos* are a fifth (C_4) and fourth (F_3) from the printed pitch, and are regular. *Infelix ego*, however, is transposed *up a tone* in the manuscripts: the scribe or his exemplar was clearly in agreement with Morley[43] that a two-flat key-signature was beyond the pale. In transposing the work, however, he did not use (or did not know of) the correct clefs which would have normalized this transposition; these would have included C_5 in the bass, the same configuration as is found in Byrd's early *Christe qui lux* setting.

A final problem of transposition concerns two pieces for eight and nine voices. *Ad Dominum cum tribularer* (a8) occurs wordless in an instrumental source (*GB-Lbl* Add. 31390), with F_4 in the bass. If transposed normally (and the F_4 clef and computer offset of 'o' would confirm this) the ranges would be TrTrMMATBB. This might appear to be untypical of Byrd, were it not for *Domine quis habitabit* (a9), also found in a wordless state (*GB-Lbl* R.M. 24.d.2). If its clefs (F_5) are to be trusted, the resultant ranges would indicate a scoring of TrTrMMAABBB. These two works are therefore curious, not least when compared with the eight-part *Quomodo cantabimus*, which is scored for normal ranges disposed MMAATTBB, as is *Diliges Dominum* (1575), for the same voices.

The F_5 clef, found in the bass of *Domine quis habitabit*, as often as not represents a transposition of a minor sixth in relation to modern pitch (as with Tallis's *In jejunio* and *Candidi facti sunt*). In *Domine quis habitabit*, however, it must be assumed to imply a *total* transposition of a fourth (as is the case with Sheppard's *Media vita* and many other works). As with the confusion of the otherwise similar F_3 and C_5 clefs, the transposing significance of the F_5 and D_4 clefs seems to have been confounded at some point during the sixteenth century, to the extent that the evidence of voice-ranges has to be used to determine which of the two possibilities is the more likely.

It should again be stressed that the foregoing problems of transposition, though of interest, must not be viewed out of context: the handful of anomalies or peculiarities discussed above are but a minute fraction of the 200 or so Latin works by Byrd, or the 800 or so Latin works by other English composers of the period c. 1485 – c. 1610.

APPENDIX 2

According to a note by John Alcock attached to his eighteenth-century score[44] of Monte's *Super flumina*, it was '... sent by him, to M^r: Bird – 1583'. Similarly, Byrd's *Quomodo cantabimus*, supposedly a continuation by way of reply, has Alcock's note '... made by M^r: W^m: Byrd, to send unto M^r: Phillip de Monte, 1584'. It is

---

43 Thomas Morley, *A Plaine and Easie Introduction to Practicall Musicke* (London 1597; facs. Farnborough 1971), p. 156.
44 *GB-Lbl* Add. 23624 (ff. 101^r and 107^r).

reasonable to suppose that these remarks derive from a lost source from whence they were copied by Alcock, and it is certainly plausible that Monte might send the piece to Byrd whose family he might have known during his visit with the *capilla flamenca* in 1554–5; though William would have been only a boy at the time, Monte might have kept up some kind of correspondence.

Yet there are two difficulties, one musical one textual, concerning the way the pieces might fit together. It is true that both are in eight parts (though Monte's forces tend to be disposed as two four-part choirs, at least at the outset), but the two works are in different, and irreconcilable, keys: Monte writes in 'plagal' g minor, normal clefs (F_4 in bass), whereas Byrd writes in F major, high clefs (F_3 in bass); neither at the written nor sounding pitches can the tonal schemes be made to connect with each other. So far as the text is concerned, Byrd starts at the words 'quomodo cantabimus' and continues to the word 'Jerusalem'. Monte, however, had already set the phrase 'quomodo cantabimus', since he had re-ordered the text of the first few verses of the psalm ('pointedly re-arranged' to deliver a recusant message, according to Kerman).

The textual inconsistency does not militate against joining up the two compositions, but the discrepancy of key does. It is easier to see Byrd's *Quomodo* as a separate work, particularly since the section 'Si non proposuero' is labelled *secunda pars*. If so, however, why did he start setting the psalm at that point; why did he write in eight parts (dismissing the slight difference in scoring and the fact that his setting is canonic); and how did the two pieces come to be together in *GB-Ob* Tenbury 389 and the 'McGhie' manuscript (the only survivors of the set of books from which Alcock presumably copied)? Whatever the solution to this intriguing puzzle, some form of collusion between the two composers seems likely; but equally, it does not seem that Byrd can have seen Monte's setting before he composed his own, otherwise, surely, he would have made them fit?

Another work with possible recusant overtones, *Ad Dominum cum tribularer*, is also somewhat problematic. The text is not given in the only surviving score[45] but can be fitted with reasonable ease except for two *cruces*: towards the end, a disconnected phrase appears, which Fellowes plausibly conjectured was underlaid to a repetition of the words 'habitantibus Cedar...', a repetition which Kerman sees as significant from the recusant standpoint.

Warwick Edwards, in volume 8 of *The Byrd Edition*, however, overcomes the problem by using a conflation of translations, a practice which has contemporary sanction, and which in this instance leads to an equally plausible solution, though it somewhat lessens the recusant import of the text. Edwards's underlay at 'Heu mihi', however, is surely incorrect. Despite the ligature marks in the instrumental version, the underlay of the phrase is clearly syllabic, the diphthong of 'Heu' being opened. Byrd's practice in the matter (see *O quam suavis* in the *Gradualia*) was not as fastidious as the humanists (or indeed Ferrabosco in his two settings

---

45 The instrumental tablebook *Lbl* Add. 31390.

of *Heu mihi Domine*) would have had it; it is for this reason that the words are less likely to derive from Lassus (who treated 'Heu' as a monosyllable, and incidentally used the Vulgate text). Certainly Byrd's setting evinces no demonstrable musical debt to Lassus, nor yet to Ferrabosco's setting of the text (which does not in any case contain the crucial second part).

As to the chronology of *Ad Dominum*, it seems unlikely to precede the decidedly inferior *Domine quis habitabit*. Kerman's judgement of the work is wide of the mark: it is a mature and richly expressive work, and of assured workmanship, though it dates from before c. 1580, when the tablebook in which it is now found was completed. It was probably omitted from the printed collections of 1575, 1589 and 1591 on account of its length and the large number of voices required.

APPENDIX 3

PITCHES AND VOCAL RANGES IN TALLIS AND BYRD: BY JOHN DUFFILL[46]

The problem was to determine the pitches of pieces in *TCM* 9 and, later, in Tallis's contributions to the Tallis–Byrd *Cantiones ... sacrae* (1575), relative to the contents of *TCM* 2, whose latter pitch was determined by the organ parts. The method used initially was to count the high and low range limits observed in the 25 Byrd items from *TCM* 2 and then to compare the other pieces under test with these base counts, using mathematical methods to assess 'goodness of fit', assuming in turn each of a range of relative differences of pitch (called 'offsets') from +7 to −7 semitones (an 'offset' is defined as the number of semitones by which a piece would have to be transposed to bring it to the base pitch of *TCM* 2 – e.g. 'offset −5' means that the test piece would need to be transposed down by five semitones, a perfect fourth). Later, the base counts were expanded to include acceptably 'set' items from the tests, for further tests using this strengthened bank. The basic range counts were made under the eight categories of High and Low limits of four voices, called for these purposes Bass, Tenor, Alto and Soprano. These labels were assigned to parts in the scores with guidance from the part-names printed in the editions – *contratenor* and *discantus* were classed as Alto, whilst the topmost part or parts were called Soprano. Most often the top part was *medius* (Mean) but there were a few variants such as *superius*, *sextus*, etc.

A computer program was written to apply the matching tests; the output, for each piece and each offset tested, was a score (positive or negative) in favour of the observed ranges belonging to the parent population (i.e. the base ranges of *TCM* 2).

In the earliest test runs of *TCM* 9 items compared with the *TCM* 2 bank, some excellent results were obtained, with scores high enough to convince of the accuracy of the offset indicated. The most popular offset was 'o', but the three Latin masses (tested movement by movement) gave very interesting results by predominantly indicating '-5' as their best offset; there were several problem pieces which did not score well. Most of the Tallis *Cantiones* (1575) likewise scored best at offset 'o'; but amongst them were some wide exceptions:

In jejunio et fletu	offset '+5'
Honor virtus et potestas	offset '-7'
Dum transisset sabbatum	offset '-5'

Despite the credibility of the best results achieved, it was also evident that the voice-ranges in the Tallis *Cantiones* and in some of the Byrd *TCM* 9 items were untypical of *TCM* 2 (this was David Wulstan's expectation, though at the time unknown to me). The most common sign of this was that the highest part (called 'Soprano' in my counts) sometimes scored badly whilst the other parts scored well at the best-scoring pitch offset. An idea of reinforcing the base counts by admitting a fifth voice ('Treble' – higher than my Soprano which was so far really Mean) was rejected because of the predictable difficulty of how to start building up the fifth-voice data. It was therefore decided to strengthen the base counts by sequentially adding in data from the best-scoring items at each of a further series of runs and thereby to expand my Soprano counts to embrace effectively two ranges – Mean and Treble – and to improve the other voices' data by increased sample sizes. The computer runs continued in this way until a saturation point was reached at which 74 of the 80 items tested were regarded as acceptably 'set', with the remaining six staying indefinite. A summary of results follows:

BYRD: MASSES

	No. of items	Results		Lowermost clef[47]	
a3	6			C_4	
a4	6	all offset -5 semitones		C_4	all with flat key-signature
a5	6			F_3	

The written top note observed (after transposition down by five semitones) was d^2, thus Mean and not Treble appears to have been the highest voice.

---

47 This clef evidence was disclosed by David Wulstan only after completion of the computer runs; it confirms offset '-5'.

BYRD: CANTIONES (1575)

a5 (5 items)

A most problematical set. All started off with offset '-3' best. Finally *Emendemus in melius* came out with '-5' best, but with '-3' still a strong competitor. *Peccantem* and *Libera me Domine de morte* were finally best at offset 'o', but with weak scores. The other two, *Libera me Domine* and *Siderum rector*, remained obstinately at '-3' and were finally left as unset. *Peccantem* and *Libera me Domine de morte* had top notes higher than d^2, so that their top parts appear to be Treble.

a6 (11 items)

All believed to be offset 'o', although *Gloria Patri* was best at offset '+2', with voices SSAATB. Believed scored for Trebles on top except in *Laudate pueri* and *Memento homo*.

a8 (1 item)

Offset 'o'; *Diliges Dominum*: top written note is d^2 – apparently Mean on top.

BYRD: REMAINDER OF TCM 9, EXCLUDING INSTRUMENTAL AND SPURIOUS WORKS

20 items, four of which gave offset '5': *Benigne fac, Petrus beatus, Quomodo cantabimus* and *Christe qui lux*. Lamentations remained problematical. The remaining items (including the dubious *Sacris solemniis* and *Similes illis*) all scored well at offset 'o'. The following pieces had top notes higher than d^2: *Peccavi, Reges Tharsis, Circumspice, Domine ante te, Domine quis habitabit* and *O salutaris*.

TALLIS: CANTIONES (1575)

No. of items	Results	Lowermost clef[48]
16	offset '+5':	
	Candidi facti sunt	F_5
	In jejunio et fletu	F_5
	offset '-5':	
	Dum transisset	C_4, with a flat signature
	offset '-7':	
	Honor virtus et potestas	C_4, no flats

48 The offsets confirm the clef evidence (received later); twelve items (the remainder) gave offset 'o'.

The following pieces had top notes higher than d^2: *Candidi facti sunt*, *In jejunio*, *In manus tuas*, *Miserere nostri*, *O nata lux* and *Dum transisset*.

Such mainly satisfying results were possible because of Byrd's adherence to quite strict range limits in *TCM* 2 and to a lesser extent in *TCM* 9, most marked in low Bass and high Soprano limits. In *TCM* 2, out of the 25 items, 21 had a low Bass limit of F and four had E, whilst in high Soprano, there were fourteen at c^2 and eleven at d^2. These severe limitations lent power to the scoring method adopted, which nevertheless inevitably suffered to some extent from the small number of observations available for accumulation of scores for each item (e.g. 10 for a five-part item). The semitone scale used below is based on $c^1 = 40$.

The range limits recorded at three stages of the work were (on the base pitch of the *TCM* 2 edition used, i.e. not transposed up a minor third to agree with modern pitch):

	Bass	Tenor	Alto	Soprano	Overall range (in semitones)
TCM 2					
	$E-c^1$ (20–40)	$A-g^1$ (25–47)	$c-a^1$ (28–49)	$a-d^2$ (37–54)	34
Range 20		22	21	17	
TCM 2 and masses					
	$E-d^1$ (20–42)	$A-g^1$ (25–47)	$c-a^1$ (28–49)	$a-d^2$ (37–54)	34
Range 22		22	21	17	
Final – All accepted results					
	$D-d^1$ (18–42)	$G-a^1$ (23–49)	$C-c^2$ (28–52)	$f\sharp-g^2$ (34–59)	41
Ranges 24		26	24	25	

The above table illustrates the remarkable stability of all ranges except Soprano which, as explained earlier, was expanded as work proceeded to include Treble and Mean voices and which also illustrates Wulstan's conclusions described above, but which I had not seen until after these results had been tabulated.[49]

The final Soprano details developed by the computer runs resemble the lower voices (ATB) in approximating to a two-octave compass; it is thus the top voice (presumably Mean) of *TCM* 2 and the masses that appears abnormal. Analysis of the Soprano ranges of all of the set items (obviously excluding those in three parts) is most interesting. First, counts of the range limits:

49 Full counts of the Byrd and Tallis items are printed with those of Ferrabosco at the end of Appendix 4 below.

Number of cases where high Soprano limit is:

		<55 (say 'Mean')			>54 ('Treble')	
		Low	High		Low	High
$f\sharp$	34	1	–		–	–
g	35	7	–		5	–
$g\sharp$	36	–	–		–	–
a	37	18	–		5	–
$b\flat$	38	4	–		3	–
b	39	5	–		2	–
c^1	40	24	– ('middle' C)		2	–
$c\sharp^1$	41	6	–		–	–
d^1	42	11	–		8	–
$e\flat^1$	43	–	–		–	–
e^1	44	2	–		3	–
f^1	45	3	–		1	–
$f\sharp^1$	46	–	–		–	–
g^1	47	–	–		–	–
$g\sharp^1$	48	–	–		–	–
a^1	49	–	–		1	–
$b\flat^1$	50	–	–		–	–
b^1	51	–	1		–	–
c^2	52	–	44		–	–
$c\sharp^2$	53	–	–		–	–
d^2	54	–	36		–	–
$e\flat^2$	55	–	–		–	4
e^2	56	–	–		–	14
f^2	57	–	–		–	8
$f\sharp^2$	58	–	–		–	–
g^2	59	–	–		–	4

Note that the two low-limit distributions resemble each other, and that the high centre of gravity for Treble appears to be about three to four semitones above the Mean, though its absolute top limit is allowed to go higher than this.

Secondly, an analysis of Mean and Treble ranges according to their top notes and the number of parts in the score, for the Byrd *TCM* 9 and the Tallis *Cantiones* pieces of more than three parts:

No of parts:	4	5	6	7	8	9
No. of items with top note:						
<55 (Mean)	13	26	2	1	0	0
>54 (Treble)	0	10	11	1	1	1
Totals:	13	36	13	2	1	1

This implies that a greater number of parts tends to push the topmost part upwards and appears to illustrate Wulstan's terraced scoring.

APPENDIX 4

PITCHES, VOCAL RANGES AND CLEF PATTERNS IN LATIN CHURCH MUSIC OF ALFONSO FERRABOSCO (THE ELDER):[50] BY JOHN DUFFILL

As before, the aim of this analysis was to look for evidence of different pitch-standards among the pieces, to try to measure pitch differences; also to study the role of clef conventions as indicators of pitch levels. Notes are referred to by their positions in the semitone scale of a standard piano keyboard, as previously.

The two Ferrabosco volumes analysed contained pieces in three, four, five or six parts, comprising 37 motets, Lamentations in four sections and one English anthem. The incomplete motets of the Appendix have not been included. The voices have been labelled Soprano, Alto, Tenor and Bass by the editor. Under his scheme there are never more than two *divisi* parts per voice. Although the original part-names are not given in the transcriptions they (e.g. *Medius, Contratenor, Altus, Tenor, Sextus*) occur in the critical notes. The original clefs are indicated, though there is no editorial reference to pitch.

Some of the pieces are sectional, but all those of a given piece do not always have the same characteristics. The unit for analysis was thus the piece, or section, if applicable. Thus the original 42 numbers appear as 68 items here. The data extracted for computer analysis of each item were: (1) the number of flats in the key-signature (always 0 or 1); (2) the ranges, expressed as the high and low observed limits for each voice-part, qualified by the original clef, and the modern part-name assigned by the editor (where only one bass part occurred it was labelled 'Bass 2' for analytic convenience); and later, as a result of analytic findings, (3) a Type, describing clef pattern.

Pieces for five or six voice-parts are by far the most frequent, scored most commonly with four clefs; doubling of parts is found most often in the Tenor part. The clef combinations used are very stereotyped, falling into two main sets; as will be seen under 'clef-sets' below, this factor became important.

The material yielded so well to analysis that the clear-cut results will be summarized first.

SUMMARY

There are two and only two pitch levels covering all of the pieces; they stand a

50 See Richard Charteris (ed.), 'Alfonso Ferrabosco the Elder (1543–1588) Opera Omnia'. This Appendix had been completed and revised (apart from one or two typographical matters) by John Duffill before his death.

perfect fourth apart. With each pitch-level is associated a set of clefs, containing four main components for the four main voice-ranges, S, A, T, B, plus two subsidiary components for intermediate, less-often used ranges.

	S	S/A	A	T	Bar	B
Clef-set A:	$\underline{C_1}$	C_2	$\underline{C_3}$	$\underline{C_4}$	F_3	$\underline{F_4}$
Clef-set B:	$\underline{G_2}$	C_1	$\underline{C_2}$	$\underline{C_3}$	C_4	$\underline{F_3}$

The main components are underlined; 'S/A' indicates a vocal range between Soprano and Alto. Scores of the clef-set B items need to be reduced by five semitones to bring them to the base of clef-set A. Clef-set A pitch base equals the pitch base of the Byrd and Tallis works previously analysed, which itself stemmed from Byrd *TCM* 2.

The counts of the overall compass of the pieces strongly suggested homogeneity of compass, which tended to a mean of 34.14 semitones, in a compact distribution with a small statistical spread:

Range in semitones	Number of pieces
32	3
33	10
34	24
35	3
36	10

A different pattern emerged, however, when assessments of the relative pitches of the pieces were made. In these counts the 'mid-compass' note was counted, for all pieces judged to have the full four-voice compass; mid-compass is calculated as the note midway between the highest Soprano note and the lowest Bass note of a piece.

Mid-compass note	Number of pieces	Clef-set
37 (*a*)	3	A
37.5	6	A
38 (*b♭*)	13	A
38.5	3	A
39 (*b*)	1	A
39.5	1	A
40 (*c¹*)	–	–
40.5	–	–
41 (*c♯¹*)	9	B
41.5	–	–
42 (*d¹*)	11	B
42.5	3	B

This distribution is clearly bimodal, the bimodality being obviously governed by clef-set differences.

Calculating the mean mid-compass notes for clef-sets A and B separately, gives a value of 37.93 for clef-set A, and 41.67 for clef-set B. This may be taken as a clear indication of a difference in pitch between the A and B clef-sets, but the difference seen here, of 3.74 semitones, is only an approximation; more precise methods were used later.

The most obvious explanation for this pitch difference is that a common pitch base applies to all of the pieces, and that transposition of some of them must be made to bring them all to the common base. As has been found with other composers' works, the clef conventions determine the transposition. In this case the clef-set B items need transposing down a perfect fourth, to what in this analysis is taken as 'basic' pitch. (The statistical tests from which the interval of a fourth was derived are described under 'correlation tests', below.)

CLEF-SETS

This pitch difference apart, remarkably good matching was found between the structure of clef-set A items and clef-set B items. The following counts are not merely of number of items, but of numbers of voice-parts using the clefs, to reflect accurately the structure of the pieces with regard to duplication of clefs. The counts are set out under their clefs in a logically descending order.

Clefs:	G_2	C_1	C_2	C_3	C_4	F_3	F_4	Totals
Clef-set A:	.	11	.	16	19	.	11	57
Clef-set B:	7	.	9	10	.	6	.	32

An obvious match is obtainable by shifting the B count one column to the right, and aligning the clef headings in the following way:

Clef-set A	C_1	C_3	C_4	F_4
Clef-set B	G_2	C_2	C_3	F_3
A	11	16	19	11
B	7	9	10	6

The *chi-squared* statistical contingency test for goodness of fit applied to this 2×4 array of counts gave the exceptionally good answer of *chi-squared* = 0.1 with 3 'degrees of freedom'. This leaves hardly a shadow of doubt that the two sample counts come from the same parent population (here describing the part and clef-structure of the pieces). Thus we can confidently propound the following equations:

	Clef-set A		Clef-set B
Soprano	C_1	=	G_2
Alto	C_3	=	C_2
Tenor	C_4	=	C_3
Bass	F_4	=	F_3

Of the 68 items, 29 were of type A and 21 of type B. Further items were classified as basically of types A or B, but with one or more clefs extra to the basic set of four. These were classified as type A* (seven items) or type B* (five items). There remained six items (with only two clef patterns) which were at first unidentifiable to types A or B; these were classified as type C. Discussion of the non-standard items can be found later at 'Further clef configurations' (p. 138 below).

DETERMINING RELATIVE PITCH DIFFERENCES

The method used was to compare pairs of frequency counts of the range limits by aligning the counts at offsets corresponding to pitch differences. To assess the virtue of a comparison the 'correlation coefficient' r was calculated. The correlation coefficient r ranges from $+1$ for a perfect match, down to -1 for a perfect mismatch (e.g. counts for 1, 2, 3 and 4 would make a perfect match with counts of, say, 2, 4, 6 and 8, whilst counts of 8, 6, 4 and 2 would form a perfect mismatch with the first count of 1, 2, 3 and 4 or with 2, 4, 6, 8, etc.). Positive values of r are therefore preferred; the nearer they approach $+1$ the better. In the nature of the case, either flush matching (i.e. zero offset) would be expected, or matching at some other interval if transposition is necessary. The results obtained were excellent: r values of 0.7 and above are absolutely convincing, and those in the 0.4 area are very good indeed.

CORRELATION TESTS

Various pairs of counts were tested for correlation, or goodness of match. At first the correlations were effected between the two sets of Ferrabosco items, and finally between Byrd–Tallis counts and Ferrabosco or between Byrd *TCM* 2 alone and Ferrabosco. All of the tests gave splendid and consistent results. In the correlation details which follow, the offset is expressed in the same way as for the Byrd–Tallis analysis (e.g. an offset of '-5' means that the notes of the second-named count and the items it represents have to be reduced in pitch by five semitones to bring them to the base of the first-named count).

The counts used for correlation tests were:

(i)   Ferrabosco, types A and A*
(ii) Ferrabosco, types B and B*
(iii) The sum of counts A and B after reduction of the types B and B* notes by five semitones
(iv) Byrd, *TCM* 2 only
(v)   Byrd–Tallis, the finally developed count

(Note that for items types A* and B* only those ranges associated with the two basic clef-sets were counted.)

Counts compared Offsets (pitch adjustment, in semitones)

	0	-1	-2	-3	-4	-5	-6	-7
Values of r:								
I with II †	-0.12	-0.23	+0.06	+0.10	+0.17	<u>+0.49</u>	-0.23	-0.13
IV with I	<u>+0.70</u>	-0.10	-0.02	-0.16	-0.22	-0.21	-0.23	
IV with II	-0.11	-0.21	+0.05	+0.10	-0.02	<u>+0.75</u>	-0.18	
IV with III †	<u>+0.82</u>	-0.07	+0.33	+0.05	-0.12	-0.08	-0.22	-0.17
V with III †	<u>+0.73</u>	-0.14	+0.20	-0.10	-0.16	-0.14	-0.23	-0.18

(† prints of these counts appear at the end of this Appendix)

Note that positive offsets were not tested; by inspection they were obviously irrelevant for I with II, but were indirectly covered in the comparison of V with II by offsets '0' to '-4'.

The best answer for the two Ferrabosco counts (I with II) of $r = +0.49$ at offset '-5', is statistically significant and entirely acceptable, being much more significant than its best competitor at $r = +0.17$. The other best results are outstandingly good, without competition and they confirm the hypothesis of the pitch difference of a fourth between the two Ferrabosco clef-sets, and the relative pitches between Ferrabosco and the Byrd–Tallis works quoted.

FURTHER CLEF CONFIGURATIONS

Examination of the ranges associated with the clefs extraneous to the two basic sets suggested (without computer runs) that these clefs fitted into the established sets in their natural and logical order, as shown below (the original main clefs are underlined):

Clef-set A	<u>C_1</u>	C_2	<u>C_3</u>	<u>C_4</u>	F_3	<u>F_4</u>
Clef-set B	<u>G_2</u>	C_1	<u>C_2</u>	<u>C_3</u>	C_4	<u>F_3</u>

The new F_3/C_4 range appears to fit between Tenor and Bass, say Baritone, whilst C_2/C_1 fits as a range intermediate between Soprano and Alto, both C_4 and C_1 in these instances requiring transposition down a fourth. These new pairings account for all but one of the eighteen non-basic pieces; the eighteenth item has F_5 for its lowest part, with F_4 immediately above – these ranges would fit as Bass and Baritone, without transposition, and must therefore be left as the sole oddity in 68 extremely orderly items.

SUMMARY OF RANGES

These are expressed in the basic Ferrabosco pitch base, which equates with the basic Byrd and Tallis base and needs upwards transposition of a minor third to bring it into line with modern pitch.

COMPASS (SEMITONES)

Soprano	35 (*g*) to 56 (*e²*)	21
S/A	32 (*e*) to 52 (*c²*)	20
(intermediate)		
Alto	28 (*c*) to 50 (*bb²*)	22
Tenor	25 (*A*) to 47 (*g¹*)	22
Baritone	23 (*G*) to 42 (*d¹*)	19
Bass	18 (*D*) to 40 (*c¹*)	22

Table 5:1: Counts, as discussed earlier, for Ferrabosco types A and A★ (shown in the X columns) and for types B and B★ (Y columns).

Note	Soprano				Alto				Tenor				Bass				Note (c¹=40)
	X LO	X HI	Y LO	Y HI	X LO	X HI	Y LO	Y HI	X LO	X HI	Y LO	Y HI	X LO	X HI	Y LO	Y HI	
E													9				20
F													24				21
F♯													1				22
G													5			8	23
G♯																	24
A					1											15	25
B♭					1											3	26
B					1												27
c					52												28 c
c♯																	29
d					11				9		7						30
e♭																	31
e					12												32
f					12		6				33						33
f♯					1						1						34
g					13		14				2		2				35
g♯																	36
a	3				2		12				1		9				37
b♭	1						1						24				38
b	3																39
c¹	6		2										4			2	40 c¹
c♯¹	4		1														41
d¹	14		10				1		7							17	42
e♭¹									5							6	43
e¹	2		2						10							1	44
f¹			4			2			35								45
f♯¹			2														46
g¹			5			15			7		10						47
g♯¹																	48
a¹			1			33					30						49
b♭¹						1		1			4						50
b¹																	51
c²								31									52 c²
c♯²																	53
d²		10						2									54
e♭²		16															55
e²		7															56
f²				2													57
f♯²																	58
g²				25													59

Table 5:2: Counts for Byrd, *TCM* 2 (shown in the *X* columns) and (*Y* columns) for Ferrabosco types A, A★ and B, B★ (the last two reduced by five semitones).

	Soprano				Alto				Tenor				Bass				
	X		Y		X		Y		X		Y		X		Y		Note
Note	LO	HI	LO	HI	LO	HI	LO	HI	LO	HI	LO	HI	LO	HI	LO	HI	(c^1=40)
D															8		18
$E\flat$																	19
E													4		24		20
F													21		27		21
$F\sharp$															1		22
G															5		23
$G\sharp$																	24
A									3		8						25
$B\flat$									1		1						26
B											1						27
c					4		6		20		85						28 c
$c\sharp$											1						29
d					6		25		1		11						30
$e\flat$																	31
e					1		24				1			1			32
f					5		13							4			33
$f\sharp$					2		1										34
g			2		6		13							3		4	35
$g\sharp$			1														36
a	6		13		1		3			1				9		26	37
$b\flat$			1							1				5		30	38
b	3		5											1		1	39
c^1	6		10							4				2		4	40 c¹
$c\sharp^1$	4		6														41
d^1	3		19							6		17					42
$e\flat^1$										1		5					43
e^1	2		3							10		40					44
f^1	1					3		3		1		39					45
$f\sharp^1$																	46
g^1						19		46		1		7					47
$g\sharp^1$																	48
a^1						3		35									49
$b\flat^1$								1									50
b^1																	51
c^2		14		2													52 c²
$c\sharp^2$																	53
d^2		11		35													54
$e\flat^2$				16													55
e^2				7													56
f^2																	57
$f\sharp^2$																	58
g^2																	59

Table 5:3: Counts for Byrd and Tallis of *TCM* 2 (reduced to pitch base of *E*); these are shown in the X columns. The Y columns show Ferrabosco types A, A⋆ and B, B⋆ (the last two reduced by five semitones).

Note	Soprano X LO	Soprano X HI	Soprano Y LO	Soprano Y HI	Alto X LO	Alto X HI	Alto Y LO	Alto Y HI	Tenor X LO	Tenor X HI	Tenor Y LO	Tenor Y HI	Bass X LO	Bass X HI	Bass Y LO	Bass Y HI	Note (c¹=40)
D													2		8		18
Eb													1				19
E													24		24		20
F													70		27		21
F#													2		1		22
G									3				13		5		23
G#									1				1				24
A									28		8		4				25
Bb									12		1						26
B									3		1						27
c					20		6		69		85						28 c
c#					1				2		1						29
d					60		25		11		11						30
eb					1				1								31
e					18		24		2		1			2			32
f					22		13		2					11			33
f#	2				4		1		1					1			34
g	13		2		15		13		2					15		4	35
g#	1		1		1		1							3			36
a	25		13		4		3			2				35		26	37
bb	9		1		2					2				25		30	38
b	8		5							1				7		1	39
c¹	27		10							18				17		4	40 c¹
c#¹	7		6							1				1			41
d¹	20		19			2				37		17		3			42
eb¹	1					1				4		5					43
e¹	6		3			2				35		40					44
f¹	5					15		3		26		39					45
f#¹	1					1				1							46
g¹	1					75		46		7		7					47
g#¹	1					1				1							48
a¹	2					39		35		2							49
bb¹						7		1									50
b¹		2				1											51
c²		46		2		4											52 c²
c#²		1															53
d²		37		35													54
eb²		5		16													55
e²		15		7													56
f²		9															57
f#²		1															58
g²		6															59

6

JOHN BALDWIN AND CHANGING CONCEPTS OF TEXT UNDERLAY

DAVID MATEER

An important consequence of the dissemination of humanist ideas among continental theorists and musicians at the beginning of the sixteenth century was the emergence of an intense concern with language and a recognition of the primacy of the text. This new word-consciousness manifested itself in the efforts of composers to adapt their rhythms to the accentual properties of speech and to pattern musical phrases according to textual syntax. Improvements in declamation were also advocated with a view to ensuring the comprehensibility of the words, and composers – aware of the advantages of syllabic over melismatic writing as a means of achieving this end – gradually abandoned the florid style in favour of a more word-dominated approach to composition. This change of attitude had a profound effect not only on the new music that was being written but also on a large body of older polyphony, of which the melismata were retrospectively subjected to a process of syllabification by later editors and scribes. In this connection Hans Albrecht has noted the increased use in continental sources of signs for textual repeats, the so-called *ditto-* (or *iterum-* or *idem-*) signs, by means of which 'it was possible to set long melodies, originally sung, one might assume, to one syllable, in a straightforward or fairly straightforward syllabic style'.[1] From a comparison of individual works as they appear in earlier and later sources – the earlier sources without *ditto*-signs, the later ones with them – Albrecht concludes that 'older pieces in later copies have their text more precisely aligned and, with the help especially of text repeats, more densely set'.

Developments similar to those on the European mainland were also taking place in England, though at a slightly later date and for somewhat different reasons. Composers here were no doubt aware of continental trends, and may have absorbed humanist ideas vicariously through the influence of French and German contemporaries, but in the main it was not so much the new learning as the Reformation that provided the impulse towards syllabic setting and

1 'Humanismus: B. Humanismus und Musik', *Die Musik in Geschichte und Gegenwart* 6 (1957), col. 902, quoted in translation in Don Harrán, *Word–Tone Relations in Musical Thought from Antiquity to the Seventeenth Century*, *Musicological Studies and Documents* 40 (Neuhausen-Stuttgart 1986), p. 89.

intelligibility. The melismatic character of much insular polyphony had constraints imposed upon it during the latter half of Henry VIII's reign, but it was not entirely suppressed, and in the 1550s and 1560s the old style had a second lease of life in the antiphons, Canticles and psalm-motets of Tallis, Tye, Sheppard, White, Parsons and William Mundy. Indeed, by borrowing textures and metrical schemes from the large-scale *Magnificat* and votive antiphon, many of these settings affirm their composers' allegiance to an earlier, more florid, phase of the native tradition. Much of this repertory survives only in sources that date from the second and third decades of Elizabeth's reign, by which time humanism had made a belated impression on English musical taste through its contact with the work of continental theorists like Zarlino and composers such as Lassus and the elder Ferrabosco. Most of these sources contain music of a wide stylistic diversity, so that the latest Byrd motets often rub shoulders with pieces by Taverner, Fayrfax, Aston and Johnson from the early part of the century. Given this juxtaposition, it is hardly surprising that the scribes occasionally carried over aesthetic principles from the more modern items they had copied and applied them extraneously to the old-fashioned melismatic works. This anachronistic process of 'humanizing' earlier music is nowhere more apparent than in matters of text underlay.

One of the most interesting and versatile of these late Elizabethan scribes was John Baldwin, an amateur composer and 'singing man of Windsor', who later became a member of the Chapel Royal.[2] He was wholly responsible for at least three collections: GB-Och 979–83, a set of partbooks probably started in the late 1570s which contains over 170 pieces, most of them vocal and sacred; 'My Ladye Nevells Booke', an important source of Byrd's keyboard music, which was finished in 1591; and his so-called 'Commonplace Book' (GB-Lbl R.M. 24.d.2) which was compiled over a period of roughly twenty years from c. 1586 to c. 1606.[3] These manuscripts are as remarkable for their catholicity of taste as they are impressive in their command of different notational styles and musical formats. Baldwin also repaired and completed the Forrest-Heyther collection of masses (GB-Ob Mus. Sch. e. 376–81) which passed into his hands around 1581;[4] in addition he copied two pieces into the Dow partbooks (GB-Och 984–8),

---

2   His career and achievements are summarized in Roger Bray, 'John Baldwin', *Music and Letters* 56 (1975), pp. 55–9. For two recent studies see Hilary Gaskin, 'Music copyists in late sixteenth-century England, with particular reference to the manuscripts of John Baldwin' (Diss., U. of Cambridge 1985), and *eadem*, 'Baldwin and the Nevell hand', in Alan Brown and Richard Turbet (eds.), *Byrd Studies* (Cambridge 1992), pp. 159–73.

3   For further details see Roger Bray, 'The part-books Oxford, Christ Church, MSS 979–983: an index and commmentary', *Musica Disciplina* 25 (1971), pp. 179–97; *idem*, 'British Library, MS Royal 24.d.2: an index and commentary', *[Royal Musical Association] Research Chronicle* 12 (1974), pp. 137–51, and the facsimile edition introduced by Jessie Ann Owens in *Renaissance Music in Facsimile* 8 (New York 1987); Elizabeth Crownfield, 'British Library MS R.M. 24.d.2 and Oxford, Christ Church Library MSS 979–83; two Elizabethan musical sources copied by John Baldwin' (Diss., U. of New York 1985); Alan Brown, '"My Lady Nevell's Book" as a source of Byrd's keyboard music', *Proceedings of the Royal Musical Association* 95 (1968/9), pp. 29–39.

4   See John D. Bergsagel, 'The date and provenance of the Forrest-Heyther collection of Tudor masses', *Music and Letters* 44 (1963), pp. 240–8, and John Milsom's introduction to the facsimile edition *Renaissance Music in Facsimile* 15 (New York 1986).

presumably in or after 1603, when their subsequent owner, Giles Thompson, became Dean of Windsor.[5] Although the *tenor* book is missing from *Och* 979–83, scholars have nevertheless used the anthology as a central source for editions of the Latin works of most Tudor composers from Taverner to Byrd. For present purposes, it is the very breadth of its chronological spectrum that makes it the ideal testing ground for an examination of changing attitudes to underlay from c. 1520 to c. 1600.

The term 'overlay' would perhaps describe Baldwin's working methods more accurately, in view of the strong evidence that there is to suggest that he copied the music above previously inscribed text. For instance, in Sheppard's *Beati omnes* (*Och* 979, no. 2) a supernumerary repetition of the text unit 'et bene tibi erit' appears beneath a portion of empty staff because the dittography was discovered only during the music copying process; moreover, occasional cramping of the underlay at times obliges Baldwin to extend the original staff lines into the right-hand margin of the page to allow the notes and syllables to regain their proper alignment at the beginning of the next line. Another difficulty with copying the text first was that the scribe could not easily estimate how much staff-space to leave for the melisma of a penultimate syllable. He could either postpone entering the last syllable of the text unit until he had copied its music – in which case the extent of the melisma would be known and accuracy of alignment assured – or he could write out the final word in its entirety at the beginning of the melisma in the hope that the singer would know to place the last syllable at the end of the musical phrase. With the first possibility there was always the risk that the scribe would forget to complete the final word after copying the music, and indeed one does sometimes find the last syllable missing from the end of florid passages. The problem with the second option was that the singer might take the underlay at its face value, i.e. construe it as indicating a terminal melisma. To avoid such a misunderstanding, and to show the final syllable's true position, the scribe occasionally repeated it at the end of the *neuma*.[6] This duplication, which is rare in Henrician sources before c. 1540, occurs not infrequently in the work of Elizabethan scribes when copying melismatic music. In such cases it appears that Baldwin also intended the melisma to fall on the penultimate syllable of the text unit; thus, in the *contratenor* of Sheppard's respond and prose *Gaude, gaude, gaude Maria Virgo cunctas* (*Och* 981, no. 98) we find 'et hominem genuisti___ti', but in the written-out repeat of the section containing this phrase the underlay is given as 'et hominem genuis—-ti'. Similarly at the end of the 'Annae mulieris' section of Tallis's *Salve intemerata* Baldwin writes 'Jesu Christi___ti' in the *superius* and *contratenor* (*Och* 979 and 981, no. 46), but when he copied the same extract into R.M. 24.d.2 he clearly indicated that the

---

5   David Mateer, 'Oxford, Christ Church Music MSS 984–8: an index and commentary', *[Royal Musical Association] Research Chronicle* 20 (1986–7), pp. 1–18.

6   The repetition may also have acted as a mnemonic aid; see Edward E. Lowinsky, 'The problem of text underlay', *The Medici Codex of 1518* (Monuments of Renaissance Music 3–5), 3 vols. (Chicago 1968), pp. 90–107.

melismata should occur on the paroxytone – 'Jesu Chris——-ti'. The evidence of printed sources further supports this view; in the *contratenor* of Tallis's *Dum transisset* (*Och* 981, no. 21) Baldwin gives the underlay as 'et Maria___a', but recourse to the 1575 *Cantiones Sacrae* shows that this meant 'et Mari——-a'.[7]

The repetition of the final syllable at the end of a phrase may also have been used by the scribe as a means of transforming what was originally a terminal melisma into a penultimate one. Vocalizing on the closing vowel of a text unit had, of course, a well-established precedent not only in Gregorian chant but also in much medieval and early renaissance polyphony. Nevertheless, sixteenth-century theorists generally discouraged the practice because it emphasized through melodic extension that part of a word that was invariably weak and in so doing offended a basic tenet of the humanist creed concerning the word–tone relationship, namely that music should be moulded to the length and brevity of syllables.[8] Although there is some evidence to show that even by the late 1540s English taste was beginning to reject terminal melismata, they persisted – along with the more usual penultimate type – until well into the first decade of Elizabeth's reign. By the mid-1570s, however, they were considered decidedly old-fashioned, and as such were unlikely to survive the modernizing tendencies of scribes like Baldwin and Dow. Thus, in the Gloria of Taverner's Mass *Gloria tibi trinitas* the treble of the Forrest-Heyther partbooks sings 'cum Sancto Spiri-NS -tusL8', but in *Och* 982 (no. 133) Baldwin effectively transfers the eight-note melisma to the penultimate syllable by repeating '-tu' at the end of the *cauda*.[9] The result is a conflation that appears to preserve the underlay of his source while at the same time presenting us with his revision of it. Similar vestigial traces of Baldwin's exemplar lie close to the surface of the instructive Example 6:1.

Example 6:1: Sheppard, *Non conturbetur cor vestrum* (II) (*Och* 982, no. 96)

---

7   It is worth emphasizing the point that in such circumstances no text repetition was intended by the scribe. This cautionary note is sounded because of statements like the following from the critical commentary to Edwin Warren's edition of Fayrfax's *Lauda vivi Alpha et O*:

'[bars] 60, 65, syllable "ma" in 60 repeated in 65, implying repetition of "praefulgidissima"'

The source under discussion is the Henrician set of partbooks belonging to Peterhouse, Cambridge (now in the University Library and catalogued as MSS 471–4); see Edwin B. Warren (ed.), 'Robert Fayrfax: Collected Works', 3 vols., *Corpus Mensurabilis Musicae* 17 (Rome 1959), III, pp. 34 and 56.

8   In the vast majority of cases it is apparent from context that theorists used the words 'long' and 'short' in the general sense of accented and unaccented. For the restricted circumstances under which the terminal melisma was considered permissible, see Harrán, *Word–Tone Relations*, pp. 140–2, 207–8, 242–3, *et passim*.

9   The symbols NS and SL indicate respectively syllabic setting and the slurring of two notes (or more if a figure is added). Hugh Benham follows Baldwin in 'John Taverner: I, Six-part Masses', *Early English Church Music* 20 (London 1978), pp. 21–2.

Here the suggestion is that the bipartite extension of the point was originally sung to the final syllable, that Baldwin altered this from a terminal to a penultimate melisma by repeating '-tis' at the end of the phrase, and that he introduced a second '-ta-' after the first rest as confirmation of this reading.[10] Thomas Morley, whose attitude to the correlation of words and music was plainly directed by the humanist aesthetic of Zarlino, seems to provide theoretical justification for such scribal intervention. Precepts such as the following, although primarily aimed at the budding composer, have clear implications for the scribe too:

We must also have a care so to applie the notes to the wordes, as in singing there be no barbarisme committed: that is, that we cause no sillable which is by nature short be expressed by manie notes or one long note, nor no long sillable bee expressed with a shorte note.[11]

Thus in the majority of cases Baldwin does not even bother to repeat the final syllable, but simply relocates it at the end of the phrase, thereby removing all trace of the original terminal melisma. In his version of Taverner's *Gaude plurimum* this happens on some 30 occasions, though at times the alterations themselves give rise to accentuation that is just as improper; at 'spem certam tradidit', for instance, melismata that occur on the final syllable in earlier sources appear in Baldwin on the equally weak penultima.[12] Baldwin's idea of what constituted good word-setting may have been derived from a study of the Tallis–Byrd *Cantiones,* a copy of which is bound up with the Christ Church partbooks; his principles of text underlay are certainly consistent with those operating in the print with regard to the rarity of terminal melismata and the melodic emphasis given to the second-last syllable of a text unit, irrespective of its accentuation.[13]

Other ways in which Baldwin dealt with the problem of terminal melismata involved the use of the *ditto*-sign ⫶⫶. In the vast majority of cases, of course, this fulfils its normal function of abbreviating the re-statement of a text unit that has already been given in full, as at the second 'gloria *haec est omnibus sanctis eius*' in the middle line of Plate 1. Similarly, if only part of the phrase is required,

10 The '-tis ta-' syllables are in effect redundant. For a literal transcription of this passage see David Chadd (ed.), 'John Sheppard: I, Responsorial Music', *Early English Church Music* 17 (London 1977), pp. 69–71; Baldwin's intentions are correctly realized in David Wulstan (ed.), *John Sheppard Collected Works I: Office Responds and Varia* (*Voces Musicales* Series 1: 6), p. 58. The phenomenon recurs in Tye's *Cantate Domino* at 'in manicis ferreis' (*Och* 981, no. 122); see Nigel Davison (ed.), 'Christopher Tye: III, Ritual Music and Motets', *Early English Church Music* 33 (London 1987), p. 72, Bass 1, bb. 153–6, where Baldwin's underlay is again reproduced unquestioningly.

11 Thomas Morley, *A Plaine and Easie Introduction to Practicall Musicke* (London 1597; facs. Farnborough 1971), p. 178.

12 Compare the edition in *Tudor Church Music* 3, which corresponds in most respects to Baldwin's version, with that in Hugh Benham (ed.), 'John Taverner: II, Votive Antiphons', *Early English Church Music* 25 (London 1981), which is based on Henrician sources and the Sadler partbooks (*GB-Ob* Mus. e. 1–5). For examples of this process at work in a more modern piece compare the treatment of 'in Domino' and 'et hoc nunc et usque in seculum' near the end of White's *Domine non est exaltatum* as given by Baldwin in *Tudor Church Music* 5, pp. 83–4, and Sadler in David Mateer (ed.), 'Robert White: II, Six-Part Latin Psalms; Votive Antiphons', *Early English Church Music* 29 (London 1983), pp. 98–100.

13 A few of Byrd's more modern motets display greater variety and sophistication in this respect; see Craig Monson's editorial notes to 'Cantiones Sacrae (1575)', *The Byrd Edition* 1 (London 1977), pp. xii–xiii.

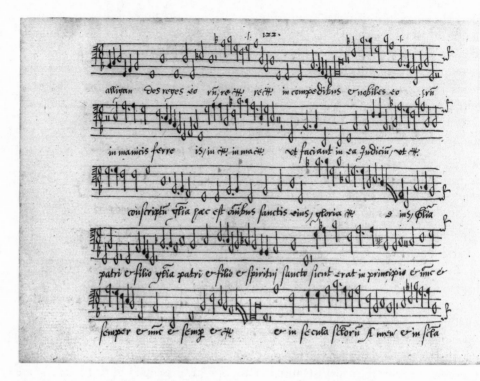

Plate 1: Christopher Tye's *Cantate Domino* (*GB-Och* 983, no. 122)

the point from which the repeat should begin is usually indicated by preceding the *ditto*-sign with the appropriate word or syllable, as at '[Ad] alligandos reges eorum re*ges eorum*' at the top of the same page. Even when the sign is used without a prefix its significance is nearly always unambiguous, as for instance, when it accompanies the repetition of a point whose texting may be inferred from a previous appearance. This having been said, however, there are clear cases where the commonly understood imperative of the *ditto*-sign to repeat underlay cannot plausibly be obeyed, as in Example 6:2.

Example 6:2: Tallis, Lamentations (II) (*Och* 979, no. 41)

Here repetition of the complete text unit is impossible because of insufficient notes; even a partial repeat consisting of 'solempnitatem' is unlikely, for had this been the scribe's intention its opening syllable would doubtless have accompanied the *ditto*-sign. Furthermore, although the melisma has the requisite number of pitches, its rhythmic structure is such that any attempt to set 'solempnitatem' to it would do serious violence to the verbal accentuation. The implication must be that in this context the *ditto*-sign has a significance additional to that which requires the singer to repeat text. This secondary meaning will become plain in the course of discussing Example 6:3, which shows two of Baldwin's manuscripts in apparent disagreement with respect to the density and location of the underlay of the same passage.

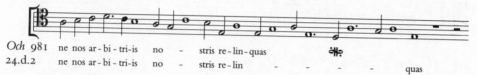

Example 6:3: Wood, *Exsurge Domine* (*Och*, no. 30; section 'Perfice illud')

The later, second reading explicitly demonstrates the scribe's predilection for penultimate melismata; the first, which is earlier and more ambiguous, might represent a terminal melisma in the exemplar being modernized, ostensibly by text repetition. However, if repetition is ruled out, as it surely must be in Example 6:2, one is bound to explore the possibility that the two manuscripts convey the same information in ways that are different only because they were copied at different times. Their readings, in fact, are not as irreconcilable as they might first appear. We have seen that the duplication of the final syllable was a common device for converting a terminal into a penultimate melisma; if the *ditto*-sign after 'relinquas' is taken to mean 'repeat the last syllable' – as opposed to 'repeat the previous word(s)' – then the reading in *Och* 981 can be equated with that in *Lbl* R.M. 24.d.2. Baldwin's initial uncertainty about the validity of some of his scribal initiatives, particularly those effecting the suppression of terminal melismata, may explain why he deferred to his exemplar by incorporating its underlay into the first reading.[14] On the other hand, the second reading of Example 6:3 shows that by the time he came to compile the Commonplace Book Baldwin had lost his earlier inhibitions, and was re-positioning melismata without compunction. If this theory is correct, the difficulties that surround the *ditto*-sign in Example 6:2 are resolved. Assuming that Baldwin's exemplar treated the untexted five-note ascent as a vocalize on the last syllable of 'solempnitatem' (as do the Sadler partbooks – the earliest and best source of Tallis's setting), then on the evidence of Example 6:3 the *ditto*-sign that follows should be regarded not as an instruction to repeat text, but rather to change a terminal into a penultimate melisma.[15]

The case for broadening our interpretation of Baldwin's *ditto*-sign to embrace this function is further strengthened by Examples 6:4–6:6, seemingly enigmatic cases.

14 Similar retention of his source's underlay has already been noted in Example 6:1.
15 The word is repeated in *Tudor Church Music* 6, p. 116, and in the edition prepared by Philip Brett (Oxford 1969), where it appears in italics as an editorial suggestion.

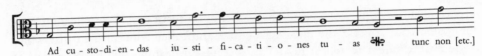

Example 6:4: Mundy, *Beati immaculati* (Och 981, no. 57)

Example 6:5: Tye, *Cantate Domino* (Och 982, no. 122)

Example 6:6: Mundy, *Vox Patris* (Och 983, no. 136)

In the first of these the sign cannot conceivably mean word repetition, with only one untexted note available. Again, Baldwin is probably following the underlay of his source in aligning the last syllable of 'tuas' with the B♭, though he uses the *ditto*-sign as a way of signalling his belief that its proper place is beneath the *A*. The curious situation in the next example no doubt arose from the omission of 'novum' from Baldwin's exemplar. The untexted minims G and *A* would then have been perceived as a short melisma sung to the last syllable of 'canticum'. The *ditto*-sign was therefore applied not to indicate a verbal repeat – for none of the previous words, all of which are of three syllables, would fit – but to ensure that the underlay was distributed 'can-NS –ti-SL3 -cumNS'. Only later was the *ditto*-sign rendered redundant by the insertion of the missing word. The last extract illustrates much the same point; the sign cannot be construed as an injunction to reiterate any of the previous text, for the melisma will not accommodate 'dilectissimi', and to repeat 'quae' and/or 'mea' would be nonsensical. Here its only justification is as a directive to the singer to vocalize on the penultima.

This new interpretation of the *ditto*-sign can be shown to apply even in instances where text repetition is not entirely beyond the bounds of possibility. I shall restrict myself to two examples only; in Tallis's *Salve intemerata* there is some disagreement among the concordances about the underlay of 'mortalibus' in the *medius* part (see Ex. 6:7).

Example 6:7: (Och 980, no. 46)

A terminal melisma is prescribed by *GB-Lbl* Harley 1709, *GB-Ob* Tenbury 356, the Sadler manuscripts (*Ob* Mus. e. 2 and the 'Willmott' manuscript at Spetchley Park, Worcester) and the earlier of the two copies in the 'Henrician' partbooks belonging to Peterhouse, Cambridge. This reading, which was also no doubt that of Baldwin's exemplar, is modified by his application of the *ditto*-sign; this advances the final syllable to the end of the phrase, which is where it is found in the later Peterhouse copy and two seventeenth-century sources – *GB-Ob* Tenbury 342 and 808. Significantly, no source calls for the repetition of text. In the two upper parts of Taverner's *O splendor gloriae* Baldwin allocates the syllables of 'assideas' in such a way as to create penultimate melismata, but in the middle voice he treats the word as a terminal melisma with *ditto*-sign. Here the function of the sign is obvious: it is to establish uniformity by projecting '-as' to the end of the point so that the three voices can finish together with the same syllable.[16]

Less frequently, the final syllable of a text-phrase may be found after – as well as before – the *ditto*-sign. The fact that their collocation has the same meaning and function as in the cases discussed above in which they appear separately, is demonstrated by Example 6:8, which gives four versions of the same passage from Mundy's *Vox Patris* as copied by the scribe of *GB-Lcm* 2035, by Sadler in the Willmott manuscript, and by Baldwin in *Och* 979 and *Lbl* R.M. 24.d.2:

Example 6:8

It is not easy to reconstruct with any certainty Mundy's original text from such divergent readings, but it doubtless shared with the grammatically correct Willmott and *Lcm* variants a common melismatic treatment of the final syllable. Predictably 24.d.2 shows that the duplication of '-la' in *Och* 979 shifts the melisma to the penultima, and confirms that the *ditto*-sign here does not imply text repetition. On this basis one would be justified in thinking that when Baldwin wrote 'oleo laetitiae ⌐ -ae' in the second bass part of Mundy's *Eructavit cor meum* (*Och* 983, no. 135), he meant 'oleo laetiti——ae'.[18] The terminal melisma

---

16 For the underlay as Baldwin conceived it, see *TCM* 3, p. 107; for Sadler's unmodernized reading, see *EECM* 25, p. 87.

17 The extract appears a fifth higher in *Lcm* 2035.

18 See Frank Ll. Harrison (ed.), 'William Mundy: Latin Antiphons and Psalms', *Early English Church Music* 2 (London 1962), p. 129 (bb. 120–1) where 'laetitiae' is repeated.

that Baldwin alters is preserved in *GB-Ob* Mus. Sch. e. 423 – usually a very reliable source, with its reading in this instance probably close to the composer's original thoughts; it also survives in the corresponding passage in the first bass (*Och* 981), with which Baldwin, for some reason, did not tamper. Another example occurs near the end of White's second *Domine quis habitabit*; according to Sadler the underlay of the first bass should read 'qui facit haec___' (*GB-Ob* Tenbury 1486), but Baldwin gives it as 'qui facit haec ⁈ haec' (*Och* 981, no. 131). Again this appears to be just an expedient for the latter to nullify what was originally a terminal melisma, thus bringing it into line with the penultimate melismata that characterize his treble and *contratenor* parts (*Och* 982 and 980) at that point.[19]

The editors of volume 5 of *Tudor Church Music* responded to the *ditto*-sign in the last example by repeating the text unit, and even recent scholars have considered this to be the only possible interpretation. Consequently, most editions that use Baldwin's manuscripts as a basic source suffer from overloaded text underlay. A prime example of this is the edition of Mundy's *Vox Patris* in *EECM* 2, which is heavily dependent on *Och* 979–83. Had the evidence of the concordances been more judiciously weighed, a less narrow view of the function of the *ditto*-sign might have emerged which would have prevented the editor from making text repetitions that the scribe never contemplated. The following verbal repeats should therefore be expunged, leaving the melismata to be vocalized on the final syllable:

EECM 2 bars		voice	text	omitted from
34–5	28–30	A	'macula'	*Lbl* R.M. 24.d.2, Willmott, *Lcm* 2035
39	77–8	A	'dulcedinis'	Willmott
40	85–8	A	'dilectissimi'	Willmott
41	90–1	A	'dilectissimi'	Willmott
44	110–13	T¹	'gratia'	*Ob* e. 423
44	112–13	A	'gratia'	Willmott
44–5	115–18	A	'gratia'	Willmott
54	182–3	A	'Libano'	Willmott
57–8	205–6	A²	'Esther'	Willmott
58	207–10	A²	'nobilissima'	Willmott
58–9	209–13	A¹	'nobilissima'	Willmott
63–4	232–3	T¹	'desiderio'	*Ob* e. 423

Furthermore, certain assumptions can safely be made about the *ditto*-signs that occur in those parts of this work for which concordances have not survived. Thus the repetition of 'gratia' should doubtless be omitted not only from the Soprano (bars 109–10 and 117–19) but also from the second Bass (bars 114–18) and second Tenor (bars 113–15). The same applies to 'nobilissima' in the two Soprano parts (bars 208–10 and 211–13 respectively) and in the second and third Basses (bars

---

19 See *TCM* 5, p. 101, parts labelled *sexta pars* and *discantus*; also *EECM* 29, p. 30, where an attempt has been made to restore the original underlay.

211–13 and 209–12); the repeats of 'desiderio' and 'coronaberis' should similarly be excised from the Soprano (bars 232–4 and 243–6) and from the second Bass (bars 242–4 and 246–9).[20]

It would be wrong, of course, to assume from the above that Baldwin denied the possibility of ever extending melismatically the final syllable of a text unit. At the end of the first line of Plate 1 the *signum congruentiae* above the dotted minim D serves to couple that note with the last syllable of 'eorum' beside which another *signum* has been placed, thereby converting what at first was a medial into a terminal melisma. However, his practice of copying the verbal text first creates a number of illusory instances, and it appears that at such times responsibility for co-ordinating the final syllable with the last note of the phrase passed to the performer.[21] To indicate this Baldwin frequently places an oblique stroke at the end of the point concerned; for instance, in the 'Gloriosa Domine' section of Taverner's *O splendor gloriae* he writes 'tua est maiestas___/' (*Och* 983), but the same passage in 24.d.2 appears as 'tua est maies—-tas'. These are to be taken neither as alternatives nor as a change of opinion; rather, the latter is a realization of the former.[22] Just as often, however, Baldwin omits the oblique, but still expects the singer to make the necessary adjustment in the text placement. Thus, when he copied Robert Parsons's *O bone Jesu* into the Dow partbooks he gave the underlay of one of the points as 'clamavi ad te Domine___' (*Och* 984, no. 53), but the same phrase in *Och* 979 (no. 54) appears as 'clamavi ad te Domi--ne'. Again, in the *contratenor* of Byrd's *Tristitia et anxietas* (*Och* 980, no. 69) Baldwin underlays the final statement of 'in dolore' in such a way as to suggest a terminal melisma, but it is evident from the 1589 *Cantiones* (no. 6) that the last syllable belongs to the end of the phrase.[23] Similarly, the word 'rex' two lines from the bottom of Plate 2 is ambiguously associated with the minim f^{1}, but reference to the opening of the motet, which is here exactly recapitulated, shows that its true position is beneath the breve e^{1}. However, when a point appears with a terminal melisma in all or most of the parts, or when some other consistency of usage can be discerned, then it is probably safe to assume that this was the scribe's intention.[24]

20 The 'gratia' in bar 117 (T^{2}) and the 'coronaberis' in bars 247–8 (S) should probably end with a terminal melisma despite Baldwin's duplication of the final syllable. This duplication has also inspired a number of editorial additions to the underlay: bb. 36 (T^{1}) 'non est in'; 83–4 (T^{2}) 'turtu-'; 185–6 (T^{2}) 'altissi-'; 247–8 (T^{1}) 'coronabe-'.

21 This notion has a solid basis in contemporary music theory; the relevant passages from treatises by Lanfranco, Zarlino, and Stoquerus are quoted in Harrán, *Word–Tone Relations*, pp. 427 and 431–2.

22 In Mundy's *Vox Patris* the phrase given as 'mihi amabilissima___/' in T^{1} (*Och* 980) was sung 'mihi amabilissi—-ma' according to the Commonplace Book. The oblique's potential as a tool for the metamorphosis of terminal melismata is obvious. *EECM* 2, p. 34, is surely correct here in following *Ob* Mus. Sch. e. 423.

23 Alan Brown (ed.), 'Cantiones Sacrae 1 (1589)', *The Byrd Edition* 2 (London 1988), p. 48, bb. 53–6.

24 See 'et insulae' in Sheppard's *Reges Tharsis et insulae* (*EECM* 17, p. 23); also 'quae Christum in utero' in Tallis's *Gaude gloriosa* (*TCM* 6, p. 127, bb. 5–8), though the point's treatment as a terminal melisma is not evident from that edition. In Wood's *Exsurge Domine* the phrase 'quam a corporibus' is set in double imitation; the alto and bass progress in parallel tenths with the melisma falling on the penultima, while the soprano and tenor, moving in parallel sixths, have a terminal melisma.

Plate 2: Robert Johnson's *Domine in virtute tua* (*GB-Och* 979, no. 5)

Baldwin's taste for penultimate melismata at times creates anomalies such as Example 6:9.

Och 979   ar-dens de-sy-de - ri - - - - - - um
Ob Tenbury 807 ar-dens de-si-de - ri-um

Example 6:9: Tye, *Peccavimus cum patribus* (*Och*, no. 120)

So anxious was the scribe to extirpate the terminal melisma that he consigned the last syllable to the end of the point without first examining the pitch structure of the phrase. In certain pieces, however, particularly those written in accordance with the demands of 'just note and accent', the scribal imposition of penultimate melismata was actually a reactionary step. For instance, in Byrd's *O quam gloriosum* Baldwin underlays 'ierit' and 'actio' so that the melisma falls not on the stressed first syllable (as it does in the print) but on the weak penultima.[25] However, this cannot have been his intention when 'actio' appears in the *contratenor*, for there

<hr />

25 Compare the 1589 *Cantiones sacrae* I, nos. 22–3, and *Och* 979–83, no. 9.

the penultimate and antepenultimate notes of the point are repetitions of the same pitch. This automatically throws the melisma back to the first syllable, so that although he wrote 'acti--o' he must have sung 'a--ctio' as the print directs. Baldwin's reluctance to acknowledge antepenultimate melismata, even when they appear in the work of an illustrious contemporary, means that only rarely does he force them on the music of previous generations (see Ex. 6:10).

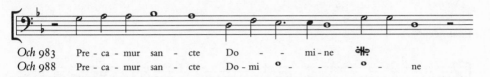

Och 983   Pre - ca - mur san - cte   Do   -   -   mi - ne
Och 988   Pre - ca - mur san - cte   Do - mi   o -   -   - o -   ne

Example 6:10: White, *Christe qui lux es et dies* (II) (*Och*, no. 78)

It is ironic that what is almost certainly the correct reading of this passage is given by Robert Dow, who perhaps more than any Elizabethan scribe sought to 'improve' the word-setting of composers by lengthening or shortening rhythmic values, dividing notes and applying slurs.[26]

Of all the measures taken by scribes to modernize the older music in their collections perhaps the most radical was the abbreviation of melismatic passages through the introduction of unauthorized verbal repeats. The trend towards more syllabic underlay becomes increasingly marked in the later collections of both Sadler and Baldwin. Thus, when the latter copied the opening of Mundy's *Maria Virgo* into 24.d.2, he inserted into the text of the first tenor repetitions of 'sanctissima' and 'gratia' that are not to be found in *Och* 979–83.[27] Similarly, in Tallis's *Salve intemerata* Sadler repeated 'permanseris'[28] and 'omnipotentem'[29] in Willmott and Tenbury 1486 at points left untexted in his earlier *Ob* Mus. e. 1–5. Morley's very general discussion of word–tone relations does not touch on the question of verbal repeats, but it is clear from certain continental treatises that they were tolerated if they formed complete or significant portions of speech, and provided there were enough notes to sustain them.[30] Baldwin indulged in unwarranted text repetition more than any other scribe; he could re-state the verbal unit either in full – for instance, after 'arma et sagittae' in the *superius* of Tye's *Miserere mei Deus* – or in part – as at 'exsurge psalterium et cithera, et cithera' in the *bassus* of the same piece.[31] The additional underlay could be

26 Both *TCM* 5, p. 170, and *EECM* 32, pp. 16–17, follow Dow. For more on his 'corrections', see Philip Brett, 'Editing Byrd – 2', *The Musical Times* 121 (1980), pp. 557–9.
27 These repeats are rightly ignored by the editor of *EECM* 2; they affect bb. 5–6 and 14–16.
28 *TCM* 6, p. 149, *Medius*, bb. 5–7.
29 Had this repeat been included by the editors of *TCM* 6, it would have appeared in the Tenor of p. 154, third system.
30 See Harrán, *Word–Tone Relations*, pp. 138–9, 151–2, 205–6, *et passim*. The repetition of single words was, however, generally deprecated.
31 *Och* 980 and 983, no. 27; this extra underlay is rightly omitted from *EECM* 33, p. 31, C¹, bb. 60–2, and pp. 37–8, B², bb. 134–6.

applied to either terminal or internal melismata; Examples 6:11 and 6:12, from Van Wilder's *Aspice Domine*, show how the sparsely texted readings of Sadler's partbooks are filled out with verbal repetitions in *Och* 979–83.

Ob e. 3   A - spi - ce   Do - mi-ne
Och 981   A - spi - ce   Do - mi - - - - - - - ne, Do - mi - - ne

Example 6:11

Ob e.1   plo - rans   plor - a - vit in noc - - - - - te
            plo - rans   plor - a - vit in noc-te   / in   noc - - te

Example 6:12

A terminal melisma could also be cancelled when text from the next point was introduced prematurely; in the treble of *O splendor gloriae* the repetition of 'pectora' precedes rather than follows Taverner's original setting of the word, because Baldwin assigns it to the descending six-note figure from the end of the previous melisma.[32] Sometimes it was necessary to alter the rhythmic structure of a line for its contours to accommodate the additional texting satisfactorily. Baldwin's adjustments are usually unobtrusive (see Ex. 6:13).

Ob Tenbury 810   in - iu - ste   e   -   gi-mus
Och 983   in - iu - ste   e   -   gi-mus   in - iu - ste   e   -   gi-mus

Example 6:13: Tye, *Peccavimus cum patribus*

Occasionally, however, the clumsiness of his adaptations makes the interference all too apparent (see Ex. 6:14).

- rens   / ac e - a - dem tu - o   pre - ci - o - sis - si - mo,   pre - ci - o - sis - si - mo

Example 6:14: Taverner, *O splendor gloriae* (*Och* 983, no. 29)

32 Compare *TCM* 3, p. 108, b. 5 (Baldwin), with *EECM* 25, p. 89, bb. 186–7 (Sadler). See also 'spem certam' and 'assumpta es' in the treble of *Gaude plurimum*; these variants, which are wisely rejected by the editors of *TCM* 3 and *EECM* 25, would have occurred at bb. 152–3 and 213–14 respectively of the latter edition. For a more modern example of this phenomenon see White's Lamentations (*a*5), and compare *TCM* 5, p. 24, bb. 2–4 (*Medius*), with *EECM* 32, p. 81, bb. 189–93 (*Countertenor*).

The text unit 'ac eadem tuo preciosissimo' should have begun at the second *D*, but Baldwin introduces it ahead of its time by setting the opening syllables to notes appropriated from the melisma on '-rens' that closed the previous point. The attempt to marry the text to this newly manufactured phrase creates a clash of musical and verbal stresses that is hardly mitigated by the rhythmic division of the second *G* and second *A* – originally a breve and semibreve respectively.[33] All scribes at some stage tinkered with the composer's rhythm to make room for supplementary underlay. Baldwin's position lies somewhere between that of Sadler, who showed considerable restraint in this respect, and Robert Dow, who perpetrated some of its worst excesses.[34]

The temptation to repeat text was particularly strong in cases where the original musical phrase was dissected by one or more rests. The ridicule to which Morley subjected such passages no doubt reflected a disapproval that was widespread among the scribes and musicians of his generation:

We must also take heed of seperating any part of a word from another by a rest, as som dunces have not slackt to do, yea one whose name is *Iohannes Dunstaple* (an ancient English author) hath not onlie devided the sentence, but in the verie middle of a word hath made two long rests ... which is one of the greatest absurdities which I have seene committed in the dittying of musicke, but to shewe you in a worde the use of the rests in the dittie, you may set a crotchet or minime rest above a coma or colon, but a longer rest then that of a minime you may not make till the sentence bee perfect...[35]

Again, this is advice for the aspiring composer, but its corollary has significance for the scribe too; if, in the course of copying a work, he encounters a rest in the middle of a phrase, he should – according to the modern view – assume the mantle of 'editor' and curtail the melisma by bringing the text unit to a conclusion at that point. This would impart meaning to the musical hiatus, thereby strengthening the syntactical bond between the text and its setting. The remaining notes of the melisma could then be sung to a repetition of all or part of the same text. A good example of this occurs in the *bassus* of Tallis's *Salve intemerata* (see Ex. 6:15).

---

33 See *EECM* 25, p. 82, Bass, bb. 128–30. A similar situation occurs at 'immortalem Filium peperisse' in the *mean* of *Gaude plurimum* (*Och* 980, no. 48), with consequent rhythmic dislocation; see *ibid.*, pp. 43–4, bb. 90–5. No edition adopts any of these readings.

34 See White's *Lamentations* (*a*5) at 'convertere ad Dominum' (first 'Jerusalem' refrain), and compare Sadler's readings in *EECM* 32, p. 80, bb. 185–95 (Tenor) with Dow's in *TCM* 5, p. 24, bb. 1–5 (Altus); also compare Dow's over-texted version of 'cor ad te semper vigilet' in the same composer's *Christe qui lux es et dies* (IV) (*TCM* 5, p. 177, bb. 5–6, Medius) with the reading in *GB-Ob* Tenbury 389 (*EECM* 32, p. 33, bb. 25–9, Mean). White's music more than most was subjected to this kind of mishandling; perhaps certain scribes could hardly believe that a composer who died as late as 1574 was capable of writing in such a conservative manner.

35 Morley, *A Plaine and Easie Introduction*, p. 178. Earlier continental theorists, also, regarded rests as an important means of clarifying the structure of the text; see Harrán, *Word–Tone Relations*, pp. 137, 157, 197, 199–201, *et passim*.

Example 6:15: Tallis, *Salve intemerata* (*Och* 983, no. 46)

The division of what were originally two breves (*G* and *F*) enables the scribe to accommodate one whole statement of the word before the *caesura*; this is then repeated in the second half of the phrase, thus avoiding the 'absurdity' of 'incorru-[rest] -ptis-NS -si-SL4 -maNS'.[36] The eradication of such old-fashioned 'hocket' effects accounts for most of the redundant verbal repeats made by Elizabethan scribes. Baldwin and Dow are among the worst offenders in this regard, but no one is entirely guiltless – not even John Sadler, who is normally a reliable witness.

Casual text repetition could also be generated by harmonic, as well as melodic, forces. In melismatic contexts the scribe might perceive pseudo-dominant to tonic relationships in the bass or leading-note to tonic motions in an upper voice as being cadential in effect, and thereby requiring closure in the underlay. Again, this type of verbal accretion probably originated in the humanist concern that the articulative power of cadences should be premised on sentence structure.[37] Morley expressed that view as follows:

Lastlie, you must not make a close (especiallie a full close) till the full sense of the words be perfect: so that keeping these rules you shall have a perfect agreement and, as it were a harmonicall concent betwixt the matter and the musicke, and likewise you shall bee perfectly understoode of the auditor what you sing...[38]

If a scribe believed that composers wrote perfect cadences only when the sense of the words was complete, then his natural reaction to untexted cadences would be to 'rectify' the omission by bringing the underlay to an immediate close and repeating the text unit, in full or in part, to the remaining notes of the melisma. Although the examples (see 6:16–6:18) of such cadentially induced repetition are all taken from Baldwin, it is not an uncommon phenomenon in the work of Dow and Sadler too.

Example 6:16: Taverner, Mass *Gloria tibi trinitas* (*Och*, no. 133)

36 The correct reading of the other sources is given in *TCM* 6, pp. 147–8. For an example involving a terminal melisma see Baldwin's treatment of the point 'dedit in opprobrium' in Tye's *Miserere mei Deus* (*Och* 979, no. 27), where the isolated six-note *cauda* is set to a repetition of 'opprobrium'. The editor of *EECM* 33 alters this to 'in opprobrium' (second Countertenor, bb. 50–2).

37 Harrán, *Word–Tone Relations*, pp. 138, 158, 197, 199–201, *et passim*.

38 Morley, *A Plaine and Easie Introduction*, p. 178.

Och 983   mi – sit   de   ce – lo,   de   ce – – lo
Ob e. 5   mi – sit   de   ce –   –   –   –   lo

Example 6:17: Tye, *Miserere mei Deus* (Och, no. 27)

Och 983   et   in   ve – ri – ta – te   tu – a, tu   –   –   –   a
Ob e. 4, Och 987 et   in   ve – ri – ta – te   tu   –   –   –   –   a

Example 6:18: White, *Manus tuae fecerunt me* (Och, no. 63)

Repeated notes in a melisma could also attract text repetition if the editor/scribe failed to appreciate that they were an intrinsic part of the old *stylus floridus* (see Ex. 6:19).

le-ten-tur et ex-sul-tent gen – tes gen   –   –   –   –   –   tes

Example 6:19: Sheppard, *Deus misereatur* (Och, no. 981, no. 3)[39]

Further examples of such verbal proliferation could be given, but those already cited should be sufficient to deter an editor from using any of Baldwin's redactions as the 'best text', at least so far as the underlay is concerned.

This study has sought to illuminate some of Baldwin's more arcane scribal practices, and to show how they relate to his primary objective of updating the underlay of the old-fashioned works in *Och* 979–83. Most of the modernizations can be detected easily with the help of concordances, but a number of pieces are unique to the collection – either in whole or in part – and it is these that present the editor with something of a dilemma. Does one practise safe musicology and produce a mere diplomatic transcription of the manuscript article which is then passed off as an edition, or should an attempt be made to restore passages suspected of being corrupt as closely as possible to their original form?[40] Given the fact that all the sources lie at an unknown number of removes from the composer's autograph, and vary in their trustworthiness as witnesses to the original texts, it is arguable that the editor has a responsibility to make such conjectural emendations as are necessary, even if the manuscript tradition depends

39 No repetition occurs in *US-NYp* Drexel 4181.
40 The problem is discussed, and the main views summarized, in Philip Brett, 'Text, context, and the early music editor', in Nicholas Kenyon (ed.), *Authenticity and Early Music* (Oxford 1988), pp. 83–114.

on a single witness. If one has some acquaintance with the various types of error or interpolation that are likely to occur, then the task of balancing the historical probabilities will be greatly facilitated.

7

SACRED SONGS IN THE CHAMBER

JOHN MILSOM

> ... the morrow after, being Friday [12 October 1537,] ... at two of the clock
> in the morning, the Queen[, Jane Seymour, was] delivered of a man-child [Edward,
> future King Edward VI] at Hampton Court beside Kingston. And the same day,
> at eight of the clock in the morning, *Te Deum* was sung in every parish church
> throughout London, with all the bells ringing in every church, and great fires
> made in every street. And at nine of the clock there was assembled at [St] Paul's
> all the orders of friars, monks, canons, priests and clerks about London, standing
> all about [St] Paul's in rich copes, with the best crosses and candlesticks of every
> parish church in London. ... and after[, ... St] Paul's choir sang an anthem [=
> antiphon] of the Trinity, with *Te Deum*, and the ninth respond [at matins] of the
> Trinity [*Summae Trinitati*], with the collect of the same. Then the king's waits and
> the waits of London played with the shawms; and after that a great peal of guns
> were shot at the Tower of London, all which solemnity was done to give laud
> and praise to God for joy of our prince.[1]

That account − ironically, a reference to the birth that ultimately had grim
consequences for Tudor church music − conveys in the most vivid terms an
impression of that music's true and original performance context. When we listen
today to works by Fayrfax, Ludford and Taverner sung by choirs such as The Taverner
Choir, The Tallis Scholars, The Sixteen or The Cardinall's Musick, it is that same
world of ceremony, splendour and solemnity that we imaginatively re-enter, a world
far removed from what goes on in most twentieth-century churches, and one which
at least some listeners no doubt would wish were still there.

---

1 William Douglas Hamilton (ed.), *A Chronicle of England during the Reigns of the Tudors, from A.D. 1485 to 1559.
By Charles Wriothesley, Windsor Herald*, vol. I (Camden Society, 2nd Series, 11; London 1875), pp. 66–7; spelling
modernized. In late medieval England, occasions of national or communal rejoicing were often marked by
the singing of the *Te Deum*; see Frank Ll. Harrison, *Music in Medieval Britain* (London 1958), pp. 65 ff., and
John Caldwell, 'The "Te Deum" in late medieval England', *Early Music* 6 (1978), pp. 188–94. Although
normally sung to its chant melody, on occasions of state a polyphonic performance is likely to have been
used; Shakespeare's report of Anne Boleyn's coronation at Westminster Abbey in *Henry VIII* (Act IV Scene I),
for example, mentions that 'the choir, / With all the choicest music in the kingdom, / Together sung *Te
Deum*'. The respond *Summae Trinitati* was sung in procession for the reception of a king and queen; see
Harrison, *Music in Medieval Britain*, p. 259. No polyphonic setting of this text is known, but the chant was
used as the *cantus firmus* of a mass by Walter Frye. For a survey of music at St Paul's in the sixteenth century
see David Scott, *The Music of St Paul's Cathedral* (London 1972), pp. 8–14.

For Fayrfax, Taverner, Ludford, Tallis, Tye, Sheppard, White, William Mundy, even William Byrd in his chorister years, that world was a reality. For composers who worked later in the sixteenth century, it had largely ceased to exist. With the passing of the Act of Uniformity in 1559 and the publication of the English Prayer Book later that year, Latin-texted ritual and votive music that had been the pride of England's choral foundations fell out of use. If it survived at all in churches, then it did so either with new English words substituted for the original ones[2] or, where liturgically appropriate, in the private worship of communities who retained the right to use Latin: the Chapel Royal and the colleges of Cambridge and Oxford. Whether or not those communities took advantage of the dispensation and allowed their choirs to sing (for example) pre-Reformation settings of the *Te Deum* and the *Magnificat* we will probably never know, for the books that were used by those choirs no longer exist, and no service-lists or first-hand accounts survive to shed light on the matter.

Yet as every editor and historian of Tudor church music knows, the Latin ritual and votive music of pre-Elizabethan England continued to circulate after 1559. Even from the limited number of manuscripts that have come down to us, we can sense how tenaciously English musicians clung to that music during Elizabeth's reign, and even into the 1620s and 1630s. Long after cathedral and church choirs had been directed towards the more sober fare of Protestant worship, people collected and re-copied the riches of the old order. More than that, new works were composed that emulated the old, some of them set to outmoded liturgical texts that were no longer part of the reformed liturgy, some with biblical texts – again in Latin – that are barely imaginable within the context of Protestant worship, and some with words that are easily construed (and were surely meant to be understood) as statements on Catholic prohibition or attacks on the Protestant faith itself. The books that contain these Latin-texted pieces, both old compositions and new, did not live in churches, but rather in private houses. The majority of them appear to have been copied by amateurs, not by church musicians. And, with a few possible exceptions, they were made for performers to use.[3]

The present chapter aims to give an introduction to those books, and to shed some light on the Elizabethan and Jacobean households to which they belonged. In the few cases where we know the identities of the copyists and owners,

---

2   See John Milsom, 'Songs, carols and *contrafacta* in the early history of the Tudor anthem', *Proceedings of the Royal Musical Association* 107 (1980/81), pp. 34–5; and John Morehen, 'The English anthem text, 1549–1660', *Journal of the Royal Musical Association* 117 (1992), pp. 69–74.

3   The most useful studies of Elizabethan music manuscripts containing Latin-texted repertory remain Joseph Kerman, 'Byrd's motets: chronology and canon', *Journal of the American Musicological Society* 14 (1961), pp. 359–82; Warwick Edwards, 'The sources of Elizabethan consort music' (Diss., U. of Cambridge 1974); and May Hofman, 'The survival of Latin sacred music by English composers, 1485–1610' (Diss., U. of Oxford 1973). Their information about the ownership, date, function, contents and structure of those manuscripts has been so fully absorbed into the musicological literature that it would be impractical to make more than a general (and generous) acknowledgement of debt to them. The present study has also benefited from the advice and comments of Alan Brown and Jason Smart.

progress has already been made in explaining why, when and where the books were made and used. Other manuscripts are more shadowy; it is often hard to penetrate the secrets of odd partbooks from otherwise lost sets, books that bear no sign of their owners' names, or merely have a pair of initials stamped on their covers. Even such obscure books, however, can sustain some close questioning. Who made them, Roman Catholics or Protestants? What criteria lay behind the choice of their contents? What performing resources, vocal or instrumental, did the compilers have in mind? Where were such books used?[4]

Those questions are asked partly with the historian in mind, but they are also bound to be of interest to the modern performer. The sound-image we habitually cultivate today of a mass by Taverner or a votive antiphon by Tallis is faithful to the conditions under which they were created: churches, choirs, ritual, magnificence. It is easy to overlook the half-century during which those conditions no longer pertained, 50 years when the music may even have been in more active and widespread use than it had been before 1559. Today we rarely consider the viability of scaled-down performances that are redolent of the Elizabethan chamber rather than the Henrician or Marian Church.

More important, it is easy to overlook the fact that the chamber context in which the old music continued to be sung and played also served as the breeding-ground for new music, works that sometimes appear to be stamped with the stylistic hallmarks of the Church but which may always have been intended for domestic use. Robert White's psalm-motets, for example, inhabit a shadowy world that might fall on either side of the divide. Possibly they were composed for use in churches, possibly for spiritual recreation in the chamber; no one knows for sure. In the case of Tallis's Elizabethan motets, and conceivably every piece of Latin-texted music that William Byrd ever composed, it is the chamber rather than the church that can lay the stronger claim. Today's performers and audiences, hungering for the sound of echoing vaults and heavenly choirs, often express a different preference. No doubt Tallis, too, would have been moved by the sound of his two Lamentations being sung by a choir in the resonant spaces of one of England's great cathedrals. But there is not a grain of evidence to show that he ever experienced the pieces in that way. In Byrd's lifetime the Mass for Four Voices would have been unthinkable in the repertory of any Anglican church choir – much to Byrd's chagrin, no doubt. Only in the nineteenth century did Byrd's masses make the move from chamber to church. Most of us find it hard not to think of those works as part of the rich legacy of Tudor church music; but this is a twentieth-century attitude, fostered partly by performers, partly by the loose terminology of publishers, editors and historians. In what follows I hope to illuminate some of the chamber contexts that provided a home for so much of what we now think of as 'Tudor church music'.

4   In the past, those questions have been directed principally to sources that include William Byrd's Latin-texted works. See for example Joseph Kerman, *The Masses and Motets of William Byrd* (London 1981), pp. 46 ff., and Alan Brown (ed.), 'Cantiones Sacrae II (1591)', *The Byrd Edition* 3 (London 1981), p. viii.

There is no better place to start than in the house of John Sadler. Thanks to David Mateer's thorough researches, Sadler has become more than just a name to us.[5] In the late 1560s, when our interest in him kindles, Sadler was a few years beyond his fiftieth birthday, and on the point of giving up his teaching career in order to take over the living of Sudborough in the diocese of Peterborough. By the time we lose sight of him in 1591 he was an old man of about eighty, had been retired from his living for more than six years, and had created two beautiful sets of music manuscripts. One of them, often known as the 'Sadler partbooks' (GB-Ob Mus. e. 1–5),[6] is the work of perhaps twenty years of collecting and copying that drew to a close around 1585. Though badly corroded by the acid content of the ink, this set none the less survives intact. Sadler's second set, begun at an unknown date and still in progress in 1591, is more ambitious in its layout, calligraphy and pictorial decoration. Few Elizabethan music manuscripts are more beautifully executed than this, and we can only regret the fact that Sadler never completed his job. Only two of the original five (or possibly six) partbooks have survived – the 'Willmott' manuscript, in private ownership, and GB-Ob Tenbury 1486.[7]

Why were these books created? David Mateer has argued that they are statements of Sadler's allegiance to the Roman Catholic Church. The repertory is certainly suggestive, for Sadler collected primarily Latin-texted music, both old and new: works from the first quarter of the sixteenth century, such as Fayrfax's *Ave Dei patris filia* and Taverner's *Gaude plurimum*, right up to pieces that are younger by 50 years or more, such as Byrd's *Deus venerunt gentes* and Morley's *Domine Dominus noster*. Mateer also detects Catholic sympathies in the ritual and biblical texts with which Sadler annotated the pages of the older set, and reads a Catholic message in some of the marginal drawings. The words taken from the Breviary are indeed hard to ignore. But the drawings are arguably more equivocal; can such tiny, stylized depictions of heads drawn into the capital letters possibly be intended as representations of the martyred Jesuit priest, Fr Edmund Campion? The musical repertory, as we shall see, was by no means collected only by Roman Catholics. And we cannot overlook the fact that all this was drawn together by an Anglican clergyman. If Sadler was indeed thinking of his impending death, expressing the views of a man who 'may well have asked to be received back into the Catholic faith' and showing remorse at having abandoned the faith of his youth through the 'guilt-ridden and penitential tone of many of the inscriptions', as Mateer suggests,[8] then we might have expected his later set of partbooks to adopt a similar tone. Its musical contents are indeed comparable. But ritual and biblical quotations, which in the older set are written over pre-ruled staves, make no appearance around the custom-ruled staves of

5   David Mateer, 'John Sadler and Oxford, Bodleian MSS Mus. e. 1–5', *Music and Letters* 60 (1979), pp. 281–95.
6   A page is reproduced in Paul Doe (ed.), 'Elizabethan Consort Music: II', *Musica Britannica* 45 (London 1988), p. xxiii.
7   A page from the 'Willmott' manuscript is reproduced in Edmund H. Fellowes, *William Byrd* (London 1936; 2/1948), pl. facing p. 72.
8   Mateer, 'John Sadler and Oxford, Bodleian MSS Mus. e. 1–5', p. 289.

the later set, where they might more easily have been accommodated. The drawings, which this time are given generous amounts of blank paper on which to flourish, cannot easily be construed as symbolic. Instead they boast their fabulous nature – a griffin, a double-headed dragon, a man-in-the-moon – not to mention their skilled penmanship and the brilliant colours that Sadler was adding right up to the time when his hand was too shaky to make further progress. Far from serving to confirm Mateer's Roman Catholic interpretation, Sadler's later set reveals only an elderly man with a taste for good Latin-texted music and handsome books – so handsome, in fact, that one wonders how often they would have been allowed within range of the spittle of singers.

A similar pride radiates from the fine partbook set copied by Robert Dow, *GB-Och* 984–8.[9] On the verso of its opening folio, each book begs the reader (in Latin) to bring clean hands to its master's treasure, 'whether you sing well or cannot sing at all'[10] – a sure indication that the books were valued no less for their visual aspect than their musical utility. The same page bears the date of 1581, which has been taken to mean the point at which copying began. This may be misleading; the various layers of repertory that David Mateer has recently identified need not have been conjoined in book form from the start, and '1581' might equally represent the point at which the various parts of the project began to come together.[11] Possibly the books were never bound permanently in Dow's lifetime, for their current binding is stamped with the initials of their second owner, convincingly identified by Mateer as Dow's friend and colleague, Giles Thomson. Since the music is copied on 'ruled paper imprinted' of the design sold by Tallis and Byrd under the conditions of their royal patent of 1575, and since the musical contents pay special tribute to Robert White, who died in 1574, it is conceivable that copying began some years before 1581.[12] Whatever that opening date may have been, the books were evidently still being filled at the time of Dow's death in 1588.

This set was copied in Oxford, specifically at All Souls College, where Dow held a fellowship. Giles Thomson apart, we know little about Dow's circle of musical friends, but in Oxford of all places we can imagine a body of people who would have valued Dow's immaculate Latin, his superb penmanship – an art he taught in the city – and his sophisticated musical tastes. Presumably the books were used at social gatherings in his rooms. A more ingenious interpretation

9 Some pages are reproduced in Philip Brett (ed.), 'Consort Songs', *Musica Britannica* 22 (London 1967), p. xx; Iain Fenlon (ed.), *Man and Music: The Renaissance* (London 1989), p. 313; and elsewhere. See also fn. 12 below.

10 This and other translations from Dow's annotations to *Och* 984–8 are taken from Morrison Comegys Boyd, *Elizabethan Music and Music Criticism* (Philadelphia 1940; 2/1962), pp. 312 ff.

11 David Mateer, 'Oxford, Christ Church Music MSS 984–8: an index and commentary', *[Royal Musical Association] Research Chronicle* 20 (1986–7), pp. 1–18.

12 On the paper used by Dow, see Iain Fenlon and John Milsom, '"Ruled paper imprinted": music paper and patents in sixteenth-century England', *Journal of the American Musicological Society* 37 (1984), pp. 147–9. The connection between *Och* 984–8 and Robert White is suggested in Mateer, 'Oxford, Christ Church Music MSS 984–8', p. 17, fn. 54. For an example of Dow's encomia to White expressed in Dow's own calligraphy, see the reproduction in David Wulstan, *Tudor Music* (London 1985), p. 304.

than this seems unnecessary. There is no pressing reason to believe that the maker
of the books projected his Roman Catholic identity on to them. There is, indeed,
no evidence to show that Dow was ever a practising Catholic. While the words
of White's five-part Lamentations (which opens the set) might indeed be read as
'thinly disguised metaphors for the bondage of the Catholic Church in England
and the hope on the part of English Catholics that their faith might be restored',[13]
Dow need not have interpreted them in that way. Possibly he placed more value
on White's restrained expressivity and decorous oratory. The fact that Dow initially
failed to connect the four sections of Byrd's *Deus venerunt gentes* – a work of far
greater significance and poignancy to the Catholics – might argue more forcibly
that he was relatively indifferent to such metaphors. It is one thing to prove
ownership of a politically sensitive text, another to claim the owner's sympathy
with its intended meaning. Even the most pointedly political of Elizabethan motet
texts were drawn from the Bible; they cannot be claimed as the unique property
of those Catholics whose oppression left them inwardly smouldering. For Robert
Dow, 'music moves the very trees and savage beasts'; 'wine and music gladden
our heart'; 'not even the words of the gloomy Jeremiah sound so sad as the sad
music of my composer'. In their original Latin, these are the comments Dow
chose to write into his partbooks. They suggest a discerning musician and an
elegant Latinist, not a Roman Catholic with a hidden agenda.

Another accomplished penman, John Baldwin, has left us the most valuable
of all Elizabethan music manuscripts, treasured today despite the loss of its tenor
partbook. Though almost identical in size and format with Robert Dow's
partbook set, and today shelved beside it in the library of Christ Church, Oxford,
John Baldwin's partbooks (*GB-Och* 979–83)[14] served a different function, one
that was possibly even further removed from the prospect of actual performance
than Sadler's or Dow's. This is the hoard of an antiquarian. Baldwin's profession
as a church singer is clearly unconnected with these books, in which he made
a point of amassing Latin-texted works that had fallen out of the church repertory,
together with a selection of pieces that had never formed part of it, such as
motets by William Byrd, a composer with whom he was closely acquainted.
From another of Baldwin's manuscripts, the so-called 'Commonplace Book'
(*GB-Lbl* R.M. 24.d.2),[15] which includes 87 double-page spreads of music put
into score, we can sense how the spirit of assembling and studying might even
take precedence over convenience to the performer. Baldwin's partbook set is
more obviously designed for practical use; we can imagine him singing from it
with friends in the privacy of his home. But it is first and foremost a personal

13 Mateer, 'Oxford, Christ Church Music MSS 984–8', p. 7.
14 One page is reproduced in Hugh Benham, *Latin Church Music in England c.1460–1575* (London 1977), pl. 7.
15 Some pages are reproduced in David S. Josephson, *John Taverner: Tudor Composer* (Ann Arbor 1979), pl. 22; and
Doe (ed.), 'Elizabethan Consort Music: II', p. xxvii; for a complete facsimile see fn. 16 below.

anthology of valued and rare music, much of which must have been hard to come by in the late 1570s, when the books were begun.[16]

Notwithstanding Baldwin's taste for ritual music of the old order and his close connections with Byrd, to date there has been no serious attempt to claim him for the Catholics. Like Dow and Sadler, Baldwin's music-books are the product of a hobby. Performance from them, if it took place at all, may have been secondary to the urge to collect, preserve and neatly transcribe. In all three men – Sadler, Dow and Baldwin – penmanship stands out as an issue of primary concern. It is possible that none of the manuscripts described so far takes us deep into the world of Elizabethan performance. For this we will have to look instead to books that are less well known, and usually far less beautifully made. Almost without exception, their copyists and original owners are now unknown.

One of the earliest is a single bass partbook from what was once a set of five, *GB-Ob* Tenbury 1464. Holding this book in the hand, the reader's first impression is of a rather grand volume. That impression quickly recedes. Despite its generous size and high-grade paper, both the music notation and the text-hands are very rough indeed, and there are many signs of carelessness or inexperience; the very first piece in the book opens with a crude crossing-out.[17] In this book, at least, one would think that it is a performer who has been at work, rather than a bibliophile and collector. Household accounts of the time are well stocked with references to payments made for 'paper for a song book' – in that instance by Sir Henry Willoughby in 1556–7 for the use of his family.[18] Surely the Tenbury partbook is tangible evidence of the use to which one such batch of paper was put.

The contents are worth describing in some detail. Three works by Osbert Parsley open the collection, two instrumental pieces followed by the Lamentations. This sets the tone of the first 30 pages of the book, where consort music rubs shoulders with motets. The copyist then turned to older English music, of the kind that John Baldwin took such pains to preserve: votive antiphons by Fayrfax, masses by John Taverner (including *Gloria tibi trinitas*, no less), and Office

---

16 The fullest published study of *Och* 979–83 is Roger Bray, 'The partbooks Oxford, Christ Church, MSS 979–83: an index and commentary', *Musica Disciplina* 25 (1971), pp. 179–97. For *Lbl* R.M. 24.d.2, see *London, British Library, R.M. 24.d.2*, facsimile with introduction by Jessie Ann Owens, *Renaissance Music in Facsimile* 8 (New York and London 1987). Although Baldwin might have amassed his hoard of obsolete Catholic church music in a spirit of uncertainty about the line of the Tudor succession, knowing that the music might again be useful after Elizabeth's death, the random and unsystematic nature of the collection makes that interpretation unlikely. A more credible example of such 'stockpiling' would be the 'Gyffard' partbooks (*GB-Lbl* Add. 17802–5); their contents are largely governed by liturgical considerations, and the books might have been partly or even wholly copied during Elizabeth's reign. Uncertainty about the Tudor succession probably accounts in part for the survival of some pre-Reformation church books, both of polyphony and plainchant; see Ronald Hutton, 'The local impact of the Tudor Reformations', in Christopher Haigh (ed.), *The English Reformation Revised* (Cambridge 1987), pp. 114–38.

17 The page is reproduced in Doe (ed.), 'Elizabethan Consort Music: II', p. xxiii. For a provisional inventory of the partbook, see Edmund H. Fellowes, *Tudor Church Music. Appendix with Supplementary Notes* (London 1948), p. 8.

18 Walter L. Woodfill, *Musicians in English Society from Elizabeth to Charles I* (Princeton 1953), p. 274. In Tudor parlance the word 'song' signifies any musical work, not necessarily one with secular words.

hymns by Tallis, Sheppard and Parsley – these complete with text-cues to the verses that would have been supplied in plainchant. The original words are provided throughout, and most of the pieces have been checked for accuracy; the words 'true and good' at the end of Fayrfax's *Aeterne laudis lilium*, for example, confirm that this has been corrected ready for performance. Rounding off the manuscript is a selection of more up-to-date Latin pieces, largely by Tallis and White. In a manner wholly characteristic of the Elizabethan amateur anthologies, secular and sacred freely intermingle. The hands that played Parsley's *Song upon the dial* presumably belonged with the voice that sang Fayrfax's *Aeterne laudis lilium*. In making the transition from one piece to the other, it is highly unlikely that the book and its owners migrated from chamber to chapel.

Were those owners Roman Catholics? There is only one piece of evidence that might argue against that conclusion. At f. 70ᵛ the copyist wrote out an anonymous setting of the words *My soul O God doth now confess*. It has previously been catalogued as an anthem, but it turns out to be a harmonization of one of William Hunnis's 'Honeysuckles' – sternly moralizing religious songs by the Master of the Children of Elizabeth's Chapel Royal, which first found their way into print around 1579.[19] The antithesis of Byrd, Hunnis proclaimed his Protestant message with zeal; during Mary's reign his plots against the Catholic regime landed him in prison. His music is not something we would expect to meet in a book made by a Catholic household. Certainly this piece stands in curious isolation amidst the overtly Catholic music that most appealed to the copyist: masses and hymns, antiphons, and works of less securely ritual or votive function, such as Lamentations and motets.

Were such pieces really being performed in people's homes? To judge from other books copied after 1558 the answer must be yes. Few Elizabethan anthologies can match the Tenbury bass partbook for its riches of pre-Reformation church music; some replace the original Latin texts, or dispense with words altogether. But the general pattern is clear. Music that had ceased to serve a useful function in the church regularly found a welcome in the chamber, alongside repertories that more obviously belonged there. By examining individual manuscripts we can sense how tastes and attitudes might differ from household to household. The more closely we look into the various collecting instincts of the men and women who made these books, the more easy it becomes to imagine the range of domestic performance contexts in which obsolete Tudor church music and Elizabethan motets were sung and played during the last quarter of the sixteenth century.

19 The tune and first stanza of Hunnis's song are given in Maurice Frost, *English and Scottish Psalm and Hymn Tunes, c.1543–1677* (London 1953), pp. 466–7. Details of Hunnis's publication are given in *STC* 13975, together with a reference to an apparently lost edition of c. 1579. Hunnis's songs may have been in circulation before publication, and the inclusion of one of them in *Ob* Tenbury 1464 does not help to fix the date of the manuscript. More suggestive is the presence of motets by Tallis in versions that are earlier than those of the 1575 *Cantiones ... sacrae*; see John Milsom, 'A Tallis fantasia', *The Musical Times* 126 (1985), p. 660. Given the emphasis on Parsley in its opening stages, *Ob* Tenbury 1464 may be connected with the Norwich area.

The owners of one set of partbooks, for example, allocated generous amounts of space to Latin-texted works adapted to English words. No doubt the set would have attracted more interest had it survived intact. Instead we have only one partbook out of five, *GB-Ckc* 316.[20] To judge from its first 60 pages, there is just a chance that the copyist began writing out music for a church choir to sing, apparently in the 1560s or early 1570s. But it is only a slender chance. Alongside *contrafacta* of Taverner's *Gaude plurimum* (which becomes *I will magnify thee O my God*) and Aston's *Te matrem Dei* (which has been turned into an English *Te Deum*), he copied three macaronic carols: Sheppard's *Of all strange news*, Johnson's *Benedicam Domino* and an anonymous setting of *A maid immaculate*. All three have pious, metrical texts that suggest use in the chamber, although any of them might have been drawn into church services during those early, musically barren years of the English rite. Less obviously the stuff of evensong are motets by Tallis, pieces that were eventually published in the *Cantiones …* *sacrae* of 1575. One of them, *Absterge Domine*, has become an anthem (*Wipe away my sins*), but two others – *Dum transisset* and *O sacrum convivium* – keep their Latin texts. Whatever the book's original purpose may have been, by f. 30ᵛ the chamber has securely taken it over, for *In nomines* by Parsons, Poynt and Tye creep in – as do different hands, latterly from the end of the sixteenth century.[21]

One partbook set that almost certainly started life under a church roof before moving into the chamber is *GB-Lbl* Add. 30480–4.[22] In the early seventeenth century the books belonged to Thomas Hamond of Hawkedon in Suffolk, for which reason they have sometimes misleadingly been called the 'Hamond partbooks'. Their earliest owner cannot be traced – a great pity, for this is possibly the only Elizabethan source still in existence that was actually created for a church choir. Which church we do not know. If the composer named 'R. Partyne'

20 A page is reproduced in Iain Fenlon (ed.), *Cambridge Music Manuscripts, 900–1700* (Cambridge 1982), p. 134.

21 For a description of *Ckc* 316 see Iain Fenlon's catalogue entry in Fenlon (ed.), *Cambridge Music Manuscripts*, pp. 134–7. No inventory of its contents has been published. Two features of the manuscript suggest a date of compilation before 1575. First, the design of its pages of printed staves differs from those issued by Tallis and Byrd under the terms of their 1575 royal patent, and would appear to be of earlier date; see Fenlon and Milsom, '"Ruled paper imprinted"', pp. 145–7. Second, the manuscript contains early versions of motets by Tallis that were subsequently published in revised form in the *Cantiones … sacrae* of 1575; see Milsom, 'A Tallis fantasia', p. 660. Later the book passed into the circle of Edward Paston; see Edwards, 'The sources of Elizabethan consort music', p. 316.

    Four adjacent pieces in *Ckc* 316 – Tallis's *Blessed are those that be undefiled* (f. 13ᵛ), Sheppard's *Of all strange news* (f. 15ᵛ), Tallis's *Dum transisset* (f. 18) and *O sacrum convivium* (f. 19) – also constitute the opening four works (in the order 3, 4, 1, 2) in a partbook from Ludlow, *GB-SRO* ref. 356 Box 519/2. The readings are close to those of *Ckc* 316. A slender, crudely made partbook, *SRO* 519/2 contains no overtly secular music. Another Ludlow partbook of similar size and roughness, *SRO* ref. 356 Box 519/4, mixes anthems with partsongs and an untexted chanson by Philip van Wilder. These books are all the more enigmatic for being unbound and badly worn. Possibly they bring us close to ephemeral forms of circulation, of the kind that must have lived in the pockets of singers. If so, they probably belonged no less to the church than they did to the chamber. The books are described in Alan Smith, 'Elizabethan music at Ludlow: a new source', *Music and Letters* 49 (1968), pp. 108–21, with inventories and datings that are in need of some revision.

22 A page of *Lbl* 30482 is reproduced in Paul Doe (ed.), 'Elizabethan Consort Music: I', *Musica Britannica* 44 (London 1979), p. xxviii.

whose evening Canticles open the set could be identified, we might get nearer to solving that interesting problem. The compiler started work with only four partbooks in front of him, all of them made from printed music-paper that was available in the 1560s. (When a fifth partbook came to be needed, its staves had to be ruled by hand.) For close on a hundred pages all we get are anthems and Service-music. Then partsongs start to appear among them: Tallis's *When shall my sorrowful sighing slack*, Johnson's *Defiled is my name*. Soon the first copyist has given way to a confusion of other hands. They wrote out consort songs, instrumental pieces, motets by Tallis taken straight from the 1575 *Cantiones ... sacrae*, and works of greater antiquity, such as Sheppard's Paschal *Kyrie / Haec dies*. Pointedly, all the Latin words have been omitted. Finally chansons and madrigals take over, again without words. Chronologically the last piece to find a home is Byrd's settings of the *turbarum voces* from the St John Passion, 'Jesum Nazarenum', which was first published in the *Gradualia* of 1605.[23]

From the untexted motets in *Lbl* 30480–4 we can identify a new category of user: the performer who valued the musical substance of a motet but had no interest in its words. At the end of Sheppard's (textless) Paschal *Kyrie / Haec dies* someone has written 'a good songe excellent' – clearly more than a sign that the music has been checked for error, since another partbook from the set describes it as 'the best songe in England'. Protestants compiled the early layer of the books, and a Protestant family continued to use the books during the 1580s, filling up blank pages with pieces for domestic music-making. The textless motets were presumably played on instruments or sung as vocalizes, perhaps using solmization syllables. Stripped of their words, they were purged of tangible links with religious faction and became, in effect, abstract music of universal appeal.[24] The only piece that points to Roman Catholic interests is the extract from *Gradualia*, which retains its text underlay, but this is clearly a late addition.

One of the copyists of *Lbl* Add. 30480–4 also had a hand in compiling *GB-Lbl* 47844,[25] the sole survivor from what must once have been a dainty and diminutive set of five partbooks. It is dated 1581. Here everything is wordless, not only motets by Sheppard, Johnson, White and Byrd, but also seven pieces taken from

---

23 The printed music-paper of *Lbl* 30480–4 is discussed in Fenlon and Milsom, '"Ruled paper imprinted"', pp. 145–7. The various layers in the books, and the hands that copied them, are analysed in Hofman, 'The survival of Latin sacred music', III, pp. 250–60. I am grateful to Jason Smart for pointing out that the composer John Franclynge, who is represented in the early layer of partbooks by the anthem *O God for thy name's sake*, may be the same 'John Frankelyng' who served as conduct at the London church of St Michael, Crooked Lane, in 1547; see Hugh Baillie, 'Some biographical notes on English church musicians, chiefly working in London (1485–1569)', *[Royal Musical Association] Research Chronicle* 2 (1962), p. 36. This may point to a London provenance for at least the early layer of *Lbl* 30480–4.

24 Further evidence for the wordless performance of motets comes from Thomas Morley: 'But I see not what passions or motions it [the motet] can stir up being sung as most men do commonly sing it, that is leaving out the ditty and singing only the bare note, as it were a music made only for instruments, which will indeed show the nature of the music but never carry the spirit and, as it were, that lively soul which the ditty giveth.' Thomas Morley, *A Plain and Easy Introduction to Practical Music*, ed. R. Alec Harman (London 1952), p. 293.

25 A page is reproduced in Josephson, *John Taverner*, pl. 21.

Costanzo Porta's *Musica in introitus missarum* (Venice 1566).[26] Although instrumental pieces open and close the book, they merely flank the run of motets and Catholic ritual music that makes up the substance of the collection. Vocalization may have been intended, for one piece has been corrected with the words 'sing menim and crotchet', and such a tiny book can hardly have been read from any greater distance than the singer's own hand. Perhaps this partbook set was created for (or by) young musicians.

Wordless copies of obsolete church music and Elizabethan motets are common in late Tudor music-books. The most celebrated collection of them appears in *GB-Lbl* Add. 31390,[27] the self-proclaimed 'booke of In nomines & other solfainge songes of v: vi: vii: & viii: parts for voyces or Instrumentes'. This rather grand volume is copied in 'tablebook' format, with the various voice-parts arrayed in all four directions, allowing performers to cluster round it. Evidently connected with Clement Woodcock, sometime choirmaster and organist at Chichester Cathedral, it was substantially complete by 1578.[28] Although the manuscript's main riches lie in its seam of instrumental works by Christopher Tye and chansons by Philip van Wilder, the book is also an important source of motets by Sheppard, Tallis, Byrd and their contemporaries. Without it we would have lost such major works as William Mundy's *In aeternum*, Byrd's *Ad Dominum cum tribularer* and the sonorous twelve-part setting of *Credo quod redemptor* by Edward Blancks. Like everything else in the book, these pieces appear without their texts – 'solfainge songes', as the title of the book says, 'for voyces or Instrumentes', to be used convivially, with as many as twelve people gathered around the book for the piece by Blancks.

Lbl Add. 31390 is an impressive tome, large and intact, and it is justly famous. Set beside it, *GB-Lbl* Add. 32377 at first seems insignificant, yet as a record of domestic music-making in Elizabethan England this untidily written partbook is no less valuable than the most handsome of Tudor music-books. An odd volume from an otherwise lost set of five, it ends with a page of pen-trials that includes the dates '1584' and '1585', and the name of 'Hugh Geare', whom Warwick Edwards has traced to the West Country.[29] In its opening stages this book, too, was a collection of *In nomines* and solfaing songs. About 50 pages

---

26 The pieces by Porta occupy ff. 5–8, and are unattributed. They are catalogued as Anonymous Compositions nos. 83, 107, 126, 141, 180, 307 and 347 in May Hofman and John Morehen (comps.), 'Latin Music in British Sources c1485–c1610', *Early English Church Music*, Supplementary Vol. 2 (London 1987). The readings of *Lbl* Add. 47844 follow the 1566 edition of Porta's introits rather than the substantially revised second edition of 1588; see P. Constantii Porta, ... *Opera Omnia, XV: Introitus missarum...*, ed. Siro Cisilino (Padua 1968; 2/1971).

27 Some pages are reproduced in Doe (ed.), 'Elizabethan Consort Music: I', p. xxviii; Stanley Sadie (ed.), *The New Grove Dictionary of Music and Musicians*, 20 vols. (London 1980), 17, p. 715; and elsewhere.

28 For a discussion and inventory of *Lbl* Add. 31390 see Jeremy Noble, 'Le répertoire instrumental anglais: 1550–1585', in Jean Jacquot (ed.), *La musique instrumentale de la Renaissance* (Paris 1955), pp. 91–114. Woodcock's possible association with the book is investigated in Edwards, 'The sources of Elizabethan consort music', pp. 96–7; see also Thurston Dart, 'Music and musicians at Chichester Cathedral', *Music and Letters* 42 (1961), pp. 225–6.

29 Edwards, 'The sources of Elizabethan consort music', p. 136.

into the volume, however, instrumental music gives way to textless copies of Sarum hymns and other ritual music by Sheppard, Tallis, Parsons and White, together with some non-liturgical motets. Soon after, words begin to be included. Presumably Geare and his friends sometimes allowed themselves more than one performance option. Today this strikes us as a casual attitude. In Elizabethan England it was perfectly normal.

Some Elizabethan music-books contain only portions of longer works. For collectors who were interested only in music for four, three or two performers, the five- and six-part repertory was of little use. They took from it what they could, by turning to pieces that included verses for a reduced number of voices. Full sections were discarded, and only the verse sections preserved. Masses were occasionally dismembered in this way, but the more usual prey were votive antiphons, *Magnificat* settings, and Elizabethan works that mimicked the traditional full/verse manner, such as Robert White's psalms and Lamentations, or William Byrd's six-part motet *Infelix ego*. All of those categories are represented in *GB-Och* 45, a tablebook of unknown origin, copied towards the end of the sixteenth century. Curiously, its owner took pains to collect different settings of the same words. No fewer than five settings of the *Magnificat* verse 'Quia fecit mihi magna' were extracted and placed side by side, as if for comparative purposes. All are for four voices; the composers are William Mundy, Sheppard, Tye, White and Taverner. The original texts are fully underlaid. One wonders what purpose such a book was meant to serve. Perhaps it was compiled for teaching inexperienced singers in a family that remained loyal to the Roman liturgy.[30]

Few of the books mentioned so far contain much by way of continental sacred music. At a time when printed repertories from abroad were becoming increasingly available in England, Elizabethan amateur musicians evidently preferred works from their native tradition, cherishing its musical content even when they cared little for the words.[31] As far as we know, only one significant foray was made into the vast riches of foreign church music. This was done by a single set of copyists: the men – and conceivably also women – who wrote out music for the Norfolk gentleman Edward Paston.[32] The Pastons were known Roman Catholics, so it is not surprising to find that their music-books are rich sources both of Tudor Catholic music, Byrd especially, and of foreign masses and motets. There are many Paston music manuscripts – an astonishingly large number,

---

30 Compare this with *GB-Eu* JZ.28, a volume of mass-prints issued by Nicolas du Chemin in Paris between 1556 and 1558. A Scottish owner apparently of the late sixteenth century compiled an index to the volume, arranged not by title of mass but rather according to the number of voices needed to sing individual sections of works, ranging from two singers to eight. The index is headed with these words: 'The Tabil off the songs in this buik as also on quhat leaff to find them'.

31 For a discussion of the limited circulation of continental sacred music in Elizabethan manuscript sources, see John Milsom, 'English polyphonic style in transition: a study of the sacred music of Thomas Tallis' (Diss., U. of Oxford 1983), ch. 3: 'Foreign music and musicians in mid-Tudor England'.

32 See Philip Brett, 'Edward Paston (1550–1630): a Norfolk gentleman and his musical collection', *Transactions of the Cambridge Bibliographical Society* 4 (1964–8), pp. 51–69. I am grateful to Francis Knights for allowing me to consult his unpublished catalogues of the Paston manuscripts.

in fact – and it is easy to imagine what they should contain: masses and ritual music conveniently laid out for use by Catholic families during their covert celebration of the Roman Offices and Mass.

The reality of the Paston books is utterly different from that image. Most of them contain a mixture of sacred and secular works; many transmit only extracts of longer works; sometimes the words are missing. Rarely is there the slightest hint that liturgical use was envisaged. Rather than supplying music for the undercover services of England's Catholics, the Paston copyists instead concentrated on producing chocolate-box-like selections of pieces, evidently with domestic music-making in mind.

Few of the Paston books can be linked with owners outside the family itself. Two that can are the sets compiled for (or subsequently owned by) Byrd's patrons, the Petres. Now known only from their bass partbooks, *GB-Chelm* 1 and *GB-Chelm* 2,[33] they contained a high concentration of sacred music, but clearly neither was designed exclusively or even primarily for chapel use. The first set, represented by *Chelm* 1, opens with Henrician works by Fayrfax, Taverner and Tallis, and later moves on to Elizabethan motets. But space is also found along the way for instrumental pieces (ff. 27ᵛ and 54), and by the end it has turned into a miscellany of anthems, *In nomines*, continental motets and Italian madrigals.[34] This book evidently dates from the decade c. 1590–1600. The second set, represented by *Chelm* 2, is roughly contemporary with it, but owes its existence to a different copyist. It, too, begins with an early Tudor work, Fayrfax's Mass *Sponsus amat sponsam*, but thereafter contains a mixture of foreign motets and chansons.

Some books from the Paston scriptorium treat Tudor church music with quite unexpected casualness. An example is *GB-Ob* Tenbury 354–8, a complete set of five partbooks containing mostly ritual and votive works composed before 1570; it may have been compiled for use by members of the Paston family themselves.[35] First comes a layer of verses extracted from works for five or more voices: four-part sections from Fayrfax's Mass *Sponsus amat sponsam*, Taverner's Mass *Gloria tibi trinitas*, settings of *Ave Dei patris filia* by Tallis (misattributed to Taverner) and Johnson, and other works of similar size and scope. Four-part *In nomines* follow, together with a batch of instrumental hymn-settings by Byrd. Then comes a layer of five-part music. It opens with an extract from Fayrfax's *Ave Dei patris filia*, and further portions of Tallis's setting of the same text (this time correctly attributed), before settling into complete pieces – including the whole of Johnson's *Ave Dei patris filia*, notwithstanding the four-part extract that had been copied earlier, transposed a fifth higher in pitch. With some five-part *In nomines* thrown in for good measure, the collection ends with Taverner's *Mater Christi* and a single

33 Chelmsford, Essex County Record Office, D/DP Z 6/1 & 6/2. A page from *Chelm* 1 is reproduced in Imogen Holst, *Byrd* (London 1972), p. 65.

34 For a description and provisional inventory of *Chelm* 1, see Fellowes, *Tudor Church Music. Appendix*, pp. 6–7.

35 For a provisional inventory of *Ob* Tenbury 354–8, see Edmund H. Fellowes, *The Catalogue of Manuscripts in the Library of St Michael's College, Tenbury* (Paris 1934), pp. 61–2.

anthem, Tallis's *Blessed are those that be undefiled*. The copyist initially missed out the words, providing only text-incipits to serve as identity tags. A second copyist added some of the missing texts, but not consistently through the set. It is hard to know what function these books were originally designed to serve, but evidently their relationship to liturgical practice was not close. Nor can such a miscellany of textless limbs and torsos be construed as the work of a dedicated collector. In a manner wholly characteristic of the Paston copyists, this set shows limited respect for the integrity of works from the Catholic past, works that scribes from a Catholic circle might most have been expected to cherish.

Curiously, it would seem that non-Catholics often acted as more diligent protectors of threatened Catholic repertories. Three such collectors will serve to round off this overview of the Elizabethan manuscript miscellanies, all of them evidently amateur musicians whose normal performing venues must have been the chamber rather than the church. The first devoted his labours to *GB-Ob* Mus. Sch. e. 423, a fat *contratenor* partbook from a set of six. It was copied during the 1580s. Huge in scope, and catholic rather than Catholic in the nature of its contents, it represents a monumental undertaking on the part of its unidentified scribe, and it would be reckoned one of our most important Elizabethan sources had its fellow partbooks survived. Divided into tidy layers of repertory, it includes a large group of votive antiphons, ritual pieces and motets by Byrd alongside blocks of consort songs, instrumental pieces and church anthems. From it we catch our only glimpse of some otherwise lost major works, including seven by Tye: *Ave caput Christi*, *Christus resurgens*, *Domine Deus caelestis*, *In quo corrigit*, two *Magnificat* settings and a *Te Deum*. No detailed study or complete inventory of *Ob* 423 has yet been published, and we can barely begin to guess who might have made it, or how this great collection of music was once enjoyed by a circle of Elizabethan amateur musicians.[36]

The orderliness of *Ob* 423 stands in striking contrast to the chaos of another ambitious six-part set, made (or owned) by a still-unidentified 'T. E.' and William Bower during the last quarter of the sixteenth century (with later additions). Two partbooks from this set survive, *GB-Ob* Tenbury 389 and the privately owned 'McGhie MS' (formerly known as the 'James MS').[37] This is a collection

---

36 Since this chapter was submitted for publication Dr David Mateer has established that the hand of *Ob* 423 is that of John Bentley, the chief steward of John Petre's estate at Thorndon, Essex. See 'William Byrd, John Petre, and Oxford, Bodleian MS Mus. Sch. e. 423', *[Royal Musical Association] Research Chronicle*, 29 (1996). I am indebted to Dr Mateer for permitting disclosure of his findings here prior to publication. I am grateful also to Bruce Barker-Benfield for sharing his unpublished notes about the paper-stock and gathering structure of the manuscript, made during the course of conservation and now kept in the Bodleian Library, Oxford.

37 Both partbooks are principally made out of ruled paper of the type issued by Tallis and Byrd from 1575 onwards. The same paper was used by Robert Dow in *Och* 984–8, and by John Baldwin in *Och* 979–83; see fn. 12 above. The McGhie MS is bound together with a copy of the *superius* of Tallis and Byrd's *Cantiones ... sacrae* of 1575. *Ob* Tenbury 389 was formerly bound with the Tallis–Byrd *discantus* partbook, but this is now detached, and located at Chicago, Newberry Library, Case-VM 2099 L63 T14c. For a provisional inventory of *Ob* Tenbury 389 (only), see Fellowes, *The Catalogue of Manuscripts*, pp. 68–70. I am grateful to Jason Smart for pointing to the presence of Bower's name on f. 1 of the McGhie MS.

that evidently grew spontaneously, with new pieces being added to successive pages as they fell into the owners' hands. Their net was cast unusually wide; vocal works are copied beside instrumental, foreign beside English, old beside new, secular beside sacred. Preferred above all else, however, are motets by William Byrd and Alfonso Ferrabosco. For evidence of the extent to which Byrd's *cantiones sacrae* were avidly collected by amateur performers before their publication in 1589 and 1591, one need look no further than this clearly utilitarian set. From the mix of genres represented in the books it is clear that the owners were by no means interested only in music associated with the Catholics.

One final partbook set stands chronologically on its own, even if its contents remind us of the Elizabethan miscellanies. There is a distinctly retrospective air to *GB-Ob* Tenbury 807–11, originally a six-partbook set that now lacks its *superius*. Votive antiphons and ritual music by Taverner, Sheppard, Tallis and Johnson make up the core of the collection, preceded by a block of motets copied directly from Byrd's *Liber secundus sacrarum cantionum* of 1591. Only in their later stages do the books betray their true date, for they include Thomas Weelkes's lament for Prince Henry, *When David heard*, which must be placed after 1612. On the basis of this and other evidence, Craig Monson concludes that the set was probably copied within a relatively short span of time shortly before 1620.[38] The copyist was evidently drawn to Latin-texted music, for he included two rare examples of Jacobean motets, Weelkes's *Laboravi in gemitu meo* and Kirbye's *Vox in Rama*. And his taste in general was for serious music, for the books contain only motets and anthems. It is hard to believe that they were compiled for a church choir; what institution around the year 1620 could possibly have found a use for works such as Tallis's *Gaude gloriosa* and Parsons's six-part *Magnificat*? That said, the copyist may have envisaged more than one singer to a part in Parsons's *Magnificat*, for he wrote out the piece twice, once into the books themselves, the second time on loose bifolia that have only subsequently been tipped into the rear of the set. This unique and unexpected occurrence demands closer investigation, as indeed does the very existence of this perplexing set of partbooks.

With *Ob* Tenbury 807–11 the flow of chamber sources of Latin-texted Tudor sacred music reduces to a slow trickle. Few Jacobean and later manuscripts contain more than remnants of the repertory – Merro's partbooks in particular deserve a mention[39] – and in none does that repertory stand out as the principal focus of the collection. For a generation of musicians too young to have heard the ritual music of Fayrfax, Taverner and Sheppard sung in its liturgical context, the appeal of such works may have begun to dwindle. As for Byrd's motets, their publication must have considerably lessened the need for circulation in manu-

---

38 See Craig Monson, *Voices and Viols in England, 1600–1650: the Sources and the Music* (Ann Arbor 1982), pp. 70–4; there is an inventory of the set on p. 75.

39 *US-NYp* Drexel 4180–5 and *GB-Lbl* Add. 17792–6, discussed (with inventories) in Monson, *Voices and Viols*, pp. 133–58. Two pages from *NYp* Drexel 4180–5 are reproduced by Monson on pp. 134–5. Pages from *Lbl* Add. 17792–6 are reproduced by Monson on p. 136, and in Philip Brett (ed.), 'Consort Songs', *Musica Britannica* 22 (London 1967), p. xxi.

script. Since those publications were themselves aimed at the private rather than the institutional market, it is to them that we finally turn for evidence of sacred music-making in the chamber.

Although we can posit church origins for some of the contents of Tallis and Byrd's jointly-published *Cantiones … sacrae*, printed in London in 1575, the book itself appealed to a secular readership rather than to church choirs. Admittedly the two composers style themselves on the title-page as Gentlemen and Organists of Elizabeth's private chapel. But mention of the queen (and the dedication to her) arises from the royal letters patent that gave Tallis and Byrd their printing and bookselling monopoly, of which this publication was the first fruit, and mention of the Chapel Royal may merely advertise the fact that Tallis and Byrd stood on the highest rung of the professional ladder. The book's title, 'Cantiones, quae ab argumento sacrae vocantur', signifies only 'songs, which from their contents are called sacred'.[40] For Tallis, Byrd and their public, motets such as these would have been regarded (in Thomas Morley's words) as 'grave and sober music', or works based on 'grave ditties'.[41] From the prefatory material we learn that sober music (according to the physicians) governs a heathy mind, and that 'whoever possesses wisdom honours music'.[42] All this recommends the book to the general reader – as do the extremely varied contents, which were clearly chosen (or specially composed) in order to impress. Every imaginable genre, style and technique is represented, and the use of canon is particularly evident.

Who owned copies of this showpiece? The queen must have possessed one, although no royal copy has survived. There was once a copy at Nonsuch Palace, in the library of Henry Fitzalan, 12th Earl of Arundel;[43] and in 1599 a copy was purchased by William Cavendish, 1st Earl of Devonshire, for use at Chatsworth.[44] There must have been copies in the libraries of the men who wrote the commendatory verses that preface the book: Richard Mulcaster, Master of Merchant Taylors' School, and Ferdinand Richardson (alias Heybourne), courtier and amateur composer. Robert Dow, copyist of *Och* 984–8, had at least access to a copy, for he cites some of its prefatory material in his marginal notes.[45] John Baldwin had a set bound in with his manuscript partbooks, *Och* 979–83; so did the unknown owner of the *Ob* Tenbury 389/McGhie partbooks. Sets of the 1575 publication, or intermediate manuscripts made from them, were available to John Sadler, John Merro, the Paston scribes, and the copyists of *Lbl* Add. 30480–4 and *Lbl* Add. 32377; in all cases the readings in their manuscripts derive

40 A facsimile of the 1575 *Cantiones … sacrae* is published by Boethius Press (Leeds 1976). For reproductions and translations of the prefatory material, see Craig Monson (ed.), 'Cantiones Sacrae (1575)', *The Byrd Edition* 1 (London 1977), pp. xv–xxvii.

41 Morley, *A Plain and Easy Introduction to Practical Music*, pp. 294, 292.

42 'Hoc tamen obtinuit communi Musica iure, / Ut quo quisque sapit rectius, ornet eam.' The translation follows *The Byrd Edition* 1, p. xxvi.

43 John Milsom, 'The Nonsuch Music Library', *Sundry Sorts of Music Books. Essays on The British Library Collections Presented to O. W. Neighbour on his 70th Birthday* (London 1993), p. 156.

44 Woodfill, *Musicians in English Society*, p. 253.

45 Boyd, *Elizabethan Music and Music Criticism*, p. 315.

from those of the print. William Heyther, professor of music at Oxford, bequeathed a copy of the *Cantiones* to the university.[46] Other owners are known only from the names that are written into surviving copies: 'Tho: Baker'; 'Ric: Langley'; one set variously inscribed 'Wilkinson', 'Thomas Fidge his booke', 'Thomas Evans' and 'Thomas Ford'.[47] Most interesting of all is the set in Dublin that was once owned by William Rokeby, possibly the man of that name who died in York in 1618.[48] Here the blank staves have been filled with consort songs, instrumental pieces, further motets, even Tallis's responsory *Videte miraculum*.

This list is made up of private owners, not of institutions and choral foundations. There is no evidence to show that copies of the *Cantiones ... sacrae* were acquired for use by the choirs of England's cathedrals or churches. When compositions from the 1575 collection found their way into manuscripts compiled for church use, they were invariably adapted to English words. Tallis's *Absterge Domine* thus became *Discomfit them O Lord, Forgive me Lord my sin, O God be merciful* or *Wipe away my sins*; Byrd's *Attollite portas* became *Let us arise* or *Lift up your heads*; and so on.[49] Even if originally composed for use by the choir of the Chapel Royal, in their Latin-texted form these motets found their principal audience in the chamber. To gain more general admittance to the church, new words were needed.

A pattern of private ownership identical to that of the 1575 *Cantiones ... sacrae* emerges for Byrd's later publications of Latin-texted music, the *Cantiones sacrae* of 1589 and 1591, the three masses of c. 1592–5, and the *Gradualia* of 1605 and 1607. If anything, there is even less likelihood that the contents of these books were sung in churches by choirs. Not only do their texts appeal implicitly or overtly to the Catholic faction. In style, scope and level of technical difficulty, the music of Byrd's later motets and Catholic liturgical music often stands in sharp contrast to the more stolid Anglican church repertory. It is surely significant that few of Byrd's post-1575 motets were converted into English anthems. The only piece that Anglican choirs sang widely to alternative English texts was *Ne irascaris*. Otherwise the list of known Byrd *contrafacta* runs to only four items: the third part of *Tribulationes civitatum*, which was sung as *Let not our prayers be rejected*; *Exsurge Domine*, which was adapted to the words *Arise O Lord why sleepest thou*; *Tribulatio proxima est*, which became *Blessed art thou O Lord*; and John Merro's copy of *Alleluia, ascendit Deus*, underlaid with the text *All ye people clap your hands*.[50] Motets from *Gradualia* are totally absent from the books used by church

---

46 Library location: *GB-Ob* Mus. Sch. f. 580–4. Heyther's bequest is described in Margaret Crum, 'Early lists of the Oxford music school collection', *Music and Letters* 48 (1967), pp. 23–34.

47 Library locations: 'Baker': *GB-Lbl* R.M. 15.b.4. 'Langley': *GB-Ob* Mus. Sch. f. 600–5 (*Superius* only), and several of the partbooks in the mixed set *B-Br* Fetis no. 1753. 'Wilkinson' (etc.): *GB-Lcm* I.E.9.

48 Library location: *EIRE-Dtc* OLS.192.n.40 (1–6); *superius, discantus, tenor* and *sexta pars* only. The identity of Rokeby is considered in Edwards, 'The sources of Elizabethan consort music', p. 193.

49 For a full list of English adaptations of the *Cantiones ... sacrae*, see Peter le Huray, *Music and the Reformation in England, 1549–1660* (London 1967; Cambridge 2/1978), pp. 104–5.

50 A full list of Byrd *contrafacta* is given in Craig Monson (ed.), 'The English Anthems', *The Byrd Edition* 11 (London 1983), pp. xiii–xiv.

choirs. They were copied neither with their original Latin texts nor with new English words. Possibly this music was rejected because of its known association with the Roman liturgy; possibly it was felt to be unsuitable for reasons of its internal musical style. A close analysis of Byrd's later motets – their voice-ranges, melodic characteristics and level of difficulty – would almost certainly show up marked differences with equivalent properties in the Anglican repertories. Such an analysis would take us closer towards understanding how Byrd's chamber style differs from the idiom of his church music, a difference that many singers today vaguely sense, but which it is hard to quantify and characterize in words. Whatever the reason, however, there is no avoiding the fact that Byrd's *Gradualia* settings – even the celebrated *Ave verum corpus* – found their way for the first time into choral evensong only during the nineteenth century.

Elizabethan England was far from being unique in providing a chamber context for the performance of motets. Throughout sixteenth-century Europe Latin-texted sacred music was used in domestic circumstances as well as in churches. No systematic study has yet been made of patterns of ownership of motet-books in Italy, France, Germany or the Low Countries, but even from the limited findings published so far we can see that private individuals were as likely to possess them as were church or chapel choirs.[51] It is highly improbable – indeed, it is unthinkable – that foreign printers issued such vast numbers of motet and mass publications solely for the ecclesiastical market. Foreign motet-books whose titles include the words *Motetti*, *Sacrae cantiones* and *Modulorum* were probably designed no less for the amateur market than for the choirs of cathedrals, churches or chapels. In the course of her research into the publications of the Venetian printer Antonio Gardano, Mary Lewis has located many examples of motet-books bound together with sets of chansons and madrigals, composite volumes that were once owned by sixteenth-century connoisseurs.[52] It is possible to trace exactly such mixed sets of foreign music in the libraries of contemporary English collectors. Several were owned by the avid bibliophiles of Nonsuch Palace, Henry Fitzalan, 12th Earl of Arundel, and his nephew John, Lord Lumley;[53] one set was probably brought into England by Sir Thomas Hoby, translator of Castiglione's *Il cortegiano*;[54] examples belonged to Sir Henry Billingsley,[55] Richard Forster[56] and 'H. Sowth',[57] all of whom

---

51 For an overview of this subject, see Christopher Reynolds, 'Sacred polyphony', in Howard Mayer Brown and Stanley Sadie (eds.), *Performance Practice. Music before 1600* (London 1989), ch. 10.

52 Mary S. Lewis, *Antonio Gardano, Venetian Music Printer 1538–1569: A Descriptive Bibliography and Historical Study. Volume I: 1538–1549* (New York and London 1988), pp. 9–16 and 123 ff.

53 Milsom, 'The Nonsuch Music Library', items 6 and 10.

54 Library location: *EIRE-Dtc* B.1.27–31, containing motet-books by Rore, Jacquet of Mantua, Phinot and Gombert, madrigals by Verdelot and chansons by Buus, all published by Gardano between 1543 and 1553. Full details in Milsom, 'English polyphonic style in transition', Appendix 3.8, no. 5.

55 Library locations: *GB-Och* 508–9, containing a run of motet and chanson anthologies published by Phalèse between 1554 and 1560; and *GB-Och* 318–19, containing motet and chanson anthologies for three voices, published by Phalèse in 1569. Billingsley also owned *GB-Och* 306–9, a run of madrigal books published by Girolamo Scotto between 1559 and 1561. Full details in Milsom, 'English polyphonic style in transition',

were amateur musicians; yet others are known to have been in English hands by 1600, although their owners have not been identified.[58] Without question it was motet-books such as these that provided English composers with models for their own publications of *cantiones sacrae* from 1575 onwards.

The conclusions to be drawn from all this are simple and clear. Although choral conductors today may browse through the riches of sixteenth-century polyphony confident in the knowledge that much of it was conceived as choral repertory, consorts of solo voices (and of instruments) may also help themselves to that same music, knowing that by doing so they too follow in the footsteps of sixteenth-century performers. Choral music was often sung or played by consorts. The reverse is less obviously true. Far less evidence exists to show that consort music was sung by choirs. The boundaries that separate authentic chamber music from church repertories may no longer be immediately obvious to us, and it may be necessary for us to re-learn how to tell them apart – for example from the subject-matter of texts, the stylistic quality of the music or the nature of early sources. By recovering a sense of the distinction to be made between chamber and church styles, we surely stand to gain. An audience that knows what is lost by hearing a string quartet by Mozart played in a concert hall by a string orchestra will surely also want to be sensitive to the losses sustained when a motet by Byrd is sung by a large body of singers in a spacious building. Church (and church-style) choirs have been pioneering and powerful forces in the revival of much sixteenth-century sacred music, to the extent that some listeners will be dissatisfied with any other mode of performance. If it is the sound of a good choir that matters most to an audience, then it will be of little consequence whether or not the repertory it sings is correctly the stuff of choral performance. If on the other hand it is the music we put first, then we can look forward to the day when works with a recent history of choral interpretation finally break free from performance styles for which they were never intended, and are returned to the chambers where they more legitimately belong.[59]

Appendix 3.8, nos. 6, 11 and 7. Sir Henry Billingsley (d. 1606), translator of Euclid's *Elements of Geometrie* (1570), was educated at the universities of Cambridge and Oxford in the 1550s. A wealthy London merchant, he was elected Lord Mayor of London in 1596.

56 Richard Forster (c. 1546–1616), physician, took the degrees of M.B. and M.D. at All Souls College, Oxford, in 1573. He acquired *Och* 318–19 (according to an annotation on the books) 'Ex dono Magistri Henrici Billingesley' (see fn. 55 above). No date is given for the transfer of ownership, but the style 'magister' may place it before 1597, the year in which Billingsley is thought to have received his knighthood. The two men shared interests in mathematics and medical practice.

57 Library location: Taunton, Somerset County Record Office, DD/SAS C/1193 8/1, containing motet-books by Gombert and Phinot, madrigals by Rore, Ruffo and Donato, and various anthologies, all published by Antonio Gardano between 1546 and 1553. I am grateful to Andrew Wathey for drawing this volume to my attention.

58 Library locations: *GB-Och* 341, containing motets by Willaert and madrigals by Arcadelt and Domenico Ferabosco, published in Venice between 1539 and 1542; full details in Milsom, 'English polyphonic style in transition', Appendix 3.8, no. 2. See also *EIRE-Dm* S3.5.50, containing motets by Victoria and Lassus, madrigals by Arcadelt, Lassus, Marenzio, Philips and Nanino, chansons by Sweelinck, and various madrigal anthologies, published in various places between 1575 and 1596.

59 I have argued this point specifically in relation to the performance of Byrd's motets in 'Byrd on record: an anniversary survey', *Early Music* 21 (1993), pp. 447–8

8

THE EDUCATION OF CHORISTERS IN ENGLAND DURING THE SIXTEENTH CENTURY

JANE FLYNN

The various aspects of the education of choristers during the first half of the sixteenth century are well summarized in the statutes of St Paul's Cathedral:

Let him [the master of choristers] have eight boys of good character and respectable kindred, whom he should maintain and educate in moral training. And also let him see that they be instructed in song and writing, and that they be able to do all things appropriate to ministers of God in the choir.[1]

The aim of choristers' education was not primarily musical; it was focused on the liturgy, the performance of which demonstrated practically the way to live a virtuous Christian life. In addition to musical skills, choristers learned to read and write English and Latin, and morals based on Christian teaching. This education prepared boys not only for musical careers, but also for many other careers, outside as well as inside the Church. Because of this, it was valuable, and choristers were not usually required to be poor as a prerequisite for admittance; Thomas Tusser, a choirboy at St Paul's under John Redford's care, was from a 'gentle' family.[2]

The training was practical, rather than academic. Choristers learned by participating in many daily services (depending on the degree of solemnity):[3] they read Scripture lessons, acted as crossbearers, censers, taperers and water bearers,[4] and sang. Mostly, they sang chant, and even those choristers whose musical skills were at a basic level could take part. While beginners sang chant,

---

1 'Is octo Pueros, bonae indolis et honestae parentelae, habeat: quos alet, et educet in morum disciplina. Videat etiam instruantur in cantu et literatura, ut in omnibus apti ad Ministerium Dei in Choro esse possunt.' Quoted in Maria Hackett, *Evidences on the Office and Duties of the Magister Scholarum, or Chancellor of the Cathedral* (London 1813), p. xii.

2 See his autobiographical poem in Thomas Tusser, *Five Hundred Pointes of good Husbandrie ... corrected, better ordered, and newly augmented to a fourth part more, with divers other lessons, as a diet for the farmer. Newly set foorth by Thomas Tusser, gentleman, servant to the Honourable Lorde Paget of Beaudeset* (London 1580). For a modern edition, see *Five Hundred points of Good Husbandry by Thomas Tusser [1573]* with an Introduction by Sir Walter Scott and a Benediction by Rudyard Kipling incorporated in a Foreword by E. V. Lucas (London 1931), pp. 202–11.

3 See Kathleen Edwards, *The English Secular Cathedrals in the Middle Ages* (New York 1949; 2/1967), p. 12.

4 *Ibid.*, p. 316.

the more experienced choristers improvised on it in a variety of ways ranging from simple to complex. Likewise, choristers' lessons in the classroom were practical, and were designed to reinforce the knowledge and expertise necessary for participating in the liturgy. They practised their lessons as a group, usually in one room,[5] reciting and listening to others, and being corrected by the master. Thus, at Wells, the choristers were to be taught 'by manifold repetition as often as, when and whenever the doing so is of profit';[6] and at Durham, Thomas Ashwell (Haskewell) was to give his choristers their music lessons 'carefully and adequately four times a day on all ferial days, that is, twice in the morning and twice in the afternoon, and shall hear their renderings, keeping from them nothing of his knowledge in these matters'.[7]

Since the principal focus of this educational method was the liturgy, one might expect that all of the liturgical changes during the Reformation would have had an effect on it. However, this was not the case during the reigns of Henry VIII, Edward VI and Mary, because the different liturgies did not last long enough to become established.[8] For example, during Edward's six-year reign, much of the new liturgical music was adapted from chant, and English versions of plainsong could be performed with the traditional improvisation techniques.[9] On the other hand, since Elizabeth remained on the throne long enough to ensure some kind of liturgical stability, a change in education at choir schools was inevitable. By about 1565, a generation of choristers had been educated without learning liturgical chant (other than psalms). Furthermore, since Elizabethan choristers were required to learn far less music and ceremony for far fewer liturgies than their predecessors, they spent more time studying in the classroom: the whole approach to music education became more academic than practical, with an emphasis on written rather than oral (improvised) exercises. And although they performed 'a modest and distinct song'[10] for the liturgy, they studied and performed elaborate music outside the liturgy.

CHORISTERS' EDUCATION BEFORE C. 1565

Masters of choristers' indentures dating from the mid-fifteenth century list the musical skills choristers were to learn, as demonstrated in Table 8:1.

---

5   See the description of the song school in J. T. Fowler (ed.), 'Rites of Durham', *Surtees Society* 107 (1902), pp. 62–3.
6   Dom Aelred Watkin, 'Dean Cosyn and Wells Cathedral miscellanies', *Somerset Record Society* 56 (Frome and London 1941), p. 102.
7   As translated by Dom David Knowles, *The Religious Orders in England* (Cambridge 1959), pp. 17–18.
8   For a discussion of the Reformation period see John Caldwell, *The Oxford History of English Music* (Oxford 1991), pp. 267–344.
9   See John Aplin, 'The survival of plainsong in Anglican music', *Journal of the American Musicological Society* 32 (1979), pp. 247–75; Nicholas Temperley, *Music of the English Parish Church*, 2 vols. (Cambridge 1979), I, pp. 15 and 25–6.
10 Royal Injunctions of Queen Elizabeth, 1559, no. 49, as quoted in Walter Howard Frere and William McClure Kennedy, 'Visitation articles and injunctions of the period of the Reformation', 3 vols., *Alcuin Club* 14–16 (1910), III, p. 23.

Table 8:1: Skills acquired by pre-Reformation choristers

date / place	plainsong	pricksong	figuration	faburden	descant	square-note	counter	organ
1430 Durham[a]		✓		✓	✓		✓	✓
1477 Lincoln[b]	✓	✓		✓	✓		✓	✓
1496 Durham[c]	✓	✓		✓	✓	✓	✓	✓
1507 Newark[d]	✓	✓			✓			✓
15?? Aberdeen[e]	✓	✓	✓	✓	✓			
1513 Durham[f]	✓	✓		✓	✓	✓	✓	
1522 Worcester[g]	✓	✓			✓			✓
1531 York[h]	✓	✓	✓		✓			
1538 Glastonbury[i]		✓			✓			✓
1538 Salisbury[j]	✓	✓		✓	✓			
1539 Lincoln[k]	✓	✓		✓	✓		✓	✓

a   See Roger Bowers, 'Choral institutions within the English church: their constitution and development, 1340–1500' (Diss., U. of East Anglia 1975), A056.
b   See William Page (ed.), *The Victoria History of the County of Lincoln* (London 1906), II, p. 436.
c   See Hugh Baillie, 'Squares', *Acta Musicologica* 32 (1960), p. 180.
d   See Cornelius Brown, *A History of Newark-on-Trent: Being the Life Story of an Ancient Town*, vol. II, *From the Reign of Edward VI. to that of Edward VII.* (Newark 1907), p. 186.
e   See Frank Ll. Harrison, *Music in Medieval Britain* (London 1958), p. 169.
f   See Knowles, *The Religious Orders in England*, pp. 17–18, and Frank Ll. Harrison, 'The social position of church musicians in England, 1450–1550', in Jan LaRue (ed.), *Report of the Eighth Congress of the International Musicological Society*, 2 vols. (Kassel 1961), I, p. 354.
g   See Ivor Atkins, *The Early Occupants of the Office of Organist and Master of the Choristers of the Cathedral Church of Christ and the Blessed Virgin Mary, Worcester* (London 1918), p. 17.
h   Peter Aston, *The Music of York Minster* (London and New York 1972), p. 5.
i   See anonymous (ed.), 'The engagement of an organist at Glastonbury Abbey in 1534', *Reliquary* 6 (1892), pp. 176–7.
j   See Betty Matthews, 'Some early organists and their agreements', *The Organ* 51 (1972), p. 149.
k   See David G. T. Harris, 'Musical education in Tudor times (1485–1603)', *Proceedings of the Musical Association* 65 (1939), p. 119.

Although not all of the skills appear on every indenture, they are always listed in the same order and therefore suggest a progressive order of attainment. Knowledge of the prerequisites of a particular skill adds to our understanding of what was involved in it. For example, choristers had to be able to read mensural music ('pricksong') before they could sing chant in a rhythmicized way ('figuration'), or could 'sight' notes on a staff that were consonant with the written chant and sing counterpoints to it ('descant', etc.).

All students, not only choristers, began their education at around the age of seven with 'song', a combination of Latin grammar and chant.[11] They learned to read and write, and memorized the psalms with their psalm tones and other Latin

11   For example, incoming students (*demis*) at Magdalen College, Oxford, were to be 'in lectura et plano cantu competenter instructi' ('competently instructed in reading and plain song'), quoted in R. S. Stanier, *Magdalen School: A History of Magdalen College School, Oxford* (Oxford 1940; 2/1958), p. 18. According to Bishop Elstow's Visitation of 1432, girls had to be instructed in song and reading before they could be admitted as nuns at Elstow; see A. Hamilton Thompson (ed.), *Visitations of Religious Houses in the Diocese of Lincoln* (Canterbury and York Society 1915), I, p. 53, quoted in Harris, 'Musical education in Tudor times', p. 109.

liturgical texts, such as the Canticles. Solmization helped them to memorize intervals,[12] which they learned how to sing in tune 'of someone that can already sing, or by som Instrument of Musicke, as the virginals'.[13] Thus, in order to be able to sing chant, they did not need to learn the letter names of notes nor how to read music. The more advanced choristers, who would be responsible for singing more music than the beginners,[14] would find the ability to read music preferable to additional memorizing. Moreover, since their improvisation techniques were based on reading the chant while they improvised a melody against it, music-reading was necessary before they could advance. They learned how to read music by using the 'gamut'. Diagrams of the gamut give both the solmization syllables and letter names of the notes: the letter names locate the pitches on the staff and the clefs F, C and G show how the overlapping hexachords ('mutations') fitted on to it. The chorister would thus be able to sing notated music once given the starting note and the clef, assisted by the solmization syllables in singing the appropriate tones and semitones that cannot be represented on lines and spaces.

The next stage in choristers' education was to learn how to read mensural music, i.e. 'pricksong'. Choristers would learn the note-values and shapes of ligatures by memorizing tables of prolation.[15] At St George's Chapel, Windsor, the various shapes of the ligature *cum opposita proprietate* were painted on one of the walls of the choristers' classroom.[16] Choristers could also learn mensuration (among other skills) by singing canons.[17] Thomas Ravenscroft's first collection of songs, *Pammelia*,[18] which has been described as 'highly retrospective',[19] and of

---

12 See Robert Vladimir Henderson, 'Solmization syllables in musical theory 1100 to 1600' (Diss., Columbia University 1969), p. 4, and Andrew Hughes, 'Solmization, § 1 European medieval and Renaissance systems', in Stanley Sadie (ed.), *The New Grove Dictionary of Music and Musicians*, 20 vols. (London 1980), 17, pp. 458–62.

13 'A shorte Introduction into the Science of Musicke made for such as are desirous to haue the knowledge therof, for the singing of these psalmes' was included at the beginning of a 1561 edition of 83 of Thomas Sternhold's Psalms; a manuscript copy of the same, dated 1561; and in Sternhold's *Whole Booke of Psalmes*, 1562 (and editions up to 1569); see Sir John Stainer, 'On the musical introductions found in certain metrical psalters', *Proceedings of the Musical Association* 27 (1900/01), p. 2.

14 At Wells and Salisbury, senior boys were responsible for singing and reading at matins, terce, sext and none; see Bowers, 'Choral institutions', p. 2030.

15 Tables of prolation are included in *GB-Lbl* Add. 21455, f. 8 (formerly f. 7), a descant treatise, and *GB-Lbl* Roy. App. 58, f. 51. The latter source contains also a diagram of the gamut on f. 32^v.

16 See Bowers, 'Choral institutions', p. 6084, and Dom Anselm Hughes, 'The painted music in No. 25 The Cloisters', *Report of the Friends of St. George's and the Descendants of the Knights of the Garter* 4 (1965), p. 282. Cf. the use of a board with mensural notation written on it in a woodcut of a sixteenth-century German schoolroom; this woodcut is reproduced in Edith Weber, 'L'enseignement de la musique dans les écoles humanistes et protestantes en Allemagne: Théorie, pratique, pluridisciplinarité', in *L'enseignement de la musique au moyen âge et la renaissance, Colloque organisé par la Fondation Royaumont en coproduction avec l'A.R.I.M.M. (Association pour la Recherche et l'Interprétation des Musiques Médiévales) et le C.N.R.S. (Centre National de la Recherche Scientifique)* ([Paris] 1987), p. 108. Blackboards with staves painted on them were used in the parish school at Bolzano during the fifteenth century; see Reinhard Strohm, *The Rise of European Music, 1380–1500* (Cambridge 1993), p. 289.

17 For example, canons would also be useful for teaching choristers the rules of consonance and dissonance.

18 Thomas Ravenscroft, *Pammelia. Musicks Miscellanie; or, Mixed Varietie of Pleasant Roundelays, and Delightful Catches of 3, 4, 5, 6, 7, 8, 9, 10 Parts in One.* (London 1609).

19 Iain Fenlon, 'Instrumental music, songs and verse from sixteenth-century Winchester: British Library Additional MS 60577', in Iain Fenlon (ed.), *Music in Medieval and Early Modern Europe: Patronage, Sources and Texts* (Cambridge 1981), p. 108

which some survive in earlier sources, includes examples which appear to be designed for choristers (such as 'Ut re mi fa mi re ut hey derry derry sing and be merry, quando veni quando coeli, whip little David's bome bome').

After learning mensuration, choristers could apply it to their singing of chant, which, by the fifteenth century, was sung in many different styles, including as a succession of equal notes and with regular mensuration.[20] And according to Thomas Morley, when chant is sung in a measured way for others to improvise against, it is called 'figuration'; he describes three ways of performing it.[21] For the first kind, singers would read the chant from a book, which presents the notes 'in one form' (i.e. chant notation), but they would sing one note long and the next short, etc. A simple two-part written piece using this technique is Thomas Tallis's *Natus est nobis* in the 'Mulliner Book';[22] the chant is written in alternating breves and semibreves. Morley's second kind of figuration presents the chant in an ornamented form, i.e. 'broken'. An example of it, described as 'plane sang figurateuff', is given by Scottish Anonymous, author of 'The Airt of Musick Collecit out of all Ancient Doctoris of Musick';[23] it comprises an ornamented version of the chant transposed up an octave, the unornamented chant (which is not to be performed), and three lower parts.[24] In Morley's third kind, each note of the chant is held for a time-value longer than a long or comprises two or more repeated notes; for example, in Richard Farrant's *Felix namque* each note of the chant is repeated in the rhythmic figure semibreve–minim.[25]

After learning how to read music and sing chant in rhythmicized ways, choristers could begin to improvise against chant. Singing in faburden was the easiest way of doing so, since, in its basic form, it involves little more than doubling the chant. According to Wylde's Anonymous, the chant is doubled a fourth above in the top voice, and doubled a third below by a third voice, except at cadences, when it is a fifth below; this produces 6-3 and 8-5 sonorities.[26] In the initial stage of learning, choristers singing the top part could have used solmization syllables: their syllables would be the same as those sung by boys on the chant. The lower

20 Mother Thomas More, 'The performance of plainsong in the later Middle Ages and the sixteenth century', *Proceedings of the Royal Musical Association* 92 (1965/6), pp. 133–4. See also, Richard Sherr, 'The performance of chant in the Renaissance and its interactions with polyphony', in Thomas Forrest Kelly (ed.), *Plainsong in the Age of Polyphony*, Cambridge Studies in Performance Practice 2 (Cambridge 1992), pp. 178–208.

21 Thomas Morley, *A Plain and Easy Introduction to Practical Music*, ed. R. Alec Harman (London 1952), pp. 169–70.

22 *GB-Lbl* Add. 30513. See Denis Stevens (ed.), 'The Mulliner Book', *Musica Britannica* 1 (London 1951), p. 8.

23 *GB-Lbl* Add. 4911.

24 See Judson Dana Maynard, 'An anonymous Scottish treatise on music from the sixteenth century, British Museum, Additional Manuscript 4911: edition and commentary', 2 vols. (Diss., U. of Indiana 1961), II, p. 277.

25 See Stevens (ed.), 'The Mulliner Book', p. 14. Another example is John Bull's *In nomine* (IX), which presents the chant in the rhythmic figure breve–breve–semibreve–minim; see John Steele and Francis Cameron (eds.), 'John Bull, Keyboard Music: I', *Musica Britannica* 14 (London 1967), pp. 86–90.

26 'The sight of faburdon with his a cordis' (*GB-Lbl* Lansdowne 763, no. 16, f. 116–116ᵛ) is anonymous, but copied by John Wylde between 1430 and 1450, and is also known as Pseudo-Chilston's treatise. The first scholar to explain convincingly the process of faburden described in this source was Brian Trowell, 'Faburden and fauxbourdon', *Musica Disciplina* 13 (1959), pp. 43–78, where he gives the text and a modern transliteration. For a music example, see Brian Trowell, 'Faburden', in Sadie (ed.), *The New Grove*, 6, p. 352, ex. 2.

part was sung with the help of 'sights': at the beginnings and ends of phrases and where possible at the ends of words, the faburdener sights (i.e. imagines) unisons with the chant he is reading and pitches his voice down a fifth; for the rest of the chant he sights thirds above (still pitching his voice down a fifth). By the sixteenth century, a similar kind of faburden had the chant in the top voice (generally associated with continental fauxbourdon), rather than in the middle. In Scottish Anonymous's faburden of the First Kind, the chant is usually transposed up an octave, and the two lower parts are calculated from it.[27] According to Morley, 'he who sung the ground [the lowest part] would sing it a sixth under the true pitch'.[28] His music example, *Conditor alme siderum*, presents the chant on the upper staff and the faburden on a staff below, 'pricked a third above the plainsong yet it was always sung under the plainsong'.[29] Thus it presents faburden in a similar way to those indicated by sight notation in books of chant.

Scottish Anonymous spends most of the discussion of faburden describing the First Kind: presumably it is the most usual form. Although choristers may have participated in other kinds of improvisation involving parallel intervals with chant, these usually require more advanced skills for the lower parts, and would presumably be sung by older, more experienced singers. For example, Scottish Anonymous's Second Kind of faburden is related to the First, but is in four parts. 'The tribill and the tenor keipis the just way of fabourdoun'[30] (i.e. the chant is in the top part and the tenor sings sixths and octaves below), but the alto and bass are free. A written example following these rules is the sixth *Laudate pueri* in Fort Augustus Abbey Library fragment A.1.[31] Although it might seem that this kind of faburden could apply only to written rather than improvised music, Guillelmus Monachus, a late fifteenth-century theorist, describes a way of improvising faburden in which the treble has the chant, the tenor sings in sixths below it, the bass sings alternate thirds and fifths below the tenor, and the alto sings alternate fourths and thirds above the tenor.[32] The alto and bass singers would have to imagine the faburden and work out their parts from it. The last phrase of Scottish Anonymous's example is actually written this way.[33] Scottish Anonymous's Third Kind comprises the First Kind in a different mode; the resulting lowest part may be used as a *cantus firmus* in a written composition. The Fourth Kind has the chant in the tenor, and the alto and treble sing in

27 Sometimes the chant is transposed up a fourth. Although the resulting pitches sung are the same as Wylde's Anonymous, Scottish Anonymous still describes the procedure as deriving from the top part.

28 Morley, *A Plain and Easy Introduction*, p. 207.

29 Ibid. Morley writes that *falsobordone* is synonymous with faburden, but he is not referring to late sixteenth-century *falsobordone*, but apparently to that described by Zarlino in *Le Istitutione harmoniche* (1558) (one of Morley's sources). See John Bettley, 'North Italian *falsobordone* and its relevance to the early *stile recitativo*', *Proceedings of the Royal Musical Association* 103 (1976/7), p. 2.

30 As quoted in Maynard, 'Anonymous Scottish treatise', II, p. 303.

31 See Stephen Allenson, 'The Inverness fragments: music from a pre-Reformation Scottish parish church and school', *Music and Letters* 70 (1989), pp. 21 and 37–9.

32 See Andrew Hughes, 'Guillelmus Monachus', in Sadie (ed.), *The New Grove*, 7, p. 816, ex. 8.

33 Maynard, 'Anonymous Scottish treatise', I, p. 138.

fourths and sixths above, respectively, while the bass sings notes that are in unison with the chant, or a third, fifth or octave below the chant; this is similar to Monachus's description of gymel.[34]

Choristers would perform faburden in the same ways in which they sang monophonic chant: either unmeasured or with figuration. One assumes that hymns that were usually notated metrically (and presumably performed that way on most occasions) would usually be performed metrically if they were sung in faburden.[35] In performances based on unmeasured chant, there could be measuring at cadences, as in Morley's example, and in some faburden parts written in sight notation.[36] According to Scottish Anonymous, 'Faburdoun is ane melodius kynd of harmony quilk dois transmut and brek sympill noittes in figuris colorat be numeris trinar and bynar conform to the way of music mensurall';[37] all but one of his examples are in either duple or triple rhythm; the exception has mensural cadences. Perhaps the direction at St Mary's, Aberdeen, that priests were to sing 'faburdon, cum mensuris' refers to rhythmicized faburden.

After choristers had learned the basic forms of faburden, they learned descant, another form of improvising against chant but using more sophisticated 'sighting', i.e. involving a choice of more than two notes (all that was needed for basic faburden). According to Wylde's Anonymous, the descanter sighted several possible notes that were consonant with the written note; he sang one of them, which, together with his choices for subsequent written notes, would produce a pleasing melody.[38] Morley describes how singers practised: Master Bold 'continually carried a plainsong book in his pocket [and] he caused me [Polymathes] to do the like, and so, walking in the fields, he would sing the plainsong and cause me sing the descant, and when I sung not to his contentment he would show me wherein I had erred'.[39] Presumably in the classroom, individual boys would practise singing descants while others sang the chant; they would learn by listening to each other's attempts and to the master's critique. For this purpose, they may have used special books of chant: the 1493 accounts at Tattershall College record a payment to 'Roberto Lounde pro notacione diversorum cantuum ordinatorum pro choristis addiscentibus discant ixd'.[40] Such

34 See John Aplin, '"The Fourth Kind of faburden": the identity of an English four-part style', *Music and Letters* 61 (1980), pp. 48–50, and Hughes, 'Guillelmus Monachus', ex. 7.

35 See Mother Thomas More, 'The performance of plainsong in the later Middle Ages and the sixteenth century' (Diss., U. of Cambridge 1969), pp. 107–13, for information on sources of these hymns.

36 Ibid., pp. 252–6.

37 Maynard, 'Anonymous Scottish treatise', II, p. 281. 'Faburden is a melodious kind of harmony which alters and breaks simple notes [i.e. chant] into triple or duple figures as in mensural music.'

38 The text is given in Manfred Bukofzer, *Geschichte des englischen Diskants und des Fauxbourdons nach den theoretischen Quellen* (Strasbourg 1936), pp. 146–9. Sylvia W. Kenney was the first to explain English descant, in '"English discant" and discant in England', *Musical Quarterly* 45 (1959), pp. 26–48. See Brian Trowell, 'Sight, sights', in Sadie (ed.), *The New Grove*, 17, pp. 307–8, for the sighted and sounding pitches for the quatreble and treble voices.

39 Morley, *A Plain and Easy Introduction*, p. 214.

40 Quoted in Bowers, 'Choral institutions', p. 6023.

books may have contained chants that were particularly useful for beginners, such as *Miserere*, a favourite for counterpoint exercises later in the century, even after it was no longer used liturgically.

Choristers began their study of descant by learning note-against-note counterpoint.[41] More advanced descanters improvised two or more notes against each note of the chant. In order to do this, it was usually necessary for the chant to be sung rhythmically; Johannes Tinctoris refers to the difficulty of improvising against flexible performance of chant.[42] Using figuration methods, the rhythm of the underlying chant remains constant, and thus the singers improvising another part against the (ornamented) chant can anticipate what the next accented note will be and choose their pitches accordingly.[43] Against a stable *cantus firmus* choristers could apply figuration techniques to the descant itself. Morley's Master demonstrates how singers practised a descant with the rhythmic figure 'crotchet, minim, and crotchet' for each note of the chant;[44] then they practised 'minim and crotchet', and progressed on to *Tripla*, *Quadrupla*, etc. (referring to 'the number of black minims set for a note of the plainsong').[45] Teaching descant 'to four minims' (i.e. *quadrupla*) was one of the requirements of Robert Haywood, the master of choristers at Christ Church, Dublin, 1546.[46] The more advanced descanters improvised melodies that carried 'some form of relation to the plainsong' [such as singing] 'with a Point or Imitation',[47] or that involved difficult proportions. Scottish Anonymous's examples show that a descant of 'tua mynnyms', for example, does not necessarily comprise two minims, but rather several notes that take the time of two minims.[48]

Although descant was discussed in terms of two voices, the procedure did not preclude more than one descanting line improvised against a chant, as is described by Juan Bermudo in *Declaratión de instrumentos musicales* (1555).[49] Roger North, discussing music in England before his time, mentions that 'divers would descant upon plaine-song extempore together'.[50] Tinctoris suggests how it was done: the singers agreed 'among themselves on a similarity of assumptions and arrangement of concords'; i.e. they followed some kind of system ruling the

41 As described in *Lbl* Lansdowne 763 (no. 16).

42 Johannes Tinctoris, *The Art of Counterpoint (Liber de arte contrapuncti)*, transl. and ed. Albert Seay, *Musicological Studies and Documents* 5 ([Rome] 1961), p. 110 (bk. 2, ch. 21, 'How all counterpoint is made ... on plainchant').

43 *Ibid.*, pp. 110–12 (bk. 2, ch. 22, 'How counterpoint is made on figured song [*cantus figuratus*]' i.e. rhythmicized plainsong).

44 Morley, *A Plain and Easy Introduction*, p. 168. One of the examples of descant which Polymathes was given by his Master to study is an example of descant to four notes by Pygott.

45 *Ibid.*, p. 171.

46 See Harrison, *Music in Medieval Britain*, p. 197, who also refers to Morley.

47 Morley, *A Plain and Easy Introduction*, p. 149. Cf. the similar description given by Henri Madin, *Traité du Contrepoint simple ou du Chant sur le Livre* (Paris 1742), p. 25.

48 See the examples of descant transcribed by Maynard, 'Anonymous Scottish treatise', II, pp. 161–79.

49 See Bonnie J. Blackburn, 'On compositional process in the fifteenth century', *Journal of the American Musicological Society* 40 (1987), p. 259.

50 Roger North, *Memoirs of Musick, Now first printed from the original MS. and Edited, with copious Notes, by Edward F. Rimbault* (London 1846), p. 68.

progression of consonances. Such a system could include the use of the faburden techniques discussed above involving a restricted number of intervals sung in a certain order, or the application of descant to faburden, with a decorated version of the chant in the top part. This appears to be mentioned in a letter from a vicar, Richard Cliffe, written between 1427 and 1432, concerning the accomplishments of a collegiate vicar: he is 'als we her say, of connyng sufficient in redynge and sigynge of plane sane and te synge a trebull til faburdun, als I have harde ye abilaste men of our kirke say and record of hyme'.[51] It seems unlikely that a vicar's ability to sing the chant up an octave or to sing in fourths above chant would be so noteworthy. On the other hand, it would be so if he could improvise a descant above the undecorated chant while the bass part sang thirds or fifths below the chant; his choice of intervals would be even more restricted than for two-part descant.

After learning how to improvise against chant, choristers learned 'square-note'. 'The evidence currently available suggests that a square is a bottom part derived from a polyphonic composition of the late fourteenth century onwards in order to be used (usually via monophonic storage) in a later composition.'[52] In the context of choristers' training, I suggest that 'square-note' applies to improvisation against such melodies, i.e. mensural melodies, that are not chant;[53] written mensural faburdens fit into this category. That choristers sang squares, in place of chant, for others to improvise a descant against, is suggested by a two-part organ Kyrie and Christe that are based on the same square as is Nicholas Ludford's feria 3 Mass.[54] Likewise, choristers may have sung squares for faburden-style improvisations. One of the squares (that is not a mensural faburden) in GB-Llp 438 (feria 4) fits with a melody on the facing page that is in unison or in thirds below it; in a faburden-style performance, this melody would be sung up an octave (cf. Morley's example of faburden), and a middle voice would sing parallel fourths above the square.

Even more advanced sighting techniques were necessary for choristers learning how to improvise 'counter', a melody below chant; these choristers would also need to be older, singing in a lower range. Wylde's Anonymous, who provides the most detailed description of how to sing below chant, gives sights depending on the range of the singer.[55] Morley describes bass descant using similar terms: 'that kind of descanting where your sight of taking and using your chords [i.e. consonances] must be under the plainsong'.[56]

---

51 Quoted in Trowell, 'Faburden and fauxbourdon', p. 71.

52 Margaret Bent, 'Square [swarenote, sqwarenote]', in Sadie (ed.), *The New Grove*, 18, pp. 29–30.

53 The term apparently derives from the appearance of the notation of the melody. See Harrison, *Music in Medieval Britain*, p. 292; Andrew Wathey, 'New sources of English fifteenth- and sixteenth-century polyphony', compiled by Roger Bowers and Andrew Wathey, *Early Music History* 4 (1984), p. 333.

54 *GB-Lbl* Roy. App. 56. Denis Stevens (ed.), 'Early Tudor Organ Music II: Music for the Mass', *Early English Church Music* 10 (London 1967), pp. 16–17.

55 See Bukofzer, *Geschichte des englischen Discants*, pp. 149–52, and Trowell, 'Sight, sights'.

56 Morley, *A Plain and Easy Introduction*, p. 164.

Older choristers also learned to play the organ. For example, in 1527 at St Martin-the-Fields, the sum of 16s 8d was paid to 'Mr. Watts for his Child to pley at organs byal that yere'.[57] Since choristers learned the organ by transferring their vocal descant skills to the keyboard,[58] it is to be expected that most pre-Reformation books for the organ contain chant to be used as *cantus firmi* for improvising on;[59] the Inventories of King's College, Cambridge, in 1506 and 1529 include an 'antiphonal pro organis'. Perhaps one of the initial ways choristers transferred their (vocal) improvisatory skills to the organ was to have someone else sing or play the *cantus firmus* for them, while they improvised an additional part. One of William Byrd's pieces is entitled 'The playne song Briefs To Be played by a Second person – playe This Ut re mee Fa Sol la: For the grownd of this lesson';[60] *Lbl* Roy. App. 56 contains a *Felix namque* presumably for two players, since the *cantus firmus* is written in chant notation at the end of the piece with the instruction 'play the playne songe in lonke'.[61] Beginners would presumably also play or sing the chant in long, equal notes themselves, and practise descants against it with the other hand.[62] They would progress to improvising more than one part against the chant, and then on to improvising against measured versions of the chant (figuration) and square-note (including pieces 'on the faburden'). Presumably the measured plainsongs and faburdens in *Lbl* Roy. App. 56 (ff. 22ᵛ and 29) and the squares in *Lbl* Roy. App. 48 were for players to improvise on.[63] The contents of the Mulliner Book may show how beginners learned to play, since there is a noticeable increase in compositional complexity of the chant-based organ pieces. Those towards the beginning of the manuscript are in two or three voices and all but one (Tallis's *Natus est nobis*) present the chant in long, unornamented notes; towards the middle, most are in three voices, some are based on the faburden, and many have breaking or ornamenting of the chant; towards the end of the manuscript, most are in four voices and are highly contrapuntal. From the middle of the sixteenth century, choristers were also trained to play viols. Although these instruments were not used during liturgies at that time, the repertory probably included improvised

57 These examples are given by Hugh Baillie, 'London churches: their music and musicians, 1485–1560' (Diss., U. of Cambridge 1957), I, pp. 146–7.
58 Daniel Boys's indenture at Worcester (1522) refers to 'Descant, tam in cantacione quam in ludicione super organum' (Descant, both how to sing it and how to play it upon the organ); see Atkins, *Early Occupants of the Office of Organist*, p. 17.
59 Such books were still being provided for organists in Italy during the late sixteenth and early seventeenth centuries; for example, *Canto fermo sopra messe, hinni, et altre cose ecclesiastiche* (1596), by Giovanni Matteo Asola. See Benjamin van Wye, 'Ritual use of the organ in France', *Journal of the American Musicological Society* 33 (1980), p. 307.
60 Paris, Bibliothèque Nationale fonds du Conservatoire, Rés. MS 1122.
61 See Willi Apel, *The History of Keyboard Music to 1700*, transl. and rev. Hans Tischler (Bloomington and London 1972), p. 149.
62 Cf. continental treatises on playing the organ that begin with examples comprising chant in long notes and descants above or below, such as 'Instructions for Beginners' in Tomás de Santa Maria, *Arte de tañer fantasia* (Valladolid 1565).
63 See David Wulstan, *Tudor Music* (London 1985), p. 259.

chant-based music, similar to choristers' vocal and organ music. *Lbl* Roy. App. 56 includes *A solis ortus cardine* scored on two staves, for keyboard, and the same piece is in *Lbl* Roy. App. 58 in four separate parts.[64]

Sources connected with choristers' education in grammar and morals provide a significant amount of information concerning choristers' 'secular' music repertory. During this period, masters of choristers taught at least elementary grammar; for example, at Cirencester, Henry Edmund's indenture of 1538 states that when the choristers were 'sufficiently instructid in their prickid songe the said henry or his deputie shall instructe & teache their accidens of gramer'.[65] The grammar books masters used, such as Robert Whittinton's *Grammar*[66] and William Lily's *Instituto Compendiaria totius Grammaticae*,[67] taught the eight parts of speech and progressed on to grammatical constructions that were demonstrated by sentences in English (*vulgaria*) with their Latin translation. Some sentences provided useful vocabulary, since students could converse only in Latin:

> What parte synges thou. Qua voce cantas.
> He is cunnynge in syngynge. Peritus est cantandi.
> My throte is hoors. Guttur meum est raucum.[68]

Many phrases consisted of proverbs and classical and Christian *sententiae* (wise sayings), which were particularly valuable because they taught morals.

Masters of choristers incorporated proverbs and *sententiae* into songs that reinforce grammatical and moral lessons. *GB-Lbl* Add. 15233 includes song-texts by masters John Redford, John Thorne, [?Thomas] Knyght, and their associates John Heywood (who put on entertainments performed by choristers), Thomas Pridioux and Miles Huggard.[69] *The Paradise of Dainty Devices* (1576), a collection made by Richard Edwards, master of the choristers at the Chapel Royal, is (rightly) considered unusual as a printed poetry miscellany, because of its 'single-mindedly didactic motive',[70] in which 'gravity, didacticism, and proverbial

64 See Kenton Parton, 'On two early Tudor manuscripts of keyboard music', *Journal of the American Musicological Society* 17 (1964), p. 82.
65 Public Record Office, E. 315/94, ff. 159ᵛ–161.
66 This book was listed in the will of Richard Sharpe, a master of choristers who died in the mid-1530s (Toullyes Offesses; Ovids Postallis; Melantons gramer; methaforfoceos; vergell; tyrens without comyt; one gmer boke; Eligens vallot; colloquium; Ysoppus fabuli; wityngtonys gmer; Adagus; Tules Pistillis), as quoted in A. White, '"Tam in cantu quam in gramatica" – Richard Sharp, an early Tudor song and grammar master', *Durham Research Review* 5 (1965), p. 4.
67 This grammar was prescribed by law in 1540, and also authorized during the reigns of Edward VI, Mary and Elizabeth I; see Nicholas Orme, *English Schools in the Middle Ages* (London 1973), p. 258.
68 John Stanbridge's *Vulgaria*, as quoted in Beatrice White, *The Vulgaria of John Stanbridge and the Vulgaria of Robert Whittinton*, Early English Text Society, original ser., 187 (London and Oxford 1932), 17; 18; 19. 'What part do you sing? He is skilful at singing. My throat is hoarse.' From 1488 to 1494 Stanbridge was master at Magdalen College School, where choristers from Magdalen College and Corpus Christi College received their education.
69 The manuscript also contains liturgical organ music, a moralistic play for choristers by Redford and two fragments of plays. An edition was published by James Orchard Halliwell, *The Moral Play of Wit and Science and Early Poetical Miscellanies from an Unpublished Manuscript* (London 1848).
70 Elizabeth W. Pomeroy, *The Elizabethan Miscellanies: Their Development and Conventions* (Berkeley, Los Angeles and London 1973), p. 53.

philosophy are conspicuous'.[71] The collection was published posthumously, and the editor's preface mentions that the poems were intended to be sung.

Examples of songs of this kind include Edwards's *In going to my naked bedde*, which has as a refrain 'The fallyng out of faithfull frends is the renuyng [renewing] of love', a *sententia* in both Whittinton's and Lily's grammars ('Amantium irae amoris redinti gratia est');[72] Francis Kinwelmerch's (or Kindelmarsh's) *By painted words*, which is based on a *sententia* included in Thomas Elyot's *Bankette of Sapience*[73] ('The greattest token and offyce of sapyence, is that the dedes do agree with the wordes, and that the persone be ever one, and lyke to hym selfe');[74] and *Yf vertu sprynge, wheras youth raynythe*, which has the single-line refrain 'Servire Deo regnare est' ('to serve God is to reign').[75] Some choristers' songs are ballads based on classical stories given a Christian focus (such as were used in the study of grammar); an example is Edwards's *Fortitude: a yong man of Ægipt, and Valerian.*[76] Others are moralizations of ballads that in their original form were not necessarily considered suitable for children; Thorne's *The hunt is up* uses exciting hunting imagery to teach salvation history.[77] On the other hand, some songs were written primarily for choristers' entertainment: Redford's *Of all the creatures, lesse or moe / We lytle poore boyes abyde much woe* is a choristers' complaint about their master (Redford himself).[78] Another category of choristers' songs seems initially to have little or no pedagogical use: love songs and laments. However, these had a place in the plays that masters wrote for their choristers, plays that were also intended to reinforce grammatical and moral lessons. For example, Redford's *Exceedyng mesure wyth paynes continewall* is to be sung in his moralistic play *Wit and Science*, in which Wit eventually conquers Tediousness and marries Science.[79]

Examples of the kinds of songs described above can be found in choristers' plays. Therefore, although little music survives for them, stage-directions, references to, and descriptions of music in plays and other entertainments provide useful information concerning choristers' secular music in general. Many vocal solos with serious or moralistic texts are accompanied, either with regals, as in

---

71 Hyder Edward Rollins, Introduction to Richard Edwards, *The Paradise of Dainty Devices (1576–1606)* (Cambridge Mass. 1927), p. lxvi.

72 See Edwards, *Paradise of Dainty Devices*, ed. Rollins, pp. 50–1. The *sententia* is from Terence, and is an example to show that 'a verbe personall agreeth with his nomynatyve case, in number and person', according to Lily's *Grammar*. See also White, *Vulgaria*, p. 39.

73 This collection 'in a litle rome [room] sheweth out of holy scripture many wise sentences', according to Elyot's list (1541) of his works to date, as quoted in Lillian Gottesman, Introduction to Thomas Elyot, *Four Political Treatises* (Gainsville Fla. 1967), p. xiv.

74 See Edwards, *Paradise of Dainty Devices*, ed. Rollins, pp. 21–2. The *sententia* is from Seneca, under the heading 'Sapience', in Elyot, *Four Political Treatises*, p. 92.

75 Halliwell (ed.), *Wit and Science*, pp. 60–1.

76 Edwards, *Paradise of Dainty Devices*, ed. Rollins, pp. 57–8.

77 Halliwell (ed.), *Wit and Science*, pp. 65–8.

78 *Ibid.*, pp. 62–5.

79 *Ibid.*, pp. 83–4.

Edwards's *Awake ye wofull Wightes* from *Damon and Pithias*,[80] or four viols, as in
Exceedyng Mesure from *Wit and Science*; these instruments, also mentioned
frequently in non-dramatic entertainments,[81] were apparently considered inter-
changeable. Three sources preserve *Awake ye wofull Wightes*: an arrangement for
solo voice and lute (an instrument rarely mentioned in choristers' plays); as a
tune on a broadside-ballad; and as the 'tenor' of a metrical hymn, *I woeful wretched
wight*.[82] If the version with the lute accompaniment were played on viols or
regals, it would be typical of the 'consort song' from this period: it is strophic,
the text is set syllabically and simply, and the accompaniment is basically
homophonic (with short interludes between phrases). Similar in style are the
fragment *Com now to mee my faithfull wife* for solo voice and three viols (four
parts), which appears to be another example of a lament from a choristers' play,[83]
and settings of two moralistic song-texts, *In youthly years* and Heywood's *What
hart can think?* for voice and lute.[84] Choristers probably played the same musical
settings of the two moralistic songs, only on viols or regals rather than lute. The
pitch of the solo vocal part of both songs shows that the accompaniments are
set for a lute tuned on D, suggesting that they were adapted from four-part
consort versions: the standard viol tuning is on D.[85] Similar arrangements were
probably sung by ensembles as well as by solo voices: the final song in *Wit and
Science* – *Remember man* (possibly a version of the moralistic ballad)[86] – is sung
by everyone on stage and accompanied by four viols. Choristers also sang
polyphonic settings: the (incomplete) setting of the last song in *Bugbears* (*Sith
all our grief*) has three parts all in a high tessitura; it lacks a bass part, which may
have been supplied by an instrumental accompaniment that would complete the

80 Richard Edwards, *The excellent Comedie of two the moste faithfullest Freendes, Damon and Pithias* (London 1571).
    For a modern edition see Edwards, *Damon and Pithias*, Malone Society Reprints, ed. Arthur Brown and F. P.
    Wilson (Oxford 1957). The first documented performance is 1564.
81 For example, at the progress of Edward VI in 1547, 'six Children richly apparelled … plaid upon the Regalles,
    and sang, with great melody, divers goodly Songs', according to John Leland, *De Rebus Britannicus Collectanea*,
    ed. Thomas Hearne (London 1770), p. 4. For other examples see Ian Woodfield, *The Early History of the Viol*
    (Cambridge Musical Texts and Monographs [3]) (Cambridge 1984), pp. 213–14.
82 See Temperley, *Music of the English Parish Church*, I, p. 35, and ibid., II, pp. 44–5, exx. 11a and 11b for transcrip-
    tions of the ballad and the voice and lute arrangement (*GB-Lbl* Add. 15117), with the text of the first stanza.
83 *GB-Lbl* Add. 4900. For a transcription see Jane Flynn, 'A reconsideration of the Mulliner Book (British
    Library Add. MS 30513): music education in sixteenth-century England' (Diss., Duke University 1993),
    pp. 578–9.
84 *Lbl* Add. 15117 and *Lbl* Add. 4900 respectively. See David Greer (ed.), *Songs from Manuscript Sources* (London
    1979), I, pp. 8–11, and Flynn, 'A reconsideration of the Mulliner Book', pp. 568–9, for transcriptions of these
    songs, respectively. Milsom's transcription of *What hart can think?* transposes the vocal line up a fourth 'to
    lute pitch', in John Ross Milsom, 'English polyphonic style in transition: a study of the sacred music of
    Thomas Tallis' (Diss., U. of Oxford 1984), II, Appendix 4.6C. Both song-texts are in *Lbl* Add. 15233, and *In
    youthful yeares* is also in *Paradise of Dainty Devices*.
85 See Mary Joiner, 'British Museum Add. MS. 15117: a commentary, index and bibliography', [*Royal Musical
    Association*] *Research Chronicle* 7 (1969), pp. 59–60.
86 The 1566 version of this ballad-text is given in Herbert L. Collmann (ed.), *Ballads and Broadsides chiefly of
    the Elizabethan Period and printed in Black-letter*, Roxburghe Club (Oxford 1912), pp. 177–9.

harmony and fill out the rests between phrases.[87] A setting of Kinwelmerch's *By painted words* (see above), entitled *O the silly man* in the Mulliner Book,[88] has a similar, high compass (d–f^2), and may have been intended for choristers to sing in four parts, perhaps accompanied by regals. Light-hearted songs, both solos and carols (in which solo stanzas alternate with refrains for two, three or four parts), are usually unaccompanied, as in *Patient Grissell* and *Horestes*,[89] where ballad tunes are specified for solo songs, and in *Damon and Pithias*, where Jack and Wyll sing alternate lines of each stanza and perhaps of the refrain (or they sing together), and Grimme the Collier sings a bass part, 'in my man's voice'. The first song in *Misogonus* – *Sing care away* – is sung 'to the tune of Heart's Ease' by a treble, a mean (the name of the voice is illegible), a 'counterfeit tenor' and a bass; the setting probably had a high tessitura.[90]

In addition to playing accompaniments, viols and regals were also used for purely instrumental music in plays. In *The Play of the Wether*, 'a song [is] played' by a group of musicians to honour the god Jupiter as he exits and before Mery Report enters;[91] in *Damon and Pithias*, 'the Regalles play a mourning song'; in *Cambyses*, two characters play the lute and gittern together.[92] Most instrumental music comprised dances, usually galliards based on grounds. Choristers who could sing descant would use their skill to improvise melodies over a repeating bass. In *Wit and Science*, a galliard based on the *passamezzo* (if I read the puns correctly)[93] was probably played on viols, since these instruments are used later in the play.

87 It survives in a manuscript (*GB-Lbl* Lansdowne 807) in five different hands. The five song-texts are written out at the end of the play, with (incomplete) music for two of them. For a modern edition see [John Jeffere], *The Bugbears: A Modernized Edition*, ed. James D. Clark (New York and London 1979). It was performed at court by boys between 1563 and c. 1570, according to Yoshiko Kawachi, *Calendar of English Renaissance Drama, 1558–1642* (New York and London 1986), p. 9.

88 Stevens (ed.), 'The Mulliner Book', p. 59.

89 *The Commodye of pacient and meeke Grissell, wherain is declared, the good example, of her pacience towardes her husband: and lykewise, the due obedience of Children, towards their Parentes* (London [1566?]). For a modern edition see John Phillip, *The Play of patient Grissell by John Phillip*, Malone Society Reprints, ed. Ronald B. McKerrow and W. W. Greg (Chiswick 1909). The play was offered for acting between 1558 and 1561, according to Kawachi, *Calendar of English Renaissance Drama*, p. 2. *A New Enterlude of Vice conteyninge the Historye of Horestes with the cruell revengment of his Fathers death upon his one naturall Mother*, by John Pikering, was printed in 1567. For a modern edition see Marie Axton (ed.), *Three Tudor Classical Interludes: Thersites, Jacke Jugeler, Horestes* (Cambridge 1982).

90 See the discussion below of Ravenscroft's settings of songs from plays written later in the century.

91 *The Play of the Wether: A new and a very mery enterlude of all maner wethers*, by John Heywood, was performed in 1533 and printed in 1533 and ?1544. For a modern edition see Heywood, *The Plays of John Heywood*, ed. Richard Axton and Peter Happé, Tudor Interludes 6 (Cambridge 1991).

92 *A Lamentable tragedy mixed ful of pleasant mirth, conteyning the life of Cambyses king of percia...* by Thomas Preston was possibly performed by the St Paul's boys in 1560, and registered in 1569–70 and printed in 1569 by J. Alde.

93 *Wyt*   Cum now, a basse!

     Honest Recreacion   Nay, syr, as for bassys,
                                   From hence none passys,
                                   But as in gage
                                   Of mary-age.
                                   …

     Honest Recreacion   Go to, my men, play.

Thus, choristers' music, grammar, non-liturgical songs, and plays – the various components of their education – all had the liturgy and moral education as their focus. This unified approach to choristers' education gradually eroded during Elizabeth's reign.

CHORISTERS' EDUCATION AFTER C. 1565

Masters of choristers' indentures dating from the late sixteenth and early seventeenth centuries[94] place a greater emphasis on instruments than before, and are generally unspecific as regards vocal and improvisational skills, because liturgical music was no longer chant-based. It was now more important for choristers to be able to read music than to memorize 'plainsong'. Most choristers still learned to read music using solfège syllables and the gamut,[95] as in Ravenscroft's manuscript 'Treatise of Musick',[96] William Bathe's *Briefe Introduction to the Skill of Song* (?1597) and Morley's *Plaine and Easie Introduction to Practicall Musicke* (1597). However, the method was not always followed, especially as instrumental music grew in importance.[97] In Thomas Robinson's *New Citharen Lessons* (1609), written as a dialogue, the Master uses the strings and frets, rather than the gamut, to teach the Scholler; all of his examples are in tablature.[98]

Choristers did not need to learn complex methods of improvising for performance during the liturgy; they needed to learn how to *write* music for the liturgy. According to Morley, 'the excellent musicians have discontinued it [descant] ... but they rather employ their time in making [i.e. composing] of songs'.[99] He also states that the term 'descant' had changed its meaning to apply to composing.[100] Thus, choristers now studied and emulated (in written form) compositional techniques demonstrated in sets of short examples written specifically for the purpose. Such examples are based on chant chosen for purely academic reasons; they merely demonstrate compositional technique, and are not

94 For example, at Westminster, 1560, 'Boys of a young age and clear voices for singing, and for teaching the art of music and also apt for playing on musical instruments, who serve, minister and sing in the choir'; as quoted in E[dmund] K[erchever] Chambers, *The Elizabethan Stage*, 4 vols. (Oxford 1923), II, p. 71. See also Brian Crosby, 'The song school at Durham', *Durham University Journal* 60 (1968), p. 67, for information on Langley song school, 1582; Mary Elizabeth Smith, 'Nathaniel Giles "from Windsor": Master of the Children in the Chapel Royal', *Notes & Queries* 225 (1980), pp. 126–7, for St George's, Windsor, 1585 and 1595; Alan Smith, 'Parish church musicians in England in the reign of Elizabeth I (1558–1603): an annotated register', *[Royal Musical Association] Research Chronicle* 4 (1964), p. 77, for the song school in Newark in the 1590s; Woodfield, *Early History of the Viol*, p. 247, fn. 78, for Peterborough, 1614.
95 See Anthony Mundy's poem, *The Paine of Pleasure, describing in a perfect mirror the miseries of man* (?1585).
96 GB-Lbl Add. 19758.
97 See Eberhard Preussner, 'Solmisationsmethoden im Schulunterricht des 16. und 17. Jahrhunderts', in *Festschrift Fritz Stein zum 60. Geburtstag überreicht von Fachgenossen, Freunden und Schüler*, ed. Hans Hoffmann and Franz Rühlmann (Braunschweig 1939), p. 127.
98 Thomas Robinson, *New Citharen Lessons, with perfect tunings of the same, from Foure course of strings to Fourteen courses...* (London 1609).
99 Morley, *A Plain and Easy Introduction*, p. 215.
100 *Ibid.*, p. 204. 'By continuance of time, that name [descant] is also degenerated into another significance and for it we use the word "setting" or "composing".'

intended as pieces in their own right. Elway Bevin, who uses one *cantus firmus* in *A Briefe and Short Instruction*, explains that he has set his examples 'downe very brief and short, and have made choice of the Plainsong of purpose, to the intent, the Learner or Practitioner may the better conceive of every particular'.[101] Presumably for the same reason, Morley uses one *cantus firmus* for 56 of his examples of two- and three-part counterpoint in his *Plain and Easy Introduction*.[102] Nathaniel Giles's 'Lesson of Descant of thirtie-eight Proportions of Sundrie Kindes' is based on the *Miserere*,[103] a frequently chosen chant, presumably because it is one of the shorter chants, and has the compass of only a fifth.[104] The very rudimentary 'Pretty Wayes: For Young Beginners to looke on' comprise fifteen short two-part pieces and one three-part piece on the same newly written 'plainsong' similar to *Jam lucis* and the beginning of the *In nomine*;[105] they demonstrate 'wayes' of writing descants to a *cantus firmus*. Canons were considered particularly valuable for learning composition; according to Morley, they 'lead you by the hand to a further knowledge'.[106] The study of sets of canons was a new pedagogical method in England at this time, according to the preface of John Farmer's *Divers and sundry waies to two part in one* (1591).[107] Other examples similar to Farmer's include the twenty 'wayes of 2 Pts in One of Tho. Woodson' (on *Miserere*),[108] Bathe's *X. sundry wayes of 2. partes in one upon the plaine song* contained in his *Briefe Introduction*, and sets by W. B. on *O lux beata* and *Miserere*.[109]

Whereas pre-Reformation choristers studied extracts of compositions, during Elizabeth's reign choristers scored and collected entire works for study and emulation; this was apparently a new procedure in England.[110] Scottish Anonymous represents a transitional stage, in that some of his examples comprise the final few bars of several pieces and some are complete vocal and instrumental pieces, such as the *Lessons* on the first two psalms and the *Report on When sall my sorrowful sighing slack* for viol consort by John Black, master of the choristers

---

101 Elway Bevin, *A Briefe and Short Instruction of the art of Musicke, to teach how to make Discant* (London 1631), p. 22.

102 Morley, *A Plain and Easy Introduction*, p. xxii.

103 *GB-Lbl* R.M. 24.d.2.

104 Peter Kolb Danner has studied and transcribed many examples of pieces based on the *Miserere* in 'The *Miserere Mihi* and the English Reformation: a study of the evolution of a cantus firmus genre in Tudor music [with] transcriptions' (Diss., Stanford University 1967).

105 *GB-Lbl* Add. 29996. See Hugh M. Miller, 'Pretty Wayes: For Young Beginners to looke on', *Musical Quarterly* 33 (1947), p. 547. Miller includes transcriptions of all these 'wayes' on pp. 555–6.

106 Morley, *A Plain and Easy Introduction*, p. 201.

107 As quoted in Lewis Pascal Bowling, 'A transcription and comparative analysis of "Divers and Sundry Waies of Two Partes in One" (1591) by John Farmer' (Diss., University of Northern Colorado 1982), p. 112. Farmer's set of canons follows Zarlino's use of canons in 'The art of counterpoint', pt. 3 of *Instituzioni Armoniche* [1558].

108 *GB-Lbl* Add. 29996. See Hugh Milton Miller, 'Forty Wayes of 2 Pts. in One of Tho[mas] Woodson', *Journal of the American Musicological Society* 8 (1955), p. 19.

109 *GB-Lbl* Add. 31391.

110 Such compositional procedures are described by Zacconi in his two books of *Prattica di Musica*, 1592 and 1619, as explained by James Haar in 'A sixteenth-century attempt at music criticism', *Journal of the American Musicological Society* 36 (1983), pp. 197–8.

at Aberdeen; all are in score and have no text underlaid. *GB-Lbl* Add. 31390, entitled 'A Booke of In nomines and other solfaing songs', includes pieces useful for study such as Christopher Tye's *In nomine* entitled *Trust*, which has five minims to a bar (cf. descant).[111] It also includes pieces by students that begin with an extract from another composer's work; for example, four of the *In nomines* begin in a similar way to John Taverner's. Likewise, a piece in *GB-Och* 1113 begins with a point from one of John Coprario's three-part viol fantasias, and one signed B[enjamin] C[osyn] is a reworking of Orlando Gibbons's four-part organ fantasia.[112] Robert White's five *In nomines* use points and direct quotes from Tye's works.[113]

The pieces in *Lbl* Add. 31390 and other similar collections dating from the second half of the century were intended for performance by choristers (not amateurs), who sang them (using solmization syllables) or played them on instruments.[114] Choristers may also have played the viols in liturgical music: the early verse- or consort-anthem with accompaniment for organ or viols dates from this period.[115] As mentioned above, masters' indentures reflect an increased use of instruments in choristers' education. There are many other references to this: at Ely in 1567 choristers were taught viol;[116] John Colden, master of choristers at Worcester 1569–81, bequeathed to his successor, Giles, 'my clavycordes and all my song Books';[117] Sebastian Westcote (d. 1582) bequeathed to the Almonry at St Paul's 'my cheste of vyalyns and vialles to exercise and learne the children and Choristers';[118] and an inventory of the song school at Newark-on-Trent (1597), includes 'five violine bookes' and 'five violins'.[119]

Thus, a significant amount of the music Elizabethan choristers learned was not focused directly on the liturgy, and in many respects music education became specialized: it was useful for musicians only, rather than for all church officers. Likewise, a knowledge of Latin grammar was no longer necessary for performing the liturgy,[120] and choristers began receiving all of their grammar education at

111 See Jeremy Noble, 'Le répertoire instrumental anglais: 1550–1585', in Jean Jacquot (ed.), *La musique instrumentale de la Renaissance* (Paris 1955), pp. 91–114.
112 Gerald Hendrie (ed.), 'Orlando Gibbons: Keyboard Music', *Musica Britannica* 20 (London 1962), no. 12. Note, dated 1987, written by G[ordon] Dodd and attached to the manuscript.
113 See Oliver Neighbour, *The Consort and Keyboard Music of William Byrd* (Berkeley and Los Angeles 1978), pp. 32–3.
114 See Neighbour, *Consort and Keyboard Music of William Byrd*, p. 27; Warwick A. Edwards, 'The performance of ensemble music in Elizabethan England', *Proceedings of the Royal Musical Association* 97 (1970/71), p. 119; and Woodfield, *Early History of the Viol*, pp. 216–18.
115 See Peter le Huray, *Music and the Reformation in England, 1549–1600* (London 1967; Cambridge 2/1978), pp. 217–25.
116 Godfrey Arkwright, 'Note on the instrumental accompaniment of church music in the sixteenth and seventeenth centuries', in *Six Anthems by John Milton*, Old English Edition 22 (London and Oxford 1900), p. 14.
117 As quoted in J. Bunker Clark, 'Dr. Gyles and the choirboys', *Diapason* 71 (1980), p. 3.
118 Public Record Office, Prerogative Court of Canterbury, 14 Tirwhite.
119 Brown, *History of Newark-on-Trent*, p. 207.
120 Only the choristers and clerks who sang at collegiate and royal chapels performed services from the 1560 *Liber Precum Publicarum seu ministerii Ecclesiaticae administrationis Sacramentorum aliorumque rituum et caerimoniarum in Ecclesia Anglicana*.

grammar schools.[121] Moreover, since grammar and moral education were so closely connected, choristers would also receive much of their moral instruction there. Nevertheless, masters of choristers' indentures still refer to a responsibility for the moral up-bringing of the boys: Thomas Giles was to see that the choristers were 'brought up in all vertue, civility and honest manners'.[122] Andrew Kempe was appointed to the Aberdeen Song School in 1570 to teach 'mwsek, meaners, and wertew'.[123] Hence, masters continued to write or at least collect moralistic, proverbial poetry. From the mid-1560s to the 1580s, many of their moralistic songs were printed in the form of broadside ballads or in books. *The Paradise of Dainty Devises* was reprinted several times with additions; other popular collections include *A Hive full of Hunnys* (1578), by William Hunnis, master of choristers at the Chapel Royal; the *Courte of Vertue* (1565),[124] by John Hall (c. 1529–66), which includes moralistic songs to be sung to the ballad- or psalm-like tunes he provides, one of which is set in four parts; and John Wedderburn's translations of German hymns and religious songs and moralizations of English ballads in *A Compendious Book of Godly and Spiritual Songs* (1567).[125] With the reading public, moralistic songs had a short-lived appeal: in collections of the 1590s, 'the moral earnestness of collections from the 1570s is entirely gone'.[126] To some extent, masters of choristers continued to collect proverbial poetry; for example, Andrew Melville, master of the song school at Aberdeen between 1636 and 1640, compiled a commonplace book containing proverbs and poems based on them.[127]

Nevertheless, it appears that moralistic songs were not used as much in choristers' education as they were earlier in the century. For one thing, choristers' plays became increasingly secularized and separated from the study of grammar and morals. From 1575 and 1576 on, the St Paul's and Chapel Royal boys respectively not only performed their plays in theatres for the public,[128] there was 'fierce commercial competition with the men's companies ... [which] accounts for the recourse [in choristers' plays] to racy comedy and vicious

121 For example, the document of appointment of Thomas Giles as master at St Paul's in 1584, states that 'the said Thomas shall suffer them [the choristers] to resorte to paules schole tow howers in the forenone and one hower in the afternoon ... that they may learne the principles of gramer, and after as they shall be forwardes learne the said catechisms in Laten which before they lerned in Englishe and other good bookes taught in the said Schole'. As quoted in Reavley Gair, 'The conditions of appointment for masters of choristers at Paul's (1553–1613)', *Notes & Queries* 225 (1980), p. 119.

122 *Ibid.*

123 Quoted in William Walker, *Extracts from the Commonplace Book of Andrew Melville, Doctor and Master in the Song School of Aberdeen 1621–1640* (Aberdeen 1899), p. xxviii.

124 John Hall, *The Court of Virtue (1565)*, ed. Russell A. Fraser (New Brunswick NJ 1961), pp. 259–64.

125 See *A Compendius Book of Godly and Spiritual Songs commonly known as "The Gude and Godlie Ballatis" reprinted from the Edition of 1567*, edited with Introduction and Notes by A. F. Mitchell, *The Scottish Text Society* 39 (repr. New York and London 1966).

126 Pomeroy, *Elizabethan Miscellanies*, p. 18.

127 See Walker, *Extracts from the Commonplace Book of Andrew Melville.*

128 Masters received money for such performances. See Smith, 'Nathaniel Giles', pp. 125–6.

political satire'.[129] Choristers' performances were now intended more for the
audience's entertainment than their own edification, and professional playwrights
such as John Lyly and John Marston began writing their plays. Edmund Pearce,
master at St Paul's from 1599, appears to have been more interested in the secular
activities of his choristers than in their liturgical duties. No sacred music by him
survives, whereas at least some of his music for choristers' plays survives in
Ravenscroft's publications, and he abused his privilege of impressing boys for
the choir by taking up boys who could act but not sing, for the theatre.[130]

Stage-directions and examples of music surviving for the plays show that
musical performances in plays were more elaborate than before. Ravenscroft's
Pammelia and *Deuteromelia* (both 1609), *Melismata* (1611) and *Brief Discourse* (1614),
include popular songs, freeman's songs, and madrigals used in plays by the St
Paul's boys c. 1597 – c. 1604.[131] Many plays include consort songs: long,
through-composed laments in five parts for solo with viol accompaniment.[132]
Furthermore, performances included pre-, *entr'acte* and finale music. The diary
of Philip Julius, Duke of Stettin-Pomerania, contains a description of music
performed before a play at Blackfriars in 1602.[133] John Marston's *Sophonisba*,
'printed onely as it was presented by the youth', contains stage-directions referring
to instrumental music during the play (e.g. 'a treble viol and a bass lute play
softly within the canopy') and *entr'acte* music (e.g. 'Organs, viols, and voices'
after Act III); other instruments mentioned are cornets and recorders.[134]

Thus, during Elizabeth's reign, music, grammar and morals began to be treated
as separate subjects, and in a specialized manner: music became the main subject
at choir schools. This training was not as valuable to non-musicians as it had
been: according to the anonymous 'Praise of Musick',[135] beginning in Elizabeth's
reign, 'those children which supplye the place of Choristers [at cathedrals], they
are of the poore and beggerly sort, whose parents are not able to pay any thinge
for their learninge'. However, choristers' education now prepared them for
musical careers outside as well as inside the church. Some taught music privately,
and some may have become town waits. It does not seem coincidental that at

129 Philip Brett, 'The English consort song, 1570–1625', *Proceedings of the Royal Musical Association* 88 (1961/2), p.
79. According to Lennam, 'the Paul's boys were quick to meet the changing demands of courtly taste in
the seventies, replacing moral interludes with the more spectacular plays based upon classical sources'. Trevor
[N. S.] Lennam, *Sebastian Westcott, the Children of Paul's, and 'The Marriage of Wit and Science'* (Toronto 1975),
p. 48. See also Linda Phyllis Austern, *Music in English Children's Drama of the Later Renaissance*, Musicology: A
Book Series 13 (USA, Switzerland, Australia, etc. 1992), pp. 35–42.
130 The Clifton suit, 1600 (Star Chamber Proceedings, Elizabeth, C 46/39), concerns the taking up of eight boys
who were in 'noe way able or fitt for singing' and who were employed 'only in playes and enterludes', not
in liturgies.
131 See Austern, *Music in English Children's Drama*, pp. 212–19. See *ibid.*, pp. 49–77, for a general description of
music in children's plays of the period.
132 See Philip Brett (ed.), 'Consort Songs', *Musica Britannica* 22 (London 1974).
133 See le Huray, *Music and the Reformation*, p. 220.
134 John Marston, *The Selected Plays of John Marston*, ed. MacDonald P. Jackson and Michael Neill (Cambridge
1986), pp. 460 and 452.
135 *GB-Lbl* Roy. 18. B. xix.

the time when the first group of choristers educated entirely during Elizabeth's reign graduated, the London waits began to expand their musical horizons;[136] by the end of the century, they were considered very fine musicians: Morley dedicated his book of *Consort Lessons* (1599) to them. Thus, the methods of educating choristers during the sixteenth century fitted the changing circumstances of musicians.

136 They no longer restricted themselves to wind instruments: in 1561 they purchased 'certain instruments called a set of vialles'; in 1568, a 'whole set of recorders', and in 1576, 'certain new instruments'. See Walter L. Woodfill, *Musicians in English Society from Elizabeth to Charles I* (Princeton 1953), p. 34.

9

THE 'BURDEN OF PROOF':
THE EDITOR AS DETECTIVE

JOHN MOREHEN

Writing several years ago in conjunction with the launch of *The Byrd Edition*, Philip Brett wisely cautioned readers to bear in mind the theory of 'the duplicity of duplicates' advanced by the former Bodley's Librarian, Falconer Madan – a theory which established as good working practice the assumption that two copies of an edition were different unless they could be proven to be identical.[1] In view of the ease with which a unique source of an early musical composition, be it manuscript or printed, can be assumed to be reliable, the astute editor might do well to extrapolate from this maxim by assuming any such source to be defective unless convinced of its accuracy.

The surviving sources of English sacred music of the period c. 1550 – c. 1640 are, almost without exception, both unreliable as to musical and textual detail and uninformative as to performing practice. No collections of liturgical music were published in England between 1565 and 1641, a period delimited by Day's somewhat wayward *Certaine notes set forth in foure and three parts* and John Barnard's no less defective *First Book of Selected Church Musick*, which contained only music by composers who were no longer living. So far as manuscript sources are concerned, most are of provincial provenance and demonstrably embody a high degree of corruption, while of the autograph manuscripts few contain music by front-rank composers. Not a note of autograph church music survives by composers such as Thomas Tallis, William Byrd, Orlando Gibbons, Thomas Weelkes or Thomas Tomkins, for instance, although autograph sources are plentiful for second-flight composers such as Robert Ramsey, John Amner, Henry Loosemore, and a host of less accomplished musicians. The suspicion that the surviving sources convey at best an imperfect picture (and at worst a thoroughly misleading one) is thus inescapable. Areas of particular unease not only encompass the nuts-and-bolts of music and verbal text, but also extend to aspects of compositional structure and many fundamental areas of performing practice. This chapter addresses a sample selection of such areas of concern.

---

1   Philip Brett, 'Editing Byrd – 2', *The Musical Times* 121 (1980), p. 558.

COMPOSITIONAL STRUCTURE

Although the desire for simplicity in the immediate aftermath of the Reformation ordained a cautious approach to form, a clear preoccupation with formal organization can nevertheless be discerned. Although it is most evident in the *ABB* structure of numerous short Edwardian and early Elizabethan anthems, it is found also in some more extended works, such as Tye's *If ye be risen again with Christ*,[2] which even deprived of its repeat runs to some 74 bars. In many instances – such as Mundy's *O Lord the maker of all thing*[3] and Tye's *If ye be risen again*[4] – the repeat is found in selected sources only. Two alternative scenarios present themselves: first, that some scribes deliberately doctored a composition in simple *AB* form so as to make it conform to the more popular *ABB* form; or secondly, and surely more plausibly, that some scribes either ignored or carelessly overlooked a direction to repeat, thus transmitting a straightforward *AB* form.[5] If we accept the latter as being the more likely eventuality, the clear possibility emerges that repeats were sometimes intended in pieces which – so far as the surviving sources are concerned – no longer contain them. The place at which such a repeat might be expected to commence is the point where a homophonic opening passage concludes with a clearly defined cadence and is followed by imitative writing. The anthems of Thomas Tallis are instructive in this regard. With the exception of *contrafacta* and psalm-tune harmonizations the majority of Tallis's anthems[6] exhibit *ABB* form, as the following table shows:

Table 9:1: Anthems by Tallis in *ABB* form.

Title	Length in bars (without repeat)	Length in bars (with repeat)
A new commandment	[30]	[53]
Hear the voice and prayer	34	57
If ye love me	26	39
O Lord give thy Holy Spirit	29	40
Out from the deep	[24]	38
Purge me O Lord	24	35

A repeat is signalled in all sources of two of the above anthems – *Hear the voice and prayer* and *Purge me O Lord* – while the presence of a repeat in certain sources only is a feature of a further two – *If ye love me* and *O Lord give thy Holy Spirit*.

2 John Morehen (ed.), 'Christopher Tye: I, English Sacred Music', *Early English Church Music* 19 (London 1977), no. 6.

3 Peter le Huray (ed.), *The Treasury of English Church Music*, 5 vols. (London 1965), II, p. 22.

4 Morehen (ed.), 'Christopher Tye: I', no. 5.

5 Repeats were often indicated by an *ut supra* direction in association with a *signum congruentiae*, rather than by re-copying in full, and could thus easily be overlooked.

6 Leonard Ellinwood (ed.), 'Thomas Tallis: English Sacred Music: I, Anthems', *Early English Church Music* 12 (London 1971).

In *Out from the deep* the repeat is fully written out in all sources, and the anthem is printed as such in *EECM* 12, thus partially concealing its *ABB* form. *A new commandment give I unto you*, however, presents a curious situation. It is clear that bars 29–51 of the *EECM* edition comprise a musical repeat of bars 5–28, though with a slightly different (and decidedly ill-fitting) text. The resulting marriage of text and note produces inelegancies such as Examples 9:1 and 9:2, where version (b) shows the variant text supplied for bars 29–51 (version (a) is the text from bars 5–28). The separation of 'know' and 'that' by a minim rest in Example 9:1(b) immediately prompts misgivings.

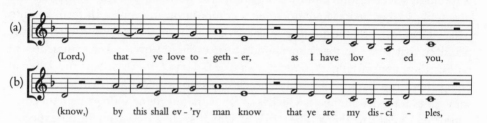

Example 9:1

Equally unconvincing is the setting of 'disciples' in Example 9:2(b), with its repeated crotchets preceding a period of rests.

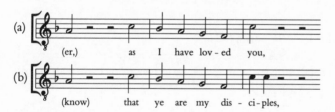

Example 9:2

Surely a *literal* textual repeat must have been intended here, thus presenting the anthem in conventional *ABB* form? John Merro, the copyist of the entries of this piece in *US-NYp* Drexel 4180–2, certainly worked from such a version, for although he re-copied bars 5–28 in full as bars 29–51 he correctly repeated the words of bars 5–28. Such exact repetition of the previous text enables the final three bars to stand as at Example 9:3(a), rather than as the textual torso 'love one to another' found in the less preferable version in *GB-Lbl* Add. 15166 and 29289 and given in Example 9:3(b). The possibility that repeats should be incorporated in some anthems of the late sixteenth century which survive today only in truncated form should not lightly be dismissed.

Several Elizabethan and Jacobean anthems are cast in the mould of *prima* and *secunda pars*, a well-established feature of many continental motets. The overwhelming majority of such anthems circulated between performers and copyists in complete form. Sometimes, however, individual sections were transmitted

Examples 9:3(a) and (b)

independently, especially in the case of semi-sacred works appearing in domestic sources. In *GB-Ob* Mus. f. 11–15, for instance, Thomas Ravenscroft's *O woeful ruins* appears complete with its second and third parts (*Those sacred walls* and *O how these graceful piles*), whereas the entries in *GB-Och* 56–60 preserve only the first part. Similarly, the two sections of Amner's *Thus sings the heavenly choir* (with its second part *The heavens stood all amazed*) appear separately in *GB-Ob* Mus. f. 20–24 and *NYp* Drexel 4180–5 respectively.[7] Yet the work's integrity as a single bi-sectional composition is confirmed beyond doubt by the *notatim* incorporation of the twelve-bar *Alleluia* which concludes *Thus sings the heavenly choir* within the sixteen-bar *Alleluia* with which *The heavens stood all amazed* ends. Clearly there are grounds for considering whether other apparently 'independent' single-section works are in reality no more than sections of much larger compositions.

The reverse phenomenon (where a work transmitted as a unified composition may have originated as two or more independent compositions) must also be considered. Such is almost certainly the case, for instance, with Byrd's only dual-section anthem, *Arise O Lord why sleepest thou*,[8] where, in common with one of his keyboard fantasias,[9] Byrd commits what Thomas Morley regarded as 'one of the grossest faults which may be committed'[10] by opening and concluding a work in different modes. As Craig Monson has cautiously observed, the two parts 'may have been conceived independently and only brought together as an afterthought'. The possibility that other seemingly unified anthems comprise merely the sum of their parts clearly cannot be discounted. Could even such a

---

7   The complete composition was printed in Amner's *Sacred hymns* (1615). The two sections, ed. J. A. Pilgrim, are published separately in Stainer and Bell's *Church Choir Library*, nos. 591–2 (London 1959).

8   Craig Monson (ed.), 'The English Anthems', *The Byrd Edition* 11 (London 1983), p. vii.

9   Alan Brown (ed.), 'William Byrd: Keyboard Music I', *Musica Britannica* 27 (London 1969), no. 27.

10 'The leaving of that key wherein you did begin and ending it in another.' Thomas Morley, *A Plain and Easy Introduction to Practical Music*, ed. R. Alec Harman (London 1952), p. 249.

masterpiece as Orlando Gibbons's *O clap your hands*,[11] the apparent neglect of which during the period 1622–44 can surely be satisfactorily explained only by its technical complexity, possibly be a marriage of two originally independent compositions? It survives today in two sources only: an isolated pre-Restoration *contratenor* partbook of London provenance,[12] and the early post-Restoration 'Gostling' partbooks at York Minster,[13] both of which transmit the anthem in its complete form. Yet the niggling doubts which are prompted by the independent inclusion of the two sections in some eighteenth- and nineteenth-century books of anthem texts[14] are aggravated by the fact that whereas the second section ('God is gone up with a merry noise') makes effective use of *Decani–Cantoris* antiphony, there is not so much as a hint of antiphony in the first section.

A further aspect of musical structure which clearly requires investigation is that of final *Amen* sections and concluding settings of *Gloria Patri*. The dovetailing of closing *Amen* settings into anthems is less common than is the case in Service settings, and usually follows a cadence chord which is delimited by a barline or *fermata* (or both). This, together with the fact that such *Amen* sections are often found only in selected sources or are for a different vocal scoring from the work which they purport to terminate, suggests that they may frequently have been later accretions. It is inconceivable, for instance, that the perfunctory three-bar *Amen* which concludes Richard Nicolson's otherwise fine full anthem *O pray for the peace of Jerusalem*[15] in *GB-Ob* Tenbury 1382 comes from the composer's pen, since it is missing from an authoritative set of partbooks closely associated with the composer and which may even be autograph for this composition.[16] Similar suspicions surround the *Amen* (found only in Ely Cathedral manuscripts) to Richard Farrant's *Lord for thy tender mercy's sake*, the addition in *GB-Lbl* Add. 17797 of an *Amen* to Byrd's *O praise our Lord*[17] that is absent in one of the Paston lute-books (*GB-Lbl* Add. 31992), the *five*-part *Amen* to William Mundy's *four*-part anthem *O Lord the maker of all thing* (but see below, p. 206), and the omission from all sources except the 'Barnard' manuscripts (*GB-Lcm* 1045–51) and a related organ-book (*GB-Ob* Tenbury 791) of the *Amen* which concludes Nathaniel Giles's *O Lord turn not away thy face*.[18]

If the detachability of an *Amen* section may perhaps suggest possible scribal intervention, might a similar presumption be made in the case of anthems which

---

11 David Wulstan (ed.), 'Orlando Gibbons: II, Full Anthems, Hymns and Fragmentary Verse Anthems', *Early English Church Music* 21 (London 1978), no. 6.
12 *Lbl* Add. 29289 (c. 1625).
13 *GB-Y* 1/1–8(S).
14 E.g. Anselm Bayly (comp.), *A Collection of Anthems used in His Majesty's Chapel Royal, and most cathedral churches in England and Ireland* (London 1769); *Anthems used in the Cathedral Church of Norwich* (Norwich 1789); W. E. Dickson (ed.), *Anthems sung in the Cathedral Church of Ely* (Ely 1877).
15 John Morehen (ed.), *Oxford Anthems*, no. A194 (London 1963).
16 *GB-Ob* Mus. Sch. d. 212–16. The *Amen* is missing also from the Lichfield sources, which were copied possibly as late as c. 1665.
17 Monson (ed.), 'The English Anthems', no. 21.
18 J. Bunker Clark (ed.), 'Nathaniel Giles: Anthems', *Early English Church Music* 23 (London 1979), no. 11.

terminate not with *Amen* but with a setting of the Doxology, *Gloria Patri*? Several anthems of the period are settings of entire psalms – usually short psalms such as Psalms 117, 133 and 134 – about one-third of which conclude with *Gloria Patri*. Such works could theoretically have served two main purposes, i.e. as anthems (with or without *Gloria*), or as Festal Psalms (with *Gloria*); this is especially likely in those cases where the start of the *Gloria Patri* is preceded by a *fermata* and a barline and is thus independent of the setting of the psalm itself. The practice of a work serving a dual purpose is explicitly confirmed by John Barnard[19] and by annotations in a Durham Cathedral tenor partbook,[20] where two different commencement points are given for Richard Hutchinson's *Ye that fear the Lord*, depending on whether it was being sung as an anthem or as a Festal Psalm. Similarly, Morley's Festal Psalm *Let my complaint* is found as an anthem in the organ-book *Ob* Tenbury 791 (c. 1630), and (without *Gloria Patri*) in some published anthem wordbooks dating from as late as the mid-nineteenth century.[21] Settings of Psalms 67 (*Deus misereatur*), 95 (*Venite exultemus*), 100 (*Jubilate*) and 98 (*Cantate Domino*) could serve yet a third purpose, i.e. that of a prescribed Canticle at Morning or Evening Prayer.

It follows, then, that *Gloria Patri* may well have been added, not necessarily by the composer himself, to some 'anthems' as an afterthought in order to give them an additional role as a Festal Psalm or Canticle (or, alternatively, that some Canticle settings or Festal Psalms may have been deprived of their Doxology in order to enable them to be sung as anthems). This suggests that editors ought perhaps to be wary of accepting the authenticity of *any* appendage to a setting of a complete psalm. Morley's *How long wilt thou forget me*[22] is a good illustration. The setting of the last verse of the psalm concludes at bar 114. There follows in five sources (for which no interrelationship can be established) an unconvincing setting of *Gloria Patri*, while a further four apparently independent sources present merely a five-bar *Amen*. Quite possibly neither ending is by Morley, especially since the *Amen* bears more than a fleeting resemblance to that which concludes Thomas Ravenscroft's setting of *O Jesu meek*.[23] Nor should suspicion necessarily be concentrated on sections with which compositions conclude, since opening sections of works, also, occasionally raise doubts. It is not yet possible, for instance, to advance any satisfactory explanation for the exclusion from several sources

19 In the index to *The First Book of Selected Church Musick* (1641), Barnard observes: 'Note that Deus Misereatur, in Mr. *Strogers* Service. The Jubilate in Dr. *Giles* Service. The Jubilate in Mr. *Gibbons* Service. Save me O God in Mr. *Birds* 1st. Psalmes. Teach me O Lord in Mr. *Birds* 2nd. Psalmes Are many times, Sung in stead of Anthems.'

20 *GB-Drc* C14, p. 164.

21 William Marshall, *A Collection of Anthems used in the Cathedral and Collegiate Churches of England and Wales* (Oxford, 1840), p. 101, and Benjamin St John Baptist Joule, *A Collection of Words to which Music has been Composed or Adapted for Use in the Choral Service of the United Church of England and Ireland as Anthems* (London, 1859), p. 88.

22 John Morehen (ed.), 'Thomas Morley: 1, English Anthems; Liturgical Music', *Early English Church Music* 38 (London 1991), no. 1.

23 Watkins Shaw (ed.), *Church Music Society Reprints*, no. 3 *revised* (London 1971).

of the five-bar opening section of the widely circulated setting of *Holy Lord God Almighty* by the elder Robert Parsons.[24]

CHORAL TEXTURE

Whereas Edwardian and early Elizabethan church music was usually composed for four-part choir, later Elizabethan and Jacobean music in the 'full' style generally follows a five-part disposition with divided countertenors. It would not be surprising if the desire to conform to changing fashion or to present a more stimulating challenge to choirs had precipitated the adaptation for five voices of music originally conceived for only four. There would have been nothing novel about such a practice. One of John Taverner's two five-part settings of *Dum transisset sabbatum*, for instance, was arranged, possibly in the composer's lifetime, for four-part men's voices, an arrangement described by Hugh Benham, as 'very skilfully done'.[25] Post-Reformation music seemingly accorded a new lease of life in this way includes William Byrd's *Prevent us O Lord*,[26] Thomas Morley's *Preces*,[27] the *Amen* section of William Mundy's *O Lord the maker of all thing*,[28] and the chorus section of Mundy's *The secret sins*.[29] Although there is no reason to believe that this type of adaptation was ever widespread, its true extent has yet to be determined. A striking example of this phenomenon is perhaps Morley's verse anthem *Out of the deep*,[30] a work whose textural integrity has hitherto passed unchallenged. It is one of the earliest post-experimental verse anthems, with solo verses assigned to a countertenor throughout, and dating in all likelihood from the 1580s. There are three instances of blatant – or, at the very least, barely disguised – consecutives,[31] while the tenor writing in the opening and concluding choruses is decidedly angular; furthermore, the settling of the tenor on an almost unrelieved *b* in the final chorus (bars 69–77) is far from convincing. These and other solecisms, all of which are unbefitting a contrapuntist of Morley's calibre, suggest that at some time following the anthem's composition unauthorized re-composition of its inner parts must have taken place.

The texture of the first chorus commands particularly close attention, since indications that something is amiss are so manifest that it is remarkable that the work has not hitherto occasioned suspicion. Not only do both chorus counter-

24 I am indebted to Paul Doe for providing a transcription of this anthem.
25 See Hugh Benham (ed.), 'John Taverner: III, Ritual Music and Secular Songs', *Early English Church Music* 30 (London 1984), p. xiii. The two versions are printed as nos. 9 and 10 of *EECM* 30.
26 Monson (ed.), 'The English Anthems', no. 8.
27 Morehen (ed.), 'Thomas Morley: I', p. 101.
28 Le Huray (ed.), *The Treasury of English Church Music*, p. 114. See also above, p. 204.
29 David Wulstan (ed.), 'Orlando Gibbons: I, Verse Anthems', *Early English Church Music* 21 (London 1964), no. 14. The chorus of Mundy's *The secret sins* as preserved in pre-Restoration partbooks at Durham Cathedral is for five voices. Some mid-seventeenth-century fragments at Lichfield Cathedral suggest that the chorus was originally in four parts, with the Lichfield tenor representing a conflate of the Durham tenor and second countertenor parts.
30 Morehen (ed.), 'Thomas Morley: I', no. 3.
31 B. 34, C^2/T; b. 50, C^1/T and T/B.

tenor parts commence in unison – an uncharacteristic redundancy – but there are other duplications, resulting in a chorus of which less than one-third is in five real parts. In Example 9:4, the five upper staves show the 'best text' of the opening chorus as represented by the surviving sources, the duplications (shown by enclosing) are conspicuous.

In bars 13–16 the interval span between the outer voices is so compressed that it is hardly surprising that subsequent adaptation could divine a fifth (i.e. additional countertenor) part only by doubling an existing one. The original version of this chorus may well have approximated Example 9:4(b), which introduces only one new note (the second f minim in the Tenor of bar 20) and which, at the same time, respects the essential contrapuntal contours throughout. The organ part of this anthem is unusually contrapuntal, suggesting that the original accompaniment may well have been for a consort of viols; is it possible that the enlargement of the chorus from four to five voices took place when the anthem was transferred from chamber to church? If this indeed was the case, how many other 'domestic' (albeit sacred) pieces may have undergone similar adaptation?

With the likelihood of such pieces having been enlarged to suit the standard MCCTB disposition of late Elizabethan choirs it is worth asking whether the texture of some large-scale works might have been *reduced* for the same reason, or, perhaps, for greater ease of performance. All the sources of Orlando Gibbons's full anthem *Deliver us O Lord* transmit it as a four-part composition, although David Wulstan's reconstruction of it as a *five*-part piece is justified not only by the harmonic incompleteness of the existing four-part version but also, and more importantly, by the ease with which extra points of imitation can be reconstructed in the 'missing' part. Byrd's six-part full anthem *O Lord make thy servant Elizabeth*,[32] too, seems to have suffered from such adaptation, for several Jacobean sources preserve it as a five-part composition. The uncertainties do not end there, however, for there is clear evidence that a variety of different five-part scorings of this anthem were in circulation. In other works the inconsistent exploitation of the overall texture is a possible clue that they, too, might have undergone adaptation. Gibbons's *Hosanna to the Son of David*, which is in *ABA* form with a closing coda, is perhaps a case in point. Although the overall texture is MMCCTTB, section *A* (bars 1–11 and 48–58) shuns the bass voice, while section *B* (bars 11–48) and the concluding six-bar coda require only one of the two tenor parts. Consequently, while requiring seven voices overall, no more than six are ever in use at one time. It seems unlikely that this represents the composer's expectations. Local musicians were certainly prepared to re-arrange compositions for more convenient scorings when the occasion demanded; evidence for this can be seen in the transference of Richard Alison's sacred madrigal *Behold now praise the Lord*[33] to the church, when its scoring was adjusted from a five-part

32 Monson (ed.), 'The English Anthems', no. 6.
33 *An Howres Recreation in Musicke* (1606); see Edmund H. Fellowes (ed.), 'Richard Alison: An Howres Recreation in Musicke', *The English Madrigal School* 33 (London 1924), no. 22.

(a)

(b)

Example 9:4

domestic grouping of SSTTB to an unorthodox five-part liturgical scoring of
MMCTB, an adjustment dictated by the fact that the notated pitch is unchanged
although the sacred version requires transposition to liturgical pitch.

ANTIPHONY

Genuinely 'antiphonal' singing (i.e. the alternate use of the two sides of the choir,
Decani and *Cantoris*) is precluded by the format of the earliest Anglican sources,
since the 'Lumley' (*GB-Lbl* Roy. App. 74–6) and 'Wanley' partbooks (*GB-Ob* Mus.
Sch. e. 420–2) and Day's print (1560/5) do not allow for different material to be
sung by the two sides of the choir. Within a decade or so of the introduction of
the 1549 Prayer Book, however, composers had embarked on the exploitation of
spatial effect through the allocation of various passages to alternate sides of the

Example 9:4 (cont.)

choir. This practice, perceived by some as a relic of Roman practices, seems to have been held in low esteem during the Elizabethan period, as a London cleric, John Field, asserted in 1572:

In all theyr order of service there is no edification, according to the rule of the Apostle, but confusion, they tosse the Psalmes in most places like tennice balles.[34]

The tennis analogy was invoked again within a decade by the Separatist Robert Browne, who, in *A true and short Declaration* (1583), attested:

Their tossing to & fro of psalms and sente[n]ses is like tenisse plaie whereto God is called a Judg who can do best and be most gallant in his worshipp.[35]

34 *An Admonition to the Parliament* (1572), section 13 of 'A view of Popishe abuses yet remaining in the Englishe Church'.
35 Quoted here from the British Library proof-sheets of the reprint in *The Congregationalist* (1882).

Antiphonal singing, which is encountered more frequently in Services than in anthems, is found in many compositions from a wide period, ranging from such unpretentious works as Weelkes's Seventh ('Short') Service[36] to Byrd's supreme 'Great' Service,[37] taking in Services by Tallis, Robert Parsons (I), Sheppard,[38] William Mundy,[39] Tomkins[40] and others *en route*. However, virtually none of the surviving sources of any of these works was copied during their composer's lifetime, and the *Decani–Cantoris* alternations, effected by copying the relevant passages into the partbooks for only one side of the choir, may well be a result of later scribal intervention. The antiphony in works such as Sheppard's First Service and Parsons's First Service is apparently authenticated by the occasional passages in up to as many as eight real parts. Although this is perhaps remarkable in the case of Sheppard, bearing in mind that the work probably dates from before the accession of Mary,[41] it is less so in the case of Parsons's Service, since its use of the 1549 text merely reflects the Elizabethan intention to restore 'the former order of King Edward'.[42] In much later works, such as Tomkins's Second Service,[43] the legitimacy of the antiphonal directions is apparently confirmed by the exchange of similar musical material between the two sides of the choir. However, with some compositions the antiphony is confined to selected sources, reinforcing the suspicion that local musicians occasionally 'improved' compositions in this way. The *Decani–Cantoris* alternations in Mundy's *O Lord the maker of all thing*,[44] for instance, are found only in Barnard's print, where they are limited to one central passage, thus imposing a somewhat incongruous imbalance in spite of Barnard's attempts to confer credibility by dovetailing the *Decani* and *Cantoris* sections at phrase overlaps. The reverse process (whereby a genuinely antiphonal work became 'full' throughout) is a considerably less likely phenomenon, if only because of the complications which concatenating two parts (from different partbooks) into a single part would have entailed, with the consequent danger of corruption through the misreading of rests. This is not to exclude the possibility totally, however. Denis Stevens has argued that sections of Tye's *I will exalt thee*[45] should be sung antiphonally, since antiphony 'is most explicit in the music itself';[46] antiphonal intent would certainly explain the overbearing repetition of musical material. And if the repetition of material

---

36 For the Morning and Evening Canticles of Weelkes's Seventh Service, ed. David Brown, see Stainer and Bell's *Church Services*, nos. 348 and 279 (London 1969 and 1968 respectively).

37 Craig Monson (ed.), 'The Great Service', *The Byrd Edition* 10b (London 1982).

38 For Sheppard's First Service Evening Canticles, ed. C. F. Simkins, see *Church Music Society Reprints*, no. 45 (London 1963). For the Second Service Evening Canticles see David Wulstan (comp.), *An Anthology of English Church Music* (London 1971), p. 59.

39 For the Evening Canticles, ed. Royle Shore, see Novello's *Cathedral Series*, no. 1 (London 1912).

40 'Thomas Tomkins Part 1: Services', *Tudor Church Music* 8 (London 1928).

41 See David Wulstan, 'New light on John Sheppard', *The Musical Times* 135 (1994), pp. 25–7.

42 Paul Doe (ed.), 'Robert Parsons: Latin Sacred Music', *Early English Church Music* 40 (London 1994), p. xi.

43 *TCM* 8, pp. 50–81.

44 See fn. 3.

45 Morehen (ed.), 'Christopher Tye: I', no. 9.

46 Denis Stevens, *Tudor Church Music* (London 1961; 2/1966), p. 61.

would justify the use of antiphony in sections of *I will exalt thee*, why not also in the same composer's *O God be merciful unto us*,[47] which, too, is characterized by considerable duplication of material? There is an alternative – albeit more sinister – interpretation, however, namely that the surviving versions of both anthems represent fully written-out copies incorporating putative antiphonal repetition that was never actually intended.

VOICE SUBSTITUTION IN VERSE ANTHEMS

In the earliest consort songs and verse anthems, which employ only a single soloist, the solo or 'singing part' is almost invariably allocated to a boy, or 'mean'. That this was the conventional grouping of the period is apparently confirmed by the Unton memorial painting (c. 1596) in the National Portrait Gallery, London (ref. 710), where a boy is portrayed singing to the accompaniment of a consort of four viols.[48] But might the incorporation of the solos in the highest partbook have been sometimes a mere notational convenience or formality? In one source the solo passages of the younger John Hilton's *Teach me O Lord*, plausibly assigned to a mean in *Ob* Mus. Sch. d. 212–16, are surprisingly notated an octave lower and assigned to a tenor. While such a transfer of verses between mean and tenor (or theoretically between countertenor and bass) is likely to have had a deleterious effect on the textural interplay, it is perhaps not particularly remarkable, since the tessituras of the two voice types lie at the approximate interval of the octave. Rather less satisfactory is the reading of Gibbons's *This is the Record of John*[49] as given in *GB-Cp* 485, where the countertenor verses are notated an octave higher for a mean; both represent unusual transpositions in that they are between voice types which lie approximately a fifth apart. An even less likely phenomenon is encountered in the York Minster 'Gostling' partbooks, where the verses of Gibbons's *Behold thou hast made my days*,[50] which in all other sources are assigned to countertenor, are copied into a tenor partbook but at countertenor pitch. The same Gostling partbooks take the process to its extreme in Morley's *Out of the deep*, where the solo countertenor verses are found both in the countertenor *and* tenor partbooks, and so could have been taken by either singer without prior warning, something which could not normally have taken place spontaneously, since it would have required a singer to have recourse to a partbook belonging to another musician, assuming, of course, that he were not singing from memory.

SERVICE–ANTHEM PAIRINGS

Little is known of the frequency with which specific Services and anthems were

---

47 Morehen (ed.), 'Christopher Tye: 1', no. 11.
48 The relevant detail is reproduced in Philip Brett (ed.), 'Consort Songs', *Musica Britannica* 22 (London 1967), p. x.
49 Wulstan (ed.), 'Orlando Gibbons: 1', no. 15.
50 *Ibid.*, pp. 24–37.

performed in any given institution during the sixteenth and seventeenth centuries. The earliest Service list to survive is, unfortunately, of post-Restoration date,[51] and although inferences as to a choir's likely repertory may be drawn from the contents of the working manuscripts of that institution (such as those used by the choirs of Pembroke College, Cambridge, and Gloucester Cathedral in the 1630s and early 1640s) such conclusions are at best speculative and at worst dangerous. The extent to which the selection of music was so ordered in a given foundation that, at a particular service, both anthem and Service setting were by the same composer can only be guessed at. Although the extent of the phenomenon is difficult to establish, there are clear grounds for believing that in the early seventeenth century certain anthems were sung in conjunction with a 'parent' Service setting. The most important authenticated example of a Service–anthem pairing is undoubtedly Orlando Gibbons's Short Service and his full anthem *Almighty and everlasting God*.[52] Such pairs of compositions were usually on the same modal or tonal centre and with an analogous vocal scoring (in this case, four parts), although there is not necessarily any thematic relationship between the two compositions. Indeed, the traditional 'misattribution' (if such it be) to Weelkes of *Let thy merciful ears*[53] – attributed elsewhere to 'Mudd'[54] – results wholly from its position in the Peterhouse 'Latter' set of 'Caroline' manuscripts,[55] where in all the relevant partbooks[56] it immediately follows Weelkes's Seventh ('Short') Evening Service, in the same hand and without attribution; moreover, the compatibility of key suggests that the two pieces may have been conceived as a pair.[57] These circumstances closely parallel those of Weelkes's verse anthem *Why art thou so sad*,[58] which in some Wimborne Minster manuscripts[59] immediately follows his Sixth Service without title or attribution. Judging from annotations in John Barnard's manuscripts the St Paul's Cathedral musician Adrian Batten seems to have relished this practice. Anthems by Batten and other early seventeenth-century composers which, according to contemporary sources, were composed for performance in conjunction with a particular Service setting are shown in Table 9:2.

51 Brian Crosby, 'A Service sheet from June 1680', *The Musical Times* 121 (1980), pp. 399–401.
52 See *GB-Ojc* 180 (index on f. ii): 'Anthem to Mr Gibons Short Servis'.
53 Edmund H. Fellowes (ed.), *Tudor Church Music* octavo series, no. 35 (London n.d.).
54 In addition to the musicians of this name listed in Watkins Shaw, *The Succession of Organists of the Chapel Royal and the Cathedrals of England and Wales from c.1538* (Oxford 1991), an earlier Thomas Mudd, 'sometimes fellow of *Pembrok hall in Cambridge*', was one of England's sixteen 'excellent Musitians' named by Francis Meres in *Palladis Tamia* (1598), f. 288ᵛ.
55 *Cp* 485–91.
56 *Cp* 489 (f. 114), 490 (f. R5) and 491 (f. R5).
57 An apparent argument against this particular pairing is that *Let thy merciful ears* is a setting of the Collect for the 10th Sunday after Trinity, which would seem to restrict the use of the associated Service setting, also, to that one occasion in the Church's year. However, it is likely that Collect settings were used much more frequently than their text would strictly seem to suggest; see John Morehen, 'The English anthem text, 1549–1660', *Journal of the Royal Musical Association* 117 (1992), p. 79.
58 David Brown, Walter Collins and Peter le Huray (eds.), 'Thomas Weelkes: Collected Anthems', *Musica Britannica* 23 (London 1966), p. 123. This volume contains all the anthems by Weelkes which are cited in this chapter.
59 E.g. P11, p. 28; in P17 it is described as 'The Anthem'.

Table 9:2: Authenticated Service–anthem pairings

Composer	Service	Anthem
Batten	Short Service	*O praise the Lord all ye heathen* (I) (a4)[a]
Batten	Short Service for Men (a4)	*Christ our Paschal Lamb* (a4)[b]
Batten	Full Service	*We beseech thee Almighty God* (a5)[c]
Batten	Full Service *Te Deum*	*Hear the prayers O our God* (a5)[d]
Batten	Short Service for Meanes	*When the Lord turned again* (a4)[e]
Child	Short Service, the whole or full service, in A	*O Lord God the heathen* (a5)[f]
Child	Whole Service, the sharp service, in D sol re	Matins: *Blessed be the Lord God* (a4)[g] Evensong: *O clap your hands* (a4)[h]
Child	Whole Service, in F fa ut	Evensong: *The King shall rejoice* (I) (a ?)[i]
Deane	Evening Service 'for men' (a4)	*O Lord God most merciful saviour* (a4)
Deane	Morning Service 'for men'	*Lord have mercy upon us*
Deane	Short Service 'for meanes' (a4)	*Lord in thy wrath reprove me not* (a4)
Weelkes	First Service[j]	*Thou art my portion O Lord*
Weelkes	Sixth Service	*Why art thou so sad*

a   See *Lcm* 1048 (f. 199ʳ), 1049 (f. 199ʳ), 1050 (f. 177ʳ), and 1051 (f. 199ʳ).
b   See *Lcm* 1048 (f. 199ʳ), 1049 (f. 199ʳ), 1050 (f. 177ʳ) and 1051 (f. 199ʳ).
c   See *Lcm* 1048 (f. 188ᵛ), 1049 (f. 185ʳ), 1050 (f. 162ᵛ) and 1051 (f. 184ʳ).
d   See *Lcm* 1048 (f. 206ʳ), 1049 (f. 182ʳ), 1050 (f. 160ʳ) and 1051 (f. 206ʳ).
e   See *Lcm* 1048 (f. 200ʳ) and 1049 (f. 200ʳ).
f   See Ralph T. Daniel and Peter le Huray (comps.), 'The Sources of English Church Music, 1549–1660', *Early English Church Music*, Supplementary Vol. 1, 2 pts. (London 1972), II, p. 93.
g   *Ibid.*, p. 94.
h   *Ibid.*
i   *Ibid.*
j   David Wulstan (ed.), *Oxford Church Services* no. S573 (London 1966).

One of the most interesting pairings in this table is that of Weelkes's First Service and anthem *Thou art my portion O Lord*. The association of these two compositions is documented in the Wimborne Minster manuscripts,[60] which cite the exact text of the anthem.[61] Despite David Brown's claims that this anthem is lost, it is clear from other annotations in the Wimborne partbooks – 'For the chorus the 4 verse of the second part [i.e. of Psalm 119] Blessed art thou O Lord' – that at least the chorus of this verse anthem survives.[62]

60   P11 (f. 65ᵛ, C), P14 (f. 71ᵛ, T) and P17 (f. 35ʳ, BD).
61   Ps. 119, vv. 57, 73, 72, 103–4 and 12; see David Brown, *Thomas Weelkes: A Biographical and Critical Study* (London 1969; 2/1976), p. 189.
62   It is printed as Anonymous Anthem no. 386, in Daniel and le Huray (comps.), 'The Sources of English Church Music', I, p. 38. The text of this extract should therefore read 'Blessed art thou O Lord' and not the opening words of the anthem, 'Thou art my portion O Lord'.

Weelkes's clear penchant for Service–anthem pairings lends credence to Brown's theory that some Services by Weelkes other than those in Table 9:2 were intended to be used in conjunction with specific anthems. On the evidence of Weelkes's musical self-borrowings, which are often extensive, Brown postulates that no fewer than five other Services by Weelkes may have been written for performance in combination with a specific anthem:

Service	Anthem
Second Service (v)	*O Lord turn not away thy face* (v)
Fourth (Evening) Service ('for Trebles')[63]	*Alleluia! I heard a voice* (a5)
Seventh ('Short') Service (a4)[64]	*O Lord God Almighty* (a7)
Eighth (Evening) Service (a5)[65]	*O how amiable* (a5)
Ninth (Evening) Service (a7)[66]	*O Lord grant the King* (a7)

In most of these cases the anthem is for predominantly the same vocal distribution as its parent Service, and while there is an undeniable circularity in Brown's argument,[67] his theory certainly deserves to be taken seriously. How far the re-cycling of material indicates linked performance must remain a matter for conjecture, however, for although the substantial closing section of Weelkes's *Alleluia! I heard a voice* recurs also at the conclusion of his Fourth (Evening) Service, it is noteworthy that similar material is found also in the composer's madrigal *As wanton birds*.[68]

Our ability to link the Services and anthems cited above is due in large measure to casual scribal annotations in manuscript sources closely associated with the composers or copied within close geographical proximity – the 'Barnard' manuscripts in the case of Batten, the Chirk Castle partbooks[69] in the case of Deane, and the Wimborne partbooks in the case of Weelkes. Most surviving sources lack obvious authority, however, and it seems highly likely that other anthems were written for use with specific Services, with their links having been lost through haphazard lines of transmission. In the Peterhouse 'Latter' set of Caroline partbooks, for instance, a Service by the Exeter musician Robert Parsons is immediately followed by the same composer's anthem *Ever-blessed Lord*; both anthem and Service are in the same key, and the anthem is described as 'A Collect for the Quire'. A more obvious indication of association between two works seems difficult to imagine. The anthem *Increase my joy*, the words of which

63 Peter le Huray (ed.), Stainer and Bell's *Church Services*, no. 327 (London 1962).
64 See fn. 36 above.
65 David Wulstan (ed.), *Tudor Church Music* octavo series, no. 96 (London 1965).
66 David Brown (ed.), *Voces Musicales* 1:7 (Oxford 1979).
67 The circularity lies in the fact that musical borrowings and extensive re-workings in anthems of material from Services (or vice versa) are inherently likely to be between works for the same number of voices.
68 Edmund H. Fellowes (ed.), 'Thomas Weelkes: Madrigals of Five Parts', *The English Madrigal School* 11 (London 1916), p. 55. It is noteworthy that the theme of longevity runs through two of the three examples: '... and ever shall be' in the Fourth Service, and 'Long may he live...' in *As wanton birds*.
69 US-NYp Mus. Res. *MNZ (Chirk). See Peter le Huray, 'The Chirk Castle partbooks', *Early Music History* 2 (1982), pp. 17–42.

follow the *Nunc Dimittis* of a Service by Robert Johnson in *GB-Cpc* Music 6.2 is yet one more example of possible linked Service–anthem pairing.

THE PRAYER BOOKS AS A GUIDE TO LITURGICAL PRACTICE

The extent to which the detailed rubrics of the 1549 and 1552 Prayer Books dictated actual liturgical practice is unclear, although there is strong evidence that they provided at best no more than a rough guide. This is the conclusion to be drawn from a scrutiny of the music apparently written between c. 1549 and the early Restoration period for use at burials. The early Prayer Books included seven specific burial texts which found favour with composers:

(1)   *I am the resurrection*
(2)   *I know that my redeemer liveth*
(3)   *We brought nothing into this world*
(4)   *Man that is born of a woman*
(5)   *In the midst of life*
(6)   *Thou knowest Lord the secrets of our hearts*
(7)   *I heard a voice from heaven*

No fewer than 81 settings of these texts can be identified, as shown in Table 9:3. If these were all intended for use at the burial service, as would on first sight appear to be the case, this would make the service an incongruously popular one with composers, a presumption which clearly requires investigation.

Table 9:3: Settings of texts for the Burial Service, c. 1549 – c. 1660

Composer	Forces	1	2	3	4	5	6	7
John Merbecke[a]	fI	✓	✓	✓	✓	✓	✓	✓
anon. ('Wanley' MSS)	f4	✓	✓	✓	✓	✓	✓	✓
Thomas Morley[b]	f4	✓	✓	✓	✓	✓	✓	✓(2)
John Alcock	f4	✓	✓	✓	✓	✓	✓	✓
John Ferrabosco	f4	✓	✓	✓	✓	✓	✓	✓
John Parsons[c]	f4	✓	✓	✓	✓	✓	✓	✓
Leonard Woodson	f6?	✓	✓	✓	✓	✓	✓	
Thomas Tomkins[d]	f4	✓	✓	✓				✓
John Foster[e]	f	✓	✓	✓				✓[f]
Michael East	f	✓	✓	✓				
Thomas Wilkinson[g]	v6	✓	✓	✓				
[John] Holmes	?[h]	✓	✓	✓				
[?Thomas] Wanless[i]	f4	✓	✓	✓				
Henry Loosemore	v				✓	✓	✓	
Adrian Batten	f[j]	✓	✓					[k]
Orlando Gibbons[l]	f5	✓						
Robert Lugge	f4	✓						
John Milton	f5	✓						
William Child[m]	f4							✓

Table 9:3 (*cont.*)

Composer	Forces	1	2	3	4	5	6	7
Randolph Jewett	f							✓
Robert Ramsey[n]	f5							✓
George Jeffries	f4				✓			
Totals:		17	14	13	8	9	8	12

a   Merbecke also provides the Burial Responses, which appear not to have been set polyphonically by any composer.

b   Morehen (ed.), 'Thomas Morley: I', no. 7. There is some doubt as to whether all, or indeed any, of the Burial Service attributed to Morley (of which the earliest complete source is William Boyce's *Cathedral Music*, 3 vols. (London 1760–78)) is genuinely Morley's work. Its only pre-Restoration source (*Ob* Tenbury 1382) contains *Man that is born*, *In the midst of life* and an otherwise unknown setting of *Thou knowest Lord*, all of which are found without attribution amongst a group of later additions to the partbook. The earliest source to name Morley is an early post-Restoration organ-book (*GB-Ojc* 315) which omits *Thou knowest Lord*.

c   In addition to pre-Restoration sources, Parsons's Burial Service survives also in *GB-Ob* Tenbury 787 (c. 1665), where it is headed 'The score of Mr *John Parson's* Funerall servis H.P.' in what was once thought to be the hand of Henry Purcell. The manuscripts' black covers inspired a tradition that these manuscripts were used by Purcell at the funeral of Charles II, at which this Service was sung.

d   Bernard Rose (ed.), 'Thomas Tomkins, Musica Deo Sacra: IV', *Early English Church Music* 27 (London 1982), no. 30.

e   *Drc* manuscripts and *GB-Lbl* Add. 30478–9.

f   The association of this item with Foster's other burial music is not firmly established. In some sources it is adjacent (or in close proximity) to settings of items 1–3, but in others it appears independently.

g   The forename 'Thomas' is supplied in *GB-Lbl* Add. 29366–8, where this anthem is described as being 'of 6: Vo:'. The text of section three departs somewhat from the standard text.

h   In *GB-Lbl* Add. 17820 (f. 105^v) *I am the resurrection* opens with a five-bar bass solo. Holmes's setting of *I am the resurrection* was included as an anthem in William Marshall's *A Collection of Anthems used in the Cathedral and Collegiate Churches of England and Wales* (Oxford 1840).

i   Although no first name is given in *Lbl* Add. 17820, this work is clearly of Restoration date.

j   Only the text is extant, the presentation of which in James Clifford's *The Divine Services and Anthems* (1663/4) strongly implies that Batten's two items are full rather than verse.

k   Batten's setting of *I heard a voice* is not the Burial Service text, but a text from the Epistle for Michaelmas.

l   Wulstan (ed.), 'Orlando Gibbons: II', no. 4.

m   C. F. Simkins (ed.), *Ascherberg Sacred Part-Music*, no. 445 (London 1956).

n   Edward Thompson (ed.), 'Robert Ramsey: I, English Sacred Music', *Early English Church Music* 7 (London 1967), no. 18 (incipit only).

The Prayer Book rubrics decree the saying or singing of *I am the resurrection* (1), *I know that my redeemer liveth* (2), and *We brought nothing into this world* (3) after 'metyng the Corps at the Church style' and as the burial party proceeds 'either into the Churche, or towardes the grave'. *Man that is born of a woman* (4), and *In the midst of life* (5) – including *Thou knowest Lord* (6) – were prescribed to be said or sung 'When they come to the grave, whyles the Corps is made readie to be layed into the earth…'. *I heard a voice from heaven* (7) was to be said or sung following the 'castyng of earth upon the Corps' by the priest. One might expect the music sources to reflect apparent liturgical intent and transmit either complete settings of all seven texts, or, possibly, grouped settings of items 1–3, 4–6 and 7.[70]

70   Items 5 and 6 above, while forming a continuous text, were usually treated separately by composers at this period. In the setting by John Alcock numbers 4–6 are treated as a single section.

While the actuality is broadly in keeping with that expectation, Table 9:3 shows that although Merbecke included a monophonic version of the complete Burial Service in his *Booke of Common praier noted* (1550), the only complete polyphonic settings to survive from the period c. 1549 – c. 1660 are the anonymous setting in the Wanley manuscripts and the settings by Morley, Alcock and John Ferrabosco.

The forces required for the various settings, too, are not always what might be expected. Admittedly, a large proportion of the compositions (including all the complete polyphonic settings) are for four voices only, in keeping with the restraint that such a sober occasion would command. Yet, with the exception of Ramsey's *I heard a voice from heaven*, it is noticeable that the burial music for larger forces survives exclusively in domestic sources, suggesting that it was not intended for use at actual burials. This certainly explains the presence in the above table of George Jeffries's *In the midst of life*, since it is a domestic work, composed '... in the tyme of my sicknes Octob. 1657',[71] and concluding surprisingly with an *Alleluia* section. The intended function of Randolph Jewett's setting of *I heard a voice*, too, is unclear, since the text, described by Clifford as 'A funeral Anthem', ends the standard text from Revelation 14 '... for they shall rest from their labours, *and their works follow them*', continuing with verse 3 ('And they sang the song of the Lamb...') and *Gloria Patri*. It would appear, then, that the assumption that settings of burial texts were necessarily written for use within the Burial Service itself is unsafe, and that funeral music was sung on other occasions.

Even if the opening procession of the priests, clerks and others in attendance were from the 'Churche style' into the church (rather than to an outdoor burial site) it is clear that much of a typical Burial Service took place outdoors. Yet it seems unlikely that musicians would have been prepared to endanger valuable partbooks by exposing them to the vagaries of the weather. (While singing from memory cannot be discounted, this seems an unlikely eventuality in the case of burials, not only because of the amount of music that was potentially involved, but also because burials with music would have been a relatively infrequent occurrence.) The isolated settings by Wilkinson, Loosemore and Jewett could not possibly have been performed outdoors, since their use of the verse style requires independent instrumental accompaniment. One possible inference is that no burial music was *ever* performed outdoors, those compositions which have survived being either for domestic use or for performance at the burial of dignitaries *within* a church building.

Some burials, notably those conducted at the Chapel Royal and those of local dignitaries, undoubtedly included music other than settings of the Burial Sentences provided in the Prayer Book. An organ-book[72] copied by Henry Loosemore for his own use at King's College Chapel, Cambridge, for instance, contains a surprisingly large number of additional pieces suitable for use at

71 *GB-Lbl* Add. 10338, f. 160ᵛ.
72 *NYp* Drexel 5469.

burials: in addition to settings by Wilkinson, Jewett and Loosemore himself of standard burial texts it includes a setting of *Like as the hart*[73] by Loosemore's Ely neighbour John Amner, and two anthems by Thomas Tomkins which were omitted from his posthumous *Musica Deo Sacra* (1668) – the verse anthem *Know ye not*,[74] composed for Prince Henry's funeral in 1612, and *Death is swallowed up in victory*, the text of which is taken from the extended Lesson at the Burial Service.[75]

STANDARDS OF PERFORMANCE

Of all the areas where there is a paucity of contemporary information, that of performance standards is perhaps the most frustrating. Any comparison of the standards of performance in the sixteenth and seventeenth centuries with those of today is dangerous, since it requires subjective interpretation of contemporary descriptions. It is clear, nevertheless, that the standards of singing and playing in cathedrals and collegiate chapels must have varied enormously at this period. Chapter records and other contemporary sources offer occasional glimpses into the performance conditions at individual establishments. Not untypical of such accounts is Joule's observation that

Bishop Hackett relates that at Buckden, the chapel of Dr. John Williams, when Bishop of Lincoln... 1621 to 1637 ... 'the holy service of God was well ordered ... with Music and Organ exquisitely ... and with such voices, as the kingdom afforded not better for skill and sweetness'.[76]

Rarely, however, is it possible to compare performance standards at more than one foundation at any given time. Accounts of the musical state of affairs in other institutions in the 1630s is provided by John Cosin, who was deeply committed to music which reflected both high standards and high churchmanship. In a report which he submitted to Archbishop Laud on the subject of general and musical discipline in Cambridge college chapels, Cosin described King's College in the following acerbic terms:

Quiremen cannot sing and are very negligent. Choristers are half mute and come without surplices. No reverence shown, and service 'posted over'.[77]

---

73 From Ps. 42, appointed for use when Holy Communion is celebrated at a burial.

74 Wulstan (comp.), *An Anthology of English Church Music*, no. 13.

75 1 Corinthians 15.54–7. See Peter James, 'Thomas Tomkins: sacred music omitted from *Musica Deo Sacra*', *Soundings* 2 (1971/2), p. 36. The presence in particular manuscripts of an unusually heavy concentration of funeral pieces can be seen elsewhere. *Lbl* Add. 17820, for instance, includes as consecutive items the Burial Services of Holmes and Wanless, while *Lbl* Add. 29366–8 includes the burial music by Gibbons and Wilkinson in addition to a Latin version of *I am the resurrection* (*Ego sum resurrectio*) by the younger Alfonso Ferrabosco. The most remarkable concentration of burial music within a single pre-Restoration source is seen in St George's Chapel, Windsor, XVIII.1.11–13 (c. 1640), which contains funeral music by Woodson, Child and Parsons, to which Croft's Burial Service was added in the eighteenth century.

76 Joule, *A Collection of Words*, p. vi.

77 F. J. Varley, *Cambridge During the Civil War, 1642–46* (Cambridge 1935), p. 25.

His account of affairs at Trinity College is only marginally more complimentary, for he wrote:

The choir is negligent and unskilful and negligent in their postures. Few bow at the name of Jesus, and some turn to the West door at the Creed. Services are scamped and mutilated.[78]

Cosin's comments were undoubtedly influenced in part by his reluctance to compliment those college choirs which might be considered to rival his own choir at Peterhouse; doubtless a certain inter-collegiate rivalry obtained even at that period.

Perhaps the most valuable source of information of this period is one Lieutenant Hamond, who in 1634–5 conducted a tour of much of England, during which he attended services at several cathedrals. His comments both on the musical resources and on the performances which he heard provide a valuable insight into the remarkably varied choral standards at this period:[79]

Lincoln Cathedral:
heere wee heard their solemne Service, the Organs, wth other Instrume^{ts}, suited to most excellent voyces.

Carlisle Cathedral:
The Organs, & voices did well agree, the one being like a shrill Bagpipe, the other like the Scottish Tone.

Lichfield Cathedral:
... the Organs, & voyces, were deep, and sweet, their Anthems we were much delighted with, & of the voyces ... that ... most melodiously acted, & performed their parts.

Hereford Cathedral:
There we heard a most sweet Organ, and voyces of all parts, Teno^{r}, Counter-Teno^{r}, Treeble, & Base.

Bristol Cathedral:
In her are rich Organs, lately beautify'd, and indifferent good Quiristers.

Rochester Cathedral:
her Organs though small, yet are they rich, and neat, her Quiristers though but few, yet orderly and decent.

Canterbury Cathedral:
... heere I saw, and heard a fayre Organ, sweet, and tunable, and a deep, and ravishing consort of Quirsters.

---

78 *Ibid.*, p. 24.
79 *GB-Lbl* Landsdowne MS 213. The extracts printed here are found on ff. 317^{r}, 323^{v}, 328^{r}, 334^{r}, 336^{v}, 350^{v}, 351^{v}, 359^{v}, 364^{v} and 375^{v}. See also *A Relation of a short survey of 26 counties observed in a seven weeks' journey begun on 11 August, 1634, by a Captain, a Lieutenant, and an Ancient, all three of the Military Company in Norwich*, ed. L. G. Wickham Legg, Stuart Series (1904) and *A Relation of a short survey of the western counties ... in 1635* ed. L. G. Wickham Legg, Camden Society, 3rd Series, 52, Camden Miscellany, 16 (1936).

Chichester Cathedral:
her Organs small, and voyces but indifferent.

Winchester Cathedral:
The Organs in this Church are not exceeding faire, nor rich, but sweet, & tunable, and sweetly playd on, by one of the rarest Organists that this Land affoords [Thomas Holmes], ... the Quiristers were skilfull, & the voices good, where they sing sweet, and heavenly Anthems.

Exeter Cathedral:
... a delicate, rich, & lofty Organ wch has more additions then any other, as fayre Pipes of an extraordinary length, & of the bignesse of a mans Thigh, which wth their Vialls, & other sweet Instruments, the tunable Voyces, and the rare Organist [John Lugge], togeather, makes a melodious, & heavenly Harmony, able to ravish the Hearers Eares.

Interpretation of such observations must have some regard for the qualifications of the observer, of course, and in the case of Hamond (unlike John Cosin) it has to be admitted that there is no evidence that he possessed musical skill.

While such glimpses into the daily workings of England's most prestigious ecclesiastical foundations are greatly to be valued, they serve also to heighten the desire for even more detailed and comprehensive information – a *lacuna* which seems destined to remain. And while some light has been shed in this chapter on select and diverse areas of performing practice, many other equally important areas of uncertainty remain unillumined by modern research.

INDEX OF NAMES AND PLACES

Dodd, Gordon, 196
Doe, Paul, 116, 164, 166–7, 169, 171, 206, 210
Donato, Baldassare, 179
Douai, 80–1
Dow, Robert, 112, 146, 155, 157–8, 165–7, 174, 176
Dryden, John, 90–1
Dublin, 177, 187
Dufay, Guillaume, 26–7
Duffy, Eamon, 45
Duffill, John, 109, 121–2, 125, 129, 134
Dunstable, John, 4–5, 9, 22–4, 27, 44, 68
Dunstan, St (Archibishop), 27
Durham, 12–13, 181–2, 194, 206

East, Michael, 107, 215
East, Thomas, 123
East Anglia, 92
Edmund, Henry, 190
Edward VI, (King), 80, 161, 181–2, 190, 192, 210
Edward VII, (King), 182
Edwards, Kathleen, 180
Edwards, Richard, 190–2
Edwards, Warwick A., 128, 162, 169, 171, 177, 196
Elizabeth I, Queen, 144, 146, 162, 167–8, 176, 181, 190, 194–5, 198–9
Ellinwood, Leonard, 201
Elstow, 182
Elstow, (Bishop), 182
Elyot, Thomas, 191
Ely, 196, 204
Epworth, 15
Erasmus, Desiderimus, 74, 77–8, 80–3, 88
Essex, 91, 174
Eton College, 11, 16–17, 20
Euclid, 179
Evans, Thomas, 177
Excetre, John, 6
Exeter, 11, 220

Fallows, David, 19, 93, 97
Farmer, John, 195
Farrant, John, 39
Farrant, Richard, 204
Fayrfax, Robert, 19, 40–1, 49–55, 57, 60, 63, 69–70, 98, 126, 144, 146, 161–2, 167, 173, 175
Fellowes, Edmund Horace, 128, 164, 167, 173–4, 212, 214
Fenlon, Iain, 18, 165, 169–70, 183

Ferabosco, Domenico, 179
Ferrabosco, Alfonso, the Elder, xii, 109 et passim, 144, 174–5
Ferrabosco, John, 215
Fidge, Thomas, 177
Field, John, 209
Fisher, John H., 95
Florence, 74
Flynn, Jane, xi, 192
Ford, Thomas, 177
Forster, Richard, 178–9
Foster, John, 215–16
Fotheringhay College, 11, 16
Fowler, Joseph Thomas, 33, 181
Foxe, John, 19
France, 178, 189
Franclynge [Frankelyng], John, 170
Fraser, Russell A., 197
Freeborn, Dennis, 90
Frere, Walter Howard, 34, 181
Frost, Maurice, 168
Froude, James Anthony, 80
Frye, Walter, 161

Gair, Reavley, 197
Gardano, Antonio, 178–9
Gardiner, Stephen, 81
Gaskin, Hilary, 144
Geare, Hugh, 171–2
Germany, 178
Gibbons, Orlando, 110, 196, 200, 204–6, 211–12, 216
Gil, Alexander, 107
Giles, Nathaniel, 194–7, 204–5
Giles, Thomas, 197
Gimson, Alfred Charles, 83, 90, 92, 95–6, 101
Glasney, 11
Glastonbury, 182
Gloucester, 35, 212
Gombert, Nicolas, 178–9
Gottesman, Lillian, 191
Grede, John, 17
Greer, David, 192
Greg, Walter Wilson, 193
Grosseteste, (Bishop) Robert, 79

Hackett, (Bishop) John, 218
Hackett, Maria, 180
Haigh, Christopher, 167
Hall, John, 197
Halliwell, James Orchard, 190–1
Hamilton, William Douglas, 161

INDEX OF MANUSCRIPT AND PRINTED
MUSIC SOURCES

Libraries are referred to by the sigla used in the publications of RISM (Répertoire International des Sources Musicales, Kassel).

F: FRANCE
Pn   Paris, Bibliothèque Nationale, fonds du Conservatoire, Rés. 1122: 189

GB: GREAT BRITAIN
Cgc   Cambridge, Gonville and Caius College, 667 (the 'Caius Choirbook'): 56–8, 65, 70
Chelm   Chelmsford, Essex County Record Office:
           D/DP Z 6/1: 173
           D/DP Z 6/2: 173
Ckc   Cambridge, King's College, Rowe Music Library, 316: 169
Cmc   Cambridge, Magdalene College, Pepys 1236: 20–1, 27, 29
Cp   Cambridge, Peterhouse (deposited in the University Library):
           471–4 (olim 40, 41, 31, 32; the 'Henrician' partbooks): 56–8, 65, 146, 151
           485–91 (the 'Latter' set of 'Caroline' partbooks): 41, 211–12, 214
Cpc   Cambridge, Pembroke College, Music 6.1–6: 215
Ctc   Cambridge, Trinity College, o.3.58: 4
Cul   Cambridge, University Library:
           Nn.6.46: 48
           Pembroke College 314: 18
CA   Canterbury, Cathedral Library and Archive:
           Add. 128/7: 19
           Add. 128/66: 19
Drc   Durham, Cathedral Library:
           misc. MSS: 206
           C14: 205
Lbl   London, British Library, Reference Division:
           Add. 4900: 192
           Add. 4911: 184
           Add. 5465 (the 'Fayrfax' manuscript): 98
           Add. 5665 (the 'Ritson' manuscript): 19, 21, 23
           Add. 10336: 54
           Add. 10338: 217
           Add. 15117: 192
           Add. 15166: 202

INDEX OF PRINTED MUSIC SOURCES

RISM identifications refer to printed collections listed in volume BI (*Receuils Imprimés, XVIe–XVII Siècles*, 1960) or in the RISM series *Einzeldrucke vor 1800*, A/I/1– (1971–).

INDEX OF WORKS CITED

Within this index compositions are listed in the following order: Latin-texted (including chant and faburden) and macaronic compositions; English anthems; Services; Preces and Festal Psalms; untexted consort music; keyboard music. Works of uncertain authorship are indicated thus †.

anonymous

Alleluia V̊ Per te Dei genitrix (*CMM* 40/40), 28

Ave regina celorum, 48

Cantemus Domino, socie / Gaudent in celis (*EECM* 8/37), 19, 26–7, 29

Conditor alme siderum (faburden), 185

Gaude flore virginali, 26

Gaudent in celis *see* Cantemus Domino, socie

In dulci jubilo, 78

Jam lucis (chant), 195

Kyrie eleison, 28

Lauda vivi Alpha et O, 19

Laudate pueri (faburden), 185

Magnificat, 19, 85, 87, 119, 162

Miserere mihi Domine (chant), 187, 195

Nesciens mater (*EECM* 8/13), 9

O lux beata trinitas (chant), 195

Salve festa dies ... astra tenet (*CMM* 40/17), 29

Salve festa dies ... qua caro Messie (*CMM* 40/65), 29–30

Sancta Maria virgo (*EECM* 8/3, *CMM* 50/8), 9

Spiritus sanctus procedens, 112

Summae Trinitati (chant), 161

Te Deum, 161–2

A maid immaculate, 179

Ah my dear, ah my dear son (*MB* 36/50), 98

Come now to me my faithful wife, 192

Heart's ease, 193

I am the resurrection ('Wanley' MSS), 215

I heard a voice from heaven ('Wanley' MSS), 215

I know that my redeemer liveth ('Wanley' MSS), 215

I woeful wretched wight, 192

In the midst of life we are in death ('Wanley' MSS), 215

In youthful years, 192

In youthly years, 192

Dunstable, John
Descendi in ortum meum (*MB* 8/73), 27, 29
Veni sancte spiritus/Veni creator spiritus (*CMM* 50/32), 7

East, Michael
I am the resurrection, 215
I know that my redeemer liveth, 215
We brought nothing into this world, 215
When David heard, 107

Edwards, Richard
†Awake ye woeful wights, 192
By painted words (= O the silly man, q.v.), 191, 193
†Exceeding measure with pains continual, 191, 192
†Fortitude, 191
In going to my naked bed, 191
†O the silly man (= By painted words; *MB* 1/79), 193

Excetre, John
Credo (*CMM* 46/80), 7
Gloria (*CMM* 46/20), 18

Farrant, Richard
†Lord for thy tender mercy's sake (*TECM* 2, p. 48), 204
Felix namque [keyboard] (*MB* 1/19), 183

Fayrfax, Robert
Aeterne laudis lilium (*CMM* 17-2, p. 47), 168
Ave Dei patris filia (*CMM* 17-2, p. 36), 164, 173
Lauda vivi Alpha et O (*CMM* 17-3/15), 19, 146
Maria plena virtute (*CMM* 17-2, p. 59), 40
Mass *Albanus* (*CMM* 17-1, p. 33), 57–61, 63, 65–8, 70, 73
Mass *O bone Jesu* (*CMM* 17-1, p. 1), 49, 70
Mass *O quam glorifica* (*CMM* 17-1, p. 64), 49, 51–3, 55–7, 60, 65, 70
Mass *Sponsus amat sponsam* (*CMM* 17-1, p. 174), 173
O Maria Deo grata (*CMM* 17-3/16), 57–8, 60, 66, 68–9
Salve regina (*CMM* 17-2, p. 26), 40

Ferrabosco, Alfonso (I)
Aurora diem nuntiat (*CMM* 96-1/4), 116
Benedic anima mea ... Domine Deus meus (*CMM* 96-1/5a), 115
Credo quod redemptor (*CMM* 96-1/10), 115, 117
Domine non secundum peccata nostra (*CMM* 96-1/15), 116, 118
Ecce iam noctis (*CMM* 96-1/16), 116
Extendens caelum (*CMM* 96-1/5b, pt. 2 of 'Benedic anima mea', q.v.), 115
Heu mihi Domine (two settings; *CMM* 96-1/19 & 20), 129
In monte Oliveti (*CMM* 96-2/21), 121
Lamentations (*CMM* 96-2/2-4), 114, 134
Peccantem me quotidie (*CMM* 96-2/30), 116
Qui fundasti (*CMM* 96-1/5c, pt. 3 of 'Benedic anima mea', q.v.), 115, 122, 125
Surge propera (*CMM* 96-2/34a), 124

Timor et tremor (*CMM* 96-2/36a), 121

Ferrabosco, Alfonso (II)
Ego sum resurrectio, 218

Ferrabosco, John
I am the resurrection, 215
I heard a voice from heaven, 215
I know that my redeemer liveth, 215
In the midst of life we are in death, 215
Man that is born of a woman, 215
Thou knowest Lord the secrets of our hearts, 215
We brought nothing into this world, 215
Burial Service, 217

Foster, John
I am the resurrection, 215
I heard a voice from heaven, 215
I know that my redeemer liveth, 215
We brought nothing into this world, 215

Franclynge, John
O God for thy name's sake, 170

Frye, Walter
Mass *Summae Trinitati* (*EECM* 33/2), 161

Gibbons, Orlando
Almighty and everlasting God (*EECM* 21/1), 212
Behold thou hast made my days (*EECM* 3/3), 211
Deliver us O Lord (*EECM* 21/2), 207
God is gone up (*EECM* 21/6, pt. 2 of 'O clap your hands', q.v.), 204
Hosanna to the Son of David (*EECM* 21/3), 207
I am the resurrection (*EECM* 21/4), 215
O clap your hands (*EECM* 21/6), 204
†Out of the deep (*EECM* 21/9; also attributed to Byrd, q.v.), 111
This is the Record of John (*EECM* 3/15), 211
Burial music (*EECM* 21/4), 218
Short Service (*TCM* 4, p. 30), 212
Second Service (Jubilate) (*TCM* 4, p. 95), 205
Fantasia [keyboard] (*MB* 20/12), 196

Giles, Nathaniel
O Lord turn not away thy face (*EECM* 23/11), 204
First Service, 205

Heywood, John
What heart can think, 192

Hilton, John (I)
Lord for thy tender mercy's sake *see* Farrant, Richard